Gendering the State in the Age of Globalization

Gendering the State in the Age of Globalization

Women's Movements and State Feminism in Postindustrial Democracies

Edited by
Melissa Haussman and Birgit Sauer

ROWMAN & LITTLEFIELD PUBLISHERS, INC.
Lanham • Boulder • New York • Toronto • Plymouth, UK

ROWMAN & LITTLEFIELD PUBLISHERS, INC.

Published in the United States of America
by Rowman & Littlefield Publishers, Inc.
A wholly owned subsidiary of The Rowman & Littlefield Publishing Group, Inc.
4501 Forbes Boulevard, Suite 200, Lanham, Maryland 20706
www.rowmanlittlefield.com

Estover Road, Plymouth PL6 7PY, United Kingdom

British Library Cataloguing in Publication Information Available

Library of Congress Cataloging-in-Publication Data

Gendering the state in the age of globalization : women's movements and state feminism
in postindustrial democracies / edited by Melissa Haussman and Birgit Sauer.
   p. cm.
 Includes bibliographical references and index.
 ISBN-13: 978-0-7425-4016-3 (cloth : alk. paper)
 ISBN-10: 0-7425-4016-2 (cloth : alk. paper)
 ISBN-13: 978-0-7425-4017-0 (pbk. : alk. paper)
 ISBN-10: 0-7425-4017-0 (pbk. : alk. paper)
 1. Feminist theory—Political aspects. 2. Feminism—Cross-cultural studies. 3. Social
policy—Cross-cultural studies. 4. Sex role—Political aspects. I. Haussman, Melissa,
1959- II. Sauer, Birgit.
 HQ1236.G4628 2007
 305.4201—dc22
                              2007000035

Printed in the United States of America

∞™ The paper used in this publication meets the minimum requirements of American
National Standard for Information Sciences—Permanence of Paper for Printed Library
Materials, ANSI/NISO Z39.48-1992.

Dedicated to Amy G. Mazur and Dorothy E. McBride,
the founders of the RNGS network,
and to our colleagues in the network.

Contents

Figures and Tables

FIGURES

TABLES

Abbreviations

AAUW	American Association of University Women
AFDC	Aid to Families with Dependent Children
AGALEV	Flemish Green Party (Anders Gaan Arbeiden, Leven, En Vrijen; since 2003: Groen!)
AIDDA	Associazione Imprenditrici e Donne Dirigenti D'Azienda (Association of Women Entrepreneurs and Managers)
ALP	Australian Labor Party
ANCI	Associazione Cumuni Italiani (Association of Italian Muncipalities)
ANTaR	Australians for Native Title and Reconciliation
ASF	Arbeitskreis Sozialdemokratischer Frauen (Social Democratic Women)
ATSIC	Aboriginal and Torres Strait Islander Commission
AVFT	Association européenne de lutte contre les violences faites aux femmes au travail (European Association against Violence against Women at Work)
AWBZ	Algemene Wet Bijzondere Ziektekosten (General Law on Special Medical Costs)
BÄK	Bundesärztekammer (German Chamber of Doctors)
BC	British Columbia
BMFSFJ	Bundesministerium für Familien, Senioren, Frauen und Jugend (Federal Ministry for Family Affairs, Senior Citizens, Women, and Youth)
BMG	Bundesministerium für Gesundheit (Federal Ministry of Health)

BMI	Bundesministerium des Inneren (Federal Ministry of the Interior)
CADAC	Coordination des Associations pour le Droit à l'Avortement et à la Contraception (Coordination of Associations for the Right to Abortion and Contraception)
CAPOW	Coalition of Australian Participation Organizations of Women
CBC	Canadian Broadcasting Cooperation
CCOO	Comisiones Obreras (Workers' Commission)
CCWI	Congressional Caucus for Women's Issues
CDU	Christlich Demokratische Union (Christian Democrats Party)
CEDAW	Convention on the Elimination of all Forms of Discrimination Against Women
CEOE	Confederación Espanola de Organizaciones Empresariales (Spanish Confederation of Employer's Organizations)
CEPYME	Confederación Espanola de la Pequena y Mediana Empresa (Spanish Confederation of Small and Medium Enterprises)
CESAF	Le Centre d'excellence pour la santé des femmes— Consortium Université de Montréal (Centre of Excellence for Women's Health—Université de Montréal Consortium)
CFDT	Confédération française démocratique du travail (French Democratic Confederation of Labour)
CFFB	Conseil des Femmes Francophones de Belgique (Council of French-speaking Women in Belgium)
CGC	Confédération française de l'encadrement—Confédération générale des cadres (CFE-CGC Cross-industry French Trade Union for Executives and Managerial Staff)
CGPME	Confédération générale du patronat des petites et moyennes entreprises (Confederation of Small and Medium Businesses)
CGT	Confédération Générale du Travail (General Confederation of Labour of France)
CHST	Canadian Health and Social Transfer
CIHI	Canadian Institute of Health Information
CLASCHES	Collectif de Lutte Anti-sexist et Contre le Harcelement dans l´Enseignement Supérieur (Organization Against Sexism and Sexuell Harassment at University)
CNDF	Collectif National des Droits des Femmes (Organization for the Rights of Women)
CNPF	Conseil National du Patronat Français (French Employers Association)

CUPE	Canadian Union of Public Employees
CVP	Christen Demokratisch en Vlaams (Flemish Christian Democrats)
CWHN	Canadian Women's Health Network
D66	Dutch social-liberal party (Democraten 66)
DACOWITS	Defense Advisory Committee on Women in the Service
DCE	Directie Coordinatie Emancipatiebeleid (Department for the Coordination of Equal Policy)
DES	Diethylstilbestrol
DFG	German Research Foundation (Deutsche Forschungsgemeinschaft)
DHHA	Department of Health and Human Service
DMWRJT	Deputy Minister of Women's Rights and Job Training
DPO	Dipartimento per i diritti e le pari opportunità (Italian Department for Equal Rights and Opportunities)
ECOLO	Frankophone Green Party
EEA	European Economic Area
EFTA	European Free Trade Association
EK REM	Enquete-Kommission Recht und Ethik der modernen Medizin (Parliamentary Study Commission on the Law and Ethics of Modern Medicine)
EMU	European Monetary Union
EOC	Equal Opportunities Commission
EPF	Established Programs Financing
ER	Emancipatieraad (Emancipation-Council)
ES	embryonic stem cell
ESchG	Emryonenschutzgesetz (Law for the Protection of Human Embryos)
EU	European Union
EWL	European Women's Lobby
FDP	Freie Demokratische Partei (German Liberal Party)
FIM	Finnish Mark
FINNRAGE	Feminist Network of International Resistance to the New Reproductive Technologies and Genetic Engineering
FPÖ	Freiheitliche Partei Österreichs (Austrian Freedom Party)
FSA	Family Support Act
GBA	gender-based analysis
GDP	Gross Domestic Product
GMOs	Genetically Modified Organisms
GST	Goods and Services Tax
INEM	Instituto Nacional de Empleo (National Employment Institute)

IU	Izquierda Unida (United Left)
IVF	in vitro fertilization
JCP	Japanese Communist Party
JDS	Japanese Grant Aid for Human Resource Development Scholarship
JEDI	Justice, Economic Dignity, and Independence for Women
KFD	German Catholic Women's Association (Katholischer Frauenbund Deutschland)
KKO	Korkein oikeus (Finnish Supreme Court)
LDP	Liberal Democratic Party
LEAF	Legal Equity and Action Fund
LO	Landesorganisationen i Sverige (blue collar union)
LSO	Legislative Service Organizations
MEDEF	Mouvement des entreprises de France (Enterpreneurs association)
MP	Member of Parliament
MUA	Maritime Union of Australia
MVM	Man-Vrouw-Maatschappij (Netherlands Feminist Action Group)
NAC	National Action Committee
NAFTA	North American Free Trade Agreement
NARAL	National Abortion and Reproductive Rights Action League
NATO	North Atlantic Treaty Organization
NC	National Commission for Equality and Equal Opportunities
ND	New Democracy
NER	Nationaler Ethik-Rat (National Council on Ethics)
NGA	National Governor's Association
NGO	Non-Governmental Organization
NKO	Nederlandse Katholieke vereniging van Ouders
NOW LDEF	National Organization of Women—Legal Defense and Education Fund
NPO	Non-Profit Organization
NT	Northern Territory
NVR	Nederlandstalige Vrouwenraad (Netherlands Women's Council)
NYTKIS	Naisjärjestöt Yhteistyössä— Kvinnoorganisationes i Samarbete (The Coalition of Finnish Women's Associations)
OECD	Organization for Economic Cooperation and Development
OIW	Office of Indigenous Women
OSW	Office of the Status of Women
ÖVP	Österreichische Volkspartei (Austrian People's Party)

PCF	Parti communiste français (French Communist Party)
PDS	Partei des Demokratischen Sozialismus (Democratic Socialist Party)
PDS	Partito Democratico Socialisto (Democratic Party of the Left)
PGD	Pre-implantation Genetic Diagnosis
PID	Pre-implantation Diagnostics (Präimplantationsdiagnostik)
PND	Pre-birth Diagnostics (Pränataldiagnostik)
PP	Partido Popular (People's Party)
PRWORA	Personal Responsibility and Work Opportunity Reconciliation Act
PS	Parti Socialiste (Frankophone Socialists)
PSOE	Partido Socialista Obrero Espanol (Spanish Socialist Workers' Party)
PvdA	Partij van de Arbeid (Workers' Party)
QCA	Qualitative Comparative Analysis
QUAWPA	Quasi Women's Policy Agency
RNGS	Research Network on Gender, Politics, and the State
RPR	Rassemblement Pour la République
SAHS/SWL	Swedish Women's Lobby
SCP	Sociaal en Cultureel Planbureau (Social and Cultural Planning Bureau of the Netherlands)
SEK	Swedish Crowns
SMIC	Le salaire minimum de croissance (minimum salary)
SNTV	single nontransferable vote
SP	Socialistische Partij (Flemish Socialist's Party)
SPD	Sozialdemokratische Partei Deutschlands (German Social Democratic Party)
SPDJ	Social Democrats Party of Japan
SPJ	Socialist Party of Japan
SPÖ	Sozialdemokratische Partei Österreichs (Austrian Social Democratic Party)
STING	Stichting Network Gezinsverzorging (Foundation of the Network for Family Care)
STTK	The Finnish Confederation of Salaried Employees
SUD	Solidaires, Unitaires, et Démocratiques
SUD-PTT	Postes, Télégraphes, et Téléphones
TANF	Temporary Assistance to Needy Families
UDF	L'Union pour la démocratie française (Center Right Party)
UDI	Unione Donne in Italia (Italian Women's Association)
UFF	Unabhängiges Frauenforum (Independent Women's Forum)

UGT	Union General de Trabajadores (Workers' General Union)
UK	United Kingdom
UN	United Nations
VEIL	Values, Equality, and Difference in Liberal Democracies (EU funded project)
VLD	Vlaamse Liberalen en Democraten (Flemish Liberals Party)
VOK	Vrouwen Overleg Komitee
VUB	Vesalius Colleg at the Free University of Brussels
VVD	Volkspartij voor Vrijheid en Democratie (Liberal Party)
WEL	Women's Electoral Lobby
WI	Women's Institute
WM	Women's Movement
WMA	women's movement actors
WMA	World Medical Association
WMO	Wet Maatschappetijke Onderstenning (Act on Social Support)
WNC	Women's National Commission
WOUW	Wijze Oude Wijvennetwert (Network for Wise Old Women)
WPA	Women's Policy Agencies
WRR	Wetenschappelijke Raad voor het Regeringsbeleid (Netherlands Scientific Council for Government Policy)
WRS	Women's Rights Services
WTO	World Trade Organization
YWCA	Young Women's Christian Association

Introduction: Women's Movements and State Restructuring in the 1990s

Melissa Haussman and Birgit Sauer

Women's movement activists have been quite successful in challenging policymaking in postindustrial democracies in the last thirty years. Representation of women in the policy process has increased and women's issues have found a place on the public agenda (Inglehart/Norris 2003). Recent research on job training, abortion, prostitution, and democratic representation shows that women's policy agencies were frequently able to mediate this process of integrating women and women's issues into policymaking (Mazur 2001; Stetson 2001; Outshoorn 2004; Lovenduski 2005).

While these findings hold true on policy debates into the 1990s, it is clear that the context for movement activism and state response has changed in major ways. Some scholars argue that a restructuring of the state itself is underway (Banaszak/Beckwith/Rucht 2003). Since the late 1980s, the women's movement[1] is said to be in decline and issues that have been top priority for activists are frequently low on national policy agendas in Western democracies. At the same time, women's movement activists have become more integrated with formal institutions in parties and governments. As a result, both the activists and women's policy agencies may be in a position to persuade decision makers to consider gender implications of policies not usually considered women's issues. This is the idea of *gender mainstreaming*, now the policy of both the United Nations Organization and the European Union, which means to consider equality between men and women on all levels of policymaking by male and female policymakers (Behning/Serrano Pascual 2001).

This book is concerned with the impact of the changes in state structures and national priorities on the effectiveness of women's movement actors in achieving their goals. It places special emphasis on the fate of state feminism—the effectiveness of women's policy agencies as inside allies for movement actors—in the era of global challenges to national politics and of state restructuring. Is there a place for state feminism in these changing times? This question is explored through in-depth analysis of specific policy debates about changes in the scope, functions, and organizations of governments in fourteen postindustrial democracies. Authors have selected issues that were among the top priorities in these countries since 1990.

In these globalizing times, scholars have agreed that shifts in the role of postindustrial states and state-society relations may vary in direction (Randall/Waylen 1998). Changing state roles and relationships are sensitive to differences in institutional settings, political culture, social cleavages, ideologies, and place in the global economy. Regardless of such variations, it is clear that among the issues that are at the top of the political agendas of all postindustrial democracies, there have been major conflicts leading to and resulting from these changes. Policymakers in many of the generous welfare states have worked to reduce budgets and selectively downsize the reach of government activities. Delegation of national responsibilities to regional and local government—decentralization and devolution—has often coincided with reduced state presence in some policy sectors. Removing responsibility for social and economic well-being from the state coincides with increased marketization of state policies. On the other hand there are also policy arenas where states have not hesitated to increase their engagement and to raise public spending, for example, in the field of family policy. There have been changes along other dimensions—constitutional reform, biotechnology policies, and immigration laws—as states seek to retain their distinctiveness and citizen allegiance in the face of globalization.

Although these state restructuring policies, as any, involve differential outcomes based on gender, state actors rarely recognize these effects in official statements. All policies and institutions in question rely on a specific gender order (Ostner/Lewis 1995), which in most cases are unequal. They can discriminate against women at work, in social security, and in political representation. They rest on the division of public and private, on government institutions and citizenship as male spheres and activities. Have women's movement actors made any progress in bringing these gender questions to policy debates?

The central question raised in this book is whether women's movement actors and "femocrats" have had an impact on top-priority policy issues that involved major changes to the state. Did the women's movement actors take positions and seek to influence policy outcomes? Was the movement able to change the policy discourse on the issues and to gender the public debates? Were the women's policy agencies able to function as transmitters between movement actors and states? In other words, did states act in a noticeably feminist way on issues that were of major national priority? Or did state feminism disappear and women's movements have no voice in these policy debates?

BACKGROUND FOR THE STUDY: CHANGING WOMEN'S MOVEMENTS, CHANGING THE STATE

Changes in state-society relations have formed a backdrop for what appear to be opposing trends in the form, location, and influence of women's movement actors and women's policy agencies. On the one hand discourse in postindustrial states constrict the "death" of the women's movements; on the other hand women's movement activism has been rather successful. It has become increasingly consolidated and institutionalized through political parties, formal interest groups, legislatures, media, academia, and bureaucracies. Women's policy agencies too have become more institutionalized. Whereas they were established, often aided by feminist activism, in response to the World Plan of Action formulated at UN conferences for women beginning in 1975, by the 1990s, these policy agencies were viewed as legitimate state structures (Mazur 2001; Stetson 2001; Outshoorn 2004; Lovenduski 2005). One of the central tasks which many women's policy agencies have taken on under the UN and later European Union direction was assessing the gender-based impact of policies and mainstreaming gender into all significant government departments, agencies, or ministries (Behning/Serrano Pascual 2001; Rai 2003). One of the most successful examples to date has been Australia (Sawer 2003).

In the 1970s, women's movement actors in Western industrial countries perceived the state as patriarchal, male-dominated, hierarchical exclusionary, and unfriendly—not at all a means for achieving feminist goals. Women's movement actors often organized autonomously outside of state and para-state institutions like parties or unions. Many movement actors did not want to influence states but to change dominant gender norms and roles, to change the political culture, and to establish an alternative public space (Banaszak/Beckwith/Rucht 2003: 20).

During the 1980s and 1990s most of the women's movements in Western democracies changed strategy and location. They focused more on formal organizations that could gain access to state policy arenas. Further, "within the women's movement there was a significant shift in the 1980s towards engaging positively with state feminism as a strategy that could be effective in furthering cause(s) of women" (Rai 2003: 20). And women's movements organized and mobilized more on the international level (Meyer/Prügl 1999).

During this process of increased state-movement interaction, states also changed and became more open to women's issues. They were responsive to women's movement demands and changed their institutional settings through establishing and strengthening women's policy agencies. These agencies may be viewed as a success of women's movement struggles for gender equality.

The next question which emerged had to do with the resources, capability, and above all the willingness of these agencies to help women's movement actors achieve their goals. Have the women's policy agencies been appropriate institutions to further women's interests and women's movement aims? Have they also helped to increase the descriptive and substantive representation of women in political institutions and policy processes? The findings of four of the RNGS volumes show that state responses have been mixed. On one hand, states have co-opted movement activists while the women's policy agencies acted only symbolically towards women's movement goals. On the other hand, states have made room for women's policy agency activities and proved to be movement-friendly. Women's policy agencies have been able to successfully gender policy debates, to include women's movement goals into the policy process, and to bring women's movement activists into national policy debates. The RNGS research shows that on the issues of abortion, prostitution, and political representation women's movement actors have been successful in 50 to 53 percent of the debates, while in job training the success was at less than 30 percent. The case of co-option was much less frequent in all the debates than dual response. The conclusion is that in Western democracies a form of "state feminism" has developed, defined as "the effectiveness of women's policy agencies in assisting women's movements in achieving their procedural and substantive policy goals" (Stetson 2001: 267).

These findings from the RNGS project have been supported by other studies in the field: "(T)he state has reshaped, relocated, and rearticulated its formal powers and political responsibilities throughout the 1980s and 1990s" (Banaszak/Beckwith/Rucht 2003: 2). This "reconfiguration of states" since the 1980s opened state institutions to women's movement actors' demands. For example, in some European democracies like Austria and Germany, the weakening of the corporatist structures and the opening of the party systems to new parties, such as the "Green parties", helped provide a new political opportunity structure for women's movement actors. As a result, women's movement actors gained public voice to put women's interests on the public agenda, to represent women's issues in the policy process, and to gender policy issues in feminist frames (Bacchi 1999).

So we have a puzzling picture: States in globalizing times appear to be less sensitive to the gender-specific nature of their policy changes than they were in the 1970s, when many economies, states, and the international UN structure were expanding their capacities (Kelly 2001). At the same time, more and more states have adopted policies of gender mainstreaming (Behning/Serrana Pascual 2001; Rai 2003).

The authors' task in this volume is to investigate cases of policymaking to see if women's movement actors and women's policy agencies have been able to participate in and gain political responses on issues which have been among the top priorities since 1990. The study intends to contribute to the question of state feminism in the era of global state restructuring as well as on the efforts and the success of the women's movements to contribute to political democratization with respect to equal representation of women in the policy process, the improvement of the status of women, the promotion of women's rights, and the reduction of gender hierarchy. We posit a set of hypotheses to guide the comparative analysis of the empirical studies.

Earlier studies of the RNGS project show that women's policy agencies can be important vehicles to translate women's movement goals into state policies and to gain access to the policymaking process. They have been most successful, however, for issues that have been on the women's movement agendas for a long time, such as abortion (Stetson 2001), prostitution (Outshoorn 2004), and equal representation of women and men (Lovenduski 2005). They have been less successful in job training (Mazur 2001), an issue less readily recognized as a women's movement goal. In this final book in the RNGS series, we ask whether there is a chance of democratizing important policies that are non-gendered, that is, whose gender impact is not obvious at first glance and gendered policy structure has not been politicized by the women's movement.

The findings in these case studies pertain to the question of a state feminist spillover from gendered issues like abortion and prostitution where many agencies successfully promoted feminist claims to non-gendered hot issues. If agencies are outside these debates, it may mean that the "male state" is unable to learn women's movement lessons and that state feminism is limited to what are now traditional women's movement issues. Or does such a result mean that state restructuring is so important that the question of gender democracy[2] can be easily neglected? On the other hand, this decline in influence may not be wholly the state's fault but due to a narrowing of movement interest range in the last decade of the twentieth century. How did the movements change during the 1990s, and has their potential to democratize states through procedural and substantive equality declined?

RESEARCH FRAMEWORK AND DESIGN: THE RNGS MODEL

The research presented in this volume grew out of the collaborative work of the Research Network on Gender, Politics and the State (RNGS).[3] The book uses the analytical framework developed by the project to explore the politics of issues of state restructuring high on national policy agendas since 1990 and to analyze these main research questions: (1) To what extent have women's movement actors been successful in gaining descriptive and substantive representation and what factors explain success and failure? (2) To what extent and under which conditions are women's policy agencies effective linkages for women's movement actors to achieve a substantive and procedural response from state institutions? The model takes the impact of the women's movement on the process and outcome of policy debates as the dependent variable. The effectiveness of the women's policy agencies and their institutional capacities form the intervening variables, whereas the characteristics of the women's movement (for instance stage, coherence around the issue, closeness to Left parties) and of the policy environment (for instance party in power, closeness or openness, issue frame compatibility) are the independent variables.

THE RNGS MODEL

Unit of Analysis: Policy Debate

INDEPENDENT VARIABLES

Women's Movement Actor Characteristics: Stage; Closeness to Left; Issue Priority; Cohesion; Location; Feminist Activism

Policy Environment: Policy Subsystem; Structure; Issue Frame Fit; Party/Coalition in Power; Counter-movement

INTERVENING VARIABLE

Women's Policy Agency Characteristics: Scope; Type; Proximity; Administrative Capacity; Leadership; Policy Mandate

Women's Policy Agency Activities: Insider; Marginal; Non-feminist; Symbolic

DEPENDENT VARIABLE

Women's Movement Impact/State Response: Dual Response; Co-optation; Pre-emption; No Response

This volume, like the others in the RNGS project, is based on an intensive collaboration among the contributors. In five meetings they discussed the RNGS model, the key concepts of the analysis, and the selection of what the group termed "hot issues". For the RNGS project, hot issues are conflicts that are among the top four to five priority issues in each of the fourteen countries. All researchers employed the same criteria and worksheets to conduct their research and classify the data. To ensure common uses of the concepts and definitions, the authors reviewed each other's work and discussed their application to the material in several workshops (see Appendix A for the worksheets).

While this book is a comparative study of women's movements' impact on policy issues of major national importance, it is also a comparison of women's movement successes or failures in different types of state restructuring policies. When authors used the debate selection criteria (see below) to determine which policy debates to study, it turned out that these debates were examples of three different types of state restructuring: downsizing, expansion of state powers, and constitutional reorganization. This allows us to compare movement influence and state feminism in conflicts over different forms of state change.

Because each case study in this book presents information according to the concepts of the RNGS model, we are able to analyze some important questions about movement activism. Are there arenas in which the women's movement is more successful than in others? Why are women's movements successfully bringing in their actors and goals in some issues, but not in others? Do different patterns of policy environments make a difference in women's movements' success? In comparing "hot issue" debates cross-nationally, this study can sort out why some governments on some issues are more responsive to women's movement demands than other governments on other issues. It can also give explanations as to why the women's movement on similar issues has been successful in one country but not in another.

The qualitative analysis allows us to shed light on processes of gendering and degendering of issues in the age of globalization. It takes various policy environments into account as well as cultural contexts and it illustrates the transformation since the 1970s of the women's movements in their engagement for democratization. The analysis also presents comparative findings on the women's policy agencies and their performance as insiders or outsiders. With this careful and small-step approach the RNGS model contributes substantially to theory building in several different areas. These include the fields of political comparison, globalization and state transformation, and the theory of women's movements.

COMPARATIVE HYPOTHESES OF THE BOOK

For the purpose of comparison of state feminism in different policy areas and in different policy environments, a set of hypotheses have been developed from the RNGS model:

H.1: More difficulties are expected for women's movement activists in gaining the substantial and procedural representation into the policy process so as to gender the debates, compared to other issues in the RNGS project.

H.2: Women's movements are more successful where women's policy agencies have acted as insiders in the process of policymaking.

H.3: Women's policy agencies with greater administrative capacities are more effective than those with lesser administrative capacities in building linkage between the movement and policymakers.

H.4: Variations in women's movement characteristics and in the policy environment explain variations in the movement's success.

H.5: Women's movement characteristics and policy environment characteristics differ from other issues. This explains the greater incidence of movement failure.

H.6: If women's policy agencies are effective linkages between movement activism and state substantive and procedural response, then variation in movement and policy environment characteristics will have no independent relation to state response, but are mediated by the women's policy agency.

H.7: Women's movement actors are more successful on the issues that expand state action and they are least successful in policy debates that involve reducing the range and scope of national institutions.

PLAN OF RESEARCH

The unit of analysis in this book is one policy debate about an issue of high national priority, among each country's hot issues. Unlike the other books of the network, this volume does not focus on one issue area, such as abortion or job training, but compares debates on different priority issues pertaining to state restructuring. Analysis of one debate per country brings the cross-national comparison to the fore. The volume contains fourteen case studies from fourteen countries: Australia, Austria, Belgium, Canada, Finland, France, Germany, Italy, Japan, Netherlands, Spain, Sweden, United Kingdom, and the USA. These countries represent four continents (Asia, Australia, Europe, and North America).

Each chapter follows a common outline. First, the author introduces the background to the issue in that country. Next is the presentation of the selection of the debate showing why the author chose the issue and the particular debate that represents that issue. This section contains evidence to support the author's assessment that the debate is among the top priorities in the country. The researchers have selected their designated debates using the following guidelines. First they identified those policy issues (at least four) on the public agenda which were the top priorities for the political system since 1990 using the following criteria: (1) *Scope*: A large portion of society would be affected by the policy and any proposed policy change. (2) *Degree of conflict*: The policy issue has engaged the major socio-political actors among political elites, political parties, social partners, interest groups, and social movements. (3) *Range of public attention*: The policy issue generated high interest of the public as demonstrated through public opinion polls, demonstrations, strikes, public conferences, media coverage, and the like. (4) *Priority among policy actors*: That is, changes in the policy issue are high on the agendas of the political executive and political party leaders. According to these criteria the researchers constructed a universe of priority issues in their countries.

The next step in this set of classification decisions was to choose from the list of top-priority issues the one that involved the greatest changes in the state. For example, these might include the downsizing of the central government in response to economic pressure, new constitutional frameworks, or extension of state policy range. Finally, if there was more than one policy debate on the issue during the period, the author selected the one that was, in her estimation, the most significant.

After the section describing how the policy debate was selected, each chapter describes the evolution of the women's movement in the country into the 1990s, pointing out changes since the 1970s in ideologies, organizational structures, strategies, and relative importance of different sectors. Following this, the main body of each chapter includes an extensive description of the policy debate—how it came to the public agenda, the dominant frame of the debate, whether the debate became gendered or degendered and who presented which statements and ideas, and the policy outcome. In particular, the authors attempt to gauge the degree of women's movement impact on the policy outcome.

The impact is assessed on two dimensions: *first*, the substantive response of the state, that is, whether or not the policy outcome met movement demands, and *second*, procedural response, that is, whether or not women's movement actors garnered representative positions in the policy debate. The impact of the women's movement is classified using a typology with four possible state responses (see table 1.1): We consider it as a *dual response* when state institutions accept women's movement actors—individual women

Table 1.1.   Typology for Women's Movement Impact and State Response

		Policy coincides with movement goals	
		Yes	No
Women involved in policy process	Yes	Dual response	Co-optation
	No	Pre-emption	No response

or women's advocacy groups—to take part in the policy debate, and the policy content coincides with movement goals. *Co-optation* means that the state only accepts women's movement actors in the policymaking process but the policy content does not answer their demands. *Pre-emption* is the case when the state acts according to movement goals but does not allow women or women's groups to take part in the debate. Finally, there is the case of *no response* when the state neither accepts women in the debate nor answers to movements' demands.

As a next step the researchers examine the women's policy agencies. The agency is described by the following characteristics: scope, type, proximity, administrative capacity, individual leadership, and policy mandate. The RNGS model assumes that these characteristics influence the potential of the agency to promote women's movement demands and to facilitate movement actors in the policy process. In the model the dimension of *scope* refers to the policy mission of the agency. Some have a cross-sectional, multi-issue approach (rather helpful in the hot issue cases), while others are a single-issue agency, which makes it difficult for them to take part in all policy debates. *Type* describes the forms an agency can take; in the different countries we find various types of women's policy agencies, such as ministries, departments in ministries, commissions or committees in parliament, or advisory councils. *Proximity* refers to the location of the agency: Is it close to the center of power or is it far away from the major locus of power? *Administrative capacity* is measured in the size of the budget and staff along with the period of mandate. The background of the *leadership* of the agency, for instance the head of the ministry, or the department is also important for the potential of the agency to promote women's movement ideas. Was or is the leader part of the women's movement? Finally, the agency's *policy mandate* determines the priorities of the agency and if the specific "hot issue" fits into its mandate.

The performance of the women's policy agency in the policy debate of high national priority then is classified again into a fourfold typology (see table 1.2): When the agency adopts the goals of the movement and is successfully gendering the debate it is classified as an *insider*. The agency acts in a *marginal* sense, if it asserts women's movement goals but is not able to insert gen-

Table 1.2. Typology for Women's Policy Agencies

		WPA advocates movement goals	
		Yes	No
WPA genders frame of policy debate	Yes	Insider	Non-feminist
	No	Marginal	Symbolic

dered policy frames into the dominant frame of the debate. When the agency does not advocate movement goals but genders the issue in other ways, it is characterized as *non-feminist*. Finally, a *symbolic* role means that the agency neither advocated movement goals nor gendered the policy debate.

The next step of the chapters is to describe women's movement actors in the hot issue debate. This part depends on the general description of the movements' development in the 1990s and points out the specific characteristics of the movement with respect to the policy debates on hot issues. Characteristics of the movement are its stage of development, the closeness to the Left, the priority of the hot issue on the movement agenda—if at all on the agenda—and the cohesion of the movement on the issue. The framework depicts four stages of development of the women's movement: emerging or re-emerging, growth, consolidation, and decline or abeyance. Closeness to the Left describes the movement's ideology and organizational closeness to parties, trade unions, and other organizations of the Left. Cohesion points to the fact that women's movement activists agree on the movement's frame on the hot issue, and priority refers to the priority the respective issue has on the movement's agenda.

In the next section the authors give information on the second independent variable, the characteristics of the policy environment in the issue. The policy environment is characterized by three dimensions, open- or closedness of the policy subsystem, the fit between the subsystem's dominant approach or frame and the frame of women's movement actors, and the party or coalition in power, especially left parties. A policy environment is classified as *open* when it has no formal rules and broad participation of interest groups or individuals in the policy debate is possible. It is classified as *moderately closed* when it is regulated and organized, when regular actors dominate the policy field but still some free agents are able to intervene. The policy environment is characterized as *closed* when it is highly codified, when participation of outside actors is limited, and if one major actor controls the policy arena. Finally the strength of a counter-movement, which in the 1990s seemed to be more likely than in the decades before, is another characteristic of the policy environment.

Finally, each chapter's conclusion covers the state response to the movement, the women's policy agency's characteristics and achievements, and the degree to which the women's movement characteristics and the policy environment explain the state's response and the women's agency activities.

WOMEN'S MOVEMENTS AND GLOBAL
STATE TRANSFORMATION: THEORETICAL DEBATES

As described above, this book adds to the debates on state transformation and state restructuring one specific aspect—how women's movements and women's policy agencies are able to influence policies of state transformation. In this section we want to locate these findings in the feminist literature on state transformation.

The work by Marianne Marchand and Anne Sisson Runyan (2000) substitutes a more specific term, "global restructuring", for globalization. The term "global restructuring" acknowledges that "we are dealing with a set of multidimensional, multispeed and disjointed processes" (Marchand/Runyan 2000: 7). *Gendering the State* draws upon Marchand and Runyan's commentary about how restructuring states become explicitly or implicitly "gendered" by policymakers in their assumptions about allocation of resources to the public or private. In traditional liberal democratic theory as often applied to industrialized states, the private sphere of home and family has typically been portrayed as the more oppressive one for women, whereas equal access to employment in and legal coverage by the public sphere has been viewed as positive (Marchand/Runyan 2000: 14–15).

Neoliberal doctrine tends to shift this equation, in which the public sector becomes the passive reflection of group interests and thereby ascribed "female" traits. In that framework, the welfare state is viewed as constituting a "drag on the global economy that must be subordinated and minimized". However, the state is alluded to in more masculinized terms as it takes on the desired "lean and mean" qualities under neoliberalism (or any other policies of state slimming); the state's increasing similarities to the private sector "as it is internationalized to assist global capital" are noted as being strengthened (ibid: 14–15). Thus, in the neoliberal ethos of restructuring, the "private" equals the private sector, where dynamism, innovation, and largely masculine traits are seen to inhere, and the best prescription for the bloated public sector is to take on the desired masculinist traits.

Under neoliberalism, the private realm, "valorized over the public sector generally", has become "highly-politicized as a site of and for restructuring processes" (ibid: 13–15). Interestingly, women find themselves in a contradictory fix, depending on whether they are supposed to be working creatures primarily of the public sector, as demanded by neoliberalism, or the nurturing caretakers of the private, as envisioned by neoconservatism. Other relevant pieces to the resexualized nature of the state-market-family-civil-society relationship under either general globalization or more specific neoliberalism are seen in the reconstitution of the meaning of the public sector. Since the 1970s, women have increased their participation in the public sphere based on both necessity and interest; yet under global restructuring and neoliberal government cutting, the public sector becomes "subordinated to private capital". Thus, even as women have become more present in the public sphere and civil society over time, including in legislatures, women's policy agencies, and movement organizations, the relative decision-making and implementing power of institutions in those sectors has declined. As so succinctly described by Marchand and Runyan, "the locus of power is shifting from the public world of politics to the privatizing, and thus depoliticizing, world of economics" (ibid: 13–15).

To this depoliticized arena we would also add the bureaucratic "councils" often employed to make the difficult decisions in states caught up in the globalizing political economy, sometimes done so as to shift the heat off elected officials. At other times, elected officials find the international infrastructure to be a convenient scapegoat, since the average citizen will not know if the fault for something really lies with the WTO, the EU, or one of the European states, for example.

As added by Anne Marie Goetz (2002), another strategy used by gender justice advocates under globalization has been to try to meet neoliberal policymakers on their own grounds, by adopting an "efficiency" criterion. For example, women in World Bank departments have argued for increasing studies of gender-based outcomes of bank programs, since this would improve the bank's overall "efficiency" in its operations (Goetz 2002: 24–66). This has sometimes gained entry for women into the public space of the dialogue, as will be shown.

It is apparent that there is no "one size fits all" theory of global restructuring. Banaszak, Beckwith, and Rucht use the term "state reconfiguration" to describe the processes of globalization and internationalization, whereby different states feel the effects of global change across different sectors and at different rates (Banaszak/Beckwith/Rucht 2003: 4). The authors describe four processes of state reconfiguration. They depict three forms of vertical shifts — the "downloading of power" to lower state levels, the "uploading" to international levels, and the "offloading" of state power to non-state actors. Another aspect is horizontal shifts, which they call the "lateral loading", the "delegation of competencies to non-elected state bodies" like executives and courts (Banaszak/Beckwith/Rucht 2003: 7).

Following the criteria for selecting priority debates related to state restructuring, the authors of this volume offer a remarkable array of important political topics for analysis. The issues described in this book represent major shifts in state activities and priorities that have close relation to major global trends. As such the research allows consideration of comparisons beyond those posed by the RNGS framework of state feminism.

In processes of state restructuring, of making changes in state-society relations states are not only shrinking but also expanding in new policy areas. The neo-liberal downsizing of states, the reduction in state budgets and state spending, the dismantling of welfare state provisions, and the transfer of state duties to the private realm of families or markets are only one form of state restructuring. The Canadian and US reforms of welfare, the reorganization of the Dutch home care system and of the Finish day care provision, and unemployment policies in Spain are examples for shrinking states. States react to the internationalization of markets and production and transform demand-oriented policies towards supply orientation. Transforming state-society relations also results in state expansion. States either spend more money in special areas like family policy (Austria and Sweden)—with the argument of demographic change—or in expanding into new policy areas and in reregulating these areas as for instance the workweek in France and biotechnology in Germany.

A third dimension of state restructuring is changes in the state apparatus, in the organization of states and reregulation of membership in nation-states. Decentralization of the nation-state in Italy, changes in the electoral system in Japan, and the reorganization of the procedures of the House of Lords in the United Kingdom are most striking examples for transformation in democratic arrangements. A new field of state expansion in the 1990s was the field of citizenship rights, redefining citizenship as in Belgium and Australia.

The concluding chapter of the book will use the fourteen data-rich case studies to construct a comparative analysis of the patterns of state feminism in the context of conflicts over the form and role of the state. The central goal of the conclusion is to assess the significance of the mature women's policy agencies of the 1990s in aiding consolidated women's movements in navigating the shifting contours of policy conflicts. This ability is analyzed with reference to the resource mobilization and policy environment characteristics present during the debates. The other extremely important aspect of this book is that along with the qualitative analysis incorporated by the four previous RNGS books, it assigns quantitative values to the variables identified in each chapter's analysis as well. Thus, *Gendering the State* continues the RNGS framework of being able to compare women's movement and policy agency influence qualitatively and quantitatively across different countries and, in this volume, across different issues as well.

COMPARING STATES, TESTING TYPOLOGIES

In the feminist literature on comparative welfare state research, one of the most debated typologies is the threefold typology of Gøsta Esping-Andersen (2001). The chapters of *Gendering the State* will contribute to this debate by adding new data on changing welfare states in the age of globalization. Esping-Andersen (2001) placed most welfare states into three categories. The first is the social democratic (usually applied to the Nordic states); the "Catholic or work merit", such as Spain and Belgium; and the "liberal individualist", including the US as the most extreme adherent and Canada as a lesser one. John D. Stephens (2001) highlights Esping-Andersen's work as characterizing first, the welfare state structure, second, the social policy type which is associated with patterns of labor market entry or exit and employment, with the intersection point of these two being the particular "welfare state regime". The different frameworks of the welfare states are useful in that they allow us to describe what could be expected from each of the three "ideal types" of the welfare state and then what happened. For example, the case studies of Finland and Sweden in the Nordic states form interesting contrasts within Type I, the Nordic case, of the "welfare state regime" in that the Swedish model particularly was based on full employment, basically by increasing the size of the public sector, and an "explicit second stage to consolidate both equality and a productivistic social policy by maximizing employment and equalizing the status of women" (Esping-Andersen 2001: 11). In contrast, while Finland is included in the "Nordic model", its unemployment policy, maternal and parental leave, and pension replacement policies have historically been lower than in Sweden (Stephen 2001: 34–35). These findings are amplified in *Gendering the State* by the chapters by Christina Bergqvist and Terhi Aalto and Anne Maria Holli, respectively, showing when and how women could make public policy debates on child care more sensitized to gender, and that the outcome was better for women in Sweden than Finland.

With respect to Type II of welfare state regimes as identified by Esping-Andersen, the Catholic or work merit welfare states, which would include France, Belgium, Austria, and Spain in this study, show a different pattern from the Nordic states. We expect less generous benefits in these states, as discussed in the chapters by Amy Mazur, Birgit Sauer, and Celia Valiente. As Esping-Andersen has suggested, welfare states with liberal leave provisions are necessary to keeping female employment and the possibility of child-rearing possible. However, fertility has declined in Spain and Italy, suggesting that the leave policies there are not sufficient to support working women and their families. Similarly, France has "induced labor supply reduction" while maintaining existing levels of social security standards. In Austria, the ascension of a rightist government has meant the recent adoption of "family benefits", which are usually consistent with a conservative view. Sauer emphasizes this in her chapter. Finally, Jantine Oldersma and Joyce Outshoorn discuss the elderly home health care and waiting list issue for the Netherlands. The Netherlands is a "border" state between welfare state regimes I and II, as can be seen by Esping-Andersen's discussion; while it could be viewed as part of the "Nordic" group with respect to having high public social security and health expenditures as a percentage of GDP, it is extremely low on the scale of percentage of labor force involved in public training measures (Esping-Andersen 2001: 10–30; Sainsbury 1999). Germany on the other hand expanded state regulation in the field of biotechnology in the context of a discourse coalition of women's movement actors and the Catholic Church.

The third type of welfare state regime, most commonly found in the Anglo-American democracies, is studied as a welfare state problem in this volume in the US and Canada, by Dorothy McBride and Melissa Haussman, respectively. In the individual-rights-oriented US and Canadian democracies, the embracing of neoliberal doctrine to "manage economic decline and domestic unemployment . . . has involved . . . greater labor market and wage flexibility" (ibid: 15). Both the reduction of welfare benefits in the US and the concomitant rise of work requirements, and the reduction of state-provided benefits in the Canadian health care system fit this model. McBride and Haussman describe in their chapters the degree to which women were able to emphasize gender differentials in these policy debates.

While the UK and Australia also belong to the "Anglo-American liberal democratic welfare state" in Esping-Andersen's framework, the chapters here by Joni Lovenduski and Barbara Sullivan, respectively, find that the hot issues of these states related to globalization actually involved new actions by the national government in the constitutional realm. These studies fall under our second category, of government expansion into new areas, to seemingly focus popular attention on a grand constitutional scheme to divert attention from economic cutbacks. A related phenomenon may be found regarding Misako Iwamoto's chapter on Japan. The Japanese welfare state has been characterized as more mixed in its underlying ideology and structure, containing in the first half of the twentieth century a mix between a "stigma attached to statutory social assistance", coupled with the tradition of relying on extended family structures for support on the one hand, versus a drive to emulate Western industrialized nations by putting in place a more comprehensive welfare state. Since the 1970s, the Japanese "ambivalence between the initial motivations for change and their potential implications" has taken center stage in the welfare policy debate, including an increased shift to emphasis on individual provision and less on following the European path (Goodman/Peng 2001). What is most interesting is that, consistent with other Asian scholars, Misako Iwamoto has found that in response to economic issues as forming part of a national crisis of representation amongst Japanese parties, the Japanese state recently undertook electoral reform so as to seem responsive to peoples' concerns.

NOTES

1. We use the term "women's movement" according to the definition of the RNGS project. The women's movement has three parts: the ideas that inspire collective behavior of women's movements, the women's movement discourse, and the women's movement actors who present the ideas in public life.

2. The concept of gender democracy has been developed by feminists in the German Green Party. The concept stresses the importance of procedural and substantive representation of women in all policy processes. The concept makes the point that although the "demos" consist of men and women, democracy is still male-dominated, or an "androcracy".

3. The authors of this volume are members of RNGS. RNGS studies the impact of women's movements on state policies on a range of issues and countries. The RNGS design used in this volume has been developed in intense discussions between the members of the network. This introduction draws in its main parts on the RNGS project outline (2003), developed cooperatively by the RNGS scholars.

2

Reevaluating the "Heart of Society": Family Policy in Austria

Birgit Sauer

Since the late 1970s, attempts for modernization have placed pressure on family policy in Austria (Goldberg 1998: 245ff.; Tazi-Preve 2003: 444ff.): Should the traditional family be supported as the "nucleus" of the society with a stress on reproduction? Or should family policy promote women's interests of reconciling care work and waged labor? These questions coincide with the two pillars of Austria's family policy: The first and most important pillar was direct financial support to families and children. This support stabilized the male breadwinner family, and was promoted by the conservative Austrian People's Party (ÖVP) (Rosenberger 1999: 760). The other pillar—supported by the Social Democratic Party (SPÖ)—aimed at public child care and at social redistribution to less affluent families (ibid: 763).

Generally Austrian family policy has favored direct monetary transfers to families, rather than the provision of public child care facilities (Walter 2004: 27; Henry-Huthmacher 2004: 33). Parents receive the funds irrespective of income (for instance family allowance for children until the age of twenty-seven). However, during the 1990s, this policy came under severe strain due to strict financial austerity measures of the SPÖ/ÖVP government. The ensuing debate over the "crisis" of the Austrian welfare state legitimized budget cuts and the government started shifting public obligations to private organizations. Along with these cuts in the state budget came the discourse on alleged *misuse* of welfare state benefits. "Accuracy of target" was the militarist metaphor for the new need-based orientation of social policy. Parental leave was one of the areas mentioned in the misuse debate, thereby undermining the place of family policy as a means of redistribution and reconciliation.

A new discourse about the importance of families and the reorientation of family policy provoked an intensive public debate. The debate emerged at the interface of a neoliberal project aimed to reduce the state deficit and shift public responsibilities to families and it provoked controversy over the decline of the birthrate and the future of the generation pact of the Austrian pension system. While the coalition of SPÖ and ÖVP jointly pushed forward in neoliberal deregulation, they differed over the fate of family policy (Rosenberger 1999: 760). However, a silent paradigm shift in family policy occurred, mainly pushed by the conservative partner in government, ÖVP, and the right-wing party in opposition, FPÖ.

In 2000 the new coalition government between the right-wing FPÖ and the conservative ÖVP came to power. It announced a "new politics" for Austria, aimed at breaking the tradition of SPÖ politics, especially the strong role of social partnership in the Austrian neo-corporatist institutional setting. Thus, the ÖVP, which represents the interests of industry, craft professions, and peasants, had the opportunity to go forward with the deregulation of the economy and the dismantling of the welfare state. Slowly the Austrian "consensus democracy" was transformed into a "conflict democracy", as the institutions of the Austrian social partnership were weakened and the Social Democratic welfare compromise was dissolved.

Family policy issues moved to the center of the politics surrounding this quest for a complete reconfiguration of the welfare state. The new government actively linked cuts in welfare state provision to support for families and renewed their claims that the family was essential to the new society. The Law on Child Care Allowance of 2001 illustrates this major shift in state-society relations. The government removed child care as a public responsibility and legitimized this strategy with the argument that the family is the best place for raising children. The law is moreover at odds with the idea of social redistribution, because all children are treated the same irrespective of the economic situation of the parents. Also, the child care allowance was to be an incentive for people with low incomes to quit their jobs and stay at home with their children. In the context of huge wage gaps between men and women this is a means to push women back to the home. Although some of the characteristics of the conservative Austrian gender regime had changed since the 1980s, the division of labor in the households remained largely untouched. Although due to part-time work female employment rates have gone up, the gender gap in the labor market has widened. Women have higher unemployment rates than men, hierarchical gender-based job segregation is strong, and the gender wage gap is still huge. In the context of the neoliberal strategy of increasing flexibility of the labor force, the debate on child care allowance can also be seen as a discursive preparation for flexible mothers *and* fathers.

SELECTION OF THE ISSUE

The five policy debates with top priority in the 1990s and at the beginning of the 2000s are EU membership, migration and asylum, the privatization of state-owned industries and public services, budget restriction, and family policy. The sources for identifying the top priority issues were the Austrian "Yearbooks of Politics" (*Österreichisches Jahrbuch für Politik*) from 1990 to 2002. The yearbooks list the most relevant policy debates at both the federal and provincial levels of the state by year. Other sources were the archives of the major daily newspapers in Austria, *Der Standard* and *Die Presse*.

Since World War II, a large section of industry, banks, and insurance companies have been state-owned. In 1993, the Austrian government launched a program toward privatization of state-owned industries and public services like Austrian mail, the state railway, electricity, and telephone. One of the major effects of privatization for the Austrian people was the reduction of jobs and the increase in prices of former public services. The measures had a major scope; they affected every Austrian household. Therefore they received high public attention not only in the media, but also in election campaigns. The issue of privatization was a top priority of the governing parties, as well as the social partners. Anticipation of the effects of higher unemployment and the increase of cost of living provoked a high degree of public conflict reflected in the media but also of conflict within different branches of the parties and in the bodies of social partnership.

Another important issue in the 1990s involved dramatic changes in the laws affecting migrants and asylum seekers, putting in place new restrictions on labor migration and on achieving asylum. The amendments of the asylum law, the foreigners' law, and the law on work permits aimed at reducing the number of foreign workers moving into Austria and restricting entrance of asylum seekers. Priority for entry was given to family members of residents, and newly immigrating persons had only restricted access to the labor market: a quota system regulated the access for jobs, especially for seasonal jobs. Further amendments in the late 1990s started a discourse on cultural difference, assimilation, and integration. Today, language courses are required for new immigrants who want to stay in Austria. The asylum law was tightened, especially the examination to get asylum. Joining the EU "Schengen Treaty", Austria took over the European policy of *Drittstaatenregelung*, which closes the country for asylum seekers who enter Austria via a so-called secure third country.

The debate on asylum and immigration was highly emotional and contested, intensifying Austria's xenophobic political culture. For example, a people's initiative against foreigners in the labor market, launched by the

right-wing FPÖ in 1993, was called "Austria first". Austrian civil society organizations mobilized against the xenophobic "Austria first" discourse: The
so-called sea of candles later in 1993 gathered more than three hundred thousand people on Vienna's streets who demonstrated in favor of "foreigners".
The debates around asylum and immigration attracted a wide range of public
attention and it was one of the issues with the highest degree of conflict in the
1990s debated both by the main policy actors and civil society organizations.

The third top issue was the debate around Austria's EU membership, which
started in the 1980s. The government's negotiations with the European Community led to fierce debates about the pros and cons of Austria's EU membership. All major policy actors—parties, unions, associations of private industry—were engaged in the debates. The governing parties were
pro-European; the Green Party and the FPÖ were against the accession. The
degree of conflict was rather high, and the Austrian population was divided.
In the obligatory referendum on the accession in 1994 two-thirds of the electorate voted in favor of the accession. Austria joined the European Union on
January 1, 1995.

The EU accession affected the whole Austrian population and it had and
still has a wide range of public attention. While the Greens changed their
opinion towards EU, the FPÖ initiated a people's initiative against the common currency euro in 1997. The people's initiative "Veto against Temelin" (a
nuclear power plant in Czech Republic), also organized by FPÖ in 2002, was
a symbolic instrument of mobilizing against the EU membership of former
state-socialist countries.

When Austria joined the EU the country was forced to a restrictive budget.
In the mid-1990s the governing parties disagreed on the direction of budget
policy. While the ÖVP sought a restrictive budget policy through cuts in social provisions, the SPÖ tried to satisfy their voters, who were afraid of loss
of jobs and drop of standard of living in the case of budget restrictions. This
conflict led to early national elections in 1995. The SPÖ was boosted by the
result of the ballot but again formed a coalition with the ÖVP. In 1996 the first
law on budget restriction—the first "economy package"—came to force. In
the negotiations on the package all major policy actors of the Austrian system
of social partnership took part.

The proposals provoked a high level of conflict in Austrian society; the
unions led the opposition and mobilized against the austerity policy. The measures were widely discussed in the media and have remained on the agenda
until the present. Fees for health care, taxation of disability pension, shortage
of state widows' pensions, and university fees are examples that show that the
scope of budget restriction was very high—most of the Austrian people have
been affected by the measures.

The debate on family policy started in the mid-1990s. Since then family policy has been one of the hot issues in Austrian politics at the national and the regional level, in major political parties, in trade unions and in family organizations, and within the Catholic Church. Family policy has also been debated extensively in the media. The decision on child care allowance and the paradigm shift in family policy in 2001 affected a large portion of society—each family with children—because the law affects the traditional family allowance for children up to the age of twenty-seven. Moreover, the changes in family policy affected also people without children because the new measures aim at a horizontal redistribution between people who have and those who don't have children. The issue also was characterized by a high degree of conflict: the shift in family policy represents conflicting ideological positions of parties, family organizations, trade unions, and churches.

Family policy also attracted a wide range of public attention and media coverage, lasting many years. Public attention was drawn for instance by the so-called family referendum in 1999, a people's initiative organized by the Austrian "Family Association", an organization close to the governing ÖVP. The initiative put the issue on the public agenda and made it one of the main topics of the national election campaign in 1999. The question of family allowances was at the top of the agendas of major policy actors, e.g., the main parties on the national level. Policy actors in the Austrian provinces, which are responsible for public child care facilities, were also engaged in the debate.

The law on child care allowance—like other measures promoted by the conservative-led family ministry in the 1990s—indicates major changes in state-society relations. While during the grand coalition the SPÖ stressed public child care as part of women's policy, the FPÖ/ÖVP coalition shifted the state's role in the care of families. Personal choice and individual responsibilities were the main metaphors used in the debate indicating the neoliberal priorities of a minimal state. The paradox is that although deregulation and reduction of public spending was in the foreground of the debate on families, in fact, the policy led to an expansion of state activities through increased state spending.

WOMEN'S MOVEMENTS IN THE NINETIES AND AT THE BEGINNING OF THE TWENTY-FIRST CENTURY

Since the late 1980s the autonomous Austrian women's movement has consolidated as a "project movement" organizing to work on specific issues. By the 1990s there were no more spectacular demonstrations and activities; rather, movement actors worked through several settled associations in close cooperation with allies inside state and party institutions (Kogoj 1998: 239). Movement organizations were state-funded, they successfully lobbied for legal change, and movement activists became part of national and provincial women's policy agencies. They have also formed significant local, regional, and national networks. For example, the issue of (domestic) violence against women has been one of the major concerns of the Austrian movement activists and they promote hotlines for victims of violence and shelters for battered women, as well as campaigns against sexual harassment and child abuse. Education and job-training agencies and counseling centers for migrant women comprise part of the women's movement networks all over the country. Feminist journals and archives, art groups, and networks of feminist researchers form a vivid women's movement culture and public (Frauenfakten 2004). Federal ministries, such as the Women's Ministry and the Ministry for Social Affairs, and local and provincial institutions support most of these women's movement projects.

Traditionally, the Austrian women's movement has had a second branch—women's organizations in parties and trade unions. The most powerful of these organizations is the SPÖ women's organization, founded in the nineteenth century. The conservative ÖVP also formed a women's association according to the party's organization principle of associations within the party, for instance for peasants, pensioners—and women. The ÖVP's women's organization has been modernized since the end of the 1990s: it was renamed as "women's offensive" and tried to mobilize a young female constituency. While the FPÖ's women's section stays in the background, the Green Party does not have a separate women's organization, but several women's movement actors hold party positions.

In the mid-1990s when the government launched the first austerity programs, movement activists together with Johanna Dohnal, the former minister for women, mobilized to form a women's party (Kogoj 1998: 253 ff.). Although the party never materialized the idea stimulated a public debate on women's issues. Thus, at the time of the so-called women's referendum in 1997 movement supporters were mobilizing and activism was reemerging. This people's initiative would for instance amend the constitution with an article on affirmative action and pass several laws to improve the situation of women (Rösslhumer/Appelt 2001: 60). The "women's referendum" was organized by the UFF (*Unabhängiges Frauenforum*—Autonomous Women's Platform), a group of female academics, journalists, and leftist politicians. Women's policy agencies on the national and on the provincial level provided support for it and it mobilized a highly politicized female constituency. Eleven percent of the electorate (644,665 citizens) voted for the "women's referendum" of April 1997, making it one of the most successful people's initiatives in Austrian history (Rosenberger 1998: 221).

Parliament debated the demands of the referendum, followed by a "women's summit" convened by women's minister Barbara Prammer (SPÖ), including the federal chancellor Viktor Klima (SPÖ) and representatives of the UFF. Nevertheless, by the fall of 1997 there was no action on the referendum's content and the UFF once again went to the streets. It organized weekly demonstrations, yet still there was no concrete response from the government (Dackweiler 2003: 146ff.). Eventually, in April 1998, however, an amendment to the anti-discrimination paragraph in the constitution providing for positive discrimination to benefit women did appear, also a request from the European Commission.

In the 1990s movement actors were close to the Left parties, namely the Social Democrats and the Greens. They were also involved within state institutions on the national as well as on the provincial level. This activist-consolidated movement of the 1990s has been in decline since the new conservative government came to power in 2000. Women's projects faced loss of state funding and the government has kept women's projects in a state of insecurity regarding their future financial support. In Vienna, the Social Democratic government has come forward to bridge the money gap of women's projects.

The movement faces other forms of powerful opposition. For instance, an ÖVP deputy, Helmut Kukacka, launched a campaign in 2000 against women's movement organizations. He persuaded a parliamentary commission to review the funding of civil society organizations by the (at that time Social Democratic) social ministry between 1995 and 1999. It examined 250 civil society organizations, more than forty of which were women's groups. Some of them were publicly summoned to prove that they did not misuse the funds for illegal activities—like supporting "secret" prostitutes (*Stichwort Newsletter* 2002: 11).

LAW ON CHILD CARE ALLOWANCE 2001

How the Debate Came to the Public Agenda

The 1990s were characterized by several changes in laws concerning families and care work. The goals of family policy in these years were twofold: the support of families to ease the reconciliation of care work and waged labor and traditional fiscal family support through direct child allowances. Throughout Austrian politics, family policy is perceived primarily as a conservative issue, a means for the ÖVP to distinguish itself from the SPÖ. Therefore family policy became an arena of competing family and equal opportunity policies of the two governing parties. In 1993 a law on pension reform guaranteed the recognition of four years of care work for pension benefits (Mairhuber 1999: 40ff.). In 1996 the law on budget reduction changed the law on parental leave benefits, providing a fixed payment instead of linking the benefit to the wage. Since 1990 parental leave benefits had been granted to women and men in waged labor up to two years as compensation for the loss of earnings in the case of child care (Rösslhumer/Appelt 2001: 59ff.).

At about the same time, the government made an effort to encourage more fathers to take parental leave and to increase their low share of 1–2 percent (Tazi-Preve 2003: 449). Since 1998 parents on leave have had the right to work; their wages reduce parental leave benefits, but the measure provides the opportunity to keep in touch with the employer (*Austria's National Report* 1998). Since then, benefits were granted up to eighteen months if the second parent is also taking parental leave.

These policies were the result of compromises reached by the SPÖ/ÖVP government in the 1990s—so-called package solutions. These packages linked different policy areas, for instance women's policy (e.g., the amend-ment of the law on affirmative action) with family measures (e.g., tax deduc-tions for children) (Rosenberger 1999: 765). While the ÖVP raised direct money transfer to families, the SPÖ raised government spending in public child care: although the Austrian provinces are responsible for public child care facilities, in 1996 the government launched a program to create more child care facilities (ibid.: 768). On January 1, 1999, the first part of the third "family policy package" was enacted.[1] It raised the fiscal support for families, especially for multi-children families, and added flexibility to the parental leave regulations according to the EU parental leave directives: three months of parental leave could be taken anytime before the child's seventh birthday, fathers got an individual right to go on parental leave, and the leave could be alternated two times between the mother and the father.

On January 1, 2000, the second part of the "family policy package" came into force. It again raised the amount of family allowance and changed fam-ily taxation towards horizontal redistribution (ibid.: 766). While vertical re-distribution reduces for instance costs and taxes for low-income households with children, horizontal redistribution shifts the tax load from people with-out children to people with children—irrespective of their income.

In the second half of the 1990s a debate on the demographic change came to the public agenda. Birthrates were in decline—the fertility rate had fallen from 1.501 per woman of childbearing age in 1993 to 1.333 in 2001 (www.statistik.at; Walter 2004: 23). On the one hand the decline of the birthrate discursively was connected to the debate on the crisis of the Austrian welfare state: falling birthrates endanger the "generation contract", the basis of the Austrian pension system. The demographic discourse on the other hand encouraged the fear that Austria might be a "dying state" (ÖVP Deputy Georg

Schwarzenberger, Nationalrat 2001) and that too many foreign children will be born.

In the mid-1990s the ÖVP-led Ministry for Families introduced a radical change in the discourse on family support through an enquete "Does the economy need family?" Since 1998, the ÖVP has repeatedly advocated stronger protections of the traditional family—for instance by amending the Austrian constitution with an article to support and protect family and marriage.

While promoting traditional moral family values, these debates also legitimized cuts in the welfare system. Legal measures, which accompanied this discursive reevaluation of the family in the mid-1990s, were changes in family taxation. Several rulings by the Austrian Supreme Court supported this policy of "negative taxation" and tax reduction for having children, which accompanied a shift from vertical redistribution towards horizontal distribution from people without children to people with children (Rosenberger/Schallert 2000: 254). This incidentally also strengthened the male breadwinner model (Dackweiler 2003: 106ff.).

Family issues played a major role in the national election campaign of fall 1999. Both right-wing parties, ÖVP and FPÖ, promised a salary for child care, which would be the same for each child and paid to all mothers or fathers, regardless of former employment. To support the election campaign of the ÖVP, the conservative Family Association launched a people's initiative on families in September 1999, which demanded parental benefits for everybody and the strengthening of families. The initiative was signed by 183,154 voters (www.familienbund.at/body/volksbegehren).

The FPÖ had started a similar campaign earlier in the province of Carinthia. Jörg Haider, the FPÖ governor,[2] argued that women should have the choice between waged labor and domestic child care and introduced a so-called children's check. According to this model, all mothers would receive a certain amount of money with which they could either buy public child care or stay at home with their children and take the money as salary for child care. The "Austrian Institute for Family Research", funded by the Ministry of Families, in 1999 conducted a feasibility study on the children's check and concluded that the model could be financed and would have horizontal distributive effects (Schattovits 1999).

In the election campaign of 1999, ÖVP and FPÖ proposed major changes in family policy. One of their main goals was to enhance care work and to create incentives for child care at home. After the formation of the Federal Cabinet in January 2000, FPÖ and ÖVP adopted the slightly different model of child care allowance and stressed that each child should get the same amount of money. The Ministry for Social Security and Generations, which then was responsible for family issues, worked on a bill presented to the Parliament and passed to the parliamentary commission on families in May 2001. In July 2001, the Law on Child Care Allowance was adopted by the ÖVP/FPÖ majority in the Austrian parliament.

Dominant Frame of the Debate

By the end of the 1990s the claim that Austrian families were in crisis dominated the family policy discourse. As Sonja Moser, ÖVP minister of families, stated: Families are endangered by social developments. Symptoms of this crisis are high divorce rates, high numbers of single mothers, a declining birthrate, a care gap, and the disappearance of the ideal family with mother, father, and several children ("Familienministerin" 1995; see also ÖVP party program: Grundsatzprogramm der ÖVP 1995). Arguments in this debate took a dramatic perspective, demanding to know the reasons for the erosion of the family and forcefully recommending solutions to the crisis.

ÖVP and FPÖ focused on the importance of the nuclear family to society as well as to the well-being of children. To these parties, in the ideal family the mother stays at home with the child and only after several years takes on, at most, a part-time job (FPÖ Minister Herbert Haupt, Nationalrat 2001; Das ÖVP-Familienbuch 1999). These parties persisted in their claim that due to pressures on parents, families are no longer able to fulfill their functions of socialization of citizens. Further, they argued that the decline of the birthrate required that family policy be a form of population policy that would promote more births (FPÖ Minister Herbert Haupt, Nationalrat 2001). Painting the picture of Austria as a "dying state", the ÖVP stressed that family policy is "policy for life" (ÖVP Chancellor Wolfgang Schüssel, Nationalrat 2001). Towards the end of the debate, the FPÖ deputy in the Austrian upper house (Bundesrat), Monika Mühlwert, and the minister for social security and generations, Herbert Haupt (FPÖ), added to this gloomy picture by claiming that the erosion of the traditional family and the lack of cozy surroundings in public child care institutions also contributed to increases in social pathologies like drug abuse and violence (Bundesrat 1999; Nationalrat 2001). With the future of Austrian society at stake, the rightist parties pledged to protect and support the Austrian family (ÖVP Chancellor Wolfgang Schüssel, Nationalrat 2001).

The ÖVP and their allies in family protection organizations made the pathologies of modern societies responsible for the sorry state of families. They portrayed adults as more and more selfish, seeing children only as a burden on their own individual freedom (FPÖ Deputy Monika Mühlwert, Bundesrat 1999). Others in the debate placed the general responsibility for the declining family on society as a whole, which did not value care work within the family (FPÖ Deputy Monika Mühlwert, Bundesrat 1999). To push the point home, ÖVP Deputy Ridi Steibl called Austria a "cold society" (Nationalrat 2001). The anti-modern theme was linked with critiques of profit-crazy private enterprise: the FPÖ and some ÖVP deputies criticized the waged labor orientation of the Austrian society and labeled private enterprise as the iron market economists (FPÖ Deputy Edith Haller, Nationalrat 2001)—for not valuing care work and for only insufficient provision of part-time jobs (ÖVP Minister Martin Bartenstein, Bundesrat 1999). Moreover, they blamed the previous coalition government, by its emphasis on waged labor for both fathers and mothers, and for degrading and devaluing care work.

When the ÖVP was in coalition with the SPÖ, however, it had promoted a form of dual breadwinner model for families. In 1996, the minister for families, Martin Bartenstein from ÖVP, stated that the aim of family policy should be to enable women to choose between family and job and to reenter waged labor after parental leave ("Mütter" 1996). The speaker for family issues in the ÖVP, Ridi Steibl, argued in favor of a dual track to improve the situation of families: first to give parents the choice to stay at home with their children by granting a child care allowance and, second, measures for the reconciliation of family and job like public child care, child minders, and part-time jobs (Steibl 2000). These arguments point to another view in the family debate— the importance of flexibility in patterns of work. "Choice" became the symbol for this approach.

This frame became part of the argument that families needed to be reevaluated. The ÖVP stressed the importance of family work—equal to wage work. In 1995, the Family Minister Moser pointed out that families are the smallest profit unit of the society and that the economy needs families for recreation and reproduction ("Familienministerin" 1995). At the end of the debate, both parties, FPÖ and ÖVP, stressed the necessity of paying parents a salary for raising children (Rauch-Kallat 2000)—although the FPÖ deputy wanted to restrict the salary only for native Austrian children. Also other organizations, like the Catholic "Institute for Marriage and Family" wanted child care recognized as valuable work (Institut für Ehe und Familie 2001). Interestingly this argument like the demand for women's choice resembles demands by women's movement actors in the early days. But in the context of neoliberal restructuring, choice, unlike the women's movement vision, evokes the connotation of uncertainty and precariousness of the labor market.

The Social Democrats, in contrast with the ÖVP/FPÖ government, viewed the problems of families in terms of poverty—especially of single mothers— and as a lack of possibilities to combine child care and waged labor for both mothers and fathers (SPÖ Deputy Alfred Gusenbauer, Nationalrat 2001). The SPÖ, together with the Greens, criticized the "conservative family ideology" of the governing parties (Green Deputy Madeleine Petrovic, Nationalrat

2001). Both left-wing parties wanted to introduce a new definition of family beyond the male breadwinner model and marriage. The Greens also fought for the rights of same sex parents (Green Deputy Ulrike Lunacek, National-rat 2001). These views differed from the ÖVP, which also demanded a rede-finition of "family" to include the rising numbers of lone parents, but still per-sisted in maintaining the importance of heterosexual marriage.

Another frame of the debate included contrasting views of justice and equal-ity. Representatives of the SPÖ, for instance the party leader Alfred Gusen-bauer and the "Austrian Children's Friends", a youth organization close to so-cial democracy, claimed the most important problem of Austrian families was the high poverty risk for people with children (Österreichische Kinderfreunde 2001; Nationalrat 2001). While the SPÖ's party program from 1998 argued that family policy must be social policy (SPÖ-Forderungen 2000), the ÖVP countered that family policy must be seen as a specific policy to support fam-ilies—regardless of family income. SPÖ representatives and children's advo-cacy groups criticized the bill for pushing women out of the labor force. Child care benefits would be too low, and it will be the person with the lower income in a partnership to go on leave—usually the women.

While the Social Democrats located the problem of families in the lack of public child care facilities and in social inequalities between families (SPÖ-Forderungen 2000; Österreichische Kinderfreunde 2001), ÖVP and FPÖ launched a new concept of justice and equality: social inequality was not a difference in family income but a difference in having children or not having children (ÖVP Minister Martin Bartenstein, Bundesrat 1999). Therefore equality needed to be established between people with and without children. Moreover, each child should be treated equally. Therefore, parental leave ben-efits were portrayed as an unjust policy towards farmers' wives, self-employed women, and students who were not eligible for the benefits before. The idea about equality changed from a conception of vertical redistribution to horizontal distribution. "Each child counts the same" was the slogan of the ÖVP (ÖVP Deputy Andreas Khol, Nationalrat 2001). The FPÖ argued in fa-vor of the child care allowance also with some references to social equality. Minister Haupt supported the child care allowance with a populist wording: the new law would end poverty of families and stop a situation where "the rich get richer and the poor get poorer" (Nationalrat 2001).

The experts who wrote the family report[3] denied the crisis of the Austrian family. Although the number of marriages and the birthrate are declining while at the same time divorce rates are rising, the nuclear family, they found, is still the main form of living together (Familie im Wandel 2000: 3). They concluded that measures against birthrate decline have to enable parents to take over responsibilities for children while being in waged labor. The report cast doubt on the claim that a salary for caring for children would be an appropriate instrument, especially since there were not enough resources to fund it adequately (ibid.: 5).

Gendering the Debate

All participants explicitly gendered the frames of the debate. The debate involved two different views of family and gender associated with the Right and Left of the political spectrum. The governing parties ÖVP and FPÖ portrayed women/mothers as victims of the economy and of the former governments, which prohibited them from exercising their right to choose between child care and waged labor; as a result women suffered from a double burden (FPÖ Deputy Monika Mühlwert, Bundesrat 1999). While SPÖ's political goal was to integrate all women—also mothers—into the labor force and to establish public child care facilities, ÖVP and FPÖ stressed the necessity of child care within the family. However, at the same time, ÖVP shifted its policy towards working mothers in the late 1990s and came out in favor of the adult breadwinner model (Steibl 2000). They reconciled the apparent contradiction by accepting women's labor only as part-time work and recommending additional earnings to the male breadwinner. The new law on child care allowances would allow women the freedom of choice between care work and waged labor (FPÖ Deputy Monika Mühlwert, Bundesrat 1999) and, presumably, restore their dignity by placing child care on a par with waged work. FPÖ Minister for Social Security and Generations Herbert Haupt—also responsible for women's affairs—stated, that because women can't afford to raise children, they leave them too early (Nationalrat 2001). He praised mothers and called women "heroines of work" (ibid.). In the discourse of FPÖ, gender intersects with ethnic or nationality biases: in the election campaign 1999, posters advertised the children's check as a salary for mothers—but only for "Austrian mothers" (Rosenberger/Schallert 2000). ÖVP and FPÖ blamed the previous government and the SPÖ women's ministers for discriminating against specific groups of women, such as farmers' wives, self-employed women, and students, who were not eligible for parental leave benefits, and increasing inequality among women.

A related frame of the right-wing parties was the idea that women had no choice about working but that the SPÖ-led women's ministry forced women into waged labor, where they suffered alienation due to assembly line work (FPÖ Deputy Monika Mühlwert, Bundesrat 1999; ÖVP Deputy Andreas Khol, Nationalrat 2001).

Quite another view of the problem of families is represented in the 1999 "Report on Families" (Bundesministerium für Umwelt, Jugend und Familie

1999) and the government's answers to the CEDAW committee (*Austria's Fifth Report* 1999). Experts, some of them feminists, centered the problems with the Austrian family in terms of discrimination and gender roles, as for instance the sole responsibility of mothers for children and the lack of shared parenthood (Familie im Wandel 2000). Representatives from the SPÖ and the Green Party also brought gendered frames into the debate. One of their main arguments was that the new law aimed at bringing women back to the kitchen and reestablishing the traditional division of labor between men and women (Anfrage der Abgeordneten 2000). The picture used was a "stone age for women". The Greens located the problem of families in gender inequality, that is, in the sexual division of labor and the discrimination against women in the labor market (Green Deputy Madeleine Petrovic, Nationalrat 2001). SPÖ Member of Parliament Barbara Prammer and former minister for women's issues demanded more "gender democracy" (Anfrage der Abgeordneten 2000).

The role of men was not neglected during the debate: some deputies claimed that the market economy did not give enough opportunities for men to take over care responsibilities by offering more part-time work opportunities (Bundesrat 1999). In the parliamentary debate, the SPÖ leader Gusenbauer criticized the proposal because it went too far in pushing fathers to take parental leave. With the low benefit and few instruments allowing men to stay connected to their employment, their overall status would drop (Nationalrat 2001).

Policy Outcome

The Austrian parliament passed the law on child care allowance on July 4, 2001. It became effective on January 1, 2002, for children born after December 31, 2001. The child care allowance is not based on income at the time of leave but is the same amount of money for each child—14.53 euro per day (BGBl I, No. 103/2001, §3,1). The parent on leave is allowed to have a supplementary income, up to the amount of 14,600.00 euro per year (ibid., § 2,1.3). Anyone who cares for a child is eligible for child care allowance *regardless of employment status*. Thus, now housewives, farmers' wives, self-employed parents, and students are eligible for child care allowances severing the link between the benefit and employment. Child care allowance is granted only for the youngest child and only if the child has regular health checks, which need to be documented in the "Mutter-Kind-Pass" (ibid., §3, 2). The benefit is paid until the child is three years old—if both parents share the care work consecutively. If only one parent is caring, eligibility for the child care allowance is only thirty months. Parents who get child care allowance have a minimum health insurance and the period of the allowance is counted in the state pension system. The benefits are financed by the family compensation funds and distributed by the national health insurance organization (Bundesministerium für Gesundheit und Frauen 2004: 57).

MOVEMENT IMPACT

Women's movement actors outside of parties were not accepted as main participants in the policy subsystem pertaining to the child care allowance. The main actors were government representatives and members of Parliament. Women deputies argued along party lines. Women from the governing parties who took part in the policy debate did not advocate women's movement goals. The women's section of the ÖVP supported the law on child care allowance and did not question the reprivatization of child care. Members of the Social Democrat women's organization such as Barbara Prammer, the former women's minister, framed the family issue in terms of women's policy and not only as children's or population policy. She actively gendered the issue in feminist frames together with women's movement actors inside the Green Party, some of them members of Parliament, like Ulrike Lunacek.

Some (feminist) experts and social scientists were engaged in family issues at the end of the 1990s, but were not invited to discuss the law on child care allowance. They claimed on one hand that child care should be recognized as work, but on the other they warned that a minimum salary would prevent fathers from staying at home with their children and that mothers would be forced to leave the job. We can conclude that women's movement actors took part in the policy debate but that the policy content did not coincide with the women's movement goals. Therefore we can value this policy debate as a case of co-optation.

CHARACTERISTICS AND ACTIVITIES
OF THE WOMEN'S POLICY AGENCY

The 1990s were the period of consolidation and expansion of women's policy agencies in Austria. In 1990, negotiations in forming the new coalition government resulted in an upgrading of the state secretary for general women's issues to become the Federal Ministry of Women's Affairs. For the first time, the ministry was allotted its own budget. In 1992 and 1993, its resources were 37 million ATS (2,688,895 euros) per year,[4] which is rather low, compared to other cross-sectional ministries. But the ministry was able to expand its staff from seventeen people in 1992 to thirty-three in 1999 (*Österreichischer*

Amtskalender 1992–2000). The minister's status also increased at the beginning of the 1990s beyond the previously limited advisory function. She gained a veto right in the Cabinet of Ministers as well as the power to initiate further women's policy initiatives. During the 1990s changes in the leadership of the Federal Women's Ministry took place: Johanna Dohnal (SPÖ), a self-declared feminist, state secretary for women's affairs since 1979 and the first women's minister, resigned in 1995. Helga Konrad (SPÖ) succeeded Dohnal.

In December 1996, Konrad started an initiative called "Fifty-Fifty": Men and women should share the same load of house and care work. Women's movement organizations supported this view, but it was highly contested in the media, by ÖVP and FPÖ, but also within the SPÖ (Dackweiler 2003: 142ff.). The intensity of the conflict forced Konrad to resign soon after this campaign and in 1997 Barbara Prammer (SPÖ) took over the office.

With the change in government in February 2000 the Federal Women's Ministry was abolished. According to the Treaty of Amsterdam, the Austrian Council of Ministers started to implement structures and measures of gender mainstreaming in July 2000 in all federal ministries. The new conservative coalition asserted that since gender mainstreaming was the order of the day there was no need for a special ministry for women. But on the level of federal ministries gender mainstreaming remains in its infancy and at the stage of "pilot projects" (Sauer 2005).

As a result of these changes, the unit for women's affairs became part of the Ministry of Social Security and Generations. The ministry was headed first by a female minister from the right-wing FPÖ (Elisabeth Sickl). She was replaced only after some months by a male appointee of the FPÖ (Herbert Haupt). In 2000, the male minister institutionalized a new unit in the ministry — the "men's unit" — equipped with staff and budget. The goals of this section are to initiate research into men's roles and needs and to support those men facing discrimination.

For the first time, family issues and women's issues were located in the same ministry. The ministry had a cross-issue task; it had a political leadership, bureaucratic staff, and its own minuscule budget. The women's section in 2000/2001 had twenty-eight people (in five departments) (*Österreichischer Amtskalender* 2000–2002). It was close to power. The women's section in the ministry had no mandate in family policy — but as a cross-sectional and coordinative unit it could have had a voice in the debate. Despite the mandate and resources, the women's policy agency took no part in the child care allowance debate and did not advocate feminist goals. The women's policy agency acted merely symbolically in the debate on the law on child care allowance.

WOMEN'S MOVEMENT CHARACTERISTICS

In the mid-1990s the women's movement was reemerging due to the formation of the UFF and the "women's referendum" and its close cooperation with the national and provincial women's policy machineries. However, since the right-wing government came to power the movement is once again in decline and under pressure. Also, in the mid-1990s a conservative populist countermovement had emerged. The "Family Association", which had organized the people's initiative on families, along with the Ministry of Social Affairs and the Ministry of Families tried to erase the women's movement view on families, not only in terms of gender roles but even in terms of domestic violence. As a result of this frontal assault, women's movement actors have become closer to Left parties, especially to the Social Democrats and the Greens.

The second-wave Austrian women's movement has had a rather skeptical view about families and stressed the authoritarian family tradition in Austria, pointing out that the family has been the locus of violence against women. Moreover, the movement challenged the concept of a nuclear family. The family had been transformed and different forms of living together should be recognized and treated the same as traditional nuclear families— for instance single parents and homosexual parents. Due to this "anti-family" perspective movement actors criticized on the one hand family policy as being conservative, but on the other hand did not engage in the family policy discourse. While the reconciliation of job and care work has always been a priority for the Social Democratic women's movement, the concerns about family allowances and demographic changes were not high on the agenda of the autonomous movement. And, although the issue rose higher on the autonomous movement's agenda by the end of the debate on child care allowance, its main focus remained violence against women, and, to some extent, abortion access, migrant women, female education, and women in science.

All in all, the movement was not cohesive on the issue. The Social Democratic women's organization had an equality position of combining family work and waged labor; some maternalist activists criticized the waged labor orientation of the Social Democratic government and movement. Nevertheless, the positions were not fundamentally divergent but more a disagreement over the salience of the issue than the frame. In any case, there was no activism from the autonomous movement actors on the child care allowance and the Social Democrat and Green Party actors were limited to making a few speeches in Parliament.

POLICY ENVIRONMENT

The issue of family policy is the responsibility of the Ministry of Families. During the grand coalition between SPÖ and ÖVP the Ministry of Families was headed by conservative ministers from the ÖVP: from 1995–1996 Sonja Moser, followed by Martin Bartenstein, 1996–2000. After the right wing parties took power in 2000, the issue shifted to the FPÖ-led Ministry of Social Security and Generations. The Ministry of Finance also had a say in the debate. The federal parliament made the final decision in the law. This policy subsystem was closed. The only outside organizations heard were conservative family organizations close to the dominant ÖVP and FPÖ. For instance, the "Family Association" offered favorable reviews on the proposed law. The "Austrian Institute for Family Research" published a feasibility study claiming that the children's check model could be financed (Schattovits 1999). The ideas of the women's movement, which supported the work/family reconciliation approach to family policy, were incompatible with the dominant frame in this policy subsystem.

CONCLUSION

Austrian family policy in the new century is a crucial component of the neoliberal project of restructuring the relation between society and state. New orientations in family policy also have an impact on equal opportunity policy because the expansion of state spending and direct money transfer to families justifies cuts in social policies that promoted a more vertical redistribution of wealth.

There are certainly contradictions in the outcome of the policy debate. The new family policy decision meets the neoliberal goal of the devolution of social responsibilities from state to society with the aim of saving money. At the same time state budgets are expanded to support this devolution process—the increased budget for family policy. Thus, the neoliberal family policy cocktail in Austria contains the reevaluation and reprivatization of care work, the shrinking of social redistribution, and the reward of having children with the discursive shrinking of welfare state expenses and selective expansion of state in terms of money transfer to families. This leads to the paradox that the state's responsibility declines, but not its budget.

The right-wing parties advocated shared family roles between mothers and fathers and used the debate on flexibility of work to give incentives to fathers to take over their parental role. While this appears at first to be a socially progressive point of view, in fact it is part of a neoliberal logic to return a public responsibility for child care to the family.

The law on child care allowance shows the more interesting dimensions of neoliberal restructuring and change of political style in Austria: rather than downloading the responsibilities to the regional governments as is discussed in Banaszak, Beckwith, and Rucht (2003), authority for family policy is concentrated at the national level. The connection of neoliberalism, conservatism, and populism also characterizes Austria's hot issue: family policy has been a means for right-wing populist mobilization and for the mobilization of emotions in politics. The Austrian women's movement didn't succeed in getting a voice in the debate and the women's policy agency acted symbolically. Thus, one of the final ironies of this case is the extent to which the right-wing parties excluded women's movement actors and at the same time justified their plan to push women out of waged labor through child care allowance by using feminist concepts and claims of another era, for instance, "wages for house and care work", shared parental responsibilities, and the possibility of choice for women.

Evaluations of the implementation of the law on child care allowance show that the number of parents who make use of the benefits has been growing constantly. While in June 2003 only 90,076 persons received benefits, in April 2005, the number was 168,000 (*Hohe Akzeptanz* 2003; *Wahlfreiheit* 2005). However, the effects of the law are ambiguous: the number of fathers who receive a child care allowance has been growing, but is still very low, 3.2 percent in April 2005 (in January 2001: 2.1 percent) (*Wahlfreiheit* 2005). Due to an amendment of the law in 2004, parents are allowed to gain money during the time of child care allowance. This measure should help mothers and fathers to be in contact with their employer; 25 percent of the parents take advantage of this. However, parents who receive child care allowance stay longer at home with their child than they had planned before (*Hohe Akzeptanz* 2003). While this makes it difficult to return to the job, the family ministry praises the law on child care allowance as a big success and has recently started a public campaign to promote the law. One of the posters says: "Great that mummy has more time for me!"

NOTES

Many thanks to Dorothy McBride, who clarified the arguments and edited the chapter. Thanks to Sieglinde Rosenberger, who contributed to the first version of the chapter.

1. The first family package was enacted in 1990; the second came into force in 1993 (Rosenberger/Schallert 2000: 253ff.).

2. Jörg Haider became known internationally for praising the "good labor market policy" of Hitler and by denying the Holocaust.

3. In 1999, the obligatory "Family Report" was published by the Ministry of Families. The research for the report was conducted by Austrian social scientists, some of them outspoken feminists (Bundesministerium für Umwelt, Jugend und Familie 1999).

4. Council of Europe, www.coe.int/T/E/communication_and_Research /press

3

Feminism and Indigenous Rights in Australia in the 1990s

Barbara Sullivan

Across the 1990s in Australia a heated public debate took place about the rights of Indigenous people. Many women and many feminists—both Indigenous and non-Indigenous—took part in this debate. Indigenous people make up only a small proportion of the total population of Australia (2.2 percent at the 2001 national census). However, they occupy a unique status as the direct descendants of those who were forcibly dispossessed of their land and subject to genocidal practices during white settlement/invasion (Reynolds 2001). Moreover, in the present day, Indigenous people continue to suffer significant disadvantage as a result of this history. National surveys consistently find that Indigenous people suffer more poverty, a much lower average life expectancy than non-Indigenous people, higher rates of infant mortality and childhood and adult illness, lower rates of school completion, higher unemployment, and higher rates of incarceration in jail and juvenile detention centers. This suggested to many Australians in the 1990s the urgency of ensuring that Indigenous people were able to exercise their full rights as citizens and of finding a just and equitable new relationship, a "Reconciliation", between Indigenous and non-Indigenous people.

This chapter aims to examine the influence of feminist voices in this debate. How have feminists organized and campaigned in relation to the rights of Indigenous people and in relation to Reconciliation? To what effect? The chapter begins with an examination of the universe of top-priority issues in Australia during the 1990s. I then select one of these for detailed study—the debate about Indigenous land rights that occurred in 1997–1998 in the wake of the Australian High Court decision in the case of *Wik*. This is followed by a review of major organizations within the Australian women's movement and of the issues and concerns pursued by them in the 1990s. I then undertake a

39

detailed analysis of the public debate which occurred about the *Wik* decision
when the Parliament debated legislation in 1997–1998. I conclude that feminist voices—aiming to advance the situation of women—did not play an important role in the debate about Indigenous rights in the late 1990s. Although
many (Indigenous and non-Indigenous) feminists were involved in the campaign for Indigenous rights, they did not work as feminists to "gender" the issue. In the context of a conservative and often hostile policy environment, activists aimed to advance the rights of all Indigenous people, women and men.
They were not successful in this campaign.

SELECTION OF DEBATE

Identifying the Universe of Hot Issues

A number of issues assumed the status of high priority issues in Australia during the 1990s.[1] One important issue was tax reform. The introduction of a
broad-based consumption tax—the Goods and Services Tax (GST)—was first
mooted in 1991 by the leader of the Liberal Party (then in opposition in the
Australian parliament). As in other Western democracies a consumption tax
was a central plank of neoliberal policy and was based on the idea that "user
pays" and that cuts in public funding could be achieved by shifting the burden from taxpayers to "consumers". The proposal for a GST was widely debated at the 1993 federal election and rejected by voters; the Liberal Party
was soundly defeated by the incumbent Labor Party and the unpopularity of
the GST was seen as the main reason for this defeat. At the 1996 federal election the Liberals—under the leadership of John Howard—campaigned more
broadly on "economic reform" and "fiscal responsibility". Labor was defeated. Over the next three years the specter of a GST was once again raised
by the Liberal Party (and vigorously opposed by the Labor Party). At the 1999
election the Liberals campaigned on a platform of encouraging economic
growth via a partial privatization of the national telecommunications industry
and tax reform, including a GST. They were reelected and a GST was introduced in 2000.

   Another "hot issue" of the 1990s in Australia was deregulation. As in other
neoliberal national contexts, this involved the reduction of tariffs (which, for
example, until the 1980s, protected Australia's agricultural and clothing industries), the deregulation of the banking and finance industries, and the
deregulation of labor markets. The latter was a particularly "hot" issue in the
late 1990s. While the Labor government began the dismantling of Australia's
centralized system of industrial relations, this process was accelerated after
the election of the Howard government. The government's aim was to break

the power of unions and thus to hobble the main opposition to labor market deregulation. This issue came to a head in 1998 when a "war on the waterfront" (see MUA 2003) led to a major strike of Australian ports, blockades, demonstrations, and public violence.

There was also a significant resurgence—and contestation—of right-wing politics in Australia during the 1990s. In September 1996 Pauline Hanson, a then Independent member of the House of Representatives, made a much publicized maiden speech in which she warned of the dangers of Asian immigrants swamping Australia and lambasted the "reverse racism" of a taxpayer funded industry servicing Indigenous people. Over the next few years Hanson became a well-known public identity and "the race debate" was widely canvassed on television and talk-back radio. Hanson's populist One Nation Party attracted significant minority support (undermining the electoral standing of the major political parties in some areas) but was opposed by large, and sometimes violent, public demonstrations (Scalmer 2001).

Another important "hot issue" in the 1990s was an Australian Republic. Like New Zealand and Canada, Australia is a constitutional monarchy. However, republicanism has a long tradition in Australia and a heated debate over this issue occurred between 1993 and 1999. In April 1993 the Labor prime minister, Paul Keating, indicated his support for a change from a constitutional monarchy to a republic by 2001 (the centenary of Australian federation). He proposed that the head of state be elected indirectly, by a two thirds majority of both houses of Parliament in a joint sitting. This issue was widely debated in the community over the next few years and by a People's Convention held in 1998. In 1999 the question of a republic was put to national referendum and defeated; while there was majority support for a republic, the republican vote was split by the issue of the indirect election of the head of state. Many republicans voted "No" in the referendum arguing that the head of state should be directly elected by the electorate.

As suggested above, one of the hottest political issues in Australia across the 1990s was the issue of Indigenous rights, especially land rights. In 1992 the High Court handed down a landmark decision in the case of *Mabo* and determined that Indigenous people could hold a common law "native title" to land that they had occupied since before white settlement. In December 1996 the High Court also extended the ambit of "native title" in its decision in the case of *Wik*. These two decisions threw into question the whole basis of the established system of land ownership and land use in Australia. They provoked significant public debate and consternation in the agricultural and mining industries (key industries in the Australian economy). In 1993 and again in 1998, the Australian government passed legislation to establish a new institutional framework for adjudicating native title. This legislation was widely contested by Indigenous rights groups, farmers, pastoralists, and miners and led to one of the longest debates ever in the Australian parliament.

Identifying the Debate for Study

All of the issues described above were "top national priority" issues in Australia during the 1990s. They affected a large proportion of society (that is, they had major scope); engaged major socio-political actors in a high degree of conflict; generated a wide range of public attention (as demonstrated through public opinion polls, demonstrations, strikes, conferences, etc.); and were a top priority issue for major policy actors such as the political executive and political party leaders. All of the selected "top national priority" issues also involved some degree of reconfiguration of state-society relations. In the case of tax reform, this involved a devolution of social responsibilities from the state to civil society; individuals were to pay less direct tax but to be more responsible for their livelihood and well-being. In the case of Indigenous rights, the High Court decisions of 1992 and 1996 clearly expanded state responsibilities—requiring the state to address historical issues, such as the white settlement of Australia, and present-day land use. It also explicitly reconfigured the citizenship rights of Indigenous people and their relationship both to the state and non-Indigenous citizens.

For this chapter I have selected one of the consistently hottest issues across the 1990s—the issue of Indigenous rights. As there are a number of different points where this issue assumes the status of "top national priority", I have limited my analysis to the public and political debate which occurred in the wake of the High Court decision in the *Wik* case (*Wik Peoples v. Queensland* [1996] 141 ALR 129). This debate began in December 1996 when the High Court decision was handed down. The end point is July 1998 when the Australian parliament passed legislation (the Native Title Amendment Act) that encompassed an administrative and political response to the High Court's *Wik* decision.

WOMEN'S MOVEMENT IN THE 1990s

In the 1990s the Australian women's movement was comprised of a diverse set of organizations and individuals. Sawer and Simms argue that it had "two faces":

> On the one hand there is the public face of glossy government publications listing the initiatives and the institutions which have been founded by government in response to feminist demands. On the other there are the continued actions of

women in small groups, often focused on the delivery of services, and the development of networks among the activists in these groups (Sawer and Simms 1993:241).

This represented the two main directions of the Australian women's movement in the 1970s and 1980s. On the one hand was the mainstream, "women's rights" approach of groups such as the Women's Electoral Lobby and of femocrats within the bureaucracy (Watson 1990). On the other hand, there were feminist groups that sought more radical change—for example in society's attitudes towards marriage, childbearing, rape, woman battering, and pornography. But the differences between these two "faces" of the Australian women's movement can be overestimated; in the 1970s and 1980s, many feminist groups obtained government funding (often as a result of femocrat support) and became involved in the feminist but non-government delivery of services to women.

At the beginning of the 1990s, there was said to be "widespread agreement" that the women's movement had become fragmented and lacked the "big picture" necessary for ongoing feminist campaigns (Sawer and Simms 1993:229). Sawer and Simms (1993) question this pessimistic view. They also suggest that many of the changes sought by Australian feminists in the 1970s and 1980s had been achieved by the early 1990s. For example, Australia had ratified the United Nations Convention on the Elimination of All Forms of Discrimination against Women; effective women's policy machinery existed at all levels of government (see also Sawer 1999); anti-discrimination laws and equality of opportunity laws had been enacted; funding for child care had risen dramatically; progress had been achieved on equal pay; significant public funding was in place for the support of feminist services addressed to women's health, housing, rape, and domestic violence; women's advocacy groups, such as the Women's Electoral Lobby, were receiving public funding; abortion was widely available and publicly funded via the nation's public health system; and women's studies courses were well established in several Australian universities (see Ryan in Caine et al. 1998:365–369).

There is certainly little evidence of a decline in women's movement activities in the 1990s. Women's policy machinery continued to operate within the institutions of the state although, as Sawer (1999) has argued, by the mid-1990s neoliberal "reforms" were impacting the effectiveness of these. Women's organizations continued to provide services for women—for example (peak organizations only), the National Association of Services against Sexual Violence, the National Network of Women's Legal Services, and the Women's Services Network. Other women's organizations addressed themselves to lobbying, advocacy, and education. One of the most important of these was the Women's Electoral Lobby (WEL). Founded in 1972, WEL pursued a range of issues across the 1990s. For example, it made submissions to government on abortion, sex discrimination and affirmative action, childbirth and breastfeeding, child support and family law, constitutional reform, welfare reform, tax (including the GST), industrial relations, superannuation, pay equity, equality before the law, education, maternity leave, federal budgets, and human rights (see WEL website, www.wel.org.au/).

Other important women's organizations in the 1990s included the National Women's Justice Coalition, which aims to promote "women's equality before the law in Australia". There were women's organizations that worked on specific issues, for example the Abortion Rights Network of Australia, or promoted the interests of particular groups of women—for example the National Network of Indigenous Women's Legal Services, the Older Women's Network, the Coalition of Activist Lesbians, the Association of Non-English Speaking Background Women of Australia, the International Women's Development Agency, and the Australian National Committee on Refugee Women. Several women's movement organizations arose in the 1990s to target the realm of public politics. For example, the Women into Politics group was (and is) a "coalition of women's organizations and individual women working towards dramatically increasing the numbers of women at all levels of public life". Emily's List financially supports the election campaigns of women running for state and federal parliament. The Australian Women's Party runs candidates in some state elections and advocates for reforms to the electoral system to ensure the equal participation of women in political life.

In the mid-1990s, the increasing deployment of neoliberal approaches in the public sphere began to significantly impact the possibilities of women's movement activities. As Sawer (1999) argues, this process was exacerbated after the federal election in 1996 when the Labor Party lost power and a coalition of the Liberal and National parties assumed government (under the leadership of Prime Minister John Howard). There was an immediate deterioration in relations between the government and women's movement organizations. As Sawer (1999) argues, women's organizations were now regarded as "special interest groups" and their ability to put women's issues on the political agenda became extremely limited. For example, in 1997 CAPOW! (Coalition of Australian Participating Organizations of Women) was defunded; this was the main networking and information-sharing group for women's movement organizations. After 1997 this role was taken over by electronic networking through Pamela's List. In 1999 many more women's organizations lost their operational funding—including WEL.

DEBATE

How the Issue Came to the Public Agenda

An Indigenous rights movement first began in Australia in the 1920s although a new phase of intense activism began in the 1960s and 1970s. In 1966 Vincent Lingiari led a walk-off of the Gurindji people from Wave Hill (Cattle) Station in protest against intolerable working conditions and inadequate wages. The protestors then began a seven-year struggle for the return of their traditional land on Wave Hill. Consequently, the first land rights legislation was implemented in the Northern Territory in 1974 (Brock 2001:2–7). However, the development of a national approach to Indigenous land rights was very slow and made little real progress during the 1980s.

In 1988 Australians celebrated the bicentenary of (white) settlement in Australia with great fanfare and expense. But at one point fifty thousand Indigenous people demonstrated in Sydney against ongoing racial inequalities and injustices. While many white Australians reacted angrily to these demonstrations, regarding them as an insult to their national pride, it is clear they provoked a new consideration of Australian history and of the injustices perpetrated on Indigenous people by white settlement. In 1988 the Labor Party prime minister, Bob Hawke, promised a "treaty" between the Australian government and Indigenous people. Unlike the USA, Canada, or New Zealand, there were no treaties made with Indigenous people during the white invasion/settlement of Australia. In 1991 the Australian government appointed the Council for Aboriginal Reconciliation; one of its prime duties was to develop the text of—not a treaty but—"Documents of Reconciliation" between Indigenous and non-Indigenous Australians. The aim was for this task to be completed by the centenary of Australian federation in 2001. At the end of 2000 the Documents of Reconciliation were presented to Australian leaders in a dramatic ceremony at the Sydney Opera House. In the same week more than 1 million people around Australia marched across bridges to indicate their support for Reconciliation.

However, it was not the movement for Reconciliation that pushed the issue of Indigenous rights to the top of the public and political agenda in the 1990s. Two landmark decisions of the Australian High Court were responsible for this. In June 1992, the High Court handed down its decision in relation to *Mabo*. Mr. Eddie Mabo was an Indigenous man who claimed ownership of his land in the Torres Strait Islands between Australia and Papua New Guinea. The High Court found in favor of Mr. Mabo and determined that under Australian common law Indigenous people could hold "native" rights to land. These rights pre-dated the white settlement of Australia in 1789 and—where

Indigenous people had remained living on or otherwise connected to their land—were retained into the present day. The High Court said that native title could be "rightfully extinguished" by the Crown—for example, by the freehold sale of Crown land—but where extinguishment had not occurred, Indigenous people could have retained their native title rights. At one sweep, then, the High Court set aside the legal fiction of "terra nullius" used to justify both the British settlement of Australia and many existing state-society relations. "Terra nullius" suggested that the Australian continent was "empty" at the time of white settlement and there were no governments, land titles, or sovereign/civilized people who needed to be taken into account (Butt et al. 2001). Thus the British crown was able to claim the territory as its own and did not need to negotiate or offer payment in compensation to the Indigenous people. As "terra nullius" was set aside in the High Court in the case of *Mabo*—and the pre-existing rights of Indigenous people were acknowledged—the whole basis of land ownership and land use in Australia was called into question.

The ensuing public debate about the implications of *Mabo* involved miners, farmers, pastoralists, politicians, and Indigenous people (and many other groups and individuals). It embraced the specific issue of land ownership as well as a more general debate about the historical injustices meted out to Australia's Indigenous people. In 1993 the Australian government—under the leadership of Labor Party Prime Minister Paul Keating—enacted legislation to address the *Mabo* decision and solve the many issues it raised. The Native Title Act of 1993 established the National Native Title Tribunal to mediate native title claims. It also specified some of the rights of native title holders (and claimants). For example, native title holders (and claimants) were to have a formal "right to negotiate" in situations where their land was to be subject to mining or compulsory acquisition for public purposes (Butt et al. 2001:97). The act also validated all Crown land acquisition since 1975 (when the Australian Racial Discrimination Act came into force). It gave native title holders a right to compensation in respect of future impairment of native title and established an Indigenous Land Fund to provide compensation where native title had already been extinguished (Butt et al. 2001:96–97).

But a number of important issues remained unsettled by *Mabo* and the Native Title Act. In particular, there was the question of whether native title was "extinguished" by the government grant of a lease (as opposed to freehold sale). This was an important question in Australia because 42 percent of the land was covered by pastoral leases granted (mainly) to sheep and cattle farmers by state and territory governments. The issue of pastoral leases was eventually addressed by the High Court in its decision in the case of *Wik*, handed down on December 23, 1996. This case—brought by the Wik and

Thayorre peoples of Queensland—involved a claim for native title over two large cattle stations that operated under a pastoral lease granted by the Queensland (state) government. The High Court found that the grant of a pastoral lease did not did not automatically extinguish native title rights or confer rights of exclusive possession on the leaseholder; the rights of pastoralists and native title holders were deemed to "co-exist" on land covered by a pastoral lease. However, the High Court also found that if there was any "inconsistency" between the rights of the native title holders and pastoralists, the rights of native title holders "must yield" (Butt et al. 2001).

In the Australian community the *Wik* decision proved to be even more controversial than *Mabo*. Pastoralists (and mining companies who saw the future implications for mining leases) as well as many politicians argued that there was now no "certainty" to land use. Without such certainty, they said, the pastoral and mining industries would be brought to a halt and the effect on Australia's economy would be devastating. The debate about *Wik* was also heightened by the publication of the findings of the "Stolen Children Inquiry" (the National Inquiry into the Separation of Aboriginal and Torres Strait Islander Children from Their Families) conducted by the Human Rights and Equal Opportunity Commission. This inquiry documented the forced removal of thousands of Aboriginal children from their families for more than a century. It described this practice as a significant abuse of the human rights of Indigenous people (a "genocide") and called for a symbolic admission of wrongdoing by government as a gesture of reconciliation. This was rejected by the new prime minister, John Howard, who feared the legal and compensation implications of an apology for past policies (and who anyway rejected what he called the "black armband" view of Australian history). The issue of an apology was widely debated in Australian society over the late 1990s (see Manne 2001)[2] and formed an intensely emotional backdrop in the Australian community to the debate about native title rights.

In 1997–1998 the prime minister attempted to formulate a legislative response to the *Wik* decision via amendments to the Native Title Act. However, his "ten-point plan" for these changes (see Butt et al. 2001:111–113) was angrily condemned by both Aboriginal leaders and white pastoralists. It was also publicly criticized by backbenchers within the government (members of the Liberal Party and National Party) and by Labor, Green, and Democrat members of the opposition parties within Parliament. The prime minister threatened a general election and a double dissolution[3] of Parliament if his efforts to implement the ten-point plan were unsuccessful. While the government had a clear majority in the lower house of Parliament, the House of Representatives, it did not have a majority in the upper house, the Senate. Here the balance of power was held by a number of minor parties—the Democrats,

Greens, and Western Australian Greens—and two Independent senators. In October 1997 the Senate voted to refer the Native Title Amendment Bill (the "Wik Bill") to its Legal and Constitutional Legislation Committee for a report on its basis in the Australian Constitution. This committee held public hearings, called for public submissions, and (in November 1997) published a report that identified several major problems with the bill.

However, after a marathon debate in both houses, the government eventually acquired the support of one Independent senator. Thus, the Native Title Amendment Act was finally passed in July 1998.

Dominant Frame of the Debate

At the beginning of the debate the dominant frame was set by the government's concern to "restore certainty" to land use in Australia without undermining the native title (and other) rights of Indigenous people. The problem, as the government saw it, was how to balance the needs of primary producers (who were a traditional mainstay of the Australian economy) with the rights and needs of Indigenous people. That there was uncertainty about land use—and about the scope and impact of native title rights on existing land use—was seen to be a direct result of both Australia's colonial history and (in particular) the High Court decisions in the case of *Mabo* and *Wik*. Consequently, there was general agreement that a "solution" had to be found. The government proposed a range of amendments to the existing Native Title Act including the validation of all existing leases; a specification of some of the rights of both leaseholders and native title holders; a modification (and reduction) of the existing "right to negotiate" held by native title owners; and the establishment of new procedures for voluntary agreements between native title holders and leaseholders and for settling native title claims. There were no attempts to argue these issues through the lens of gender (images of women, gender relations, challenges to male domination, etc.).

At the end of the debate, a year later, the dominant framing of the issue was basically the same. There had been a tinkering with the details of the proposed legislation—314 amendments to the original bill were accepted—but the overall problem (and "solution") was unchanged. No gender issues were raised.

Gendering the *Wik* Debate

While women parliamentarians (including feminists) were important actors in the debate—particularly in opposing the bill in the Senate—they made no attempt to gender the debate. In several hundred hours of parliamentary debate there is no comment on gender differences in relation to the native-title bill. Moreover, to do so would have been deeply problematic if not inappropriate. There *is* a small academic and policy literature addressed to the particular needs and concerns of Indigenous women in land rights negotiations. McGlade (2001:140–45), for example, argues that land rights policies developed by the federal government in the wake of the *Mabo* decision "fail to recognize Indigenous women, and arguably perpetuate a level of systemic discrimination". Brock (2001:1) draws attention to "the gendered nature of Aboriginal knowledge and relationships to the land" and considers the implications of this for the determination of land rights within the Australian political and legal system. In the 1970s when the first land rights legislation was implemented in the Northern Territory (NT) "(institutional) structures and the assumptions they reinforced made it difficult for women to present and articulate their rights to land" (Brock 2001:9). The NT Act did not take full cognizance of women's rights in land or of matrilineal lines of descent and inheritance (Brock 2001:8). Brock says:

> Assumptions were made in the early claims that. . . . rights to land were handed down through the male line and that men held primary spiritual responsibility for the land. The bureaucratic structures within which claims were pursued ensured that this interpretation predominated. The Northern and Central Land Councils, which were established to help traditional owners with their claims, were almost totally male institutions in their early days. The anthropologists and lawyers hired to research and prepare claims were also predominantly men. (Brock 2001:9)

By 1979–1980, however, some of these problems were being recognized and addressed (Brock 2001:9–10). Brock suggests that national and state processes for claiming native title do not appear to disadvantage Aboriginal women[4] although some problems remain particularly in relation to the protection of significant sites that are the responsibility of women (Brock 2001:10–11).

In the mid-1990s this issue was brought to public attention by a long and protracted campaign conducted by a group of Ngarrindi women who opposed the construction of a bridge to Hindmarsh Island in South Australia; the women claimed that the bridge would destroy significant sites of "women's business". This campaign involved both state and federal levels of government and eventually led to the establishment of a royal commission. Consequently, the Ngarrindi women lost their fight and the bridge was constructed. Brock says, "This case, more than any other, has brought before the Australian public the complex issues involved in the politics of land and the gendered nature of Aboriginal relationships with the land"(Brock 2001:14–15; see also Bell 2001).

Toussaint and others (2001:157–174) looked at how the land rights of Indigenous men and women have been represented and negotiated in three different state arenas. They did not find any evidence that women's interests had
been neglected. But Toussaint and colleagues (2001:174) also make an important intervention: they argue for the "centrality of the state as a major determinant of outcomes for all members of Aboriginal communities as they attempt to deal with the legacy of colonial history". That is, in land rights
negotiations it is the attitude of the state—and the extent to which it is dominated by mining and pastoral interests—that will determine the outcome for
all Indigenous people (men and women).

In the case of the *Wik* debate, it seems clear that the rights of all Indigenous
people were under threat and that the state was a major factor actor in this
process. In this context, it would have been an inappropriate feminist strategy
to "gender" the *Wik* debate.

Policy Outcome

The Native Title Amendment Act was passed by the Australian parliament in
July 1998. It provided for a significant modification of native title rights, for
example by specifying and extending the grounds for permanent extinguishment of native title by current land use agreements; by modifying the "right
to negotiate"; by allowing a range of pastoral and government activities without consultation with native title holders; and by making it harder for Indigenous people to make native title claims.

Women's Movement Impact

As suggested below, women's movement organizations did not advance a
specifically gendered analysis of the ten-point plan or Native Title Amendment Bill. The women's organizations that campaigned in support of native title—and against some of the amendments proposed by the Howard
government—did so on the basis of a general concern for the rights of Indigenous people (male and female). So if the question is "Did the policy
outcome coincide with women's movement goals?" the answer is no.
Women's organizations—like many Indigenous organizations—argued
that the amended Native Title Act was racist and represented a further dispossession of Indigenous people. It can be said, then, that the women's
movement impact was *co-optation*; individual women (especially feminist
politicians) were inside the Parliament but there was no policy satisfaction.

Women's Policy Agencies—Characteristics and Activities

The main women's policy agency at federal level[5] (in the 1990s) was the Office of the Status of Women (OSW). The precursor of this *insider/bureaucratic* agency was established in 1974 and maintained a continuous existence to the present day although (depending on the type of party holding government) often with a less marginal relationship to centers of power (see Sawer 1998). In the period under review in this paper, the OSW was located within the Department of Prime Minister and the Cabinet—that is, in *close proximity to the major power centers* in their institutional setting. It had a *medium administrative capacity* with some staff, separate divisions devoted to different project areas, and a moderate budget (see below).

During the *Wik* debate, the OSW was a multi-issue agency but did not have any specific (or visible) role in relation to Indigenous rights or native title. In the 1980s, largely in response to lobbying by Indigenous women and the white women's movement (see Sawer 1990 and Moreton-Robinson 2000:156–57), the OSW had become quite active in relation to the needs and concerns of Indigenous women. An Indigenous Women's Taskforce was appointed (see Daylight and Johnstone 1986) and several important conferences were held (Moreton-Robinson 2000:157). As a consequence of the Taskforce Report, an Aboriginal Women's Unit was also established inside the Department of Aboriginal Affairs.

In 1990 the Department of Aboriginal Affairs was abolished and the Aboriginal and Torres Strait Islander Commission (ATSIC) was formed. This became the peak representative Aboriginal body in Australia (McGlade 2001: 144). ATSIC played an important role in Aboriginal affairs and was "self-determining" to the degree that it is elected by Indigenous people; is the main policymaking body in Indigenous affairs; is the principal advisor to government; and has its budget allocated by the ATSIC regional councils (McGlade 2001:144). The Aboriginal Women's Unit became the Office of Indigenous Women (OIW) located within ATSIC (Moreton-Robinson 2000:157).

In 2001, McGlade (2001:145) expressed concern about the lack of women's representation on the ATSIC Board and about the lack of address of Indigenous women's issues within ATSIC. She (McGlade 2001:145) says the purpose of the OIW was to advise on the impact and effectiveness of programs on Aboriginal women. But the OIW was disbanded in 1997—at the same time the *Wik* debate was getting under way. This occurred as ATSIC faced significant budget cuts (up to $453 million) and as concerns arose that women's issues needed to be mainstreamed because they "were not getting sufficient corporate attention across ATSIC" (Turner cited in McGlade 2001:145). McGlade (2001:145) says that following the closure of the OIW,

ATSIC managers throughout Australia were required to implement a number of strategies to ensure women's issues were properly addressed. To date, however, there "has been no assessment or report into the effectiveness of these measures" (McGlade 2001).

Regarding the possibilities of any co-operation between the OSW and OIW during the 1990s, Moreton-Robinson (2000:157–58) says that although a dialogue took place between the OIW and the OSW, there was virtually no policy development between the two offices, because their priorities and issues were different. By 1997, however, when the *Wik* debate was under way, it was clear that the changed political climate was impacting heavily ATSIC, the OIW, and the OSW. All these bodies sustained significant budget cuts in the wake of the 1996 federal election when, after a long period of ALP (Australian Labor Party) rule, a conservative coalition government was elected. The so-called special interests of women and Indigenous people were no longer a high priority of social policy. Indeed, these were now often represented— particularly by neoliberal "economic rationalists" within the government—as contrary to good government.

In her recent review, Anne Summers (2003) has described some of the effects of Howard's policies after his election in 1996 and the significant re-shaping of women's policy machinery and of units devoted to gender equality. In 1997 the budget of the OSW was slashed from $5.58 million to $3.68 million and its staff numbers were more than halved (Summers 2003:5). At the same time the budget of the Human Rights and Equal Opportunity Commission was also slashed and the sex discrimination commissioner was forced to resign; her post remained unfilled for fourteen months. The Women's Bureau in the Department of Employment, Education, Training and Youth Affairs—a unit that had tracked trends in women's employment for more than thirty years and had been a strong advocate for equal pay—was also abolished.

Summers argues that the influence of the OSW was already in decline before Howard assumed office. However, Howard's impact on the OSW was wider than the budget cuts. In 1997 the *leadership* of the OSW changed significantly; Pru Goward, a journalist and friend and supporter of Prime Minister John Howard, was appointed head of the OSW.[6] She had no obvious ties to the Australian women's movement. In press interviews at the time of her appointment, Goward said she was a feminist but one concerned with "reclaim[ing] feminism from the Left"; the problem with the Left, she said, was that it regarded women only as oppressed victims. Her brand of feminism was "for the young women of today who want to embrace competition, business and success . . . for the mothers who want to stay home and look after their children; for tolerance, diversity and a recognition that there are many paths to (women's) fulfillment" (*Green Left Weekly* 1997). She refrained from any

criticism of government cuts to child care (although these cuts were in the order of $349 million in the 1997 budget). On Australian affirmative action
laws addressed to women in the workforce Goward said "we tried that & it
didn't work".

During the *Wik* debate the OSW made no public comment on Indigenous
rights or native title. The activities of the OSW, can, therefore, be classified
as *symbolic* on this issue (that is, it is not an advocate for women's movement
goals).

Women's Movement Characteristics

In 1997–1998 the Australian women's movement was very diverse, *cohesive*
(in relation to common goals), and in a stage of *consolidation*; that is, its organizations had structure, endurance, and regular support and were institutionalized in community and government arenas. The women's movement
was also *close to the Left* via its strong association with the Australian Labor
Party; many women's movement activists were members of the ALP and,
while not usually holding internal power positions, had some influence on
party policy.[7] In 1996, for example, the ALP introduced affirmative action
quotas to ensure that women would occupy at least 35 percent of parliamentary seats held by the ALP by the year 2001. In 1996–1998, however, the ALP
occupied the opposition benches in federal parliament. Feminists (although
not necessarily women's movement activists) were now also visible members
of the other major political party—the Liberal Party of Australia. In
1997–1998, during the *Wik* debate, the Liberals were the dominant partner in
a coalition federal government. Feminists were also prominent members of
minor parties such as the Australian Democrats and the Greens. As suggested
above, the minor parties held a balance of power in the Senate in 1997–1998
and thus, together with the ALP, played an important role in the *Wik* debate.

At the same time, it is clear that the issues raised by *Wik* were a *low priority* for the white women's movement. In 1997–1998 groups such as WEL, arguably the most important women's lobby group in Australia, were fighting
on a number of different fronts (see Sawer 1999; Summers 2003). For example, they were campaigning against the GST and against the massive cuts to
child care being implemented by the new federal government. Indigenous
rights were also not completely off the agenda of the white women's movement. WEL, for example, was involved in organizing Reconciliation discussion groups and in supporting the establishment of legal and other services for
Indigenous women (Personal communication from Marian Sawer). By 1999,
WEL also had a national policy explicitly supporting "reconciliation and native title".

Some individual members of women's movement organizations were clearly regarding the debate about *Wik* as a high priority. For example, in the South Australian WEL newsletter of February 1998 (no. 228) Deborah Mc-Culloch argued that native title was a "women's issue" and she urged WEL members to become active in the debate (for example by joining a Reconciliation group, lobbying members of Parliament, and supporting groups like Australians for Native Title and Reconciliation (ANTaR) and Women for Wik). Many women's movement activists were prominent members of groups such as ANTaR that explicitly lobbied for Indigenous rights during the *Wik* debate.

An interesting development in this regard was the formation in 1997 — from within ANTaR — of a group called Women for Wik. This group was "inspired" by a call at the National Reconciliation Conference by the wife of the governor general,[8] Lady Deane, for women to "take a lead in bringing the reconciliation process back on track" (see Women for Wik 1997). Lady Deane argued that, as women were the ones who held families together, they were also best suited to the task of achieving a reconciliation between Indigenous and non-Indigenous people in Australia. While the emphasis on women's traditional gender roles did not represent a feminist call to action, it is clear that many women, including some well-known non-Indigenous feminists (for example Elizabeth Evatt), were prepared to organize — as women — in support of Indigenous rights. Women for Wik was launched in Sydney "as a partnership between indigenous and non-indigenous women" (Gorton 1997). At the launch three Aboriginal women from the "stolen generation" shared their experiences as children taken away from their parents and the effect on their adult lives. This was said to have "opened the hearts and minds of the 500 women who attended" the launch; it also explicitly linked the *Wik* debate and the struggle over Indigenous land rights with the history of colonial appropriation and atrocity.

Women for Wik groups then formed in other capital cities and regional centers. Many high-profile women lent their public support to this group. In 1997 more than fifty women's organizations[9] endorsed a submission, prepared by Women for Wik, to the Senate committee investigating the Native Title Amendment Bill (see Women for Wik 1997). This submission argued that parts of the bill were "completely unacceptable in a democracy". Of particular concern were attempts to extinguish native title, to remove native title holders' "right to negotiate", and to impose a too onerous threshold test on native title claimants (see Women for Wik 1997). Women for Wik argued that the bill would bring the reconciliation process to an end.

It is interesting to note here the absence of any gendered analysis of issues in the *Wik* debate. Women for Wik was a group that mobilized support for Indigenous rights *by* women (but *for* Indigenous men and women). To this end it formed an explicit coalition with women's movement organizations without also engaging in conventional women's movement claims (for women). As suggested above, this would appear to be an entirely appropriate political strategy (given the policy context). It also represents the fruit of a long-standing debate between white feminists and Indigenous women in Australia. In the 1970s the Australian women's movement "demonstrated a particular lack of appreciation" of many of the particular concerns of Indigenous women (Reade 1994:218). While lip service was given to the involvement of Aboriginal women in feminist struggles, there was a glaring lack of understanding for the reasons why Indigenous women would not want to be involved in the (white) women's movement. Reade (1994:218) argues that feminists of all persuasions "seemed to find it threatening and too complex to comprehend that Aboriginal women identified the oppression of their race (both men and women) as taking priority . . . (and) white feminists were compelled to tackle the idea of being oppressors themselves". Dealing with white women's complicity in (historical and contemporary) practices of racism and colonialism was clearly difficult for many white feminists. This was an issue raised repeatedly by Aboriginal women (O'Shane 1976; Lucashenko 1994; Huggins 1998; Moreton-Robinson 2000). As Pat O'Shane (1976:33) argued, "sexist attitudes did not wipe out whole tribes of our people, sexist attitudes are not slowly killing our people today—racism did, and continues to do so". The unwillingness of white women and feminists to come to terms with the inheritance of racism and the oppression and exploitation of black men made it difficult for the white women's movement to understand the struggles and analyses of Aboriginal women (Curthoys 1992:443).

By the late 1980s and 1990s—and certainly by the time of the *Wik* debate—this situation was perhaps changing as sections of the Australian women's movement began to embrace a politics of difference (see Gunew and Yeatman 1993), to advance a critique of white privilege and to engage in coalition politics with Indigenous women. This may partly explain why, during the *Wik* debate, the women's movement worked generally in support of Indigenous rights and did not attempt to gender the debate.

Policy Environment

There were several different policy actors involved in the *Wik* debate—political parties, Indigenous rights groups, native title bureaucrats and lawyers, and mining and pastoral industry actors. However, the policy environment is dominated by the formal structure and rules of the federal system of government. Thus patterns of interaction were determined by the Australian

Constitution, by accepted parliamentary procedure and a party system dominated by two major political parties. It is notable that Indigenous voices (but
not women's voices) were almost completely closed out of this environment;
although the Howard government "consulted" with Indigenous leaders (particularly the National Indigenous Working Group), at the time of the *Wik* debate there were no Indigenous members of the Australian parliament.

During the *Wik* debate a Liberal-National Party coalition government was
in power. These parties represent the interests of business and rural people in
the Australian political system. While the Howard government had a clear
majority in the lower house (the House of Representatives), it did not have a
majority in the upper house (Senate). Thus the government needed to negotiate for support in the Senate from Independents and members of minor parties. Taken together, this means that the policy subsystem is moderately
closed; participation is limited to regular (government party) actors although
there are some free agents around (non-government party actors). The *frame*
used by dominant actors in this policy environment is not compatible with the
goals of women's movement activists in relation to the *Wik* debate; women's
movement actors sought an extension and/or consolidation of native title
rights while dominant actors in the policy environment want to limit these.

CONCLUSION

There is no evidence in this particular debate to support the broader claim that
the Australian women's movement—as an actor in its own right and via
women's policy agencies—is able to impact the conduct of high-priority national issues. The main women's policy agency in this policy arena—the
OSW—was placed close to the main arenas of power but played no part in
the *Wik* debate. Within the women's movement, some individuals and organizations campaigned on the issues raised by *Wik* and by amendments to the
Native Title Act debated in Parliament during 1997–1998. However, it is clear
that these issues were not an important general priority of the women's movement at the time particularly as it was already battling on a number of fronts
opened up by the election of a conservative government federally. It seems
likely that women's movement activists who saw Indigenous rights as a priority in this period both formed and joined non-feminist organizations such
as ANTaR and Women for Wik. Certainly women's movement activists seem
to have decided that it was inappropriate to engage in any specific "gendering" of the debate; a general support for native title and Indigenous rights was
regarded as the best strategy for advancing the interests of Indigenous men
and women. It is also clear that the policy environment was dominated by

forces hostile to any extension or entrenchment of Indigenous rights. In this context, women activists engaged in the campaign for Indigenous rights—and participated in the parliamentary debate—but were unable to have any significant impact on the final form of the Native Title Amendment Act of 1998.

The context for Indigenous rights has not improved in the years since 1998. The Howard government still holds office and has made a number of significant inroads into Indigenous self-determination. For example, in March 2005, ATSIC was abolished and Indigenous programs were "mainstreamed" within other government departments. In the last seven years there has been an emerging culture of agreement-making that has allowed Indigenous people to derive some benefit from the development of resources on countries with native title claims. At the same time, however, the bodies formally responsible for representing native title claimants have been inadequately resourced by the Australian government and this has resulted in ongoing but avoidable extinguishment of native title (see www.antar.org.au/). Three High Court test cases decided in 2002 (Ward, Anderson, and Yorta Yorta) have also effectively wiped out the possibility of native title recognition for many Indigenous people. The vast majority of Indigenous claimants now face an almost impossible burden of proof in meeting the criteria and standards of evidence required in native title determinations (see Wright 2003:3).

NOTES

I am grateful to Marian Sawer for generous advice and comments on an earlier draft of this paper.

1. These hot issues were identified by reviewing the "Political Chronicles" for the Commonwealth of Australia in the quarterly *Australian Journal of Politics and History*, 1990–2000.

2. By 2001 all state governments and many local governments had apologized. The federal government has expressed its "regret" but continues to refuse to apologize.

3. Only half the Senate seats are elected in a normal general election. In a "double dissolution" all Senate seats come up for election, thus increasing the government's chances of obtaining a majority in both houses of Parliament.

4. But Brock says it is also "not possible" to research this in depth while so many claims remain to be determined (Brock 2001:11).

5. Women's policy agencies also exist at state and territory levels of government.

6. Goward resigned from this position in 2000.

7. Where the ALP took up women's movement ideas this was usually not acknowledged and the ideas were usually "adjusted" to fit the party line.

8. The governor general is the queen's representative in Australia's constitutional monarchical form of government. As such, the governor general represents Australia's "head of state".

9. Including the YWCA, WEL, Union of Australian Women, and the National Women's Justice Coalition.

4

Speedy Belgians: The New Nationality Law of 2000 and the Impact of the Women's Movement

Alison E. Woodward

The reproduction of citizenship is a key task of the state. All state action can be tested against this. . . .

—Herman van Gunstren (1992: 119)[1]

Immigration issues fundamentally touch on state-society relations, as they concern the membership and rights of citizens. Who in a given society is a member of the polity and able to enjoy rights as well as carry out duties? The question of who is included as a Belgian nearly led to constitutional crisis at the end of the twentieth century. Increasing integration in the European Union, unresolved political integration of non-EU citizens, and the rise of a racist Far Right party politically inflamed the issue of migration and inclusion in the 1990s and led to a series of major debates around citizenship and the notion of being Belgian in Europe.

What it means to be a member of the Belgian polity has been in constant evolution since Belgium was founded in 1830. In the nineteenth century, Belgium was primarily a country of emigration. It had a narrow conception of access to political citizenship (Lefebvre 2003). Universal male suffrage came first in 1919. Women only gained full political citizenship in 1948. The twentieth century saw increasing restriction on citizenship, just as the country evolved into an interesting migration destination. European Union integration and the idea of European Union citizenship made Belgium an even more attractive political and economic magnet for migrants, but at the same time required Belgium to reconceptualize its own notions of citizenship.

Historians observe that even if membership is a central issue for the state, the legal construction of nationality is an issue for political elites (Caestecker and Rea 2002: 117). The theme of citizenship does not grab public attention in the same way that immigration policy and refugees do. However, the construction of the Belgian citizen and the construction of the immigrant are intimately tied to each other. On the one hand Belgium has been grappling with citizen identity related to linguistic identity, trying to pacify its language conflicts in a country with three official languages (Dutch, French, and German). Living together as ethnic-linguistic communities structured political debate and led to a change from a unitary to a federal structure by the end of the 1990s. On the other hand, increasing immigration posed new questions about living together, which had little to do with the classic linguistic cleavages but posed the question of what it meant to be a Belgian much more pointedly.

The foreign population in Belgium has remained below 10 percent since 1950 (Centrum voor Gelijke Kansen en racisme bestrijding 2000; Algemene Directie voor Werkgelegenheid en Arbeidsmarkt 2003; Foblets et al. 2002). At present 8.2 percent of residents in Belgium are foreign citizens. (Center for Equal Opportunities and Opposition to Racism 2005). Thanks to the immigration stop in the seventies, only family reunion and directed skilled labor migration has been tolerated. A larger proportion of the "foreigners" in Belgium have been residents for ten years or longer than in many other Northern European countries. France, Holland, Denmark, and Sweden have had a more active policy of soaking up permanent residents and the children of these residents into the polity than Belgium has. They actively encourage their slumbering potential citizens to naturalize.[2] The Belgian policy and practice regarding its foreign population has been restrictive and unwelcoming in comparison. This stiffened in the face of rising unemployment and economic difficulties.

Belgium's immigrant population includes both post-colonial (Central African) and "guest labor" (Mediterranean, North African, and Turkish) migration. The Belgian public discourse around the issue of the non-Belgian population underlines only the labor aspect of migration. In the last twenty years, the term "immigrant" has also been semi-synonymous with Islam or referring to those originating from Turkey or Morocco, even if these groups make up a relatively small proportion of the total foreign citizens. Belgians have a spectacularly incorrect picture of the composition of their "immigrant" population, vastly overestimating the presence of Moroccans and Turks (Billet et al. 1998; Morelli et al. 1998). The fact that a large proportion of foreign citizens are the spouses of Belgian citizens, tax refugees from neighboring countries (the Dutch), and third-generation children from Mediterranean member states of the European Union (Italy, Spain, and Portugal) as well as employees of multi-national and international organizations is seldom emphasized.

The state pursued a benign guest worker policy towards labor immigrants and family reunification, despite increasing societal tensions in big cities related to socio-economic problems connected with absorbing non-European immigrants and refugees. The state neglected its role in societal integration, and in developing policy frames which would privilege social peace. Bloemmaert and Verschueren (1998) made an extended analysis of the latent racism present in policy language. The term commonly used for the multi-colored and global group of people who have not been in Belgium for three generations is "migrant", they point out, yet most of these people have no plans of going anywhere. They lampoon the use of the term "illegals" to refer to those on Belgian soil without valid papers. People cannot be "illegal", even if their presence can be against the law. These people are, as Castles (1984) once pointed out, "Here for Good". However, the lack of state initiative provided fertile ground for the growth of grassroots resentment organized in Far Right political parties that aimed to send immigrants "back home" while Belgians returned to their ethnic roots. A slogan of the Flemish Far Right party *Vlaams Blok* indicates how deep the state-societal crisis was, demanding that Belgium explode (*België barst*) on the basis of nationalistic and immigration grounds.

SELECTION OF DEBATE

The Universe of Major Policy Issues in the 1990s in Belgium

A number of major issues challenged Belgian policymakers in the nineties arising from Belgium's integration in a new European context and the resolution of long simmering linguistic conflicts. A review of the political highlights of these years (in the Annual Political Yearbook published by the political science journal *Res Publica* 1990–2001),[3] reveals that the issue of the reform of the state and federalization of the three linguistic and three territorial communities dominates the political agenda throughout the decade, but these institutional reform issues do not move the public in the same way as other questions (Billet 1998).

The following five policy issues all occupied important places on the political agenda during the decade and fulfill the requirements of scope, conflict, relevance for political parties, priority, and public attention: reform of the police and justice system, immigration and citizenship policy, the rise of the Far Right, the reform of the Belgian state to a federal system, the divestment of state-owned companies such as Belgacom and Sabena, and adjustment to EMU (European Monetary Unit) requirements and food and farming issues (infections in chickens, pigs, hormone-free meat, etc.).

Naturally many of these debates are interlocking, and one political problem may impinge on several areas of policymaking. It is hard to identify *the most* salient issue in terms of changes in state-society relations, but one can rank them in terms of public salience and political priority. If the issues are ranked in terms of their scope, the degree of conflict, the level of public attention to the issue, and the priority for major parties, the federal reform and the divestment of state-owned companies do not fulfill the criteria of high level of public attention as well as the others. The economic restructuring to lower the deficit and reach the norms necessary to join the European Monetary Union, as well as to fulfill the competition requirements by divesting itself of public monopolies was an issue which led to conflicts for the industries involved and mobilized the labor unions. While one could argue that this led to a marketization of state tasks, the reforms did not capture public passion to the same degree as the other issues. The food and farming issues were limited in time and did not initiate state-society changes.

Two issues are virtually equal in terms of scope, conflict, public passion, and party priority: those around the justice system and around immigration issues. Both involve changing societal and state relations. The controversies around the corruption of the Belgian justice and political system revolved around a number of crimes committed during the decade and the incapacity of the state to resolve them in an efficient manner. These included the assassination of André Cools (1991), the political corruption scandals in terms of bribes that led to the resignation of major political figures (Agusta-Dassault affairs), the problematic prosecution of child murderer Marc Dutroux (1997), and a number of other scandals. Some of them also touched on food safety (murder of a veterinary inspector and contamination of chicken feed). Public frustration culminated in demonstrations and protest marches of a scale seldom seen in post-war Belgian society. The questions raised touch on the fundament of trust in political institutions, but they seldom received satisfactory answers within the political system. The policy debate framed the problem as a need for reform of the justice system and the rules of conduct in politics and solved it by changes in procedure in public administration. The proposed reforms that resulted from these events did not fundamentally challenge state-society relations.

While justice issues touched on societal trust in the state, the issue of the rise of the Far Right, immigration, and the pressures of globalization on society and the state's capacity to deal with these pressures had far-reaching implications for state-society relations. Certainly if politicians were asked about the issue of highest priority of the nineties it would be the electoral success of the Far Right, voting rights for migrants, and their social integration. This question has been high on the agenda of all of the political parties in Belgium, although particularly on the Flemish side. At stake was the identity of

Belgium itself, as it lost power on the European level and was in crisis in terms of who had citizenship rights. This issue had a dramatic effect on one of the most fundamental issues in state identity: membership in the polity.

This issue is the most clearly indicative of changing state-societal relations during this time period because citizenship rights at the micro-level of the Belgian polity are linked to the pressures of European integration. The European Union's neoliberal requirements for freedom of movement for the labor force, goods, and trade have had far-reaching consequences for Belgium's self-conception as a state. The requirements of integration brought about the restructuring of enterprises in the economy, but also affected the terms of membership in the polity. The passage of the Treaty of Maastricht (1992) guaranteeing the political rights of citizens of the European Union had far-reaching consequences for Belgium's sense of political sovereignty, as in Belgium, suffrage is considered not only a right of citizens, but also a duty since voting is mandatory.

Selection of Discrete Policy Debate: The Nationality Law Reform of 2000

Immigration and integration of migrants' political citizenship and asylum were conflicted throughout the period from 1990–2001. In the course of the decade, the procedures for both immigration and naturalization were revised several times. The nationality law of 1984 was revised in 1991, 1993, 1995, 1998, and 2000. Immigration issues were the subjects of public investigations by special commissions of Parliament including one on the Traffic in Women 1993. The constitution was also revised several times around issues of immigration and citizenship. There were many discrete debates meeting the criteria of salience, importance, and a resolution in an official state decision.

For a single debate with a concrete result related to both European integration and reflecting the reconfiguration of state-societal relations (from a restrictive citizenship regime to one of the most liberal in the advanced world, lacking any restrictions in terms of integration linguistically, in terms of knowledge or culture), the debate around the nationality law is a good choice. Its *scope* deals with the fundaments of membership in the political community with its attendant rights and duties. The debate about a radical revision of the rules for naturalization and the way that citizenship decisions are handled that surrounded the passage of *"The law of 2000 changing certain conditions of Belgian nationality"* is most significant as it brought the debate to a (temporary) halt and led to the enfranchisement of large numbers of people. It is important because

- It demonstrates a change in state control of the nature of state identity brought about in part by processes of integration into a European Union offering cross-national citizenship privileges

- It provides a new vision on the nature of the Belgian polity and the requirements for belonging
- It resolves temporarily the demands of progressives for a resolution of the paradox of European versus non-European citizens living on Belgian soil
- It results in a dramatic change in policy and the most liberal naturalization regime in Europe at the time of its adoption

Although the initial debate remained within the chambers of Parliament, and a matter for elites, it generated a *high degree of conflict* both within the government and with the Far Right and Christian Democrat opposition, who were opposed to the new regulations for differing reasons. A resolution of the debate was *essential for major policy actors* as the resulting compromise provided the lynchpin for the governing coalition. This specific moment in the ongoing policy debate did not directly elicit a *large interest in the general public*, although it was highly visible in the elite media. However many other debates on this issue that had excited the general public did not lead to a policy decision. The result of the debate, a new citizenship policy, did lead to wide media attention.

WOMEN'S MOVEMENT IN THE NINETIES

The Belgian women's movement in the nineties can be characterized as increasingly consolidated (Meier 2005; Celis 2001; Celis and Meier 2001) and institutionalized. It maintained its characteristics of strong cleavages on linguistic grounds, and in terms of its relation or non-relation to religious and political parties. The pressure of women's organizations and the increased stature of the women's movement in the political process thanks to the establishment of women's policy agencies in the mid-eighties at the federal level and in the late nineties at the regional level led to new resources, and many individuals were able to make women's activism into a paying activity. The period is characterized by restructuring and repositioning in a new political landscape.

The increasing federalization of the Belgian state meant that by the end of the nineties only a few Belgian cross-language women's movement activities remained. The activity and number of autonomous informal groups continued to decline, marked for example by the disappearance of the Flemish left-feminist journal *Schoppenvrouw* in the mid-nineties and the demise of the alternative women's house (offering shelter, plus office space for a wide variety of women's movement/feminist activist groups) on the Rue Blanche in

Brussels. However, an index compiled by the women's information center Amazone counted more than nine hundred organizations either devoted specifically to women, or with women's issues as one of their concerns (Amazone et al. 2002). Organizationally, the French- and Dutch-speaking umbrella organizations for women's formal organizations from the political parties, social partners, and autonomous sector (*Nederlandstalige Vrouwenraad* [NVR] and *Conseil des Femmes Francophones de Belgique* [CFFB]) increased their professionalism. Even if the groups had fewer visibly active members, professionals continued to organize their issues.

During this decade the autonomous umbrella organization on the Flemish side (*Vrouwen Overleg Komitee* [VOK]) celebrated its twenty-fifth anniversary. It published statistics showing a steadily decreasing attendance at its annual Woman's Day on November 11, but it continued to carry out analyses of politics and evaluations of the ministries responsible for women's issues and to publish a yearly list of demands. After 1995, the demands also evaluated the government in terms of the UN Platform for Action launched in Beijing.

The foundation of the federally funded women's house Amazone in 1995 is a powerful indication of the improved logistical situation of the women's movement. Both the Dutch- and French-language official Councils of Women (NVR and CFFB) have their headquarters there, as do numerous smaller organizations on all aspects of women's affairs. The documentation center and information service of the Flemish women's community got new quarters and stronger staffing in 2000 financed by the Flemish government, while the French-speaking community's library also grew. Women's studies, which was primarily a women's movement activity in the eighties, also became more institutionalized, with university programs established by the beginning of the nineties, and recognized and supported, if in limited terms, by the end of the period. Courses for credit in gender studies were offered in all Flemish universities by the end of the period and centers for gender research were established at several universities. While the women's movement may have been less visible on the streets, it was more present in lobbying and providing information on issues. The consolidation of the women's movement and new institutional actors supports an impression that the movement was perhaps less radical, but in fact the demands remained constant in comparison to previous periods.

In the nineties, economic issues, which have always been a focus for the Belgian women's movement, remained a priority. Representation of women in economic and political decision making also remained at the top of the bill of demands. In politics, this resulted among other things in the passage of dramatic legislation for quotas on electoral lists (Meier 2004). However, an increasing interest in the situation of women outside of Belgium (Afghanistan,

Africa, the countries of migration) also characterized the nineties. The issues were framed in the context of human rights and gender justice. Staff were delegated to work on global issues, and commissions on migration continued their work inside the two councils of women. This was certainly stimulated by the preparations for the UN Conference in Beijing in 1995 and the required review process of Beijing Plus Five. As the sexual traffic in women became more obvious in Belgium and evidence of violence against women of all backgrounds increased, global connections were more and more emphasized. A high point in Belgian women's movement expression of global concerns was the International World Women's March of 2000. The European phase culminated in Brussels. This event, which drew thousands of participants to Brussels, was barely covered in the media.

THE DEBATE ON THE NATIONALITY LAW

How the Issue Came to the Public Agenda

While the debate about the nationality law in 1999–2000 is relatively discrete, it is related to a number of other issues. On November 24, 1991 (Black Sunday), the Flemish Far Right achieved a significant electoral victory by running on a platform that was explicitly anti-foreign and anti-unified Belgium. The progressive (Socialists, Greens, Left Catholics) population reacted with manifestos and demonstrations demanding voting rights for foreign residents (Hand in Hand March in 1992). A highly placed female member of the Catholic ruling party (W. DeMeester) made a controversial statement in 1992 that voting rights should be extended to non-Belgian resident populations. Although shot down by the party establishment, this event opened the discussion that would be temporarily resolved with the revisions of the nationality law in 1999–2000.

It was the European Union Treaty of Maastricht (1992) that really put the issue of political rights for long-term residents on the agenda, however. A Council of the European Union 1994 directive to implement the treaty required that citizens of the other EU member states should have the *right* to participate in local elections. For Belgium this created a problem.[4]

The directive was problematic and required a constitutional amendment of Article 8 to modify the requirement that only Belgian citizens *can* and *must* vote. The possibilities under consideration were a change in the law to allow only European citizens or those where there was a bilateral accord to vote, or a more open change that would remove the requirement of national citizenship for participation in elections (which would create a possibility for other non-EU foreigners). The problem in the political post–November 1991 context was that a EU citizen with one year of residence would be able to cast a vote, while a non-EU citizen who had been legally in the country for thirty years but had not become a citizen would be unable to vote. Actors such as the Center for Equal Opportunities and Anti-racism lobbied for a change that would allow non-EU citizen residents voting rights. A second debate concerned the fact that voting was considered a duty of citizenship rather than a right. Why should Belgians be forced to vote while EU citizens were offered a choice? Some proposed that voting should become voluntary.

The Catholic/Socialist coalition government attempted to address this with a reform of the nationality law in 1998. At the end of October 1998 there was a vote on the amended Article 8 of the constitution, which *allowed* citizens of the European Union to vote and noted that the right can be expanded to other persons resident in Belgium. This was not satisfactory to the more progressive voices in Belgium, including parts of the women's movement in Flanders (VOK). They demanded full political participation for non-EU residents. Thus the debate remained open for them, even if a policy decision had been made.

The 1999 June elections led to a surprise change in the governing coalition from the long-term ruling Christian Democrats to a rainbow group of Greens, Liberals, and Socialists. This brought the festering paradox of the coupling of political duties and rights to Belgian nationality to a head. For the Greens, the issue of political rights for long-term foreign residents was non-negotiable.[5] All of the partners underwrote the need for an "open society" in the government's foundation declaration. It was stated that

> The integration of foreigners forms in a wider perspective together with a realistic and humane asylum policy and the fight against racism and intolerance one of the three pillars which the government has chosen for to make Belgium an open and tolerant society.[6]

Political representation and citizenship received a place of priority in the platform of the new federal government of 1999. A proposition of law was submitted under the emergency procedure in the late fall of that year. The Liberal Party was unwilling to decouple the issue of citizenship from the issue of political franchise, while the Green parties lambasted citizenship procedures as being too restrictive and discriminatory as they were based on vague ideas of social integration in the Belgian nation.

The proposition to reform "a number of conditions concerning Belgian nationality" resolved this by making it possible to acquire both citizenship *and* the *duty* to vote through a vastly simplified procedure that met the demands of European treaties for speed, efficiency, and justice. In principle, non-European citizens would be able to acquire citizenship in Belgium after three years of legal residency and approval from the magistrate. This judicial review of applications was limited to one month (later extended to three months).

Dominant Frame of the Debate

The debate occurred in a frame of legal regulation. The questions to be discussed were, what are the time limits to achieve political and citizenship rights in Belgium, and what procedures should be followed? By attempting to keep the discussion purely in legalistic terms, proponents could avoid the political minefield of "voting rights for non-EU citizens", but they also could keep other issues outside the frame, such as gender. A main component of the frame is the question of whether potential candidates for naturalization must demonstrate any proof of "integration". A controversial part of old law had been the concept of will to integrate. It was never concretely described by the lawmakers and was seen by opponents as a method to hinder access to citizenship rights. Previously the estimation of integration had been left to the judgment of the various authorities from the most local to the Chamber of Deputies, who could fill in the concept to include everything from the length of time in Belgium, schooling in Belgium, eating habits, to marriage.

One of the active proponents of change, the federally sponsored Center for Equal Opportunity and Anti-racism (initiated in 1989 and established in 1993) argued that the only criterion for citizenship should be legal residency in Belgium. This criterion became the proposition in law. Other frames that appeared include discussions of the injustice of the unequal treatment of un-integrated European Union citizens compared to assimilated adult non-Europeans[7] who would be subjected to lengthy inquiries to obtain citizenship and political rights. A shadow issue was the hope that enfranchisement of new publics would weaken the impact of the Far Right. Not unexpectedly the Flemish Vlaams Blok party was extremely active in the debates, introducing a new frame of security issues by coupling international criminal networks and terrorists to the amended law. Vlaams Blok attempted to obstruct the passage of the law with a steamboat of amendments in the debate in the Chamber of Deputies (De Kamer *Handelingen* 33 18 January 2000).[8] Given the relatively concise and closed nature of the debate on this proposal of law, the frame remained virtually the same throughout the debate, namely to achieve a legal fix to the paradox of immediate voting rights for European Union citizens while long-term non-European Belgian residents had no rights.

Gendering the Debate

For years left-leaning and feminist women had demanded an improvement in the political position of non-European populations as an issue of human rights that also had a gender angle. Considerable research as well as the positions of organizations such as the European Women's Lobby also emphasized that immigration has a female face (Ackers 1997; Lenz et al. 2002). The demand for voting rights for everyone with five years' residency on Belgian soil was an official demand of the Flemish autonomous women's movement (VOK) in 1995, 1998, and 1999, while the Dutch-language council of women and its French counterpart both devoted special commissions to issues around migration and human rights and considered these issues high priority. That immigration had taken on an increasingly feminized face (even if it had always been gendered) was also an issue for the human rights experts in the women's movement and the organizations concerned with immigrants and aid to developing countries. The sexual traffic in women, the position of wives of long-term foreign residents whose papers rested on their dependent relationship, violence against women and children in these dependent relationships, and the mistreatment of female household personnel working illegally in Belgium came increasingly into the news in the nineties thanks to the efforts of these actors. However, the obvious links between the debate around a more flexible citizenship law and the women's movement human rights issues were not exploited by these actors with the exception of the VOK. It is clear that a potential result of the new law would be to allow female spouses to claim citizenship in their own right on the basis of a much shorter residency than was formerly the case. This would help women who needed to escape from abusive relationships without losing their residency rights. But this argument does not appear in the debate around the law.

While the women's movement's arguments are not explicitly mentioned in the transcribed debates, the sessions in the Commission on Justice (around 25 percent female), the Commission on Naturalization (which was also 20 percent female), and in the Senate and the Chamber of Deputies demonstrate an extremely active participation of female representatives in support of the new law, or making contributions. One can say the debate had a gendered face due to the participants, even if the participants did not explicitly frame the implications of the reform in terms of gender and differential impacts on men and women. The frame utilized was not one launched by the movement, but the achievement of the law could help improve the situation of women. Thus outside the halls of government, the women's movement fought for a situation that would provide political rights to non-European women, but in the context of the nationality debate as it was framed, they did not engender it.

Policy Outcome

The law, which was proposed by the government, was accepted by the majority with opposition from all non-government parties in March of 2000 and passed into effect in May of 2000. The law became known as the *Snel-Belg-wet* or the Speedy Belgian Law.[9] The change in the law had immediate consequences with a large jump in requests for naturalization.[10] It was now possible for persons who had been legally residing in Belgium for three years to request naturalization. An administrative review of the request under a strict time limit would lead to a recommendation for or against citizenship based on reports from the state security office, the immigration service, and the police and courts. There were no requirements for knowledge about Belgium or for evidence of integration.

Women's Movement Impact

The women's movement in Belgium had become increasingly institutionalized, and also registered success in increasing the number of women in political decision making. These activities had an impact on this debate as vocal participants in the debate in Parliament had women's movement backgrounds. Several had been active in commissions on migration issues in the councils of women (CFFB and NVR). Thus individuals who could have advanced women's interests were accepted in the policy process. However, there is not much evidence that they also constructed the citizens they were speaking for in an explicitly gendered way. The wish that foreign populations could have political rights was also a demand of the women's movement, if not a high-priority demand. Thus there is symmetry in something highlighted as a social problem by the women's movement, out of their concern for social justice and human rights, and the decision made to simplify access to citizenship for all legal residents. Ultimately the demand coincided with the policy, but the direct recognition of the ways in which it could address the gendered nature of immigration and dependency was never taken up in the public debate. Interventions by both male and female parliamentarians made no explicit references to the gendered nature of citizenship requests. Thus we can speak of a situation of weak dual response, as the policy content corresponded with a priority of the women's movement, and individuals with women's movement backgrounds participated in the decision making. Even if they did not explicitly gender the debate, they furthered women's interests.

Women's Policy Agency Activities and Characteristics

By the commencement of the debate, there were women's policy agencies at the national, regional, and provincial levels in Belgium, which could have been concerned with the issue. Most relevant for this debate is the federal level, although there is interaction with the regional ministries. At the federal level the responsibility for "women's interests" rested with the Ministry for Labor and Equality of Opportunity between Men and Women. In the period under consideration the responsible ministers (Miet Smet (CVP) until 1999 and Laurette Onkelinx (PS) (1999–2003)) were both respectively also vice prime ministers and avowed feminists. Under Smet, the ministry had a unit devoted to equal opportunities with special focus on aspects of women in the labor force, women in decision making, and violence against women. The focus of the equal opportunities directorate changed somewhat under Onkelinx, with a greater emphasis on social exclusion and poverty among women, international issues, and the application of mainstreaming within Belgian policymaking.[11] The ministry finances research and projects and also subsidizes the non-profit association of Amazone and the councils of women.

A federal advisory body composed of lay experts from both the autonomous and integrated women's movements, the Council for Equal Opportunities for Men and Women, which had been preceded by several other advisory bodies, was established in 1993. This body had the power to review legislation both on demand by ministers and through its own initiative. These agencies had the mandate to review policy horizontally, which increased throughout the period, thanks to the commitment to carry out gender mainstreaming. Thus the women's policy machinery had a cross-sectional potential. However, the localization of equal opportunity support staff within the Ministry of Labor, as well as the priorities of the respective ministers, has meant that the actions of the agencies have been primarily around employment and equal treatment issues. Attempts to shake up the gender composition of the public administration have met with resistance, even if both ministers have made efforts to do so (Nelen and Hondeghem 2000). During the period under consideration, neither the advisory bodies nor the minister took any public stance on the issue of naturalization and its eventual gender impact.

Both the Chamber of Deputies and the Senate have advisory bodies devoted to equal opportunity issues (called *Advies comite voor de maatschappelijke emancipatie* and *Advies comite voor gelijikekansen voor vrouwen en mannen van de Belgisch Senaat*). These bodies have been fertile ground for discussion around the issues of human traffic and prostitution, the rights of the child, and the situations of women in work and families and their social security or lack of it. Despite a demonstrated interest in international topics, especially in the case of the Senate, there is no direct evidence of intervention in the naturalization discussion.

The women's policy agencies did not play an active role in gendering this policy debate, even though in general their work was promoting women's movement goals. Thus for this debate their role must be categorized as symbolic at best.

Women's Movement Characteristics

To the extent that one can speak of a *Belgian* women's movement by the end of the nineties, given the increased federalization, it is probably best to speak of an increasingly consolidated movement that had succeeded in finding institutional footholds thanks to the election of more and more feminist politicians, and the establishment of women's policy agencies in the different branches of government. The established organizations are implicated in offering advice on issues such as the debate discussed here, although they are understaffed, and do not always frame questions in compatible terms. The specific situation of female migrants began to receive earmarked attention with the founding of groups to support studies and campaigns for immigrant girls and women.[12]

Although all political parties have women's organizations, the women's movement throughout the period has been closest to the progressive Center Left. Many of the main feminist figures came from the left wing of the Flemish Christian People's Party (CVP now CD & V) and from the Green parties (AGALEV and ECOLO). The Socialist parties in Belgium were less conspicuous in their support for feminist issues in the nineties. However, leaders of the autonomous movement in Belgium frequently had trade union backgrounds. The national ministries responsible for funding women's activities were in the hands of Center (Christian Democrat) to Left (French Socialist) ministers. At the regional level the responsible ministers were Green, Socialist, or (briefly) progressive Christian Democrat. The movement itself was Left in spirit, even if obvious ties to the Socialist parties were weak. Opposition to women's movement ideas in the nineties was primarily indirect, using the tactics of ridiculing woman's issues, or killing them softly through media silence. The Flemish Far Right party had a more virulent anti-feminist stance, but most of their energy was directed toward immigration issues.

During this period there was a substantial increase in female representatives in both houses of the legislature. These women were active members of the bodies considering the new legislation. Not incidentally, two very active spokeswomen (Meyrem Kaçar (AGALEV)-Senate and Fauzaya Talhaoui (AGALEV)-Chamber of Deputies) were Belgians coming from Turkish and Moroccan backgrounds. They had been active in feminist movements both within their parties and within the autonomous women's movement around issues of migration. These actors lie in between women's movement action and women's policy agents given their background and involvement in the parliamentary women's commissions.

Policy Environment

The regulation of citizenship is the concern of the Ministries of Justice and the Interior while the rules are legislated by Parliament. Whereas earlier discussions about changes in the nationality law had occurred in the Commissions of Social Affairs or Domestic Affairs, this debate was restricted to a closed policy subsystem in the national parliament. Discussion took place in the Commissions on Naturalization and Justice in both the Chamber of Deputies and the Senate, before being voted on in the plenary sessions of the two chambers. Applications for naturalization are submitted at the local level. Each individual naturalization request is voted on as a law by the Chamber of Deputies.

An important semi-public actor in the debates on citizenship has been the Center for Anti-racism and Discrimination, which is a semi-autonomous arm of the government. It acts as a watchdog and makes recommendations about improvement in the social situation of immigrant populations in Belgium.

The subsystem for debate on this issue can be characterized as being moderately closed because the debate occurred within the process of legislation and those with a voice had to be members of Parliament and of the appropriate commission. As we have seen above, women made up almost one-fourth of the participants. When the initial discussion on voting for European citizens and its relation to nationality began, the government was a coalition between the Christian Democrats and the Socialists from both sides of the linguistic frontiers. After the election of 1999 a new coalition of French and Flemish Liberals, Socialists, and Greens came into power in the executive branch and had a majority in the two houses of Parliament. In this new government women increased their representation.

CONCLUSION

Compared to debates in the seventies and eighties in Belgium, the context of politics for women's interests in the nineties was radically different. Thanks to the establishment of a women's policy machinery and the institutionalization of the women's movement, as well as to a gradually increasing representation of women in political bodies, gender issues were more visible than ever before. This chapter has examined the extent to which the entrenchment of the women's movement actors and interests in the state has an effect on a top issue of the political debate that was not explicitly gendered from the first. In this case we looked at citizenship and migration in Belgium and discovered mixed results. The issue of citizenship and migration could clearly have taken on a gendered face. Indeed, many of the *cause célèbres* during the decade involved female victims,[13] but these possibilities were not exploited explicitly, perhaps because of the negative framing of non-Belgians by the Far-Right. It could be that by approaching the citizenship issue in a "non-gendered" fashion, participants strategically avoided being harmed by the tactics of the Far Right, while still achieving their end of enfranchising new Belgians.

Questions about the status of female brides and their treatment, rights of divorced women to their children, and the traffic in foreign women were never far from the newspapers and thus the political agenda. However, the debate around enfranchisement of long-term residents and the resulting Speedy Belgian Law did not become an issue for the women's policy machinery and the women's movement. While the policy result coincided with high-priority issues of the women's movement, movement organizations also did not play an active role in the debate. The inclusion of more women representatives in both the Chamber of Deputies and the Senate allowed a place for their voices. An analysis of the debates as well as the reports from commissions shows that individual women were extremely active in countering the arguments of the Far Right, and spurring the passage of this controversial law. Yet it would be hard to argue that their contributions "gendered" the debate or framed it in the way the issues were discussed within the women's movement. The political strategy of attempting to seal this explosive issue into the hermeticism of legal article nitpicking resisted social framing as a gendered issue. It was the Far Right who inserted women by name. They constructed migrant women as potential criminals who might be come citizens (the crimes mentioned included sexual preference abortions and genital operations carried out on children) or as marriage criminals who are used as pawns to bring in illegal aliens on spurious family grounds. By not rising to the bait and negatively gendering the debate, women politicians may have been acting strategically.

We can conclude here that even if the debate only marginally mentioned women, the result of liberalizing citizenship agreed with the agenda of the women's movement. Thus the women's movement could claim a mild situation of dual response, while the Belgian women's policy agencies had a passive or symbolic role in this particular debate, despite their mission to mainstream gender. While we cannot talk about an awareness of gendered citizenry and migration in this debate, it is also clear that women's presence was important both substantially and in terms of representation. They emphasized the human rights aspects of the debate (even among female members of the opposition) and represented not only the female electorate but also the immigrant female electorate.

The passage of the law easing naturalization led to a jump in requests for naturalization and has remained controversial. In one year almost twenty-five thousand people joined the polity (Van Eylen 2001). The law was evaluated in a report submitted to the Chamber of Deputies in 2002 and presented by a female rapporteur of Turkish origin from the Socialist Party. This report was passionately debated. Since the beginning of the new law in May of 2000, some 247,000 new Belgians have been created in the various nationality procedures

(*De Standaard* 15 June 2005) even though many requests are denied. The anti-racist organization Objectief claims that the effect of the Speedy Belgian Law has been minimal, and can only be held responsible for around eighty-five thousand of the new citizens (*De Standaard* 4 February 2004). The majority of the new Belgians are of either Moroccan (43 percent) or Turkish (12 percent) origin (*De Standaard* 21 September 2005). New Belgians are concentrated in big cities, and early analysis indicates that their participation in local elections has changed the face of city government in several big towns (Jacobs 1998, 2001) The original reason for the crisis in 1999, the demand for voting rights for non-EU citizens, achieved a final resolution with a new electoral law (Migrant Voting Rights Law, March 2004) permitting residents who have lived five years legally in the country to vote if they ask permission at their city hall. This went into force in the city elections of 2006. While no one knows exactly what the electoral consequences will be, it is clear that the number of new Belgians and the newly registered "migrants" will make a substantial difference in urban centers such as Antwerp and Brussels (*De Standaard* 21 September 2005). The Speedy Belgian Law is under evaluation because of administrative problems, although the present minister of justice, Laurette Onkelinx, who was formerly responsible for the WPA, sees no reason to reconsider the main lines of Speedy Belgian Law (*De Standaard* 28 April 2005). Thus those hoping to politically empower long-term residents of foreign origin in Belgium including women have in the last five years won on both counts, irreversibly changing the meaning of what it is to be Belgian.

INTERVIEWS

Chris Zwaenepoel, Anne Grauwels, Maggie Poppe, Nadine Plateau

ABBREVIATIONS

Women's Movement

NVR (*Nederlandstalige Vrouwenraad*)
CFFB (*Conseil des Femmes Francophones de Belgique*)
VOK (*Vrouwen Overleg Komite*)

Political Parties

AGALEV (Flemish Green Party)
CVP (Flemish Christian Democrats)

CD&V (New name for Flemish Christian Democrats)
ECOLO (Francophone Green Party)
SP (Flemish Socialists)
PS (Francophone Socialists)
VLD (Flemish Liberals)

NOTES

1. Herman van Gunstren 1992: 119 cited in Foqué 2002: 21. My translation.

2. According to data from Eurostat cited in Caestecker and Rea 2002:114, between 1990–1997 the Netherlands took up about 7 percent of its foreign population per year into its citizenry, while the Swedes succeeded in naturalizing 6 percent. The figure for Belgium stagnated at circa 3 percent per year.

3. D'Haese and Van Den Driessche 1991; Deweerdt and Falter 1992, 1993; Deweerdt 1994, 1995, 1997, 1998, 1999, 2000, 2001; Platel 1996.

4. In Belgium, all Belgian citizens are obligated by law to cast a vote in elections. A second Belgian peculiarity is that individual requests for naturalization are a matter for the legislature rather than the public administration, and must be voted on as laws.

5. The Greens made the promise of political rights for non-Belgians a priority and demanded that they be included in the government statement if they were to participate in government. They underlined the unfair comparison with European citizens. It should be noted that the Green Party achieved more than gender parity in its appointments to cabinet posts in the new government.

6. Regeerakkoord juli 1999, Chapter 4, "Een open samenleving afdeling 1 integratie" (cited in Kaçar 2002: 134), my translation.

7. It should be noted that children born on Belgian soil and resident for a required number of years were allowed to declare their nationality. There are three ways to become a Belgian national: a declaration of nationality open to those born and raised in Belgium or married to a Belgian, naturalization, and nationality choice.

8. Bert Laermans of Vlaams Blok insulted the AGALEV reporter (of Moroccan background), by accusing her of personally speaking only for her potential Moroccan supporters, and raised the question of dual citizenship, which had nearly doubled between 1989 and 1999. The Blok repeatedly call the AGALEV group a "foreigner party".

9. Decoo (2000) says, "Door sommigen smalend de snel-Belg-wet genoemd". This nickname is only known on the Flemish side, where the problems associated with the law are spotlighted by active members of the Christian Democrat and Far Right opposition.

10. At the end of the nineties there were around thirty thousand requests for all kinds of citizenship yearly. In the first two years of the new law requests were around sixty thousand (Center for Equality and Anti-racism in Begium 2004). This has been dramatized in the press by actions of the CVP representative Jo Vandeurzen, who is

characterized as "holding on to the issue like a bulldog" (Van Eylen 2001) and who began submitting amendments to the law almost as soon as it was passed. He was also the one who publicized the fraud that seems to be paired with the quicker process, as a number of cases in which the authorities had reason to advise against nonetheless were approved.

11. In 2003 this unit became an autonomous body, the Institute on Equality for Women and Men (Kingdom of Belgium 2004).

12. Flanders began subsidizing a support point for immigrant girls and women (*Steunpunt allochtone meisjes en vrouwen*) in 1999. This is an umbrella of organizations of immigrant women to help them organize education and self-help . This unit is only indirectly connected to the state, and became operational in November 1999, thus too late to have a substantitive role in this debate.

13. Three celebrated cases with unexplored gender aspects include Samira Adamu, a Nigerian asylum seeker whose application was refused. She was forcibly repatriated and died in a struggle with her guards on the plane in 1998. Loubna Benaïssa was a teenage girl of Moroccan origin who was brutally murdered by a Belgian connected with the Dutroux affair (1997). Tabita was a five-year-old girl repatriated without an adult companion to Kinshasha.

5

New Federalism and Cracked Pillars: The Canadian Health Insurance System under the 2000 Romanow Commission and Beyond

Melissa Haussman

The Canadian Medicare system of universally insured and publicly funded health care was begun as a national program by the Medical Care Act of 1966. While there has always been controversy over the program's administration, first conducted by doctors concerned about income lowering and since the 1980s by governments anxious to cut costs, there has been solid agreement about the Canadian principles embodied in the policy. The largest percentage of the population by far receives provincially administered insurance; federally administered insurance typically is involved in the cases of prisoners or military personnel.

BRIEF HISTORY OF THE CANADIAN MEDICARE SYSTEM

The establishment of the national public health insurance system followed sets of events at the federal and provincial levels. It is important to point out that constitutionally, the bulk of the power to regulate health care in Canada lies with the provinces. The main way in which the federal government can affect provincial conditions is through its constitutional "spending power," which involves federal-provincial transfer payments (to provincial governments, institutions, or individuals) (Tuohy, 1999: 38–44). At least through the 1970s, the federal spending power typically involved categorical grants, where money was provided to provinces for specific types of purposes, for example building hospitals. After that time, the preferred mode was a consolidated block grant.

There were four principles enshrined in the Medical Care Insurance Act of 1966. They were (1) "the scope of benefits should be all the services provided by general practitioners and specialists"; (2) the "plan should be universal . . . covering all residents of a province on uniform terms and conditions"; (3) "the plan must be publicly administered by either the provincial government or non-profit agency"; and (4) "each provincial plan should provide full transferability of benefits when people are . . . absent from the province or move to another province" (Taylor, 1990: 147).

The introduction of government-funded health insurance was at its heart a "bargain between the state and the medical profession" (Tuohy: 55–56). The "founding bargain" entailed in the Medical Care Insurance Act, which followed the Royal Commission on Health Services in 1964 gave much autonomy to the medical profession, represented by the provincial medical associations, in deciding the fee schedules of all items provided. Thus, "Canadian medicare essentially underwrote the costs of the existing system, based . . . upon private fee-for-service medical practice and public or voluntary not-for-profit hospitals" (Tuohy: 204). While individual physician discretion was reduced under the Medicare system, the collective autonomy of the profession was retained. Similarly, individual physicians who chose not to participate in the government-sponsored fee-for-service plans were free to set their own rates (known as "extra billing") and collect those fees directly from patients. Different provinces dealt with extra billing in various ways, some forbidding it sooner than others (Tuohy: 204–206).

All provincial governments tried to wrestle with the issue of the fact that health care expenditures were one of the largest portions of their budget (the other being education), and all struck some kind of commission between the mid-1980s and 1990s to look at ways to lower the cost to government of the publicly insured health care system. Successive federal governments did the same, most recently (and comprehensively in terms of its recommendations for change) embodied in the Romanow Commission, named after its chair, former Saskatchewan Premier Roy Romanow, which consulted with the public from 2000–2001 and reported back to the House of Commons in 2002.

SELECTION OF DEBATE

The selection process for the Canadian hot issue entailed narrowing down the possible universe of major policy issues from the 1990s onward to include those having a significant scope in terms of changing state-civil-society relations, a high degree of conflict, a wide range of public attention, and a high degree of interest among policy actors. The universe chosen includes five issues, three of which dealt with Native issues deemed unresolved in the "new" 1982 supreme Charter of Rights and Freedoms, one of which concerned expanding the Canadian history of number one trading partner relationships with the US to more sectors and with Mexico under NAFTA, and the issue of health care reform.

The first issue considered is that of the issue of constitutional reform entailed by the "Charlottetown" round (so named because the Canadian national founding document, the British North America Act of 1867, was signed in Charlottetown, Prince Edward Island, and this new proposal was also framed there). This set of actions was pursued almost in desperation by Conservative Prime Minister Brian Mulroney, who wished to have the issue of constitutional reform favoring French-speaking Quebec and Native Canadians as one of his legacies. The previous round, which would have entailed more sweeping discrete changes to the 1982 Charter of Rights and Freedoms, the Meech Lake Accord, had ended in a feud between an eastern and a western provincial premier. Prime Minister Mulroney had placed great importance on this type of constitutional reform for its own symbolic sake of including groups who were left out of the tightly controlled, insider negotiations producing the 1982 Charter of Rights and Freedoms.

The second issue is that of aboriginal rights in Canada, focusing on a set of decisions concerning land claims. The first relevant decision here was that of the Supreme Court in the 1997 *Delgamuukw* case, which affirmed aboriginal land rights, and the second element was the 1999 treaty between the federal and British Columbia governments regarding land claims by the Nisga'a people. The degree of conflict was high and public attention, particularly in the West and among relevant policy communities, was high.

As with constitutional arguments concerning the role of the historic "French fact" in Canadian confederation, the arguments between the Nisga'a tribal council and the federal government of Canada date back to the 1890s, just after confederation in 1867, when the Nisga'a band established their first committee devoted to the purpose of negotiation of territorial rights. The issue was not satisfactorily resolved during the twentieth century, with an important Supreme Court case (*Calder*) affirming in 1973 that there was a "possible existence of Aboriginal rights to land and resources."[1] After negotiating in some "250 consultation and public information meetings in northwestern BC," and with the federal, provincial, and tribal representatives from 1991 onwards, a final agreement was reached and signed in summer 1998. Under this agreement, the Nisga'a band was given $190 million (Cdn) in cash and 1,930 square kilometers of land, valued by federal negotiators at $36 million.[2]

The third potential issue that could be detailed as the "hottest" in Canada from the 1990s onward included the attempts from the late 1990s to repair the damage done by (often) Anglican-run boarding schools for the purpose of assimilating Native children, operated throughout much of the twentieth century. The scope of the issue was provincial and territorial, national and international, involving the worldwide Anglican Communion.

The fourth potential issue was that of the transformation of the 1989 Free Trade Agreement between Canada and the U.S. into a trilateral agreement, with Mexico having been "added on" to what was already the number one trading partnership between the other two states. This occurred under the North American Free Trade Agreement or NAFTA, implemented in 1994. The scope of the issue included actors across provinces and the US and Mexican states, as well as the three national governments. Public attention was high and the degree of conflict was high, as groups such as the Council of Canadians was formed to oppose it for the harms that were perceived to accompany "free" trade (or more accurately, the gradual, selective lowering of tariff barriers across different sectors).

POLICY DEBATE

The debate chosen has been that of "rationalizing" the Canadian Medicare (publicly insured) system, or making it more "cost-effective" as framed by policymakers. In its most recent form, the debate moved to the public agenda during the second Liberal term in the 1990s, from 1997 onward, with different commissions on health care reform, culminating in the most recent and far-reaching, the Romanow Commission of 2000–2002. This discussion centers on the inputs to and outputs of the commission from 2000–2003.

WOMEN'S MOVEMENT IN THE 1990s

Generally, the "movement" which had previously been discussed as a "national" one, often viewed as headquartered in the National Action Committee, NAC, in Toronto, had devolved for various reasons into affinity- or identity-based groups. NAC's success until the late 1980s had been largely predicated on being able to use "insider politics," such as Advisory Council meetings and recommendations regarding women's rights inclusion in the 1982 Charter of Rights and Freedoms reform. During the constitutional negotiations, a smaller group of women including lawyers and past presidents of the organization split off to form the "Ad Hoc Constitutional Committee," which then lobbied Parliament to include previously agreed-upon reforms.

By the middle of the 1990s, the "national" women's movement in Canada was more specific about which "nation" it represented; whether it saw itself as emanating largely from an Anglophone, Francophone, or First Nations base. Disappointment with federal government actions and in losses incurred while lobbying through NAC as the peak organization meant that by the decade's end it was more correct to speak of women's organizations with various national identities within Canada (such as aboriginal, Asian, francophone, etc.) and affinity groups such as gay rights groups, for example. While NAC is still important within the women's movement community, the model of having one "peak" association represent hundreds of different groups to the federal government had become viewed as unwieldy. Another trajectory within the Canadian-based women's movement, particularly since the advent of the Charter of Rights and Freedoms in 1982 and increased power of the Supreme Court, is the professionalization and specialization of certain women's groups in the legal community. One of the lead groups in this capacity is LEAF, the women's Legal Equity and Action Fund.

The women's movement by this time displayed the characteristics of women's movements in many Western democracies of having achieved many of its gains in the 1970s and early 1980s by enjoying a good working relationship with federal and often sub-national governments. This relationship was based both on cohesiveness of issue concerns but probably mainly by growing budgets during Keynesian times in which social movement groups usually found themselves funded fairly adequately and not in competition with each other as under the neoliberal hatchet. While it probably is not true that the Canadian women's movement was in abeyance as such by the 1990s it did seem to have taken on newer forms, geared towards the necessity of lobbying in new and distinct venues, not just in the legislature. Part of this was based on distrust of the budget cuts through the mid-1990s. Part of it though involved recognizing new faces of power, which included a newly strengthened Supreme Court and other avenues involving transnational activism (such as at the UN and for worker rights in North America in the face of NAFTA). Another set of "new faces" in the power grid for the women's movement to contend with, given that provinces and municipalities had to shoulder new budget responsibilities, were sub-national loci.

The stage of the women's movement during the 1990s and beyond is described as one of consolidation. While the overall women's movement was relatively close to power (when defined in the typical political science terms of closeness to federal judiciary and Parliament) the specific women's health care sector was even closer to power, having received much funding to set up the women's Centers of Excellence infrastructure. It conducted much of its research within the overall framework of priorities for change given by the National Forum Report in 1997 and then reaffirmed in the Romanow Commission Report of 2002. To this extent, the opportunities for gendering the language occurred within the terms of the national debate, managed mainly by the Romanow Commission, which had already been set forth for it by the Liberal government. Overall, in this policy instance, the specific women's health movement discussed here is described as consolidated and cohesive. The cohesive label would be far less true of the women's movement generally in Canada from the 1990s onward.

THE ROMANOW RECOMMENDATION

How the Debate Came to the Public Agenda

Since the 1970s, questions about the cost of the "input" and "output" factors of Medicare became high-profile ones on the national public agenda. Concerns have been voiced about factors such as the federal-provincial mix of tax revenues and cash contributions and doctors' fees on the input side. Beginning in the 1970s, a sense of "health cost spiral permeated the whole system, including . . . the upper echelons of the Finance Department" (Taylor: 152–153). Much of this was due to the framework in which provincial governments had virtually open-ended health budgets, where prices were determined by doctors and hospital boards. Also, the 1966 Medical Insurance Act's requirement that the federal government match the provincial spending on a 50 percent basis meant a price spiraling over which the federal government felt it had no control.

By 1977, with high federal deficits, the Trudeau Liberal government started changing the cost-sharing formula with the provinces, to reduce its own cash outlay. Under the new Established Programs Financing Act (EPF), the federal government increased the "tax point" portion of the federal-provincial distribution formula to half. In this system, provinces got to raise revenue from personal taxes up to 12.5 percent after the federal government "vacated" this area of tax jurisdiction. The EPF switch from cash and categorical grant funding to 50 percent "tax point" and block grant funding represented the "most massive transfer of revenues (and therefore the substance of power) from the federal to the provincial governments in Canadian history" (Taylor: 153–154).

By 1984, the provinces of Ontario, Alberta, and Nova Scotia allowed doctors to extra-bill insured patients, with about half of the physicians in the latter two provinces doing so. This had been deemed inexcusable under both Conservative and Liberal governments, and during the Trudeau Liberal mandate of 1980–1984, Health Minister Monique Begin introduced the Canada Health Act. The core of the act was to end the practices of user fees charged by provincial governments to patients admitted to hospital inpatient or outpatient departments, and of extra-billing by opted-out physicians to publicly in-sured patients (Taylor: 166–168). The five conditions were framed as public administration, comprehensiveness, universality, portability, and accessibil-ity. One of the "most significant new stipulations" covered in the act, as passed by the House of Commons in 1984, was that "a province must provide reasonable compensation for all medically necessary insured health services." It also included a strong financial penalty for provinces who still allowed user fees and extra-billing, whereby the federal government could withhold from the cash payment to a province "an amount equal to the total amount of extra-billing and user charges authorized by the province" (Taylor: 170–172).

While provincial budgets became increasingly squeezed after the 1984 Canada Health Act, provinces mostly remained committed to the Medicare system. At about that time, in the 1980s and 1990s, "every province estab-lished a task force or commission to give policy advice on issues of health policy" (Tuohy: 97). Important shared components in all the provincial re-ports' recommendations, with varying emphases, were "the shift from institutionally-based to community-based care, a reallocation of functions among health care personnel, a decentralization of decision-making to re-gional councils (representing a variety of interests in the health field), and a broadening of focus . . . on determinants of health beyond the health-care delivery system" (Tuohy: 97).

Overall, Tuohy has termed the functioning of the health care system in Canada as an exemplar, "more than perhaps any other nation in the late twen-tieth century," of the "logic of an accommodation between the medical pro-fession and the state" (Tuohy: 203). Within this framework, "provincial gov-ernments were the 'single payers' for most medical and hospital services; a single government plan in each province covered a comprehensive range of medical and hospital services, and no private insurance alternatives for cov-erage of those services existed."

When the Liberals returned to power in 1993, Prime Minister Chretien an-nounced that yet another national study on health care would take place. While it was initially conceived as a federal-provincial undertaking, the provinces refused to participate, suspicious of what they viewed as further federal intrusion into their policy areas. Ultimately, as noted by Tuohy, the for-um's report of February 1997 was a "solid endorsement of Canadian Medicare . . . (arguing) that key features of the system, including 'public funding for medically-necessary services, the 'single payer' model, the five principles of the Canada Health Act and a strong federal/provincial/territorial partnership' must be protected" (Tuohy: 96). The National Forum on Health Care stated that "the current level of public funding was sufficient for the ex-isting scope of the program." However, it highlighted key areas that needed

to be further brought into the national Medicare system of publicly paid services, including long-term home care (especially acute since provinces were
closing hospitals at a rapid rate) and pharmaceuticals. While none of these
proposals became feasible or acted-upon during the short term, they all returned as main recommendations of the next major federal commission on
health care, the Romanow Commission of 2000–2002.

The other major set of changes, not endemic to the social policy area of the
budget but impacting it the most, was the change in federal-provincial funding transfer policies during the 1980s and 1990s, including a central component, which was tax policy. Based "entirely on a deficit-reduction agenda,"
the Liberal government elected in 1993 created a new program of the Canadian Health and Social Transfer (CHST). It combined the EPF program (itself
a block grant) and other social assistance transfers into yet a narrower block
grant in which education and health, the two most expensive provincially
funded and administered policies, would be forced to compete with each
other for funds for the first time. The coercive mechanism of the new CHST
formula, replacing the EPF one, was that the cash component of the revenue
transfer was based on provincial compliance with the Canada Health Act and
on the province "providing social assistance without a minimum residency requirement" (Tuohy: 92).

Important data from Tuohy show that "total transfers for health care as a
proportion of provincial health spending decreased from 40% in 1975 to 33%
in 1974." Therefore, in that same period, "federal fiscal leverage over provincial compliance with the terms of Medicare declined from 40% to 12% of total provincial health care expenditures" (Tuohy: 92). The overall effect was
to "increase federal fiscal leverage in the health field while reducing overall
federal contributions to provincial budgets for social programs" (Tuohy: 92).

Therefore, by the time the Romanow Commission of 2000–2002 was
struck, it was apparent that large remaining gaps in federal-provincial agreement over public funding of home care, pharmacare (outside of catastrophic
care), and mental health care continued. The "add-ons" to these recommendations were mental health care services and some areas of primary care (although not reproductive services, which constitute the single largest area of
primary care).

Dominant Frame of the Debate

From the federal government's point of view in 1993, health care was an in-
flated social policy commitment which needed reform in order to balance the
budget. It was presented publicly as a non-gendered issue. There were at least
two facets to health care as a seemingly large chunk of social policy spending

in Canada. The first set of arguments was that mounted by the federal government midway through its first mandate of the 1990s, since it had run on a platform of fiscal austerity in 1993. Probably the central cost-cutting mandate in the first Chretien government of the 1990s belonged to Finance Minister Paul Martin, who looked for ways to cut the deficit, but not necessarily through spending cuts. For example, "he thought that economic growth would meet the Liberals' target deficit of 3 percent of GDP; his officials spent a year convincing him that the target could not be met that way" (Evans, 2000: 36).

Interestingly, one economist has demonstrated that health-care costs rose "during the first quarter century of Medicare" (1966 to the late 1980s) at a fairly steady rate. This rate was described as slower than at any time since the 1960s. The better explanation for the fiscal squeeze is thus claimed to be the fact that the economy contracted during the 1980s. As Evans has concluded, if the economy kept up its 1960–1980 rate of growth into the 1980s, Canadian spending of 7.5 percent of GDP on health care would have remained constant, not increasing in the 1980s to 10 percent of GDP (Evans: 36). Moreover, it was pointed out that Canada, in a model similar to the European countries, "learned in the 1970s to limit the growth of our health-care system to match our then rates of general growth" (Evans: 36–38). However, on a different scale, Canadian versus OECD spending on health care between the 1960s and 1980s diverged. Overall in Canada, the share of national income devoted to health care increased strongly prior to the introduction of universal medicare insurance, then stabilized with its beginning in 1967. The spending then surged again during the recessions at the beginning and ending of the 1980s, "when health-care spending continued to grow while the general economy did not" (Evans: 38).

Gendering the Debate

The view from women's organizations, not surprisingly, was that health care as a social policy typically provided by the state is an inherently gendered policy and thus cuts to it have worse outcomes for women. For example, the views advanced included that over their lives, women generally interact with welfare state institutions more, since women are still paid less, are more likely to be single mothers, and therefore are more heavily impacted whenever welfare state institutions are cut. With regard to the health care system, women's reproductive capacity and statistically longer lives were also framed as relevant factors, mainly within women's movement organization discourses. From the beginning of the 1990s debate with the creation of the National Forum in 1994 through the Romanow Commission Report in 2002 and the ensuing First Ministers' Accord of February 2003, the following issues were the primary ones debated within women's policy and movement circles. They were that women had greater needs from the state-funded insurance system (covering provision of services) particularly in areas of reproductive health, pharmaceuticals, home care (as both disproportionate recipients and providers), and services regarding mental health and amelioration of domestic violence. In the "Overview on Women's Health" prepared by (the Department of) Health Canada, it was stated that "the National Forum on Health commissioned 30 papers on various aspects of the determinants of health. Unfortunately, there is little gender analysis in any of these sources."[3]

Similarly, in the "Overview of Women's Health," it was noted that "the 1995 Beijing Platform for Action states, 'the major barrier for women to the achievement of the highest attainable standard of health is inequality, both between women and men and among women' (United Nations, 1995)."[4] From the start, strong rhetorical linkages were being made between UN-based language and the need to more completely "gender," in a positive way, health care provision in Canada.

Groups such as the Canadian Women's Health Network (CWHN) gendered their responses to the Romanow report and to global forces shaping the delivery of health services in the following ways. For example, it was noted that "women consume between 60% and 70% of pharmaceuticals around the world."[5] With respect to the issue of home care, the CWHN lauded the commission report for recommending the establishment of a Home Care Transfer Fund to fund care in post-acute and palliative situations and in cases of mental health requirements. It was also stated that "three out of four home caregivers are women between the ages of 50–65 years, with 10% over the age of 75."[6]

Other points were raised in the CWHN responses to the Romanow report that while well intentioned, still displayed male biases in their formulation. One such example with regard to mental health provisions to be covered was that the bulk of them concerned those affecting men disproportionately, such as schizophrenia, bi-polar disorders, and dementia, rather than depression, more often found in women.[7] Another issue raised frequently was that while committing to increased funding in primary health care, the government ignored one of the most important such areas for women, that of guaranteed access to reproductive care.

Women's health policy organizations, most directly the Canadian Women's Health Network, the National Coordinating Group on Women's Health Care, and the Centres of Excellence for Women's Health Care, officially clashed with some of the Romanow Commission's seemingly obligatory nods to the efficiency frame. As a government organization, the Women's Health Bureau within the Department of Health could not be so directly confrontational although it funded some of these organizations and hosted conferences at which critical voices were heard. These organizations emphasized the difference in insurance coverage of what were deemed to be medically necessary services versus those demoted to the ancillary category disproportionately affected women, due to women's greater needs for health care services over their lives. They publicly hoped that an outcome of the Romanow Commission Report would not be to "blame" women for using the health care system more.

These organizations also talked about the increasing privatization found in the health care system, which typically denied services to those who only had the means to pay through Medicare (publicly provided) insurance. Examples of such privatization were noted in the wealthy provinces of Alberta and Ontario. Women's groups noted this public-private dichotomy in terms of affordability and the contradiction to the founding legislation of public Canadian health care insurance in 1966 (Medical Care Act) and reiterated in the 1984 Canada Health Act.

Fuller noted that under a privatized system, "Canadians would be able to use the hospital for procedures that had been delisted (dropped from coverage) by provincial governments, cosmetic surgery, and workers' compensation services covered by private insurers" (Fuller, 1998: 242–243). On the other hand, some shortcuts to the universal Medicare coverage system have already been seen without privatization, such as delisting services and the imposition of "user fees," such as those required for free-standing abortion clinics in some provinces.

Overall, the micro-frames advanced by the women's health policy community showed a moderately close fit to the overall federal government's (including the Romanow Commission's) issue frame of decreasing costs but increasing pharmaceutical and home care coverage.

POLICY ACTION ENDING THE DEBATE

Policy Outcome

This is defined as the incorporation of certain aspects of Romanow recommendations into the First Ministers' Accord of February 2003, regarding federal-provincial agreements on which aspects of the Romanow recommendations to prioritize in implementation. These priorities included getting $1.5 billion from the federal government to finance publicly funded diagnostic services, and $16 billion from 2003–2008 to cover the priority issues of primary health care reform, home care reform, and catastrophic drug coverage supplements.[8] These three issues had been highlighted by women's agencies and groups as having high priority for women; however, reproductive services were not mentioned in primary health care reform.

The policy outcome is termed *co-optation* where the federal government planned to make changes to the systems of service billing and health insurance payments in any event, and included some of the women's groups goals.

From a completely elite-dominated perspective, from which institutes are given the policy latitude to perform which areas of health research they wish and decide who leads the teams, probably not surprisingly, three of women's top goals (home care, pharmaceuticals, and primary care) are included in the final Romanow document and the First Ministers' Accord of 2003. Within the accord, which increases health care funding through 2008 by $34.6 billion from the federal government to the provinces and includes in its five priority areas two of those most consistently mentioned by women's groups, home care and catastrophic drug coverage, there is good news. Nearly half of the $34.6 billion ($16 billion) goes to three priority areas of primary health care, home care, and catastrophic drug coverage. Overall, federal to provincial transfers are to be increased by "9.5 billion over the next five years" (through 2008).[9] The First Ministers' Accord, taking into account the most pressing needs for change as illustrated through the Romanow report, was a clearly delineated policy decision.

WOMEN'S MOVEMENT IMPACT

The impact of the women's health care community should be separated into short- and long-term components. The short-term components were seen in affecting the frame of the Romanow report although not in the degree wished by the National Coordinating Group on Health Care Reform and Women (formed in 1993). Evidence supporting their influence on the final recommendations includes attention paid to "user fees, medical saving accounts, de-listing of services, greater privatization and (the creation of) a parallel system" as inconsistent with the Canadian values of universal health care coverage as expressed in the 1984 Canada Health Act. Overall, the report "rejected a system where money, rather than need, determines care" and one with a "one-size-fits-all approach to health care delivery."[10] These statements were lauded in the National Coordinating Group's response document as recognizing diversity in Canadian health care clients, thus potentially helpful for women. The acknowledgment of diversity seemed positive especially in light of the report's recommendations for greater funding for provincial transfers in the areas of home care, mental health, prescription drugs, and primary care.

Overall, the Coordinating Group's report highlights its disappointment with the fact that the report of the Romanow Commission did not choose to offer a gendered analysis of the health care system. Therefore, "it fails to consider women's places in the health care system and the consequences of health care reforms for women in different locations throughout the system."[11] The Coordinating Group's response openly wondered why, since (the Department of) Health Canada recognizes gender, sex, and culture as three of twelve determinants of health due to their effects on the structure and impact of the system, the Romanow Commission Report did not choose to view gender in the same way.[12]

As for the Canadian Women's Health Network (also formed in 1993), its activities included publishing the Canadian Women's Health Network newsletter, widely available in and outside of Canada. Other foci were frequent public speeches at venues such as the federally sponsored "Public Consultation on the Future of Health Care," Toronto, May 2002 and putting out press releases and giving interviews to print- and broadcast-based news. Some of these activities, such as research presentations made at the government's "Public Consultations" clearly fit in with an agenda driven by the government to give the appearance of widespread public input. This would fit the definition of "co-optation" of women's movement organizations as mentioned by Professor Armstrong.

The overall frame emphasized by these representative women's health group coalitions was that any changes envisioned to the health care system must not reduce the historic Canadian commitments to the values of universality, access, public administration, portability, and equality of administration. The micro-frame advanced by this policy sector was to ensure a public governmental acknowledgment that preserving fairness in the future could only happen if previously gendered practices in health care delivery and insurance were eliminated or strongly reduced.

In its response to the Romanow Commission, *Reading Romanow* (April 2003), the National Coordinating Group on Health Care Reform and Women paralleled the eleven-chapter structure of the Romanow report by describing when each area of concern was related to gender and whether it proposed a solution or not.[13] The findings were summarized in the section, "What Is Missing from the Royal Commission's Final Report?" in four points. Under the overall statement that "the results of the Royal Commission and the subsequent Accord quite clearly fail to provide a gendered analysis of health care," the four points were listed, that, first and second, "the Report fails . . . to consider long-term care, chronic care, or care for people with disabilities or older Canadians, the majority of whom are women," and "to discuss the critical role reproductive health services play in primary health care for women."[14] For example, the Romanow report and the subsequent First Ministers' Accord of February 2003 give ideas and money for reforming primary health care without a mention of reproductive health care, one of the key areas of primary care used by women and lagging in service provision.

In many ways, the Coordinating Group in the national public eye and the Canadian Women's Health Coalition more in the women's media outlets provided the most publicly feminist and politicized version of the Romanow Commission and its recommendations.

CHARACTERISTICS AND ACTIVITIES OF THE WOMEN'S POLICY AGENCY AND QUASI WOMEN'S POLICY AGENCY (QUAWPA) SECTOR

Towards the end of its mandate in August 1993, the federal Conservative government created the Women's Health Bureau within (the Department of) Health Canada. Under the Liberal government which followed, beginning in November 1993, the emphasis on women's policy agencies shifted away from the historic "women's sector" as demonstrated for example by the Departments of Status of Women Canada and the Advisory Council to a more "mainstreaming" approach. This latter interest was shown in the introduction of gender-based analysis (GBA) for application throughout the federal bureaucracy in 1995.

Another initiative of the Chretien Liberal government from 1993 onwards was the creation of "Centres of Excellence" for research in various policy fields and responded to pressure from certain women's movement organizations to create such centers for women's health research. The five Centres of Excellence, involving different areas of research on women's health, began in 1996. These specific university-linked centers represent the Canadian regions in the cities of Vancouver, Winnipeg, Toronto (the "national" office, although not in the national capital), Montreal, and Halifax, as well as the Institute of Gender and Health.[15] The five centers, which were funded through 2001–2002, involved academics, researchers, physicians, community health centers, and "policymakers," left undefined.[16] These centers were mandated to put forth their research findings and "other information on women's health." As was noted by Professor Pat Armstrong, the director of the Coordinating Group on Women's Health and Director of the York University-based Toronto Center, the creation of these centers was a "double-edged sword." On one hand, it provided women a ready source of funding and a framework within which to put forth their findings and recommendations under the National Forum and Romanow Commission.

However, this structural closeness could also mean that the centers' research was sometimes viewed as "government property" and thus sometimes taken out of context to support recommendations that the centers themselves would not support.[17]

Within the Department of Health, the Women's Health Bureau is mainly policy-oriented, working with other divisions and branches of the department to highlight gender as a significant research variable.[18] Following along the lines of the overall regionalization of health care responsibility under federal and provincial mandates in the 1990s, the Women's Health Bureau was assigned the role of liaison with the Centres of Excellence in Women's Health. Given that only the Women's Health Bureau is located in a "line department," it alone is termed a WPA, while the rest of the centers and committees are described as "quasi women's policy agencies."

The term "QUAWPA" is used to describe the fact that the centers, being organizations created with a sunset provision to go out of existence after various dates, could be termed "quasi agencies." The designation is also used to show that the agencies were not created directly in the traditional way that women's policy agencies, such as Status of Women Canada and the Woman's Program in the Secretary of State's Office, were, with direct budget lines administered through central agencies such as the Treasury Board. Instead, these organizations were "mediated" by being created through the Department of Health, Women's Health Bureau. It is likely that the reasons for this structure involved a desire for greater policy autonomy, especially in light of the downsizing of traditional women's policy machinery that had been happening since the 1990s.

As firmly government-established entities, the WPAs and QUAWPAs had to toe the line between reporting their research and sounding too critical of the government which created them. The effect of the WPAs and QUAWPAs in this policy reform contained in the Romanow Commission recommendations is described to be one of co-optation, where they played a largely symbolic role.

WOMEN'S MOVEMENT CHARACTERISTICS IN THE 1990s

By the 1990s, it is clear that a large sector of feminist activists and health care providers had become interested in the future of publicly insured health care in Canada. These women (and some men) had worked to create a policy focused community that could have input on the seemingly annual prescriptions for changes in the health care services delivery system that emanated from federal and provincial governments. Sometimes eliding the lines between "policy" and "movement" groups, in at least two cases, the National Coordinating Group on Health Care Reform and Women and the Canadian Women's National Health Network, had mandates and personnel from both sides of the fence. For example, many notable personages as well as organizations belong to all three organizations; some work for one of the Centres of Excellence (the women's policy agency framework) yet may help write a report attributed to either the Coordinating Group or the Canadian Health Network, for example.

The Canadian Women's Health Network describes itself on its website as "a national, voluntary bilingual organization of individuals and groups concerned with women's health. . . . after over fifteen years of informal networking, the CWHN was officially launched in May 1993 by women representing over 70 organizations from every province and territory." The group states that its membership includes "health care workers, educators, advocates, consumers and other Canadians committed to . . . better women's health."[19] The National Coordinating Group was formed in that same year. Other groups working with the Coordinating Group included many unions, such as the Ontario Council of Hospital Unions (CUPE), the Health Research Project at the Ontario Federation of Labour, and the British Columbia Hospital Employees' Union.

Another women's network which describes itself as movement-based yet also policy-focused includes the Working Group on Women and Health Protection. Women's movement groups affiliated with this working group have included Breast Cancer Action Montreal, the Breast Cancer Prevention Coalition, the Canadian Health Coalition (not a women's group specifically), the Canadian Women's Health Network, DES Action Canada, the Birth Control Federation of Quebec, Health Action International (Canada), and the World Alliance on Breastfeeding Action. There were other issue-oriented groups helping with the working group which one would describe broadly as "sunshine in government"–oriented, with a public focus generally, including the Alliance for Public Accountability and the Consumers Association of Canada. According to its website, the Working Group on Women and Health Protection worked closely with the National Coordinating Group.[20]

THE POLICY ENVIRONMENT

The environment was at once wider, in that it involved the creation of new agencies (such as the "sunsetted" Centres of Excellence) but also more restricted in that it was conducted mainly at the elite level involving academics, physicians, members of hospital boards, and parliamentarians. While the

Romanow Commission traveled across Canada to hear from various "stake-holder groups," as it called them, this forum was so familiar to the weary Canadian public that many saw it as a "show of democracy" only. The House of Commons was basically only tangentially involved in approving the commission's report.

The policy environment in this instance is described as having been moderately open based specifically on the women's health movement sector. The government in essence helped create a corporatist framework to "roundtable" this policy and to ensure a relatively limited set of inputs. The Left was not in power (indeed not even an official parliamentary party for part of the debate, without the minimum number of seats). The dominant women's health movement and government frames were largely compatible with each other. There was no strong public counter-movement, although there was certainly pressure from across the US border from insurance and health care providers having a presence in Canada.

CONCLUSION

The involvement of a newly created set of women's policy agencies, created for the specific purpose of helping to do research as the federal Liberal government saw itself as spearheading health care reform, was mainly a new policy model although vaguely reminiscent of the ad hoc elite model by which women preserved some rights clauses in the 1982 charter. It is clear that creating new agencies with a set of feminist interests and conducting research based on feminist values is a good thing. It is too bad that the centers are going out of existence; one would hope that a similar set of institutions could be retained to monitor the implementation of the Romanow and First Ministers' recommendations.

It could be said that the role of the women's policy agencies here (the QUAWPAs, not so much directly the Women's Health Bureau, the WPA) was that of insider, primarily because they were created for the particular end of health care reform. In terms of the movement impact and state response, it would seem to be one of co-optation, where the centers, the network, and the Coordinating Group performed vital tasks of interest aggregation from various women's groups, a not insignificant favor to the federal government. Also not insignificant was that the federal government got much of its research performed "on the cheap," at a considerably lower cost than the Chretien-government-created, private CIHI (Canadian Institute of Health Information), which has taken over health care statistics gathering from its previous domain, the public agency Statistics Canada.

Since the QUAWPA framework in essence knew where the ground was laid by the recommendations of the National Forum, it could adjust its policy frames and suggestions to be consonant with the three areas of reform high-lighted by the forum, the Romanow Commission, and the First Ministers' Ac-cord: primary health care, home health care, and pharmaceutical insurance. The women's agencies and organizations, however, clearly have much dis-agreement with the way in which some of the resources are spread around these priority areas, which makes the need for an ongoing watchdog agency with teeth more paramount.

To summarize the variables in the RNGS model for this particular study, they are as follows. The women's movement overall was seen to be in a state of consolidation amongst multiple "pillars." These included the Anglo-Canadian centered movement in Ottawa and Toronto; the Native-centered movement, particularly in the Territories, Quebec, BC, Manitoba, and parts of the Atlantic provinces; and French-speaking women's groups centered largely in the province of Quebec but also with some presence in Ottawa. Similarly, an "allophone" sector grew during the 1990s, with various movement groups reflecting South and East Asian women, African women, and the internal struggle in NAC described above. In addition to being consolidated across many socio-linguistic pillars by the 1990s, the specific women's health sec-tor is here described as being close to power, having health care reform as a high priority (although low priority outside the sector), and being cohesive within the sector, less cohesive outside the health sector. This specific set of women's health community actors is described as being close to the Left. The political environment is described as (relatively) open to the women's health sector, the Left was not in power, the women's health care movement frame was compatible with the government's dominant frames, and there was not an overtly strong counter-movement. The latter was likely true because of the high-profile presence of Commissioner Romanow, a long-term Canadian public servant at both the provincial and federal levels. The appointment of such a senior person to chair the commission undoubtedly sent signals out to the transnational insurance and health care communities who opposed the Canadian model that the federal government would not budge on the core Canadian principles of universality, portability, public administration, and comprehensiveness. The WPAs acted mainly in symbolic fashion, given that their input was used selectively to confirm the actions that the Romanow Commission and then the federal government generally wanted to take. Thus, the impact of the WPAs is described as co-optation.

In terms of updating the Romanow recommendations through 2005, the federal government signed a ten-year health "deal" with the provinces in Sep-tember 2004, "promising $41 billion" towards implementing health care reform.[21] This commitment by the federal government included an additional $18 billion to be provided through 2014, an increase of $3.5 billion for transfer payments to the provinces from 2004–2006 (and a boost of the transfer increment by 6 percent each year) and $4.5 billion through 2010 to reduce waiting times for hospital procedures. As described, the compromise involved "Ottawa putting up more money and the provinces agreeing to national standards for wait times on some medical procedures."[22] The Canadian Broadcasting Corporation's (CBC) report on the September 2004 agreement notes that (former Health Commission Chair) Romanow said some provisions of the agreement went beyond what he recommended" (for example waiting times for hospital procedures were not signaled among his priority recommendations).[23] The federal-provincial cash transfer was much higher than what Romanow called for, and a provision to ensure that 50 percent of the population has access to primary care (by 2011) was a bolder strategy than called for in the Romanow report.

Overall, the Canadian Health Coalition positively assessed the increased federal contribution to the health care system but decried the continuing lack of accountability mechanisms. It approved of other elements of the 2004 Federal-Provincial Ten-Year Plan that went beyond the recommendations of the Romanow report, including the fact that the plan agreed to "provide first-dollar coverage by 2006 for short term acute home care and community mental home health care." On other key provisions of the Romanow recommendations, such as a pharmacare strategy (comprehensive federal prescription drug coverage), the Canadian Health Coalition noted the inadequacy of the ten-year plan's commissioning of a "study" for the issue, to report back by June 30, 2006. It also noted that elder care was not mentioned in the 2004 plan, despite the fact that it was a priority area of the Romanow recommendations and that "long-term care is a sector that is being rapidly privatized."[24] As with the Romanow recommendations, there is some good and much yet to be accomplished with the follow-up ten-year plan, released in September 2004.

NOTES

1. Department of Northern and Indian Affairs Canada, "Chronology of Events Leading to the Final Agreement with the Nisga'a Tribal Council," website, www.ainc-inac, .gc.ca, accessed 5/17/2004.

2. Ibid., and Burke Lewis, "The True Cost of the Pending Nisga'a Deal May Be Far Higher than Acknowledged," in *B.C. Report*, accessed at website, www.axionet .com, 5/15/2004.

3. Lewis, ibid.

4. Good descriptions of the increasing NAC and federal government antagonism are found in Lisa Young, *Feminists and Party Politics in Canada* (Vancouver, BC: UBC Press, 2000); Leslie Pal, *Interests of State* (Montreal: McGill/Queen's University Press); Jill Vickers, Pauline Rankin, and Christine Appelle, *Politics As If Women Mattered* (Toronto: University of Toronto Press); and Sylvia Bashevkin, *Women on the Defensive* (University of Toronto Press, 1998).

5. Health Canada, "National Forum on Health—An Overview of Women's Health," in *Canada Health Action: Building on the Legacy—Volume II—Synthesis Reports and Issue Papers*, n.d., accessed via web, www.hc-sc.gc.ca, 4/28/2004, p. 2.

6. Ibid., p. 1.

7. Jackie Kennelly, "The Global Drug-Pushers: Globalization Is Not Good for Women's Health. Here's Why," Canadian Centre for Policy Alternatives, BC, *CCPA Monitor*, July/August 2002, accessed through www.policyalternatives.ca website, 4/2004.

8. Jean Ann Lowry, "Why Having a National Home Care Program is a Women's Issue," *The Canadian Women's Health Network Magazine*, Spring/Summer 2002, Vol. 5, No. 2/3; accessed via the CWHN website, 4/2004.

9. Canadian Women's Health Network, "Reading Romanow: The Implications of a Final Report of the Commission on the Future of Health Care in Canada for Women," revised and updated edition, National Coordinating Group on Health Care Reform and Women, April 2003, Chapter 8, accessed on the www.cwhn.ca website April 2004.

10. Department of Finance, Canadian Federal Government, Budget Plan 2003 (Chapter 3), "Building the Canada We Want," p. 1–6.

11. Health Canada, "2003 First Ministers' Accord," Factsheets 2003, www.hc-sc.gc.ca, accessed 4/2004. Note that this has also recently (in early June 2004) become a bone of contention in the federal election race, with the Conservative leader Stephen Harper pledging to increase transfers even more than was already agreed to under the previous Liberal government.

12. "Building on Values: The Future of Health Care in Canada," Final Report of the Commission on the Future of Health Care in Canada, cited in the National Coordinating Group on Health Care response to the Romanow report, "Reading Romanow: The Implications of the Final Report of the Commission on the Future of Health Care in Canada for Women," revised and updated edition, April 2003 (authors Pat Armstrong, Madeline Boscoe, Barbara Clow, Karen Grant, Ann Pederson, and Kay Willson), p. 7.

13. Ibid., p. 7.

14. Ibid., 7–8.

15. Professor Patricia Armstrong, "A Women's Guide to Health Care Debates," *Canadian Women's Health Network News*, Spring/Summer 2002, Vol. 5, No. 2/3, accessed via the web, www.cwhn.ca, 3/2004, p. 1.

16. Pat Armstrong, Madeline Boscoe, Barbara Clow, Karen Grant, Ann Pederson, Kay Willson, Olena Hankivsky, Beth Jackson, Marina Morrow, and the National Coordinating Group on Health Care Reform and Women, "Reading *Romanow*: The Implications of the Final Report of the Commission on the Future of Health Care in

Canada for Women," revised and updated edition, April 2003, accessed from the CWHN website, www.cwhn.ca, 2004.

17. Ibid., p. 53.

18. The Canadian Women's Health Network, *Network Magazine*, Kike Ehigiator, Institute Liasion, Canadian Institutes of Health Research, "Institute of Gender and Health: A Year in Review," Spring/Summer 2002, Vol. 5, No. 2/3, accessed via web, www.cwhn.ca/network-reseau/, 4/28/2004.

19. Ibid; None of the centers have had clinical responsibilities; they have solely been involved in research concerning "women's health issues and research them, produce health data that are sensitive to gender differences, provide analysis, advice and information to governments, agencies and individuals involved in health policy, and help define a women's health research agenda for Canada." The division of responsibility has been as follows: The Maritime Centre of Excellence for Women's Health, located at the Grace Health Centre and administered by Dalhousie University has the research function to conduct "gender analysis of policy," and to research "women's perceptions of the social determinants of health and determinants of priority or marginalized women." The Centre of Excellence at the Universite de Montreal Consortium (CESAF) researches "women in non-professional roles in the health system, immigrant women and the health needs of Aboriginal women." The Prairie Women's Centre of Excellence researches "the Impact of Selected Determinants of Health on Women, the Effects of Health Reform on Women's Health, and Policy and Program Models to Improve Women's Health." The BC Centre was mandated to research projects which will "improve the health of women who face disadvantages" (with eight grounds of possible disadvantage listed). Interestingly, only the BC Center was described as having been "created by feminist researchers" along with health providers, community groups, and policymakers dedicated to improving women's health. The last center, defined as a "national network" and arguably the largest and best funded, has been located at York University, Toronto, which has pursued "work on health systems and women's health, and the transformation of work and its impact on women's health." Interestingly, studies under this project have been authored by some academics most critical of health care downsizing and the federal Liberal government's policies in particular.

20. Telephone interview with Professor Pat Armstrong, August 2004.

21. www.hc-sc.ga, Department of Health, Government of Canada, updated 6/4/2002.

22. The Canadian Women's Health Network, "Canadian Women's Health Network's Submission to the Commission on the Future of Health Care in Canada," December 2001, p. 3, accessed at www.cwhn.ca, 3/2004.

23. The Working Group on Women and Health Protection, accessed through the Canadian Women's Health Network website (www.cwhn.ca), 11/2004.

24. "PM, Provinces Sign $41B Health Deal," CBC News Online, www.cbc.ca/news, September 16, 2004, accessed October 23, 2005.

6

Debating Day Care in Finland in the Midst of an Economic Recession and Welfare State Downsizing

Terhi Aalto and Anne Maria Holli

The fall of the Soviet Union in 1991 had a great impact on both Finnish foreign policy and domestic politics. Although never a part of the Socialist bloc and insisting on a formal neutrality, Finland, a parliamentary democracy with a multi-party system and a mixed economy, had had a cooperation pact with clauses about mutual assistance in periods of armed conflict with the neighboring Soviet Union since 1948. When the Communist regime there was dismantled, the cooperation pact was unobtrusively discontinued and the Finnish political leadership turned their gazes to the West, to the European Union. Four years later, in 1995, Finland joined the EU together with Austria and Sweden.

An important consequence of the political and economic turmoil in Russia and simultaneously declining global economies was the loss of a third of the Finnish export markets. These and other factors led to a more severe economic recession in Finland than in any other OECD country in the early 1990s. In 1991–1993, the GDP fell by almost 12 percent, more than ever in peacetime since 1917 (Hiilamo 2002, 192). During the same period, the number of the unemployed more than quadrupled, from under 4 percent to over 18 percent, as first the industry and, following that, the public sector started to reduce personnel. The economic crisis challenged both the idea and the practices of the Finnish social policy model.

Consequently, during the first half of the 1990s the Social Democratic, "women-friendly" welfare state was forced to make choices about how to reconfigure social benefits and the role of the state. The solution was found in exceptionally stringent cutback policies and a restructuring of social policies both at state and municipal levels. Approximately 70 percent of the cutbacks were directed at social policy (Kautto 2000, 44–45; Hiilamo 2002, 194). The resulting "welfare society" is more streamlined and less generous than its predecessor, delegating more responsibility for providing welfare upon individuals, families, the municipalities, the market, and the third sector, with a much diminished role reserved for the state (e.g., Lehtonen 2000; Julkunen 2001, 2002).

Today, researchers disagree on whether Finland can still be called a "welfare state" or not. However, most of them agree on the fact that the expansion of the welfare state has stopped and a new era is emerging in the field of social policy. For example, the well-known feminist social policy expert Professor Raija Julkunen (2002, 42) has claimed that although the Finnish welfare state has not altogether lost the foundational characteristics that used to contribute to its acknowledged status as "women-friendly", today it is much more difficult to characterize it as such, since there have been small shifts toward a more family-based welfare model.

In this chapter we present an analysis of a major debate during 1994 over a day care reform which had been agreed upon in 1991, prior to the recession. This reform, finally implemented at the beginning of 1996, gave an absolute universal social right of access to publicly provided day care for children aged three to six years. Both nationally and internationally, this was a remarkable measure for recognizing public responsibility in child care. Faced with the recession, the Center Right government suggested delaying the day care reform's implementation until economic times got better. The chapter concerns this debate, analyzing the policy impact and attempts to gender the debate by representatives of the Finnish women's movements and women's policy agencies within the government.

SELECTION OF THE POLICY DEBATE

Identifying the Universe of Hot Issues

It has been claimed that *the economic recession of the 1990s* was not only the most serious economic crisis in Finland since the Second World War but the most important crisis in political terms as well (Aslama et al. 2002, 11). In 1992, the Finnish unemployment rate was one of the lowest in Europe, and, in 1993, it had become one of the highest. The need to pay unemployment allowances to an ever-increasing portion of the labor force stretched the budgetary capacities of the state at the same time as a decline in income taxes considerably diminished the state's resources. Social spending as a proportion of the GDP increased by almost 10 percent between 1990 and 1993 before the budget cutbacks started to make an effect.

The consequences to individual citizens were no less drastic: their available income diminished by 12 percent and their private consumption by 13 percent during the worst years of the recession. Also, while income differences had traditionally been small, they began to grow rapidly in the latter half of the 1990s, thus exacerbating the social divisions between different groups in Finnish society (see, e.g., Uusitalo 2002). It has been estimated that in the long run the brunt of the costs of the economic crisis were born by the poor, the unemployed, the sick, the elderly, the young, the marginalized, and the less affluent families with children (Kiander 2001; Julkunen 2001).

First the Center Right government (1991–1995)[1] and then the so-called Rainbow government (1995–1999)[2] tried to remedy the situation by cutting down public expenses: public spending was downsized by 58 billion Finnish marks (FIM) during the 1990s. The reforms targeted all the public sectors in principle, but social policies were affected in particular; they were downsized by 40 billion FIM by governmental measures (Julkunen 2002, 38). The Center Right government's hard line caused much dissension and political conflict, for example, strikes and threats to that end by the trade unions as well as public demonstrations by the unemployed. The public attention the crisis attracted was also considerable both during and after the crisis years (e.g., Aslama et al. 2002).

Another hot issue debated in the early 1990s concerned *Finnish membership in the European Union*. As early as in summer 1990, Finland, along with the other member countries of the European Free Trade Association (EFTA), had started negotiations about the formation of the European Economic Area (EEA). After Sweden decided to apply for membership in the European Union, Finland followed suit a year later in 1992. A referendum took place in October 1994, with the results showing 57 percent of the citizens in favor of EU membership, 43 percent opposed to it. The issue divided opinions strongly, with a large part of the political elites and the more well-educated and affluent social groups supporting EU membership and the farmers in particular against it. In the debate, arguments about economic advantages were put against those stressing national interests in agricultural policy and continued sovereignty (Paloheimo 1998). The issue divided the political parties as well, resulting in a new conflict dimension in Finnish politics, i.e., that between the Eurocrats and the Euroskeptics (Nousiainen 2000). Membership in the European Union from 1995 also brought many institutional and substantive changes in Finnish policymaking (see, e.g., the articles in Raunio and Wiberg 2000).

Compared with these two debates (the economic crisis and the following welfare state reconfiguration and the EU membership), all the other hot issues of the 1990s in Finland appear much more limited in light of the RNGS selection criteria. The question of *membership in the European Monetary Union* (EMU) in the second half of the 1990s did not particularly interest the citizens, although it was a highly prioritized goal by the authorities. Abandoning formal neutrality in favor of *a closer affiliation with the NATO or a military cooperation within the EU* has been a more debated and contested issue, but one that has not wholly been resolved yet. In addition, there were two pieces of legislation that during the 1990s and early 2000s were subject to conflicts and much public attention. The first concerned *the construction of a fifth nuclear plant*, which was debated twice (in 1994 and 2001), the proponents of nuclear power achieving victory the second time around. Also *homosexuals' right to register their partnership*, in order to have the same formal rights as married heterosexual couples, was twice debated in the Parliament (in 1996 and 2001), incurring heated dissension between the sexual liberals and conservatives. The government's bill, proposing partnership registration rights but not adoption rights to homosexuals, was finally adopted in 2001.

Identifying the Debate for Study

Given that the second criteria for debate selection emphasizes that the researchers should choose an issue that involved much change in state-society relations, the economic recession and the social spending cutbacks were evident choices. However, this involved the problem as to *which* specific debate to target. Dozens, even hundreds of cutback decisions were made during 1991–1995 in particular, by a strategy of "creeping disentitlement" (van Kersbergen 2000, 28–30), small steps producing significant changes by their accumulation. The single biggest area of cutbacks was the decrease of state subsidies to the municipalities (14.5 billion FIM), but the decisions to that end were mostly made after the economic situation had started to improve in the late 1990s. The next biggest targets were the unemployment benefits (5.5 billion FIM), financial support for families with children (5 billion FIM), and housing subsidies (5 billion FIM) (Kiander 2001, 90–91).

However, we decided to exclude the issue of unemployment benefits, since an earlier study (Holli 2001) already analyzed one of the relevant reforms (1993) during the economic recession with the aid of the RNGS approach. We felt that it would yield valuable information in terms of comparative analysis to select a debate from another policy branch in the same period instead.

Consequently, family policy, especially day care policy, was selected for a detailed analysis in this study. Providing public day care was estimated to make up 23.9 percent of all spending in family policy in 1993 (Anttonen 1999, 95; Committee report 1995, 4, 47), and thus, it was prime material for

cutbacks. The day care issue was also relatively prominent in the public debates about the welfare cutbacks: for example, in the biggest newspaper of the
country, the day care issue occupied (with 6.2 percent share) a sixth place
among the most discussed topics (Parikka 2002). At a more principal level,
municipal day care has been considered perhaps the most important public
social service in Finland, and the one that provides the cornerstone of the
"women-friendly" welfare state model.

The day care issue had been high on the political agenda ever since the
1960s. Systematic, nationwide day care policy slowly emerged in the beginning of the 1970s as a result of increasing pressure by the women's movements in particular to organize daytime care for the children of working mothers. After several committees had investigated the issue, the Day Care Act of
1973 was pushed through primarily with the support of the left-wing parties
(Välimäki 1999). In the act, arranging public day care was made a statutory
obligation of the municipalities. During the 1970s and 1980s the number of
municipal day care places expanded rapidly.

At the same time, however, demands for a corresponding financial support
system for the home care of one's own children became louder. The number
of people working in the agricultural sector was still quite high in Finland (in
1970, 20 percent), and for their children, municipal day care institutions were
not a solution because of long distances and the sparse population density in
the countryside. The powerful Center Party, supporters mostly coming from
the agrarian population, consequently pushed for a development of a national
system of home care support. The demands were backed by other representatives of agrarian and/or conservative interests, such as the Christian League,
the Rural Party, and part of the National Coalition Party (Välimäki 1999).

In the beginning of the 1980s a historic compromise was made between the
ruling Social Democrats and the Center Party concerning the child home care
allowance, as the Act on Child Home Care Allowance finally took effect in
1985. "The dual strategy" adopted emphasized the interconnectedness of municipal day care and the home care allowance. The latter was regarded as a
compensation for *not* using one's right to a place in the municipal day care.
This also meant that the children's home care allowance was based on the
same universalistic principle as day care, not dependent on the level of income.[3] The home care allowance soon became a popular alternative for families, especially those with children aged zero to two years.[4]

The level of the home allowance benefit was raised considerably in the end
of the 1980s and the early 1990s. Similarly, the subjective right[6] to a place in
municipal day care or alternatively the right to the home care allowance for
children under three years was implemented in 1990. At the beginning of the
1990s, the Finnish system for the care of small children had reached its

all-time height in terms of scope and level of public compensation for child care expenses (Hiilamo 2002, 203).

Out of the universe consisting of all the day care debates during the 1990s, we selected the enactment of the subjective right to municipal day care for children aged three to six years as our hot issue analysis. The creation of subjective rights was without doubt the most important reform in day care policy in the 1990s, as it made publicly provided, affordable day care places a legal right for all parents. The issue was debated for years, reaching its peak in 1994, in the middle of the economic recession and the outset of the gradual processes for welfare state reconfiguration. The expansion of day care rights represents a process where the proposed cutbacks met with a particularly strong resistance and caused conflicts over the adopted policy line.[6]

WOMEN'S MOVEMENT IN THE 1990s

From an international perspective, second-wave feminism emerged in Finland relatively late, during 1973–1977, and then in a rather weak form (Bergman 1999, 2002). The main reason for this was that Finland had already experienced a homegrown second wave in the late 1960s. From 1966 to 1970, Association 9, a sex role movement influenced by rising student radicalism and Nordic sex role research, mobilized Finnish women (and some men) for a more balanced division of gender segregated roles and tasks. Its ideas were also soon integrated by the women's party sections (especially of the Left), and then by political parties at large (Jallinoja 1983; Holli 1988; Alanen 1981; Nupponen 1968). Also the expanding welfare state was able to integrate many of the initiatives into its agenda early.

It has been claimed that working through established political channels and structures is typical to Finnish (and other Nordic) feminism (Bergman 1999; Gustafsson et al. 1997) In Finland, the "double strategy" adopted has entailed the central role played by women's party sections and a moderate feminist grassroots movement seldom resorting to radical actions. In addition to some local level feminist organizations and networks, there has been only one nationwide independent feminist organization since 1976, the League of Finnish Feminists (*Naisasialiitto Unioni*). Lobbying for women's rights with a distinctive radical feminist emphasis, the organization also acts as an umbrella for various self-help projects and cultural activities.

Women's economic independence and political power were prominent goals all along, with bodily rights and violence against women appearing on the women's movement agenda only from the 1980s onwards. Also, whilst the ideology has typically emphasized similarities between the sexes in a liberal framework of "gender equality", in the 1980s there was a momentary turn towards a cultural feminist stress on women's specificity and "difference" (see, e.g., Holli 2003; Bergman 2002; Jallinoja 1983). According to Bergman (1999, 2002) this could be seen, for example, in the new emphasis on women's culture and in a strong women's peace movement.

From the late 1980s, there has been a visible trend to women's institutionalized cooperation across party and organizational lines in Finland (Bergman 1999), first apparent in the establishment of NYTKIS, the Coalition of Finnish Women's Associations for Joint Action in 1988. It consists of all the women's party sections, the Central League of Finnish Women's Organizations, the League of Finnish Feminists, and the academic Society for Women's Studies. Their joint membership is more than six hundred thousand persons, i.e., over 20 percent of the female population of Finland. Initially, NYTKIS used to act as an informal network, deciding however to formally organize in the early 2000s. It utilizes rotation of leadership and consensus-oriented decision-making procedures in its activity. The aim is to promote women's political participation and gender equality, lobbying political parties, the government, and the Parliament in specific issues.

In 1991 NYTKIS was followed by another women's cross-party alliance when women MPs decided to establish a network of their own within the parliament in the aftermath of the world-record high in women MPs and a simultaneous shift in governmental power to a Center Right coalition. Acting as an unofficial parliamentary standing committee, the network investigates and lobbies for issues considered as important to all women regardless of party affiliation within the Parliament (Ramstedt-Silén 1999).

The outset of the economic recession in the early 1990s can be regarded as a watershed for the Finnish women's movement in several ways. The movement became less visible in public, more fragmented, more specialized and professional, and to an increasing degree organized in informal networks instead of formal associations (Bergman 1998). Although many women's constituencies at the beginning of the 1990s were critical of the social spending cutbacks and to some degree mobilized to defend "the Finnish women-friendly welfare state", the protests relatively seldom translated into practical proposals in day-to-day politics (Holli 2001, 207–209). This can be explained by the politically divided character of Finnish feminism. When the party political conflicts between the Right and the Left are at a peak, the affiliated women's political organizations find it harder both to engender issues and to mobilize on gender grounds (Holli 2001, 2003).

However, during the 1990s women did mobilize for some issues and in some specific contexts. The Finnish women's movement continued to apply its old state-oriented strategies but now with the themes more carefully chosen, concentrating on issues of women's bodily integrity (rape, violence against women, prostitution, and pornography), gender equality policy (e.g., the reforms of the Equality Act), and the reconciliation of family and working life. To note, these were also issues which mainly did not entail major ideological dissensions between the different branches of the women's movement as they very much tended to share views of what "women's issues and interests" were in politics (see also Kantola 2004).

Paradoxically, women's mobilization was also channeled via one of the most established political structures, namely elections. This came to affect especially the presidential elections of 1994 and 2000. At both occasions, the female electorate tended to align behind the female candidates, often abandoning old political convictions to do so. Parts of the women's party sections and well-known woman politicians also crossed the party lines to join a woman candidate's camp. As a result, Ms. Elisabeth Rehn (the Swedish People's Party) surprisingly ended as a runner-up for presidency in 1994, and Ms. Tarja Halonen (the Social Democratic Party) was elected the president of the republic in 2000.

In conclusion, gender as a political category seems to have gained in importance in Finnish politics during the 1990s, competing with party affiliation and sometimes even overcoming it in women's decisions from a political standpoint. Both gendered voting patterns and the high proportion of women in parliamentary politics contributed to this phenomenon. Furthermore, new institutionalized forms of women's cross-party cooperation helped mobilize women on specific issues during an era when many of their past achievements were seen as being threatened.

DEBATE: THE SUBJECTIVE RIGHT TO MUNICIPAL DAY CARE, 1994

How the Issue Came to the Public Agenda

A subjective right to day care for children aged zero to two years had been in force in the country since 1990. In 1991, the Parliament had also passed a law on the extension of the subjective right to day care to all children under school age. The act was supposed to gain force in 1993. Because of the economic recession, these plans were changed, however, as demands for cutting public spending—especially social spending—got louder. Despite protests, the Parliament decided in 1992 to postpone the implementation of the day care right until January 8, 1995. During the years 1993 and 1994 plans to further delay the implementation of the day care reform were clearly in the air. The issue reached its peak in the fall of 1994 in connection with the handling of the state budget for the next year, which also was to be the election year. Because of the financial difficulties faced by the state and the municipalities, the government proposed delaying the day care reform again, until 1997.

The idea for postponing the promised day care rights was initiated by bureaucrats in the Ministry of Finance. The minister of finance, Mr. Iiro Viinanen, was a widely known opponent to "lavish" social spending and thus also to the extension of the subjective rights. Similarly, the central cooperative organ of the Finnish local authorities, Kuntaliitto (the Association of Finnish Local and Regional Municipalities), had actively been lobbying against additional legal obligations for the municipalities which would increase their financial burden and limit their self-governance. The plan for postponement was supported by the governing parties with the opposition parties consisting of the Social Democrats, the Left-Wing Alliance, and the Green Party, protesting loudly against it.

The bill met also with strong resistance during the autumn of 1994 as women across the party lines and the Network of Women MPs in particular mobilized to defend the day care rights. As part of their campaign, the women MPs' network agreed on a joint pro-day care statement, which signified a radical break away from the official government position especially for the governing Center and National Coalition Party women deputies. After the statement was made public, the day care issue was strongly profiled as a women's issue in the media and the political arenas.

The subjective rights package included, however, two components: the day care right and the child home care allowance right. This came to be the decisive factor from the perspective of women's cooperation, reflecting the old schisms between the proponents of municipal day care and the defenders of home care. The cleavage became visible when, realizing that it was not possible to pull through both reforms at the same time, the majority of the active women MPs decided to prioritize the right to municipal day care. This was unacceptable for the Center Party women, who insisted that the women's front should hold on to the home care reform as well. This dissension partly broke down the women's cooperation in Parliament.

The disagreements also resulted in an extraordinary, conflict-ridden handling in the Social Affairs and Health Committee of the Parliament. While government-sponsored bills usually pass the parliamentary process without bigger changes, this time the responsible committee succeeded in overturning the proposal to postpone day care rights. After this, in December 1994, the day care issue got top national publicity as minister of finance Mr. Viinanen, immediately threatened his resignation. This would have meant the fall of the government, as Prime Minister Esko Aho later stated (STT 1994).

Dominant Frame of the Debate

Interestingly, none of the policy actors questioned the system of municipal day care as such or denied that it was a public responsibility to provide for day care services (see also Kantola 2004). Instead, what was seen as problematic was the extension of the financial burdens of the municipalities and the binding nature built into the subjective right. While initially the discourse was constructed as a conflict between the proponents and the opponents of cutbacks, in the later stages a cleavage emerged between the pro-day care and the pro-home care allowance activists.

In the reports submitted by a ministerial working group in spring 1994, the issue of day care was predominantly framed as a question of the needs and interests of the larger society (societal discourse). Firstly, day care was seen as a pedagogic and educational institution, where children would participate in stimulating and inspiring activities and learn important basic social skills. Day care also had important functions in promoting social equality and preventing the emergence of social problems for the children of low-income and underprivileged families. Secondly, the reports emphasized the positive effects of municipal day care for economic growth and the labor market, as it ensured the availability of an adequate labor force and thus contributed to the competitiveness of the national economy. The child home care allowance, in contrast, was linked neither to labor market utility nor to economic growth, but was seen as adding to the choices available for individual families. All in all, the reports stressed the multitude of alternatives as the basis of the Finnish child care policy, covering the diverse needs and life situations of families. However, these diverse circumstances or needs were not analyzed further, neither was there any impact assessment (Committee report 1994a, 1994b).

The governmental bill (Gov. prop. 211/1994), which proposed the postponement of the subjective rights, originated in the same "societal discourse" adopted by the ministry but took on an opposite, savings approach. The bill was very brief in style. The only argument explaining the postponement was a phrase which was customarily utilized during the recession years: the bill was put forward "because of reasons related to the state economy and also taking into account the financial situation of the municipalities." The effects of the proposal were inspected for the part of the employment situation, the availability of day care places, and the households. In case there were not enough day care places, postponing the subjective right to day care would lead to two alternatives: either families would have to purchase care services from the private market, which would cause more expenses to the household, or "the parents would have to stay at home" to take care of their children.

The arguments in defense of day care during the parliamentary hearings did not bring any substantively new elements into the discussion. It was pointed out that municipal day care was a service branch with a high labor intensity, as 85 percent of the costs of day care were labor costs. "The European card" was also played, as the pro-day care activists claimed that postponing the day care right of three- to six-year-olds would reduce their possibilities for pre-school education, which in turn would lead to falling behind the European (read: EU) countries where pre-school education started a lot earlier. This argument was used to persuade right-wing MPs, most of which were pro-EU, to join the pro-day care front (Gov. prop. 211/1994, Parliamentary documents 1994).

Towards the end of the parliamentary debate, the frame changed to some extent to include the city versus the countryside dimension. Municipal day care was identified with cities and the urban way of life and the home care option with farmers and an agricultural way of living. This shift reflected the escalating confrontation between the political parties, as the Center Party mobilized to defend the home care allowance and, thus, the interests of its own electorate.

Gendering the Debate

Gendered concerns were brought forward throughout the debate. Women's interests were clearly an important part of the dominant frame, not a separate issue lobbied by feminist actors (see also Kantola 2004). There was a visible tendency to make references to men as well, so as to indicate that day care issues should be a concern of men, too. While the bureaucratic and governmental policy preparation displayed a relatively gender-neutral approach, some other policy actors (politicians, especially women MPs, and trade unions) clearly framed the issue in gendered terms. In contrast, the opponents of day care rights, i.e., the representatives of employers' associations or the municipalities, totally ignored the gender aspect.

The governmental bill did not contain any gendered observations or arguments. Also, the reports written by the ministerial working group on day care were mostly gender-neutral, which is customary to Finnish official documents. In the ministerial reports on day care, this principle was especially applied to home care, which was linguistically depicted in gender-neutral terms, home care being given to the child by "the parents" or "the family", not by a mother or a father. Home care was also referred to as "the traditional form of child care". It is noteworthy that, although the home care allowance is a subsidy predominantly utilized by women, this gender aspect was not even mentioned.

Certain references to gender can, however, be found in the section of the working group report where the importance of the municipal day care system was highlighted, by pointing to two of its merits for the promotion of gender equality. Firstly, the day care system secured an adequate supply of labor by facilitating the sharing of caring responsibilities between the public sector and the family. Secondly, the day care system was credited for having created the conditions for women's full labor market participation. Organized day care had made it possible for both parents of small children, especially women, to be in paid work, the working group stated. The report noted, however, that the day care system should not be regarded as an instrument for moving women in and out of the labor market at will. That is, women should not be treated as a secondary labor force that should time their work after the demands for more or less manpower (Committee report 1994a; cf. also Holli 2001, 201–202).

The day care issue became more gendered as it moved out of the bureaucratic arena and into the Parliament. During the preparation of the issue in the parliamentary committee various interest groups were consulted or voluntarily offered their comments. By far the most gendered statement was that by one of the trade unions, STTK. Representing, among others, middle-salaried white-collar women, STTK had been an active defender of women's issues in working life. The organization opposed the plans to postpone the day care rights, motivating its standpoint mainly with gender equality concerns. Participation in the labor market was seen as the key to women's equality with men via the economic independence it made possible. Organized day care was a prerequisite for women's wage work. STTK also reminded the public authorities of their duty to promote equality "especially by changing those conditions that stand as barriers to gender equality" (Equality Act, 4 §; STTK 1994). In addition to the STTK, other trade unions also argued for gender equality and the implementation of the day care reform.

Also the parliamentary standing committee emphasized the objective of gender equality as one of its main arguments for not delaying the day care reform. According to the committee, the availability of day care was, in addition to the meal service at schools, maybe the most important factor influencing the state of gender relations, since it was women who still in practice were responsible for the care of small children. This notion was added to the report by Tuula Kuittinen, a Center Party MP who also at the same time served as the chair for the Council for Equality. The committee pointed out that reconciling work and family life in such a way that both parents had an equal opportunity to work and care for children should be set as the goal of the day care policy (Parliamentary Committee of Social Affairs and Health 1994).

Gender played a prominent role in the parliamentary plenary debates and its significance even intensified towards the finale. Also in the House the question of gender equality was clearly framed as women's opportunity to participate in the labor market. On the one hand, taking away the right to day care would mean taking away women's possibility to work. On the other, wage work was seen as a necessity, not an option one chose after a long consideration. The need for day care was a fact, since 80 percent of Finnish women with small children had full-time jobs. For them, day care was a basic social service and an essential condition in life, that "belongs to the soft sphere of life, which actually is, however, part of the hard sphere", as one Social Democratic woman MP stated (Gov. prop. 211/1994, Parliamentary documents 1994). The obvious connection between work and day care also made the women MPs critical of the savings discourse of the government. For example, Prime Minister Esko Aho had painted a picture of the day care issue where some people were working hard to get money while some others were all too eager to find ways of spending it.

A marked feature of the parliamentary debates was the strong agitation by the pro-day care women MPs toward other women MPs. They saw day care as a common interest over which all women should be united. Already early in the autumn the conflict over the day care issue had been proclaimed as a test for the women's network on "whether the women in the parliament which has the world record in women MPs are able to cooperate", as stated by Outi Ojala, a Left-Wing Alliance woman MP (Gov. prop. 211/1994, Parliamentary documents 1994). The existence of common interests on this issue was partly denied by the Center Party women in particular, who argued that, above all, the possibility to choose was in the interest of women. One Center Party deputy, a young woman, accused the opposition women of "trying to monopolize women's opinions" (Gov. prop. 211/1994, Parliamentary documents 1994, MP Maria Kaisa Aula). These dissensions illustrate the old conflict between various parts of the Finnish women's movement over the relative importance of day care versus home care (cf. Tyyskä 1995).

In the debate, home care was not motivated with moral arguments about women's proper place being the home. Instead, the home care front utilized a choice discourse (Kantola 2004), stressing that the home care allowance would open up choices for women and families to arrange child care according to their individual needs and preferences. The home care activists also emphasized that the home care option did not necessarily mean maternal or even parental care, since the parents could go to work and receive the allowance anyhow—instead, the only condition was that they did not take their children to municipal kindergartens, but to a granny in the neighborhood instead.

Near the finale of the discussions in Parliament there appeared an intense pressure by some leading male government politicians towards the "dissenting" women MPs of their own parties, with the intention to keep the women in line with the government's original proposal. It seems that the pressure politics developed even Machiavellian characteristics. Many women MPs interpreted the interference as being not a question about money but about prestige: "This does not mean we are ripping the budget proposal apart, and still Mr. Viinanen, the minister of finance, threatens with his resignation. The reactions of the minister of finance as well as those of the prime minister are getting out of hand. This is about prestige, about the fact that women have dared to take their own stand" (Gov. prop. 211/1994, Parliamentary documents 1994, MP Pirjo-Riitta Antvuori, National Coalition Party).

At the end of the debate many opposition women expressed disappointment over the breakup of the cooperation within the women's network. There were many accusing fingers pointed at the Center Party women, "who would not stick to women's common objectives". The Center women, on the other hand, were disappointed with the women MPs' network. According to Tuula Kuittinen, the women's network had not listened to the Center Party women but had pushed its own policy through in the name of the majority, without paying attention to dissenting voices (Gov. prop. 211/1994, Parliamentary documents 1994).

Policy Outcome

The conflicts over the day care reform were in the end solved by a government compromise between the National Coalition Party and the Center Party, a solution which at least partly was initiated by the Center Party women. In the compromise, both the day care and the home care rights were postponed, but not by one and a half years as the government had suggested, but instead by half a year only for both, until January 1, 1996.

Women's Movement Impact

The day care debate has later been viewed as a triumph for the women's movement and a proof of women's ability to cooperate. However, it is evident that the day care debate certainly was not a victory in absolute terms either for women or the women's movement. In RNGS terms the debate can nevertheless be regarded as a dual response by the state.

In descriptive terms, women were very well represented throughout the policy process as bureaucrats, NGO and trade union representatives, experts, and politicians. The Parliament had 38.5 percent women MPs, a world record at the time, and 64 percent of the participants in the plenary debates were women. Despite a female majority in the policy preparation process, the women seldom explicitly represented women's constituencies, although one woman (Annukka Paasikivi, Center Party activist and chair of the Association for the Promotion of Children's Home Care) was included in the ministerial working group under the title "homemaker". The women's movement was rather represented via women MPs who, seeing themselves expressly as women's representatives, actively defended what they saw as "women's interests" in child care. Institutionally, the mobilization was channeled via the Network of Women MPs (see also Ramstedt-Silén 1999).

Whether the women's movement attained its goals is a more complicated question. After some consideration, we have classified the debate as a policy success. Considering that women co-operated both across the party lines and the government/opposition divide and that the women's front was partly able to block the proposed postponement of the day care right makes the outcome positive from the perspective of the women's movement. Indeed, both the day care activists and the defenders of the home care allowance won in relative terms, as it was decided that both subjective rights would be extended.

Women's Policy Agency Activities

The Council for Equality between Men and Women was established in 1972 as a permanent, advisory committee charged with the task of proposing reforms for gender equality. It was a national, cross-sectional, politico-administrative body with limited administrative capacity having a small budget and a secretariat as its main resources. From 1986, the Council for Equality was located under the Ministry of Social Affairs and Health. Hence, it was actually inside one of the main arenas for policymaking on day care.

The politically nominated council reflected the composition of the Parliament, having a non-Socialist majority at the time. During 1992–1995, the chair of the council was Tuula Kuittinen, MP (Center Party). Although active in the Center Party Women, Kuittinen had not at least in public profiled as a feminist. On the other hand, the secretariat of the council, headed by feminist Eeva-Liisa Tuominen, had since the 1970s been more oriented to the Left (see, e.g., Holli 1991).

Day care issues were part of the policy mandate of the women's policy agency, but in practice they had not been high on its agenda since the 1970s. The strategy of the council was to lift new issues to the political agenda and shift its attention elsewhere when successful. In the 1990s the prioritized areas were, for example, violence against women and prostitution and trafficking. By contrast, day care issues were in the background. Although the council gave some statements on both social policy and day care policy, these were mostly at a very general level. The council was concerned about the effects of the cutback policies for women, but it did not pinpoint any concrete cutback proposals by the government for a more detailed scrutiny.

However, the chair of the council, Tuula Kuittinen, MP, played an active role in the debate within the parliamentary standing committee. Being a "triple agent", a woman MP, vice chair of Center Party Women, and chair of the Council for Equality, Kuittinen's role poses a thorny problem for the RNGS methodology. Since the Council for Equality did not have a concrete standpoint on the day care issue and Kuittinen herself did not motivate her actions in the Parliament with reference to the council, we can conclude that in this instance, she did not act as an agent for the council. Thus, as the council did not insert gendered concerns in the actual day care debate, it did not act as a link between the women's movement and the state either (symbolic role).

From 1987, the Council for Equality shared responsibility over equality policy with the equality ombudsman, a cross-sectional, judicial, independent official in charge of supervising the Equality Act. She or he was the formal head of the Equality Office placed under the Ministry of Social Affairs and Health, sharing the staff with the council. In 1994, the ombudsman was Tuulikki Petäjäniemi, a former National Coalition Party MP with a professional background in an employers' association. The ombudsman's policy mandate includes issues which touch on the interpretation of the Equality Act. In this case, however, the ombudsman was not consulted nor voluntarily commented on the day care issue (symbolic role).

Women's Movement Characteristics

At the beginning of the 1990s, the women's movement was in a stage of consolidation and the day care issue was a high priority on its agenda. At the outset the movement was relatively cohesive on the issue, but as the debate unfolded, a division over the day care versus home care options emerged, with the left-wing women, Green Party women, and part of the National Coalition Party women supporting the former and the Center Party women the latter. The counter-movement was strong, consisting of the government, the governmental parties, the Ministry of Finance, and the representatives of the municipalities.

Policy Environment

In the 1991 parliamentary elections, the left-wing parties had suffered an electoral defeat which decreased the proportion of Socialist MPs to 33.5 percent and forced the Social Democrats into opposition for the first time in more than twenty years. The new Center Right government (1991–1995, consisting of the Center Party, the National Coalition Party, the Swedish People's Party, and the Christian League), led by Prime Minister Esko Aho, basically adopted a reactive policy approach to the sudden economic crisis by attempts to promote the interests of private enterprise and balance the budget deficit by cutbacks in public expenditure.

Day care legislation was prepared in the Ministry of Social Affairs and Health, which was also responsible for other forms of family policy. The principal actors besides the ministry were other governmental bodies, the municipalities, and especially their cooperative organ, Kuntaliitto, the Parliament, the biggest parties, and the Ministry of Finance. Other actors included the social partners and their central organizations, although they were not so central in day care policy as in the social insurance sector. The position of nongovernmental organisations was fairly marginal, even though they were not completely excluded from the policy process. All in all, the Finnish social and health care sector has formed a rather established and stable network of relations that can be called "a policy community". That is, the participants have not greatly varied according to issue (Mattila 2000; Uusikylä 1999).

The day care legislation was submitted as a budget law, which means that the draft bill was prepared in relative secrecy by bureaucrats from the Ministry of Social Affairs and Health in cooperation with the Ministry of Finance. In general, during the recession in particular the preparation process of laws became more closed as the government for the sake of efficiency cut down on large representative inquiry commissions in favor of "one-man committees" and increasingly legislated by means of budget laws (Mattila 2000). In conclusion, taking into account both the process characteristics and the nature of the policy network, the policy subsystem can be evaluated as moderately closed in this debate.

The policy subsystem had a "societal discourse" approach to the day care issue, with a strong emphasis on its economic and social advantages. So did the government, although conceptualizing the matter from an opposite, savings angle. Representatives of the women's movement and other pro-day care activists basically utilized a gendered variation of the same "societal" discourse, thus making for a compatible frame fit.

CONCLUSION

In this chapter, we have analyzed one day care debate as part of the more comprehensive "hot issue" policy debates concerning the severe economic recession and welfare state downsizing in Finland. The study shows that the Finnish women's movement was very active in the debate and succeeded in inserting its goals into the legislation (dual response), partly blocking the proposed long delay to the subjective rights to day care and home care. As a result, municipal day care was actually extended in the era of social spending cutbacks (see also Julkunen 2002; Parikka 2002). The outcome can partly be explained by the widespread popularity and acceptance of public day care but our analysis also points out the critical acts (Dahlerup 1988) performed by women's movement actors in its defense.

However, women's policy agencies played merely a symbolic role in the success. The finding challenges the RNGS proposition that women's policy offices would be necessary to advancing women's interests within the state. In the Finnish case, the lack of WPA activity was mainly due to the fact that the Council for Equality chose to prioritize other issues during the early 1990s, letting the established policy subsystem together with the political parties and women's party sections worry about day care policies. To note, this strategy was particularly justified in the light of there being a high number of women MPs and new institutionalized forms of women's cross-party cooperation which held day care a clear common priority.

In our case study, the Women MPs' Network together with individual women MPs appeared as the main representatives of the women's movement. Also other analyses (Holli 2002, 2003, 2004; Aalto 2003; Holli and Kantola 2004) have pointed at their prominent role in promoting women's interests in public policymaking in Finland during the 1990s. Being inside the Parliament, both the network and the "critical mass" of women MPs were able to monitor public policymaking and interfere as needed. Their attempts to gender legislation did not always yield results, especially if the issue divided women's opinions and they could not secure enough support from either the governmental or the opposition parties (see Holli 2003). In this debate, however, the women MPs from various parties managed to join forces with the opposition left-wing parties against the right-wing governmental line. Even after the confrontation between the day care issue and the home care issue divided the women's front, women managed to push for a compromise between the governing parties, thus securing a positive outcome.

Comparing the results of this single debate with the other RNGS analyses of Finnish policymaking during 1991–1995, at the peak of the recession, and in the context of Center-Right governmental power (Holli 2001; Holli and Kantola 2004), some other critical notions emerge. Two debates resulting in women's policy success both displayed a high mobilization of the women's movement (high priority of issue, a relatively cohesive movement with the left-wing women's organizations included) in a moderately closed policy subsystem, whereas the only policy failure combined a closed policy network with a very weak mobilization by women (low priority, divided movement). In summary, the results of this case study also conform to Holli's (2002, 2003; see also Aalto 2003) claim of there being a definite tendency towards women's movement success in Finland if it only manages to mobilize to a sufficient degree in an open or only moderately closed policy environment. By contrast, left-wing or right-wing power plays a lesser role. The exact influence of policy subsystem closure and the mechanics of a question being defined as "a women's issue" worth mobilizing for in the Finnish women's movement still remain open.

The matter of subjective rights to day care was not ultimately resolved in this debate taking place in 1994, however. In the following spring of 1995, the issue reemerged in connection with the negotiations over the new government coalition as the drafts for the governmental program again included the postponement of both subjective rights. The right to publicly provided day care for children aged three to six years was left in peace, however. For the home care right, things turned out less well, as the extension to three-year-olds was put off until 1997 and the level of the allowance itself was cut back 25 percent.[7] In 1997 the child care system faced a more profound structural change and the idea of extending the right to home care was in practice buried altogether. The subjective right to day care is still in place in Finland, despite many attacks since then toward dissolving it.

NOTES

1. It consisted of the Center Party, the conservative National Coalition Party, the Greens, the Swedish People's Party, and the Christian League.

2. The Rainbow government was a wide coalition consisting of the Social Democrats, the Left-Wing Alliance, the National Coalition Party, the Greens, and the Swedish People's Party.

3. In practice, the child care allowance has developed into a form of basic economic security for lower-salaried women and women with an insecure labor market status (see Anttonen 1999).

4. In 2000, 44 percent of children aged zero to two years were cared for with the help of the home care allowance, 22 percent were in municipal day care, and 2% used the private child care allowance (a new support form introduced in 1997). The rest were infants under the age of one year either of whose parent was paid an earnings-related parenthood allowance. For children aged three to six years, the numbers were respectively 15 percent (home care allowance), 62 percent (municipal day care), and 4 percent (private child care allowance) (Trends in Social Protection in Finland 2002, 104).

5. The term "subjective right" refers to individuals' unconditional right to certain social benefits or services. For example, the parents can even receive financial

compensation for loss of earnings from the municipality if it is not able to offer a day care place for the child (see KKO 2001). It should be noted that a universal social benefit (or service) can be, but not necessarily is, a subjective right. The former refers to a benefit that is available to all citizens who fulfill certain conditions regardless of their economic status. The latter is a strongly compelling legal category that gives the citizens an absolute right to obtain the benefit in question. In Finland, in addition to day care rights, only a few social benefits (e.g., certain services for disabled people and emergency medical care for all) have been given the status of a subjective right.

6. For a more detailed analysis of Finnish day care and home care debates, see Aalto 2003 and Kantola 2004.

7. On the continuation of the day care debate, see Aalto 2003.

Thirty-five-Hour Workweek Reforms in France, 1997–2000: Strong Feminist Demands, Elite Apathy, and Disappointing Outcomes

Amy G. Mazur

Reflecting trends in other postindustrial democracies, the highly state-centered welfare state model in France has shifted significantly in response to global economic crises and pressure to downsize government in the 1980s and 1990s. Governments of the Left and the Right have adopted a more neoliberal approach to economic policymaking while still maintaining a typically French emphasis on state actors (Hall 2001; Schmidt 1996). For example, the major argument given by Socialist Prime Minister Jospin for the thirty-five-hour workweek reforms in 1997 was situated within this neoliberal logic—to reduce unemployment and to allow private firms more flexibility. Yet the tradition of state-mandated vacation and reduced workweeks has continued to be an important social right in France. In 1981, under the historic arrival of the Socialists to power, the workweek was reduced to thirty-nine hours and state-mandated vacation increased from four to five weeks. Political parties of the Left and the Right in the 1980s and 1990s discussed a move toward a reduced workweek and the 1986 Loi Robien, adopted under a right-wing government, provided financial incentives to businesses to negotiate shorter workweeks: a first step toward the 1998/2000 reforms that finally shortened the workweek to thirty-five hours for all full-time employees.

The thirty-five-hour workweek reforms were seen by many as a revolutionary change that promised to impact the daily lives of French men and women as well as the economy (Laurent 2000; Lemaître 1999). The formulation process was highly complex with first the adoption of a general framework law in 1998; next negotiations between the state and the social partners of the specific process of shortening the workweek that resulted in the adoption of a second law in 2000; and, finally, the actual branch- and firm-level negotiations that would make the thirty-five-hour workweek a reality for all

French employees, including management and employees in small business, by January 2002. Quality of life and gender issues, which tend to be taboo in discussions of employment policy in general in France (Méda 1999), were given secondary importance when Jospin first proposed the reforms in 1997 and throughout the debates, despite the presence of well-developed and relatively strong feminist demands for considering gender issues outside of a purely neoliberal approach. As the chapter will argue, the feminist actors who presented positions in the thirty-five-hour workweek debates were not given entry to the policymaking arenas, parliament, or social partner consultation. In addition, the Deputy Secretary of Women's Rights and Job Training, the major women's policy agency at the time of the debate, was conspicuously silent in the mainstream employment arenas. The impact of the women's movement on the reform process, therefore, was *pre-empted* and the women's policy agency activities were *marginal*.

Part one provides the rationale for selecting the thirty-five-hour workweek debates as the "hottest" issue on state-society reconfiguration for analysis. The women's movement in the 1990s is mapped out in the second part. In the third part, the debates and outcomes of the thirty-five-hour workweek reform process, efforts to gender the debate frame, women's movement impact, women's policy agency activities, and the characteristics of the women's movement and the policy environment at the time of the debates are examined.

DEBATE SELECTION

Identifying the Universe of Hot Issues

Given the general hotness of government affairs in France and the particular dynamics of policy issues in the 1990s, potential hot issues were divided into two categories using the four criteria of scope, conflict, public attention, and elite salience—hot debates and hottest debates.[1] Although many of the debates in the hot category were controversial and generated public debate, the four dimensions of hotness, discussed below for each hot issue, were at higher levels than the other policy issue for the following four issues.

1. Reform of Citizenship and Immigration, 1990–1998

First under the right-wing government and conservative Interior Minister Charles Pasqua and then under Michel Debré, the right-wing government tightened up citizenship requirements and immigration laws that set off a series of protests culminating in the occupation of a Parisian church by illegal immigrants, *sans papier*, in 1996–1997. The new Socialist government responded with a volley of more progressive laws through the Weil report and the reform of the nationality code in 1998. The laws strike at the notion of French citizenship and democracy for many, particularly with regards to the movement toward a tolerant multi-cultural society. As Schain (1996) and others assert, the immigration issue was highly controversial with the rise of the extreme right-wing National Front tending to set the agenda beginning in the late 1980s and into the 1990s. Immigration policy debates in the 1990s necessarily place the future of French democracy and the state of the French party system at its center and hence while they may not mobilize as many people as socio-economic policy issues, they draw equal levels of public attention.

2. Subsidies to Private Schools and Funding of Public School Infrastructure, 1993–1998

Less of a wedge issue than immigration, education reforms traditionally ignite French citizens (e.g., Ambler 1996). The first controversy in 1993–1994 over repeal of the Falloux law that restricted public funding of private schools was ended by a constitutional court decision. A second wave of student-led protests against the poor funding and provisions of public schools pushed the government to act in 1996 and a third wave of protests around Socialist Minister Claude Allegre in 1999 brought together the same coalition of parents, teachers, and students to ask for a more effectively run educational system. Less preoccupying of an issue for the French political party system, but just as capable of mobilizing hundreds of thousands of citizens, the education policy debates that raged in the 1990s tapped into deep-seated feelings about French republican education.

3. Government Downsizing, 1993–1997

The right-wing governments under Balladur and Juppé sought to introduce neoliberal reforms to downsize the state that had been high on the agenda of the right-wing political parties: privatize nationalized industry, deregulate public services, and significantly reduce social security coverage. As such, the scope of the reforms implicated most of the active population as well as the larger French tradition of *dirigisme*. While greatly exacerbated by the economic crisis of the mid-1990s these reforms were very unpopular. Not only did a wide range of actors mobilize both for and against the reforms, but hundreds of thousands of citizens protested to express their discontent culminating in the society-wide work stoppages and demonstrations in the fall of 1995. While the privatizations were not undone, many of the social security reforms were stopped or minimized as a reaction to the social movement against neoliberal policies.

4. Thirty-five-Hour Workweek, 1997–2000

Seen by some as an opportunity to rethink the structure of work and daily life and by others as a way of being more competitive in the global economy by reducing unemployment, the two Aubry laws adopted in 1998 and 2000 involved all of the social partners and were center stage of French public opinion for three years. Between the various actors consulted and the number of groups that protested against the impending reforms over a half a million people were involved at some level with the reforms. The employers association (MEDEF) and the management union (CGC) led large demonstrations for the first time ever. Tireless press coverage also kept the highly complex and excruciatingly technical reforms in the public eye. The laws set off huge conflicts between labor and management as well as the Left and the Right: conflicts that echoed many of the historical divisions of French industrial relations and society more generally.

Identifying the Debate to Study

The four debates are more or less at the same level of intensity with regards to the four criteria. In terms of the second set of selection criteria, the issue that involves major changes in state-society relations, all four policy issues clearly involve some level of reconfiguring the state. The two Aubry laws that put into place the thirty-five-hour workweek present the most extensive change in state-society relations out of the four. Involving a highly complex process of work scheduling and restructuring overseen by a wide variety of state actors and ironically freeing up firms to a certain degree to better compete in the global economy, the implementation of the thirty-five-hour workweek presents the most clear-cut case of state reconfigurations out of the four top-level policy debates. As many French observers assert, it is these two reforms that have the promise to engender profound change not just within the economic realm but also in the lives of French men and women outside of the paid economy (Laurent 2000:16).

RENEWAL OF WOMEN'S MOVEMENT ACTIVITIES IN THE 1990s

Contrary to the predictions in the late 1980s that feminism was dead in France, the 1990s saw a renewal of women's movement activities that departed from many of the detrimental dynamics of the 1970s and 1980s.[2] Overcoming the deep divisions over strategy and coalition-building and a certain propensity for anti-system stances and uniquely Paris-based action, broad-based coalitions of women's movement and non–women's movement groups, called *collectifs* or *coordination,* new free-standing groups, and individual actors mobilized around specific policy reforms. Men were often accepted or even encouraged to participate, in the name of *mixité*, a position that abandoned the notion of certain women's movement actors on the Left that feminist action could only be pursued by women. While some of the 1970s activists were key leaders in the new campaigns, younger women became involved and some new groups were founded by women in their twenties and thirties.

A major trend in women's movement mobilization in the 1990s was issue-based movements that were formed to promote a specific policy objective. In most cases, the movement achieved some level of policy satisfaction. In some cases, the movements continued after the specific policy was adopted; in others the *collectif* dissipated, often due to what the leaders of the movement saw as a failure in the final policy outcome. In all, an estimated 140,000 people were mobilized by the various activities pursued by the issue-specific women's movements in the 1990s (e.g., lobbying, organization building, letter writing, demonstrating). While the women's policy offices in the 1990s served as important partners in some of the policy areas, they were not always crucial to the success of the women's movement mobilization. Moreover, the ministerial-level offices and women's rights administration did not appear to undermine the activities of the women's movement actors, as some critics of the powerful women's rights ministry under Yvette Roudy (1981–1986) had feared (Mazur 1995b).

This new issue-specific activity was most prominent in the following four policy areas: Anti–sexual harassment policy through the *Association des Violence Faites Contre les Femmes au Travail* (AVFT) in the 1900s and more recently, a new group based in Paris universities, CLASCHES—*Collectif de Lutte Anti-sexiste et Contre le Harcelement dans l'Enseignement Surpérieur.* The *Coordination National pour le Droit à l'Avortement* (CADAC) was founded in the early 1990s to defend women's reproductive rights It was from these successes that the leaders of the CADAC created a more broad-based umbrella organization, *Collectif National des Droits des Femmes* (CNDF) that participated in broad range of feminist campaigns. Beginning in 1992, in the context of persistently low levels of women's representation in elected office, new groups and collectives allied themselves with prominent female political leaders and many non-women's movement groups to push for reforms that would actively promote parity of men and women in office. The movement dissipated with the final adoption of the new reforms in 2000, partially as a result of the absence of real sanctions to compel political parties to put forward female candidates.

Women's movement actors also mobilized around smaller issue-based campaigns, at the national and sub-national levels, on for instance, violence against women, prostitution, parity in education, anti-sexist language, and migrant women's rights, particularly in Marseilles. French women's movement actors across many of the areas took advantage of transnational feminist networks, developed through the European Union and United Nations, to strengthen their campaigns. The EU gender equality policy process, however, was much more central to women's movement mobilization in the 1990s than the transnational links to United Nations women's policy conferences, the Women's March, and CEDAW (Gaspard Interview).

One final important difference between the women's movement in the 1980s and the 1990s is the declining influence of women's movement actors inside left-wing political parties and the trade unions. Weak and isolated women's commissions tend to elaborate feminist positions on women's policy issues without actually getting directly involved with the campaigns or having any success in convincing their leadership to place the feminist positions on the group's agenda.[3] In contrast to its women's movement activities in the 1980s, with the exception of the anti–sexual harassment movement, the CFDT's women's commission was absent from most of the campaigns of the 1990s (Allwood and Wadia 2002, 2000; Trat and Zylberberg-Hocquard 2000). Far removed from women's movement activities in the 1980s and early 1990s, women within the CGT, in the wake of the large mobilization in 1995, revived a collectif, *Femmes-Mixités*, within the Confederation (Ibid.). The women's commission in the Socialist Party was also missing from the women's movement campaigns of the 1990s. For example, the party was not entirely supportive of the new voluntary measures to compel parties to present women candidates (Baudino 2003 and Bird 2003). In 1999, Yvette Roudy, longtime Socialist Party feminist, created a new free-standing organization to promote women in leadership positions, *Assemblée des femmes*, partially as a response to the apathy of the party and its women's commission to the new parity regulations (Interview, 2001).

THIRTY-FIVE-HOUR WORKWEEK REFORMS, 1997–2000

How the Debate Came to the Public Agenda

Workweek reduction had been on the public agenda numerous times in the 1980s and 1990s; however, such an extensive reduction had not been considered. Neither the reform on work-time by the Socialists in the early 1980s nor the Robien law, adopted under a right-wing government in 1996, generated the same degree of controversy and public attention. While the 1986 law, exonerating employers who reduced full-time work from paying social security taxes, served as a touchstone for many in the controversy that was unleashed in 1997, the debate on the thirty-five-hour workweek did not begin until the Socialists, in a coalition with the Communist Party and the Greens, took control of the government in 1997. The new prime minister, Lionel Jospin, first mentioned reducing the workweek to thirty-five hours in the context of the electoral campaign for the National Assembly in May 1997. Jospin supported reducing the workweek in the 1995 presidential elections, but only to thirty-seven hours (Lemaître 1999). First hinted at by Martine Aubry, minister of employment and solidarity, in an August 1997 Council of Ministers meeting, Jospin formally announced his government's intention to present draft legislation at a tri-partite meeting on employment policy held at the government's initiative and attended by representatives of organized labor and management on October 10. The prime minister elaborated that reform would consist of two texts: first a framework law (Aubry I) that would establish the general process for reducing the workweek to thirty-five hours for firms and a second law (Aubry II), based on assessments of the reduction process by the social partners, that would stipulate the details of reducing the workweek to thirty-five hours (*Le Monde* 10/12–13/97).

Dominant Frame of Debate

Although the reform process was not entirely complete with the adoption of the second Aubry law in January 2000, given that not all firms had brought their work-time policies in line with the new stipulations,[4] the intense society-wide debates on the thirty-five-hour workweek ended with adoption of Aubry II. Jospin's speech to the social partners in October of 1997 determined that the formulation of the reforms would take place through the established channels of employment policy decision making: the Parliament and formal social partner consultation, with the minister of social affairs orchestrating negotiations and parliamentary discussions. Jospin's speech also firmly situated the thirty-five-hour workweek reforms in the context of the rising problems of unemployment and the need to develop "new paths" to make firms more successful and develop France's economy more generally. Alongside the issue of workweek reduction, he discussed new polices on retirement, youth employment, and wages. More than improving workers' rights or French citizens' quality of life, the reforms were presented as a response to economic imperatives (*Le Monde* 10/12–13/97).

Jospin's remarks set the frame of discussions from the beginning to the end of the debate on the thirty-five-hour workweek reform: the shortening of the workweek as a way of promoting France's economy. Organized labor and business and the major political parties reacted to this economic framing, following their own established positions in tri-partite negotiations that opposed left- and right-wing policy actors. On one hand, organized management (the CNPF, the association that represented large business, called MEDEF after 1999, the CGPME, the confederation of small businesses and the management union, and the CGC) and the two right-wing parties in opposition, the UDF (Center-Right party) and the RPR (more conservative Gaullist party) opposed what they saw as the extreme reforms throughout the debates in the name of over-taxing and burdening private businesses. On the other, organized labor (the two major left-wing confederations, the CGT and the CFDT, and smaller unions like SUD) and the political parties in the left-wing coalition, the *gauche pluriell*, tacitly supported the reforms, but also demanded for stronger policy to protect workers' rights and place the financial burden of the reforms on the employers. Quality-of-life arguments about how the reforms might improve the everyday lives of French citizens were brought up in the policy discussions; however, they were of only secondary importance. Reconciliation of work and family and gender equality issues were even more peripheral to the debate. As the analysis shows below, this dominant employment frame set the parameters of the discussions on both laws in both the tri-partite arena of state-social-partner negotiations and Parliament.[5]

Dominant Frame on Aubry I: October 1997–June 1998

The sides of the debate were quickly drawn following the tri-partite meeting on employment and the subsequent Council of Ministers meeting that officially presented the bill proposal (*Le Monde* 10/12–13/97). Jean Gadois's highly public resignation from his position as head of the CNPF was the opening salvo in what quickly became a heated debate. For businesses and the Right, the law presented too much, too soon. The CNPF, under its new leader, demanded immediately for a delay of at least one year. On the Left, Nicole Notat, the head of the CFDT, announced the union's support for flexibility, no longer a "taboo", as long as worker interests were defended in negotiating the reductions (*Les Echos* 1/27/98). For the CGT and the Communist Party (PCF), the major issue was maintaining the same level of salaries with reduced work hours, including minimum wage (SMIC) earners (Ibid.). The Greens pushed for an even shorter workweek of thirty-two hours. In the end, the original bill proposal was not greatly altered even with the right-wing's referral of the first law to the Constitutional Council, which gave it a clean bill of health (*Le Monde* 6/12/98).

Dominant Frame on Aubry II: July 1998–January 2000

The major areas to be clarified in the second round of legislation were the specific timetable for reduction; wage issues, such as minimum wage, overtime, and annualization; part-time work; management reduction; finalizing public financing; and organized labor's role in negotiations (*Le Monde* 10/29/99). Given that the first law had left many controversial issues unsettled and the adoption of the second law would essentially set into motion the mandatory part of the process, the controversy and opposition was ratcheted up much higher on the second law. As the headline of *Le Monde* articulated a month prior to the opening of the "parliamentary marathon" (Nouvel Observateur 12/16/99): "Reduction of Work-Time: The Battle Is Just Beginning." Right-wing parties and employers unions continued their vocal opposition to the law, focusing particularly on the costs of the reforms passed on to employers. The Greens, Communists, the CGT, and other left-wing trade unions also continued to defend workers' rights and status in the process. The activities of the two opposing sides culminated in two demonstrations organized on the same day to mark the opening of the parliamentary debates turning out twenty-five thousand business supporters and ten thousand pro-labor demonstrators in Paris and the provinces (*Libération* 10/5/99). Demonstrations into the fall, mostly in favor of the laws, mobilized an additional twenty-five hundred people (*Libération* 11/14/99, 12/16/99 and *Le Monde* 12/1/99).

In the parliamentary debates in the National Assembly, the most vocal opponents to the bill proposal were the Greens and the Communists (*Financial Times* 10/8/99). As with the first bill, the right-wing parties attempted to block the law in the Senate, with no success (*Le Monde* 12/1/99). While the dominant frame of the debates remained focused on economic issues of employer versus worker interests, some lip service was paid to the impact of the reductions on improving the quality of life through more flexibility in balancing work and family. Martine Aubry, for example, opened the first session of the National Assembly by drawing attention to the quality-of-life issues.

> The major stakes of this bill proposal are in the search for a balance between work-time, time for oneself, and time for others, which lead to an improvement in the quality of life in work as well as in personal life. (*National Assembly* 10/5/99: 105–200)

Aubry's speech neither changed the frame from the immediate economic concerns of the social patterns or, as the next section shows, provided an opportunity to discuss seriously gender equality and reconciliation of home and work life. The final law was voted into law on December 15, 1999. Unlike the first law, the right-wing's referral to the Constitutional Council did result in the modification of several passages, but nothing crucial was eliminated from the final law (*Libération* 1/2/00).

Gendering the Debate[6]

Despite the promise of Martine Aubry's opening speech to the National Assembly, gender issues that for many feminist observers were part and parcel of any discussion of reducing work-time were relegated to a highly marginal position in the parliamentary debates and were virtually non-existent in the public controversy that was waged between business and labor outside of the legislature. From start to finish, the dominant economic frame drove the wide range of issues discussed.

Gender considerations were barely mentioned in the formal debate arenas until after the adoption of the second law in June 1998. Up until Aubry II, the only actor involved with the mainstream process to mention links between gender equality and women's rights issues had been Prime Minister Jospin in his speech at the tri-partite meeting in 1998 (Pigalle 2000: 191). His statement was neither picked up in the French press nor reflected in the content of the policy debates. This gender-blind approach was carried through in all of the debates on the first law, including expert analysis of areas of the law that would necessarily imply women's rights, like part-time work (*Le Monde* 9/9/98), or widen existing inequalities between different groups (*Le Point* 2/14/98). The social partners in their formal and informal evaluations of the first law and their contributions to the second did not raise any gender issues on the reforms. Neither of the representatives sent by the labor confederations to present their official positions on the draft legislation to the National Assembly's Commission on Cultural, Social, and Family Affairs (CCSFA) mentioned gender equality issues. Representatives from the left-wing trade union SUD-PTT and the CGT did not raise gender issues in their critiques of the Aubry laws in interviews with the Communist newspaper *L'Humanité* (9/22/99 and 9/24/99).

Reflecting the absence of any formal demand by organized labor for the inclusion of women's rights issues, the bill proposal prepared by Minister Aubry, presented to the social partners, and sent to Parliament in July 1999 had no specific reference to gender equality issues or women's rights (Bill proposal no. 1786, 7-18-99). Gender considerations were taken up in the hearings of the Cultural Affairs Commission in the National Assembly in its report on the first law in March 1999 (Gorce 1999a) and its report on the Aubry ministry's draft legislation (Gorce 1999b). In the first report, women's work issues were mentioned in three different parts of the report, one out of eighty-eight pages. Two out of the three passages mentioned that marginal part-time work was in the majority filled by women: "part-time work is also a major cause of the segmentation of the work world and an increasing precariousness, in particular form female wage earners" (12). The third brief mention was made by the Socialist Deputy Cathérine Génisson. She was also the author of a government report published in July on equal employment between men and women (Génisson 1999). She argued that the current definition of management time would hurt women managers' attempting to combine work and family duties. Although the point about the gendered nature of part-time work was included in the introduction of the report, there was no recurring discussion of the issue.

In the second report on the draft law (Gorce 1999b), the introduction did not touch upon gender equality, but gender issues were raised three times on 3 out of 453 pages. These mentions included the abolition of the ban on women's night work in the name of equal employment (132–33), insertion of a required rest for pregnant women managers (137–38), and the issue of the predominance of women as minimum wage earners (245). While the first and third discussions were related to gender equality issues that had been articulated by the women's movement, and speakers made reference to the Génisson report, the second mention was made in the context of a protectionist approach to women workers as mothers, criticized resoundingly by feminists for being detrimental for women's rights. Three amendments were made by the commission on gender equality in this report; two were accepted—an amendment that strengthened part-time work contracts that was intended to benefit women and an amendment that introduced the principle of equal employment in the negotiation of work reduction in the firm.

The commission's treatment of gender issues was basically replicated in the National Assembly during two out of the eighty-eight sessions, for the first round of debates in the lower house with little elaboration from the opposition deputies. There were no other additional gender issues raised during the rest of the debates in either house of Parliament. The press coverage of the debates did not mention the gender-specific discussions of the reforms in Parliament (e.g., *Le Monde* 23/8/99 and 9/22/00). Only a handful of articles mentioned equal-employment issues as they related to workweek reduction (e.g., *Libération* 1/9/99, *Entreprise et Carrières* 10/12/99, *Le Monde* 9/15/99).

Policy Outcome

Setting the general framework for the workweek reduction, the major points of the first law included the following stipulations: 1) all firms with twenty or more employees must establish the length of the legal workweek at thirty-five hours by January 1, 2000, and by January 1, 2002, for business with less than twenty employees; 2) social partners must begin immediately to negotiate the process for reducing the workweek at the branch and firm level; 3) work-time reduction could be calculated over the entire work year; 4) rules about official full-time work periods and rest time; 5) rules about part-time work— reduction of employers' social security dues for negotiating part-time contracts; 6) the government must make an interim report on thirty-five-hour implementation to Parliament and a report on reduction in the civil service (Law no. 98–461, 6/13/98 and Lemaître 1999). Five implementing decrees were adopted as well on government aid to firms (*Libération* 5/21/98).

The second law filled in the gray areas of the first with regards to part-time work, managers, generalized state funding of work-time reduction, and the process of negotiations. The final law had thirty-seven articles and was four times the length of the first law. There were eleven chapters on the following topics: legal length of work and overtime; distribution and alternation of work-time; rules for managers; part-time work and temporary contracts; rules for leaves; time-savings accounts; training and work-time reduction; development of negotiations and reduction of employer contributions; judicial stipulations; wages; application to agricultural professions; and diverse stipulations.[7]

The first article, in chapter 4, strengthened the development of a contract for part-time work. Although it did not mention gender issues, the formal discussion on the article was situated in the context of the high incidence of women in part-time work. Article 19 in chapter 8 was clearly about gender equality, stating that all thirty-five-hour workweek agreements must include "measures aiming to ensure equal employment between men and women, and particularly to strike down discrimination in hiring." It also stipulated that the objectives in the plans for the following year must cover the "principle of equal employment between men and women."

Women's Movement Impact

Although gender issues had a highly marginal position in the debates on the thirty-five-hour workweek and were only peripherally treated in the final law, a range of women's movement actors developed a position on the thirty-five-hour workweek during the debates. The two clauses on gender equality captured some of the feminist demands; however, the women's movement actors who actually developed and articulated these positions were not given direct entry to the mainstream employment arenas of the work reforms. Only one female policy actor in the two arenas, Socialist Deputy Cathérine Genisson, a longtime Socialist Party leader who had not been involved with women's rights activities of the Socialist Party, formally forwarded women's movement positions in the two arenas on the debate. The impact of the women's movement during this period was, therefore, *pre-empted*.

The Génisson report on equal employment, contracted by Prime Minister Jospin in 1998, was the major conduit for feminist positions on equal employment developed by the women's movement to be introduced into the mainstream arenas on the thirty-five-hour workweek. The list of the individuals and groups interviewed for the report was a "who's who" of the feminist network on equal employment. Delphine Lévy, the administrator who coordinated and wrote the report for Génisson, reiterated the extent to which the report reflected the positions of the women's movement, particularly on part-time work (Interview). While the Génisson report was cited in the parliamentary commission's report on the second Aubry law and in the National Assembly debates on the two amendments (Gorce 1999a, 1999b), none of the women's movement actors were invited to present testimony on the commission's hearings on the law or to formally comment on any of the government's bill proposals.

A range of women's movement actors with feminist agendas not only developed a specific stance with regards to issues of work-time reduction and reconciliation of work and family issues, but they also attempted to gain access to the official policy discussions to bring gender considerations to the fore of the debate. Building from the analyses of feminist researchers, femocrats, and feminists in unions that had been developed in the 1980s around the issue of equal employment policy, an increasing number of women's movement actors looked to the thirty-five-hour workweek as a potential for promoting gender equality. On one hand, rethinking work-time in the context of balancing work and home obligations had the potential of addressing what so many feminists had identified as the major causes of gender-based discrimination—the gendered division of labor in the home. On the other hand many women's movement actors hoped that reducing the workweek would help women who had been trapped in part-time work more generally. Feminist researchers had contributed to a growing literature on women's work since the end of the 1970s. In the 1990s, many had turned their attention to the reconciliation of work and family for both men and women.[8] Feminists also realized the potential for the negative impact of workweek reduction on women; many asserted the need to formally insert statements of equal employment principles into new reforms.

The feminist position on the thirty-five-hour workweek was articulated as early as March 1997 at the first National Conference on Women's Rights sponsored by the *Collectif National des Droits des Femmes*. A working group attached to the collectif was set up to discuss work-time issues. Its "argumentation on the reduction of work time" represented positions broadly held by the equal employment network on the thirty-five-hour workweek that were included in the Génisson report and her subsequent interventions defending gender equality issues in the parliamentary debates. In the essay, reference was made to the tri-partite meeting at which Jospin first announced the impending reforms to the social partners. The CNDF working group's paper first identi-fied the problem of gender inequities, then argued for a framework law on the reduction of work-time, proposing a thirty-two-hour week (CNDF 1997: 4–5).

In June 1997, the Upper Council on Equal Employment, at the initative of one of its members, feminist sociologist Jacqueline Laufer, issued a report on the impact of the reduction of the workweek on women's rights (Pépin 1999 and Laufer, Interview). In November of the same year a CNDF-sponsored demonstration attracted six thousand people in favor of the thirty-five-hour workweek as long as it took into consideration gender issues and women's rights (*Libération* 11/19/97). While much of the women's movement was pre-occupied with the parity reform campaign in 1998–1999, the CNDF re-sponded to the gender silences of the first Aubry law with an "open letter" to Minister Aubry signed by 120 prominent individuals. The letter presented the position held by the various women's movement actors, stating that "the law on work-time reduction represents a great hope for women. The extra time could become an important lever in the fight for sharing domestic roles" (*Le Monde* 10/7/99). Although not specifically discussing work-time reduction, several conferences and meetings linked equal employment issues to in-creased efforts in gender mainstreaming at the European Union level in 1998 and 1999. These developments in EU mainstreaming policy certainly rein-forced the feminist positions being articulated at the time of the debates.

Reflecting the marginalization of gender issues to the policy discussion and to the final policy outcome, the Ministry of Labor website in 2003 highlighted five provisions of the second law (www.35h.travail.gouv.fr/). The text neither mentioned the stipulations about the process of negotiations nor the gender-specific clauses of the second law, which essentially had taken verbatim the three amendments proposed by the Socialist-dominated Cultural Affairs Commission.

Women's Policy Agency Activities and Characteristics

Except for the report by the Upper Commission on Equal Employment in 1999 on work-time reduction and the indirect support given to Cathérine Génisson for the report on employment equality—a member of the Deputy Minister of Women's Rights and Job Training (DMWRJT) coordinated and wrote the report and numerous femocrats working for the Women's Rights Services (WRS) in Paris and the provinces were interviewed—none of the women's policy agencies articulated a position on the reduction-of-workweek reforms during the three years of debates. Minister of Women's Rights and Job Training Nicole Péry was actually present for some of the parliamentary debates, without participating in the debates. She was not asked to appear before the parliamentary commission that reviewed the government proposals in 1999 either. The peripheral gendering of the debate and the modest feminist outcomes of the second Aubry law took place without the direct involvement of any of the women's policy agencies. Their activities were therefore marginal to the debate.

In the first five months of the Jospin government, there were no ministerial-level women's policy agencies. The women's rights administration—the national-level Women's Rights Services (WRS), territorial offices at the regional and departmental levels, and Upper Council for Equal Employment—operated without any presence in the Jospin cabinet. Following a CNDF-sponsored November demonstration which contributed to the mounting criticism of the Jospin government for not including a women's rights portfolio in its cabinet. Jospin appointed well-known feminist academic Genevieve Fraisse as interministerial delegate of women's rights. With no formal decision-making capacity, a minute staff, and far removed from the women's rights administration, Fraisse's actions were highly constrained. She resigned in frustration just several months later.

The powerless post was replaced by a deputy minister, based on a political appointment, at the same level of women's rights ministers since the 1980s. The new Deputy Minister of Women's Rights and Job Training was under the authority of Martine Aubry's powerful ministry. As a result, Nicole Péry could not make decisions that would go against her minister's stance, particularly on the thirty-five-hour workweek reform. The Péry ministry was distant from decision-making power given that it was far removed from the prime minister and quite marginalized within the ministerial pecking order of the Aubry ministry. Feminists had argued that Aubry was not a great supporter of feminist causes. It was known by many that she did not want her laws to be diluted by feminist issues given the extent to which the dominant social partners were apathetic, if not hostile to, gendered analyses of the employment world. Thus, Péry was unable to introduce a feminist voice in the formulation of the laws. It is no coincidence that the impetus for gender issues in the debates came from Génisson in Parliament and not Nicole Péry's office. Péry herself was not a feminist activist; she had neither participated in the activities of feminists within her party nor actively supported women's movement issues outside of the party.

Despite her inaction on the thirty-five-hour workweek, Péry became immediately engaged in a variety of activities to reenergize the women's policy machinery, particularly in the context of coordinating France's national action plan for the United Nations' Beijing Plus Five conference (DMWRJT 2000), which was specifically on empowerment and the rising demands of the parity movement. By 1999, Péry's office had developed a multi-issue program, including a proposal for a new law on equal employment policy. The renewed leadership rejuvenated to a certain degree the extensive women's rights administration; its budget went from 75 million francs in 1998 to 80.5 million in 1999 (DMWRTJ 2000: 20). The Péry ministry's administrative capacity, therefore, was relatively high. New parliamentary delegations for women's rights were created in both the Senate and the National Assembly as a part of this revitalization and the ministry began to develop a formal process of systematically injecting gender into the collection of official government statistics (Blum 1999). In response to the increasing pressure to meet EU gender mainstreaming imperatives, the ministry also put into place a systematic reporting of gender-specific budgets across all ministries as well.

Women's Movement Characteristics

Overall by the end of the 1990s women's movements in general were in a consolidation and growth period. The specific movement on the thirty-five-hour workweek was also in a period of growth, with the development of organizational support in the CNDF for unified feminist demand on the thirty-five-hour workweek, a relatively large demonstration, and the open letter on the thirty-five-hour workweek. Individual women's movement actors have continued to be quite active in assessing whether the negotiated workweek reductions have actually promoted gender equality (e.g., Lurol and Pélisse 2002). The women's movement on the thirty-five-hour workweek had close ties to the Left. While on one hand, trade unions joined the CNDF and the Socialist Party gave nominal support to the collectif, on the other, the issues advanced by the women's movement on the thirty-five-hour workweek were neither placed on the general agendas of the trade union confederation nor articulated officially by spokespeople from the unions in the debate on work-time reduction. Still, the thirty-five-hour workweek issue was a high priority for the movement and the women's movement actors that mobilized around the issues were quite cohesive in terms of their shared definition of the issue. Whereas there was no counter-movement on the issue, the apathy of the mainstream employment policy actors toward gendered feminist arguments served as an important obstacle.

Policy Environment

The consistent dynamics of the employment policy subsystem throughout the debates indicated a closed policy subsystem. The social partners and Socialist Party government officials from the Ministry of Social Affairs dominated the dynamics. The only other actors that were allowed to enter were the Communist Party and the Green Party since they held minority status in the left-wing governing coalition with the Socialist Party. The issue frame fit between the micro-frame of the women's movement and the dominant frame of the debate was incompatible, given the refusal of employment actors to gender a policy issue that for many seemed to be inextricably linked to balancing gender roles in work and family. Indeed, gender-biased universalism appeared to be the norm throughout the policy discussions. The governing majority had moderate left-wing control over policy decisions, given that the *gauche plurielle* left-wing government was in power alongside right-wing President Jacques Chirac, although his party's opposition did not significantly change the final content of the laws.

CONCLUSION

In the end, the women's movement had a certain degree of success, particularly given the long-standing tradition of the employment policy actor to be resistant to gendering their approaches and mainstreaming women's rights. The activities of the women's movement, orchestrated by the CNDF, were clearly instrumental in getting the highly resistant minister of social affairs to allow feminist amendments to be added to a set of reforms that had been inextricably linked to her reputation in the world of employment policy. Departing from the key importance of the women's policy agencies in articulating feminist positions on equal employment policy, the women's policy agencies played a minor supporting role in the insertion of women's rights issues into the heated policy debates from 1997–2000. Pressure from the EU on gender mainstreaming and the development of a national action plan for the United Nations may have been more important sources of leverage than the women's policy offices. Certainly Nicole Péry had her hands tied in terms of being able to challenge her minister's pet reforms.

Going against the conventional wisdom that French women's movements are weak, anti-system, and divided, the movement around the thirty-five-hour workweek demonstrated a relatively high level of unity and decisive action. Still, due to the resistance of the more powerful mainstream policy actors, women's movement positions had to be snuck into the debate through a parliamentary subcommission with little impact on the actual frame of the debates. While the thirty-five-hour workweek reforms were not framed in terms of providing an opportunity for men and women to better balance work and home, and in doing so promote society-wide gender equality, the inclusion of the two feminist-movement-based articles provide an opportunity for the implementation of equal employment principles in the radical reshaping of work-time launched by the Aubry reforms. In this perspective, the partial women's movement victories are formally registered in this momentous shift in economic relations in France and, hence, may have the potential to lead to more significant change down the road. Still, given the absence of a gendered frame overall and of the feminist actors who forwarded a gendered approach to workweek reform from the policymaking arena on the reforms, the neo-liberal shift being articulated through the thirty-five-hour workweek reforms occurred outside of any significant gender perspective.

Since the adoption of the Aubry reforms, most firms in France have made the transition to the thirty-five-hour workweek. In many cases, the shortened work-time has been translated into additional vacation days rather than a change in weekly work schedules. Reports have indicated profound challenges of managing work in the context of divergent individual schedules. The reduction has not produced the desired economic outcomes—unemployment has remained high and the French economy has not received any significant jump start. With the election of a right-wing president and Parliament in 2002, there has been a softening of regulations and firms have been encouraged to opt out. Despite popular support for the thirty-five-hour workweek, policymakers, in part responding to poor economic performance and pressure from the EU and the international community, have placed the possibility of complete repeal on the political agenda.

The record too has been mixed for promoting gender balance in work-time plans. On one hand while analysts point to the potential for the firm-level negotiations to manage the thirty-five-hour workweek to make a new space for the social partners to discuss reconciling home and work obligations for both men and women, in reality the actual negotiations to reduce work-time did not deliver what many had hoped for. A study of work-time negotiations in which fifty-two union representatives and appointed negotiators (*mandatés*) were interviewed, showed that equality between the sexes tends to be mostly a woman's affair (Defalvard, Lurol, and Polzhuber 2005). That is, female negotiators tended more than their male counterparts to bring in gender equality either in terms of equality in employment or reconciliation of home and work time for men and women and that when reconciliation was discussed in the negotiations it was for the most part discussed for women and not for men. The outcome was seldom any real formal treatment of gender equality in the final agreement, beyond the symbolic mention of the principle of equality. In addition, in smaller firms where there was no union representative but an appointed negotiator, women tended to be in these positions "by default", due to their marginal position in the firm and not as a result of their efforts to bring a gendered perspective into the negotiation process (Ibid.).

Thus, the absence of a strong statement about bringing equality issues into the negotiations in the Aubry laws as well as the gender-neutral frame in the debate has appeared to carry through to implementation. Since 2002, the new Ministry of Parity and Equal Employment under Nicole Ameline did not change the approach of her left-wing predecessor either. If anything, thirty-five-hour workweek negotiations were given even less attention under the upgraded ministry. Instead, equal employment laws and equal pay were the major employment focus of both the new ministry and the Women's Rights Services with little mention of how work-time management was linked to gender equality issues (Mazur 2005). Despite the reality that the thirty-five-hour workweek appears to be framed in terms of women's opportunities and not gender equality, younger men do tend to join their female counterparts in bringing gender equality issues into the discussions, thus suggesting as Defalvard, Lurol, and Polzhuber do, that a generational shift may actually be the driving force in changing the frame of discussions. Rising numbers of younger men taking daddy leave also reflect this trend. In the final analysis, more than the work of the WPAs or women's movement actors, the thirty-five-hour workweek may only become an effective tool in promoting gender equality as a new generation of men and women enter the workforce.

REFERENCES

Allwood, Gill, and Kursheed Wadia. 2000. *Women and Politics in France*. London: Routledge.

Allwood, Gill, and Kursheed Wadia. 2002. "French Feminisms: National and International Perspectives." *Modern and Contemporary France*. 10(2). 211–223.

Ambler, John. 1996. "Conflict and Consensus in French Education." In *Chirac's Challenge: Liberalization, Europeanization, and Malaise in France.* New York: St. Martin's Press. 199–230.

Appleton, Andrew. 1996. "The Limits of the Maastricht Referendum and the Party System." In *Chirac's Challenge: Liberalization, Europeanization, and Malaise in France.* New York: St. Martin's Press. 301–324.

Barrère-Maurisson, Marie-Agnès, Martine Buffier-Morel, and Sabine Rivier. 2001. *Partage des temps et des tâches dans les ménages.* Paris: La Documentation Française.

Baudino, Claudie. 2003. "Parity Reform in France: Promises and Pitfalls" *Review of Policy Research*. Fall. 385–401.

Bird, Karen. 2003. "Who Are the Women? Where Are the Women? And What Difference Can they Make? Effects of the Gender Parity in French Municipal Elections." *French Politics*. 1(1). 5–38.

Blum, Catherine. 1999. *Les Situation respective des femmes et des hommes: Statistiques Pertinentes*. Report of the working group. Women's Rights Service and Deputy Minister of Women's Rights and Job Training.

Cameron, David. 1996. "National Interest, the Dilemmas of European Integration, and Malaise." In *Chirac's Challenge: Liberalization, Europeanization, and Malaise in France*. New York: St. Martin's Press. 325–382.

Cerny, Philip G., and Martin A. Schain, ed. 1980. *French Politics and Public Policy*. London and New York: Methuen.

Cerny, Philip G., and Martin A. Schain, ed. 1985. *Socialism, the State and Public Policy in France*. London and New York: Methuen.

CNDF. 1997. *Propositions de revendications pour les femmes à transmettre à non élue-s*. Document transmis par le CNDF. July–August.

DATAR. 1999. "Seminaire: Mise en Oeuvre du Principe d'égalité des chances entre les hommes et les femmes." Report of the Seminar. Mimeo. CNSAEA/ENGENDER.

Defalvard, H., M. Lurol, and E. Polzhuber. 2005. "Les inégalités de genre dans le passage aux thirty-five heures: sources et resistances." *Travail et Emploi*. No. 102.

DMWRJT. 2000. *Conférence de Pekin, Cinq ans après: La Mise en oeuvre par la France des recommandations de la 4ième conférence mondial sur les femmes*. Paris: Documentation Française.

Duchen, C. 1986. *Feminism in France from May 1968 to Mitterrand*. London: Routledge and Kegan Paul.

Fagnani, Jeanne. 1996. "Family Policies and Working Mothers. A Comparison of France and West Germany," In Janice Monk and Dolors Maria García-Ramon, eds., *Women of the European Union: The Politics of Work and Daily Life*. London: Routledge. 126–137.

Fagnani, Jeanne. 1998. "Recent Changes in Family Policy in France: Political Trade-offs and Economic Constraints." In Emerek Drew and Mahon, eds., *Women, Work and the Family in Europe*. London: Routledge. 58–67.

Fouquet, Annie, and Claude Rack. 1999. "Les Femmes et les Politiques d'Emploi." *Travail Genre, et, Sociétés*. No. 2 November. 47–70.

France. New York: St Martin's Press.

Gauvin, Annie, and Henri Jacot. 1999. *Temps de travail, temps sociaux: Pour Une Approche Globale*. Paris: Economica.

Génisson, Cathérine. 1999. *Davantage de Mixité Professionnelle pour Plus d'égalité entre hommes et femmes*. Rapport pour le Premier Ministre.

Gorce, Gaëtan. 1999a. "Rapport d'Information déposé par la Commission des Affaires Culturelles, Famliales et Sociales sur l'application de la loi n° 98–461 du 13 juin 1998 d'orientation et d'incitation relative à la réduction du temps de travail." No. 1731. 6/22/99. National Assembly. Online archive, www.assembleenat.fr/dossiers/ttravail.asp. 88 p.

Gorce, Gaëtan. 1999b. "Rapport fait Au Nom nom de la Commission des Affaires Culturelles, Familiales, et Sociales sur le projet de loi (n° 1786) relatif à la reduction négociée du temps de travail." No. 1826. 10/1/99. National Assembly. Online archive, www.assemblee-nat.fr/dossiers/ttravail.asp. 453 pp.

Guyomarch, Alain, Howard Machin, Peter A. Hall, and Jack Hayward. 2001 (or 2002, s. p. 3). *Developments in French Politics*. Basingstoke: Palgrave.

Hall, Peter. 2001. "The Evolution of Economic Policy." In A. Guyomarch, H. Machin, P. A. Hall, and J. Hayward, *Developments in French Politics*. Basingstoke: Palgrave. 172–190.

Jenson, Jane. 1996. "Representations of Difference: The Varieties of French Feminism." In M. Threlfall, ed., *Mapping the Women's Movement: Feminist Politics and Social Transformation in the North*. London: Verso. 73–114.

Jenson, J., J. Laufer, and M. Mauruani. 2000. *The Gendering of Inequalities: Women, Men and Work*. London: Aldershot.

Jenson, J., and M. Sineau. 2001. "France: Reconciling Republican Equality with 'Freedom of Choice'" In Jenson and Sineau, eds. *Who Cares? Women's Work, Childcare, and Welfare Redesign*. 88–117.

Jenson, Jane, and Celia Valiente. 2003. "Comparing Two Movements for Gender Parity: France and Spain." In L.A. Banaszak, K. Beckwith, and D. Rucht, eds. *Women's Movements Facing the Reconfigured State*. Cambridge: Cambridge University Press. 69–93.

Junter-Loiseau, Annie. 1999. "La Notion de Conciliation de la vie professionnelle et de la vie familiale: révolution temporelle ou métaphore des discriminations?" *Cahiers du Gedisst*. No. 23. 73–98.

Keeler, John T. S. and Martin Schain, eds. 1996a. *Chirac's Challenge: Liberalization, Europeanization, and Malaise in France*. New York: St. Martin's Press.

Keeler, John T. S. and Martin Schain. 1996b. "Mitterrand's Legacy, Chirac's Challenge." In *Chirac's Challenge: Liberalization, Europeanization, and Malaise in France*. New York: St. Martin's Press. 1–22.

Lanquetin, Marie-Thérèse, Jacqueline Laufer, and Marie-Thérèse Letablier. 2000. "From Equality to Reconciliation in France." In Linda Hantrais, ed., *Gendered Policies in Europe: Reconciling Employment and Family Life*, London: Macmillan. 68–88.

Laufer, Jacqueline. 2003. "Equal Employment Policy in France: Symbolic Support and a Mixed Record." *Review of Policy Research*. Fall. 423–442.

Laurent, Agnès. 2000. *Les 35 Heures: Un Nouveau Style de Vie*. Geneva: Minerva.

Lemaître, Frédéric. 1999. *Les 35 Heures*. Paris: Flammarion.

Les dossiers thématiques. 2000. Hommes et femmes face á l'emploi. No. 17.

L'Etat de la France. 1991–2001. Paris: Editions La Découverte & Syros.

Levy, Jonah. 2001. "French Social Policy in the Age of High Unemployment." In A. Guyomarch, H. Machin, P. A. Hall, and J. Hayward, *Developments in French Politics*. Basingstoke: Palgrave. 191–210.

Lurol, Martine. 1999. "Quand les Institutions Se Chargent de La Quesion du Travail des Femmes, 197–1995." *Travail Genre, et, Sociétés*. No. 1, April. 179–199.

Lurol, Martine. 2001a. "Le Travail des Femmes en France: Trente ans d'évolution des problématiques en sociologie (1970–2000)" *Documents de Travail: Centre d'Etudes de l'Emploi* . No. 7, March. 4–33.

Lurol, Martine. 2001b. "35 Heures: Les Disparités entre hommes et femmes." *Quatre Pages: Centre d'Etude de l'Emploi*. No. 48, November.

Lurol, Martine, and Jêrome Pélisse. 2002. "Les 35 heures des hommes et des femmes." *Travail, Genre, et, Société*. October.

Majoni d'Intignano, Béatrice. 1999. *Égalité entre femmes et hommes: Aspect Economiques*. Report of the Prime Minister's Council on Economic Analysis. Paris: Documentation Française.

Maruani, Margaret. 2000. *Travail et Emploi des Femmes*. Paris: La Découverte.

Mazur, Amy G., 1995a, *Gender Bias and the State: Symbolic Reform at Work in Fifth Republic France*. Pittsburgh: University of Pittsburgh Press.

Mazur, Amy G. 1995b. "Strong State and Symbolic Reform in France: le Ministère des Droits de la Femme," In Stetson and Mazur, eds., *Comparative State Feminism*. Thousand Oaks, CA: Sage Publications. 76–94.

Mazur, Amy G. 2001. "Gender-Biased Universalism Resists State Feminist Approaches to Gendered Equality," In Mazur, ed., *Making Democracies Work: State Feminism, Women's Movements, and Job Training Policy*. New York: Garland Publishing, Taylor & Francis Group.

Mazur, Amy G., and Andrew Appleton. 2001. "France at the Crossroads: An End to French Exceptionalism," In H. J. Wiarda, ed., *European Politics in the Age of Globalization*. Orlando, FL: Harcourt College Publishers. 92–135.

Mazur, Amy G. 2005. "Gendering the Fifth Republic," In A. Cole, P. Le Galès, *Developments in French Politics*. Basingstoke: Palgrave Macmillan. 212–229.

Méda. Dominique. 1999. *Qu'est-ce que la richesse?* Paris: Champs/Flammarion.

Méda, Dominique. 2000. *Le Temps des Femmes*. Paris: Flammarion.

Mény, Yves. 1992. *La Corruption de la République*. Paris: Fayard.

Miné, Michel. 1999. "La loi sure les 35 heures á l'épreuve des droits des femmes." *Travail Genre, et, Sociétés*. No. 2, November. 91–110.

Pépin, Michel (coordinator). 1999. "Réducation de Temps du Travail: Une Chance pour l'égalité professionnelle," *ANACT: Travail et Changement*. October 7–17.

Picq, Françoise.1993. *Les années-mouvement: libération des femmes*. Paris: Seuil.

Pigalle, Céline. 2000. *Femmes au travail. De qui se moque-t-on*. Issy-les Moulineaux: Prat Editions.

Schain, Martin. 1996. "The Immigration Debate and the National Front." In *Chirac's Challenge: Liberalization, Europeanization, and Malaise in France*. New York: St. Martin's Press. 169–198.

Schmidt, Vivien. 1996. "Business, the State, and the End of Dirigisme." In *Chirac's Challenge: Liberalization, Europeanization, and Malaise in France*. New York: St. Martin's Press. 105–142.

State. New York: Oxford University Press. 87–110.

Stetson, Dorothy McBride. 1987. *Women's Rights in France*. New York: Garland.

Tiersky, Ronald. 1997. *France in the New Europe: Changing yet Steadfast*. Belmont, CA: Wadsworth.

Toinet, Marie-France. 1996. "The Limits of the Malaise in France." In *Chirac's Challenge: Liberalization, Europeanization, and Malaise in France*. New York: St. Martin's Press. 279–300.

Trat, Josette, and Marie-Hélène Zylberberg-Hocquard. 2000. *La Participation des femmes aux instances de décision des syndicats à different niveaux*. Study conducted for the Women's Rights Service/GEDISST–CNRS.

LIST OF INTERVIEWS

Women's Rights Service: Martine Buffier-Morel, Fabienne Grizeau, Sandrine Dauphin, Catherine Laret-Bedel, Françoise Gasser, Béatrice Borghino (PACA)
Deputy Minister of Women's Rights Cabinet: Delphine Lévy
Mainstream Employment Administration: Catherine Pone (Currently at Renault)
Women's Movement Actors: Maia Surduts (CNDF); Monique Dental (Ruptures); Marie Victoire-Louis (AVFT); Chirstina Lunghi (Arborus), Françoise Gaspard (Parité), Jacqueline Laufer (CSEP Sociologist); Martine Lurol (Sociologist); Mariette Sineau (Political Scientist); Yvette Roudy (Socialist Party Deputy); Martine Lignière-Cassou (President of the Women's Rights Delegation, National Assembly/Deputy for the Socialist Party); Florence Montreynaud (Co-founder of the Les Chiennes de Garde and La Meute)

LIST OF ACRONYMS

AVFT (*Association des Violence Faites Contre les Femmes au Travail* [Association against Violence toward Women at Work])
CCSFA (National Assembly's Commission on Cultural, Social, and Family Affairs Parliamentary Commission on Cultural and Social Affairs)
CEDAW (Convention on the Elimination of All Forms of Discrimination against Women)
CFDT (*Confédération Française Démocratique du Travail* [French Democratic Confederation of Workers])
CGC (*Confédération des Cadres* [Confederation of Management])
CGPME (*Conseil Générale des Petites et Moyennes Entreprises* [General Council of Small and Medium Enterprises])
CGT (*Confédération Générale du Travail* [General Work Confederation])
CLASCHES (*Collectif de Lutte Anti-sexiste et Contre le Harcelement dans l'Enseignement Surpérieur* [Collective against Anti-sexism and Sexual Harassment in Higher Education])
CNDF (*Collectif National des Droits des Femmes* [National Women's Rights Collective])
CNPF (*Conseil National du Patronat Française* [National French Employers Council])
DMWRJT (Deputy Ministry of Women's Rights and Job Training)
MEDEF (*Mouvement des Entreprises de France* [Movement of French Enterprises])
RPR (*Rassemblement Pour la République* [Rally for the Republic])
UDF (*Union pour la Démocratie Française* [Union for French Democracy])
WRS (Women's Rights Services)

NOTES

The research for this chapter was made possible by a grant from the National Science Foundation No. 0084570. I would like to thank the people I interviewed from 2001 to 2003 for this project who gave me priceless insights (see interview list at the end of the chapter) as well as members of the Research Network on Gender, Politics, and the State (RNGS) for giving me important feedback on the project, particularly Melissa Haussman, Birgit Sauer, and Dorothy McBride. Special thanks go to the archivists at the Women's Rights Service in Paris for all their time and help.

1. The State of France reviews (l'Etat de la France) were one of the major sources for hot issue selection. Published on an annual basis, this series brings together France's top scholars to identify the major social, cultural, economic, and political events. Each annual volume includes a chronology of major national events and short analyses of them. Annual editions were consulted from 1990 to 2001. Given the Anglo-American industry of analyses of France, it was also important to consult the English-language literature on French politics and society. Since 1981, an edited volume of leading French politics experts provides an overview and evaluation of the major policy issues and social trends of the previous five years (Cerny and Schain 1980, 1985 and Keeler and Schain 1996a). As such, these volumes serve as systematic analyses of the policy issue universe of a given time period. Additional English-language assessments of recent policy trends were also consulted to cross-check the State of France reviews and the French Policy series (Tiersky 1997; Mazur and Appleton 2001; Guyomarch et al. 2001).

2. For women's movement trends in France see for example Picq (1993); Jenson (1996); Mazur (1995a); Duchen (1986); Allwood and Wadia (2002); Stetson (1987). To supplement the analyses of more recent trends, interviews were carried out from October 2001–June 2003 with policy actors in the Deputy Ministry of Women's Rights, the Women's Rights Services, and the Ministry of Employment and Solidarity as well as feminist members of the National Assembly, leaders of several women's groups, and feminist academics. The interviews were open-ended and focused on the positions of the WPAs and women's movement actors on the thirty-five-hour workweek and the dynamics of the women's movement in the 1990s.

3. All of the women's movement actors and individuals in the women's policy agencies interviewed pointed to the decline in political party and union support for the women's movement in the 1990s.

4. In 1999, over twelve hundred firms had already reduced employees' workweeks to thirty-five hours (*Libération* 1/12/99).

5. Electronic versions of the laws, parliamentary debates and documents for the second Aubry law for both houses and for the Senate on the first Aubry law as well as Minister Aubry's speeches were available online for the parliamentary debates (www.assemblee-nat.fr/dossiers/ttravail.asp). Citations from parliamentary debates, commission reports, etc., are referred to by the chamber of origin—Senate or National Assembly. Social partner positions throughout the debate were traced through na-

tional daily newspaper reporting on the negotiations in press clipping files at the Institute of Political Studies on work-time reduction.

6. Word searches for "women" and "equal employment—égalité professionnelle" were conducted on the electronic versions of the debates, speeches, and laws to identify the presence of gendered positions.

7. Author's translation from text of law, no. 2000-37, 1/19/2000.

8. For an excellent overview of the development of feminist studies on women's employment since the 1970s see Lurol (2001a). For research on work-time issues see for example Barrère-Maurisson et al. (2001); Fagnanini (1996, 1998); Gauvin and Jacot (1999); Junter-Loiseau (1999); Lanquetin et al. (2000); Majoni D'Intignano (1999); Méda (1999, 2000).

8

Women, Embryos, and the Good Society: Gendering the Bioethics Debate in Germany

Kathrin Braun

The 2000/2001 "Bioethics Debate" was one of the hottest policy debates throughout post-war Germany.[1] It covered issues such as genetic testing, euthanasia, and human cloning. The main focus however was on pre-implantation genetic diagnosis (PGD)[2] and embryonic stem cell research[3] and the question of whether the 1991 Embryo Protection Act (*Embryonenschutzgesetz*, ESchG) should be revised in order to legalize these technologies. The ESchG is criminal law, prohibiting surrogate motherhood, egg donation, embryo donation, embryo research, germ line manipulation, reproductive and "therapeutic" human cloning, and hybridization. It prescribes that all eggs fertilized within an IVF procedure must be transferred to the woman from whom the eggs had been taken and the number of embryos transferred is limited to three. No fertilized egg may be stored or destroyed. Consequently, according to the law, there must not be any "surplus" embryos in Germany. The debate began around 1995 and was left up to the parliamentary decision on the new Stem Cell Act in January 2002. What was at stake here was the question of who should decide on the boundaries of research and the application of new biomedical practices: the state, the medical profession, the scientific community, or the individual? Thus, the bioethics debate was at heart a debate on relations between state and society with regard to science and technology.

At the same time, it was a debate on German identity and German history: What lessons were to be learned from the Nazi medical crimes? Should society outlaw any practices that come close to the notion of a "life not worth living"?

The debate was marked by a high level of public attention and an unusual constellation of actors: political parties, Parliament, the administration, and the public were deeply divided on the issue. Interestingly, feminists argued largely along the same lines as the churches and pro-lifers. This paper will argue that the exceptional structure of the policy environment enabled women's movement actors to gender the terms of the debate.

SELECTION OF DEBATE

Identifying the Universe of Hot Issues

In Germany, policy debates often take place in the sphere of civil society, frequently generated by protest movements like the peace movement, the environmental movement, or the feminist movement (Dryzek et al. 2003; Rucht 2001). Given the diffuse character of civil society as an arena for policy debates it is hard to gauge the intensity of issues. Additionally, there are permanent issues, which continue to concern people even in the absence of a clear-cut policy. During the period under study (1990–2001), pensions, health care reform, and unemployment formed such "issues without policies" in Germany. On the other hand, we find "ad hoc issues," which cause tremendous media attention but then vanish rather quickly.

To short-list some of the hottest issues, I used a study based on the *Politbarometer* (Hennig 1999), searched the Internet version of *Die Zeit*, the prime weekly paper in Germany, interviewed an expert from the press archives of the German parliament, and did a small survey among nine experts on political participation and the public sphere in Germany. In addition, I looked at the subject matter of parliamentary study commissions since 1990, particularly those that were established for more than one legislative period and the establishment of governmental advisory commissions, particularly permanent commissions. Combining these indicators, the list of the top four hot issues in Germany since 1990 includes unemployment, genetic technology and bioethics, German unification and its implications, and immigration and asylum.

German Unification

German unification represented the most radical transformation of the Federal Republic of Germany since 1948 and had enormous implications for the economy. The process of taking over the state economy of Eastern Germany into a market economy entailed a dramatic rise in unemployment rates, debts, and taxes. In that, it clearly affected a large portion of the population, although the educational system, the academic system, child care, and welfare in Eastern Germany underwent far more transformations than did the Western German institutions.

The unification process, of course, was on top of the agendas of the executive, the Parliament, political parties, and interest groups, such as the trade unions. Yet there was no high degree of conflict on the question of whether or not German unification should take place. The most controversial issue in this context was probably the future unified abortion law.

German unification was a process which fundamentally changed state-society relations, in particular in Eastern Germany. It was important in the sense of major scope, top priority of policy actors, and wide range of public attention; however, it was not really "hot" in terms of intense public controversy.

Unemployment

Unemployment was continuously high in Germany throughout the 1990s; unemployment rates did not fall below 10 percent from 1996 onwards. The issue therefore affected a large part of the population. It was also high on the agenda of the executives, trade unions, and industry leaders, prominently addressed throughout a series of election campaigns, and broadly covered by the media. According to opinion polls, it was a top-priority issue for the population (Hennig 1999). However, there was not really a policy and even less a policy debate within the period under study. Unemployment policies in the 1990s were highly incremental, hardly visible, and often merely symbolic. It was not until 2002, when Chancellor Schröder set up the so-called Hartz Commission[4] that the administration started to design an employment policy. Thus, although no doubt unemployment was a hot issue in Germany in the 1990s that was also about changing state-society relations; in the absence of a policy decision, it is not the subject of inquiry here.

Asylum and Immigration

Immigration bothered many people in Germany throughout the 1990s. In 2000, 12 percent of the population were immigrants (BMI 2001) and in this sense, immigration policy would have affected a large part of the population. One of the most controversial policy debates in this area concentrated on restricting the constitutional right to asylum in the early 1990s, a policy heavily contested by human rights groups, trade unions, and parts of the churches. Despite these protests, the constitutional guarantee to asylum eventually was restricted 1993.

Another debate centered on the issue of naturalization. In 1998 the Social Democrats/Greens' administration suggested facilitating naturalization by offering immigrants and their children German citizenship without dropping their original citizenship, a proposal which provoked an outcry by the Christian

Democrats. In the end however, the New Naturalization Act was passed in 2000.

Asylum law and immigration clearly meet the criterion of "hotness" in that it was an issue of major scope, high degree of conflict, wide range of public attention, and top priority of major actors. It is more difficult to say, however, whether immigration policy specifically changed state-society relations. It was more about the question of *who* should belong to German society than about deregulation, downsizing government, or devolution from state to civil society.

Biotechnology/Bioethics

Biotechnology has been a hot issue in Germany since the 1980s. In the 1990s, use of genetically modified organisms (GMOs) became an issue and to some extent it still is one today. In 1994 a new protest movement emerged, mobilizing against the Bioethics Convention by the Council of Europe, which would have allowed embryo research and research on human subjects without their personal informed consent, practices that reminded many people of the medical crimes in Nazi Germany. The protest grew so strong that the German administration did not sign the convention when it was set up for ratification in 1997. The most intense debate in this issue area, however, emerged in the late 1990s on PGD and later on embryonic stem cell research. The conflict reached an extremely high level of intensity and conflict both in the public sphere and within governmental institutions. For months it was front-page news every day (Graumann 2002). A series of high-ranking constitutional organs were engaged, such as the president of state, Johannes Rau, the Chancellor, Gerhard Schröder, several federal ministers, and the Parliament. In May 2001 Chancellor Schröder established the National Council on Ethics as one of two permanent governmental advisory boards in Germany. In January 2002, a new Stem Cell Act was passed, which included the establishment of the Central Ethics Commission on Stem Cell Research. In regards to state-society relations, this decision confirmed the authority of the law in relation to societal interest groups and professional self-control.

Thus, biotechnology and bioethics, though not as sustained a concern as unemployment, have been hot issues in Germany since the 1990s. The political journal *Das Parlament* stated that "genetics and biotechnology have penetrated the public discussion to an extent comparable to the fierce public arguments in the 1950s about the civil and military use of nuclear power" (*Das Parlament* 2001).

The bioethics debate clearly meets the criteria of "hotness" and transforming state-society relations. First, it was a debate on deregulation insofar as it dealt with the question of whether or not to abolish the legal ban on certain practices. Second, it was about shifting responsibilities from state to civil society in the sense that decision-making authority, according to some actors, should be handed over from the law to research associations or the Chamber of Doctors. Third, policymaking shifted a certain degree from traditional constitutional organs such as Parliament and government to new bodies such as the newly generated National Council on Ethics (NER) and the new Central Ethics Commission on Stem Cell Research. Although these bodies are not really located in a sphere beyond the state or take the form of a "network", they represent a new style of policymaking as they strengthen the role of non-governmental experts in the policy process.

Women's Movements in the Nineties

The literature on the German women's movement in the 1990s notes processes of pluralization, professionalization, and institutionalization on the one hand, and some sort of decline or stagnation on the other (Jansen 1998; Hagel/Schuhmann 1994; Holland-Cunz 2000). More optimistic scholars hold that the movement was merely taking a breath (Gerhard 2000). Ilse Lenz (2001) describes its status quite aptly as one in which "much is happening, but nobody knows that anymore" (Lenz 2001: 211).[5]

Compared to the 1970s and 1980s, the movement in the 1990s is said to be more diverse and at the same time less ideologically divided. It does not focus on only one or two issues anymore, such as abortion rights or violence against women, and the ideological differences between radical and Social Democratic feminists are not as significant as they had been before. (Hochgeschurz 1998: 166; 182). In the 1980s, a process of institutionalization had taken place which resulted in a series of local agencies for gender equality, federal and state ministries for women or gender equality, and university chairs for women's or gender studies. It entailed a decline of more informal forms of policymaking such as marches, sit-ins, and the like. At the same time, however, other movement sections focused on developing a feminine language, sexuality, spirituality, or value system and countless so-called autonomous women's projects emerged. Neoliberal economic policy and the decline of the welfare state in the 1990s have jeopardized the existence of these projects, most of which depended on public funding. Counter-movements were weak in the 1990s. Pro-lifers were comparatively few in number and moderate in action and no influential political actors openly argued that a woman's place is the home.

In short, the German women's movement in the 1990s was institutionalized to some degree, highly professionalized, less informal, more differentiated, and less ideologically divided as compared to earlier decades. It might be considered moderately close to the Left in that a number of women's movement activists engage in trade unions or leftist parties, concentrating on equality in terms of employment, wages, and social security. Yet there are also women who actively promote women's interests in the Christian Democratic Union as a Center Right party. On the other hand, there is still a considerable number of women's movement activists engaged in women's projects such as women's refuges, groups supporting women refugees, women-with-disabilities groups, or the feminist network against genetic and reproductive technologies, Reprokult. These initiatives keep a certain distance from leftist organizations and vice versa. Ideas and concerns of this movement faction, such as violence against women, genetic and reproductive technologies, lesbian sexuality, or women refugees' rights, have only very reluctantly been adopted by the Left. Altogether, the German women's movement might be considered as moderately close to the Left both in terms of organization and of ideology.

According to the literature, the movement is in decline, or at least stagnation, when compared to the 1970s. However, looking at issue-specific activities like the bioethics debate, we get a different picture. As this article will argue with regard to this issue area we may instead speak of the reemergence of *a* (not *the*) women's movement.

Genetic technology and reproductive medicine had been an issue for radical feminists in the late 1980s and again in the late 1990s, when a new issue-specific network structure was established and existing groups and organizations, such as the Association of Women Doctors, held meetings and conferences on the issue. It was not a uniting issue, but rather one which was high on the agenda of some activists and organizations; hence it was of moderate priority for the movement in general.

THE BIOETHICS DEBATE

How the Issue Became Part of the Public Agenda

The bioethics debate entered the public sphere in 1995, when the medical superintendent of the gynecological hospital in Lübeck, Klaus Diedrich, asked the hospital's ethics commission for permission to perform PGD. PGD had not been an elaborated practice when the ESchG was passed and is not mentioned therein. The committee replied that PGD was *legally* prohibited but the ban was *ethically* wrong (Kollek 2000). Over subsequent years, the case for PGD was supported by a number of actors, mainly policymakers and actors from the medical profession. In 1999, the Bioethics Commission of the state Rhineland Palatinate published an influential report, the so-called Caesar Report, presenting arguments in favor of PGD (Caesar 1999). Disagreement as to whether or not the ESchG allows PGD led to suggestions to produce a new act on reproductive medicine. In March 2000, the German Chamber of Doctors (BÄK) published a paper (BÄK 2001) recommending that application should be restricted to so-called high-risk couples; the couple should undergo counselling; and the case should be presented to an ethics committee run by the Chamber of Doctors. Thus, the chamber was arguing for professional self-regulation instead of state control. In sum, the issue of deregulating the ESchG was put on the agenda by experts and professionals.

In May 2000, the federal minister of health, Andrea Fischer (Greens), organized a huge symposium meant to prepare the ground for a prospective act on reproductive medicine. At the same time, a new Parliamentary Study Commission on the Law and Ethics of Modern Medicine (*Enquete-Kommission Recht und Ethik der modernen Medizin*, EK REM) started work.

The public was divided into two issue-specific "camps": a techno-optimist alliance, comprising the Liberal Party, large parts of the research community and the medical community, and parts of the Social Democrats, Socialists, and Christian Democrats, and a techno-skeptical alliance, formed by the vast majority of the Green Party, disabled people's associations, the churches, pro-lifers, feminists, some biomedicine skeptics from the medical community, and parts of the Socialists and the Social Democrats, and the Christian Democrats.

In May 2001, the subject of debate moved from PGD to embryonic stem cell (ES) research. Again, the issue was put on the political agenda by professionals, in this case the German Research Foundation, who now argued in favour of ES research (DFG 2002), and two biomedical researchers, Oliver Brüstle and Otmar Wiestler, who planned to import embryonic stem cell lines for research purposes from Haifa. The ESchG prohibited the creation of embryonic stem cells, but it did say nothing about importation. Whether or not importation was legally and morally appropriate was heavily debated up to the eventual enactment of the Stem Cell Act in January 2002.

Dominant Frame of Debate

Whereas throughout the 1990s, the debate on biomedicine had been largely framed in terms of risks and benefits, from May 2000 onwards it tended to focus on questions of autonomy on the one hand and human dignity, non-discrimination, and protection of vulnerable groups such as disabled people and women on the other. I will call this issue frame the "autonomy-versus-the-good-society frame". Proponents of the new technologies referred to both individual autonomy and autonomy of research, stressing that neither state nor religion were entitled to interfere into freedom of research or people's private lives. To them, the moral status of the human embryo was a matter of personal beliefs, as MP Edzard Schmidt-Jortzig (FDP), former minister of justice, put it:

> We live not in a totalitarian regime and not in a dictatorship, but in a liberal so-
> ciety. . . . I believe that only the path of responsible and free research can do jus-
> tice to our claim to progress as a civilization, our demand for improvement, and
> our need to not want to stand still. (EK REM 2002a: 271ff., 273ff.)

The good-society frame, on the other hand, was promoted by a variety of political actors such as feminists, pro-lifers, and people with disabilities who, if
anything, shared the idea that biomedical technologies could not be judged
exclusively from an individualistic point of view. They emphasized the implications these technologies might have for the basic values of society, such
as respect for human life or the life chances of disadvantaged social groups
such as women or people with disabilities. In particular, they saw the "good
society" as a society that does not reiterate the Nazi concept of "life not worth
living", as President of State Johannes Rau indicated in his celebrated "Berlin
Speech":

> I am ever mindful of the way that history helps us—and not just us Germans—
> to realize what happens when standards are shifted, when humans are made
> from subjects into objects. Whoever begins to instrumentalize human life, who-
> ever starts to decide when a human life is or is not worth living, is, in reality, on
> a track without end. (Rau 2001: 19; 26)

Gendering the Debate

Up to May 2000, women's movement actors found themselves mostly outside
the policy subsystem, with little influence on the terms of the debate. The
Berlin Symposium in May 2000 (BMG 2001), however, provided an opportunity for them to enter the stage. Here, many feminist panellists cautioned
that practices requiring "materials" derived from women's bodies such as egg
donation, embryo donation, and embryo research threatened to instrumental-
ize women (Schneider 2001; Berg 2001). Others argued that fertility problems were rather caused by social factors such as the need for women to postpone childbearing due to hardships for working mothers (Hauffe 2001).
Reproductive medicine, in this view, was seen as offering inadequate technical solutions to problems that in fact are rooted in gender inequality. Furthermore, feminists critiqued the medicalization of pregnancy (Weiss 2001) and
argued that genetic and reproductive technologies would impose social pressure on women to produce "proper" children (Fränznick 2001; Graumann
2001b). The liberal feminist Monika Frommel (2001) took a different stance,

arguing that embryo protection and the rationales behind it would, in the long run, jeopardize women's right to abortion. Still others argued—however without referring to gender—that egg donation, embryo donation, or surrogate motherhood belonged to the realm of private life, into which the state was not entitled to interfere unless the fundamental rights of other individuals were seriously affected (Coester-Waltjen 2001; Zumstein 2001).

The symposium provided a forum for feminists from both "camps", turning them into significant actors in the policy process. It thereby contributed to opening up the policy subsystem and provided an opportunity for gendering the terms of the debate.

Another such opportunity was opened up by the Parliamentary Study Commission on Law and Ethics of Modern Medicine (EK REM), established in May 2000. Feminist members of the commission managed to address a series of gender issues in the final report, which, for instance, stated that

> Chronically ill or disabled children can worsen the career prospects and present an additional risk of poverty for women in particular, because in most cases it is the woman who bears the main responsibility for caring for the children, and marriage and family no longer provide sufficient social protection. The putative chance to avoid sick or disabled children via pre-implantation genetic diagnosis, however, implies the danger that women will be pressed to take up this technology in order to secure the birth of a healthy child. . . . In this sense, pre-implantation diagnosis is a technical solution for a socially generated problem, and this solution could itself exacerbate the problem. Priority should instead be given, by means of social policy, to lifting this burden from women. (EK REM 2002b: 243)

Around May 2001, a new gender-based argument emerged, introduced by Wolfgang Schäuble (2001) (CDU), former minister of internal politics. Drawing on the research of biologist and Nobel Prize winner Christine Nüsslein-Volhard (2001), Schäuble argued that the embryo *in vitro* was not really human life, because, without the mother, it could not grow into a human being. This argument bears a formal resemblance to radical feminist arguments in the 1980s that the woman was not a passive carrier but in fact played an active part in the development of a new human being. Whereas, however, those feminists had argued that human development outside the womb would lead to increasing control over women's lives, eugenic selection, and manipulation (Hofmann 1998), Nüsslein-Volhard and Schäuble concluded that creating embryos outside the womb was perfectly acceptable. They thus referred to feminist ideas but put them into a different context.

Many of these gender-based arguments reappeared in the big parliamentary debate on biomedicine on May 31, 2001. MP Pia Maier (PDS), for instance, a socialist feminist, cautioned that a ban on PGD might endanger women's rights to self-determination (Deutscher Bundestag 2001: 16899 D). Other MPs held that it would be less damaging for a woman's health to undergo PGD than to abort a genetically defective fetus (Deutscher Bundestag 2001: 16900 A; 16932 A; 16933 A/B). Opponents of PGD pointed at the threat of instrumentalizing women as resources (Deutscher Bundestag 2001: 16929 A) or of imposing new social pressures on women (Deutscher Bundestag 2001: 16928 D; 16929 A; 16919 D; 16917 A). Additionally, they claimed that the demand for PND and PID had its origins in gender relations in society (Deutscher Bundestag 2001: 16920 A; 16922 A), and called for gender equality as an alternative solution.

Throughout the debate, the dispute over whether or not there was an inconsistency between abortion law and embryo protection law played a crucial role. Feminists in both camps insisted on a woman's right to abortion. Pia Maier (PDS), referring to the autonomy frame, claimed that

> To treat a fertilized egg and a living human as equivalent bearers of a right to protection stands opposed, in my opinion, to the right of women to self-determination. . . .Women should continue to be masters of their own bodies. (Deutscher Bundestag 2001: 16899D)

On the other side, Andrea Fischer (Greens) contradicted the alleged analogy between abortion law and embryo protection law because "with PGD . . . there is no pregnancy that could cause a crisis in which the claims to life would have to be weighed against one another" (Deutscher Bundestag 2001: 16890B).

It was exclusively MPs from the left-wing parties (SPD, Greens, and PDS), all of them but one being women who introduced arguments referring to the ideas and aspirations of the women's movement. Note, however, that there was as much disagreement on the issue among feminists as among Social Democrats, Christian Democrats, and Socialists in general.

When the focus of the debate shifted from PGD to embryonic stem cell research and from general problems of genetics and reproductive medicine to the status of the embryo, opportunities for introducing gendered arguments dwindled. Indeed, to some degree a degendering process took place. When Minister of Culture Julian Nida-Rümelin (2001) made the argument in a newspaper article that human embryos lack self-esteem and consequently human dignity, he caused a storm of protest in the German public. However, although abortion was a central topic in this dispute, there was barely any mentioning of women, let alone the social context in which women get involuntarily pregnant or have an abortion. Both proponents and opponents tended to focus on "the embryo" as a given entity, without ever questioning the social, cultural, economic, or institutional circumstances of its existence. When it came to the question of importing embryonic stem cells, the two governmental ethics commissions, the Parliamentary Study Commission and the National Ethics Council, each presented an opinion on the issue. The Parliamentary Study Commission once again pointed to the threat of women being instrumentalized as a resource (EK REM 2002a: 142/43; 118), whereas the National Council on Ethics (NER 2001) did not mention this topic. Both reports discussed the question of an inconsistency between embryo protection law and abortion law (EK REM 2002a: 90ff.; NER 2001: 10ff.; 22), and did so by explicitly referring to women's rights.

In January 2001, Parliament was to decide on the question of import of embryonic stem cell lines, making a choice between three inter-factional motions, one of which referred to the issue of instrumentalization of women. In the plenary debate, the ideas and aspirations of the women's movement were not as present as they had been in the May 2001 debate. It was mainly two women MPs from the Socialist Party who addressed gender issues. Pia Maier (PDS) again insisted on women's individual reproductive autonomy:

> To the right of women to self determination belongs, as I understand it, the right for oneself to decide: for or against having children, for or against hormone treatment, for or against the use of her eggs for research. (EK REM 2002a: 282)

Her party colleague, Petra Bläss (PDS) countered, this type of autonomy might quickly turn into the commercialization of women's body materials (EK REM 2002a: 277). Apart from these two speeches, little reference was made to gender.

However, for the first and only time in both debates, men's issues were addressed when MP Monika Griefahn (SPD) maintained that the need for assisted reproduction was to a large extent caused by male infertility, which, she held, was in turn due to environmental poisoning. Instead of funding reproductive medicine, she said, politics should rather provide for a more healthy environment (EK REM 2002a: 261).

Apart from experts and MPs, a series of individual women and women's organizations in civil society were engaged in the debate. In November 2001, Reprokult, a feminist network of individual women and formal and informal women's organizations opposed to genetic and reproductive technologies, held a conference entitled "Reproductive Medicine and Genetics: Women between Self-Determination and Social Standardization" (Reprokult 2002), attended also by women MPs. The German Association of Women Doctors (Deutscher Ärztinnenbund 2001) published a declaration in February 2001 highlighting the dangers of PGD to women's health. Between May and November 2001, the German Catholic Women's Association (KFD) collected

178,300 signatures in favor of retaining the ESchG, however without explicitly referring to gender. The Working Group of Social Democratic Women (ASF 2001) declared that PGD would not solve women's problems but increase the problems of people with disabilities. In November 2001, a so-called Citizen Conference on Genetic Diagnosis was organized by the Hygienic Museum in Dresden (Bürgerkonferenz 2001). A group of ten women and nine men intensively debated PGD and genetic testing and eventually presented a final opinion which exhibited a clear-cut gender gap: All of the women and two of the men voted against the legalization of PGD, mainly out of concern about potential implications of PGD for women in terms of social pressure and health risks.

In conclusion, the terms of the bioethics debate have become gendered to a certain degree, due to women experts, women MPs, but a few men MPs too, mostly from the Left parties, and women's organizations and networks in civil society. They were concerned about women's reproductive autonomy, women's health, the threat of social pressure on and instrumentalization of women imposed by genetic and reproductive technologies, societal gender relations as a stimulus for the development of ethically problematic technologies, and the medicalization of pregnancy and its alienating implications for women.

Remarkably, however, the process of gendering did not extend to the inclusion of men's issues. Men's aspirations, anxieties, and responsibilities towards genetics and reproductive technology remained largely unexplored.

POLICY OUTCOME

In the parliamentary debate of January 30 in 2002, the majority of MPs voted for the motion proposed by an interfactional women's "troika" formed by Maria Böhmer (CDU), Margot von Renesse (SPD), and Andrea Fischer (Greens). This motion formed the basis of the eventual Stem Cell Act. It allowed for importing human embryonic stem cells under certain conditions, among them that the stem cell lines must have been produced prior to a certain deadline, so as to prevent the destruction of additional human embryos. Moreover, import was required to not violate the provisions of the ESchG.

After the decision, public debate came to an end. The Stem Cell Act was passed in April 2002 and enacted in July. The final outcome did not include any explicitly gendered provisions. The Stem Cell Act changed state-society relations in so far as it deregulated embryonic stem cell research to a certain degree. It allows the import of human ES cells for research purposes under certain strict conditions. In these cases it shifts authority from criminal law to a departmental research facility, the Robert Koch Institute, as the new licensing authority. In addition, a new ethics committee was established in order to evaluate applications. Thus, modes of political steering shifted to some extent from law enforcement to licensing and evaluation.

MOVEMENT IMPACT

Women were accepted as legitimate actors within the debate. In the May 2001 parliamentary debate, 43 percent (eighteen out of forty-two) of the speakers were women; in the January 2002 debate it was 42.5 percent (seventeen out of forty). Women made up 41 percent (twenty-eight out of sixty-eight) of the experts at the Berlin Symposium, more than half of them identified as feminists or engaged with gender issues. Forty-two percent of the members of the EK REM (eleven out of twenty-six) were women and 32 percent (eight out of twenty-five) of the members of the NER. In comparison, the percentage of women in Parliament at that time was 31 percent. Throughout the debate, a certain redefinition of the notion of an "expert" became apparent. Whereas before the Berlin Symposium the debate had been marked by the dominance of male experts from the life sciences, jurisprudence, or theology, now being an "expert" could include being a social scientist, a midwife, a social worker, or a psychologist. This enlarged the opportunity of women to participate as experts in issue-specific parliamentary commissions. In addition, the EK REM was chaired by a woman, MP Margot von Renesse (SPD). What is more, women were taken seriously and actively influenced the direction of the policymaking process. The fact that three women authored the final compromise on stem cell imports might serve as an indicator of the acceptance of women as legitimate actors.

Did actors from the women's movement achieve their goals? Women's movement actors managed to introduce arguments referring to women's interests and women's social status into the parliamentary debates, the reports of the National Council on Ethics, and the Parliamentary Study Commission. The final decision on stem cell research, however, was not explicitly gendered.

Women's movement actors were deeply divided on the issue. On the one hand we find individual women supporting women's movement ideas—however no women's organizations—who had favored a liberalization of the ESchG and did not achieve this goal. On the other hand, we see both individual movement actors and movement organizations who had opposed a revision of the ESchG. They did get what they had wanted to some extent: a preservation of the ban on PGD, egg donation, and technologies based on the use of human eggs, such as the production of embryonic stem cell lines. Additionally, both camps had successfully strived to preserve a woman's right to abortion. We might therefore speak of a dual response to the women's movement in this debate.

WOMEN'S POLICY AGENCY ACTIVITIES

In the 1990s, Germany had a Federal Ministry for Women's Affairs as well as a number of women's ministries on state level. Reproductive medicine and embryo protection were under federal responsibility; therefore I will concentrate on the federal level. The first Federal Ministry for Women's Affairs was established in 1985. Subsequent administrations each included a Ministry for Women's Affairs or Gender Equality or a special department within a combined ministry for women *and*, for instance, youth, senior citizens, family, health, sports, or social issues. The minister gets appointed by the chancellor. From 1998 to 2002, the Federal Ministry for Family Affairs, Senior Citizens, Women, and Youth (BMFSFJ) was lead by Christine Bergmann (SPD), who clearly articulated feminist aspirations. Women's or gender equality affairs form only one part of the ministry, with some staff but no separate divisions or field offices. The ministry funds some research into gender issues and a series of women's organizations such as the German Council of Women. Its administrative capacity thus is medium.

The Women's Ministry's scope is cross-sectional in that the minister is charged to influence draft bills by each federal ministry if women's affairs are affected. Christine Bergmann elaborated policies on gender equality in public administration, violence against women, trafficking in women, and day care facilities.[6] One of her most ambitious projects was to achieve an affirmative action act for the private sector of the economy. The project failed due to lack of support from the chancellor. The BMFSFJ did not belong to the powerful ministries in German politics. A running joke in Germany says that the competencies of the BMFSFJ are as small as its name is tall. When it came to coalition talks among the SPD and the Greens after the general elections in 2002, none of the coalition partners was eager to take over the BMFSFJ. Thus, the proximity to power centers is distant.

Christine Bergmann did not engage in the bioethics debate, although her official policy mandate could have covered the issue. We find statements by the other federal women ministers such as the minister of justice, Herta Däubler-Gmelin (SPD), the ministers of health, Andrea Fischer (Greens), and later Ulla Schmidt (SPD), and the minister for research, Edelgard Bulmahn

(SPD), but not a single public word from the minister for women. Thus, the ministry acted in symbolic fashion.

CHARACTERISTICS OF THE WOMEN'S MOVEMENT

The women's movement in Germany traditionally takes a skeptical stance on science and technology. In the late 1980s it was nearly unanimously opposed to genetic and reproductive technology. A number of huge conferences took place and an international feminist network against human genetics and reproductive medicine, FINNRAGE, was founded (Hofmann 1998). Feminists warned that reprogenetics, as they termed it, would reinforce patriarchal control over women's lives, contribute to the alienation of women from their procreative capacities, and open the door to a new form of eugenics. Women were constructed as gatekeepers whose task was to keep the door shut.

In the 1990s, however, activists had to realize that women were not only victims of reproductive technologies but also consumers. Additionally, they were increasingly concerned about how to oppose reprogenetics without jeopardizing women's right to abortion (Graumann 2002).

However, the network structure in the issue area of genetic and reproductive technology reemerged in the late 1990s, and with it, interestingly, former ideological conflicts between liberal feminist ideas on the one hand and an alliance of socialist, radical, and cultural feminist ideas on the other. Women's movement actors who advocated liberal feminist ideas, such as individual freedom of choice, supported the policy of liberalizing the ESchG. This faction was made up of individual women, mainly experts or MPs. Other women's movement actors opposed the policy, advocating typically socialist ideas, such as social support for disadvantaged groups, and typical ideas of cultural feminism, such as skepticism towards science and technology as means of controlling and alienating women. The techno-skeptical faction consisted of individuals, organizations, and networks. If we understand the women's movement as an organized structure, we have to note that this issue-specific women's movement was a) reemerging, b) opposing the policy at stake, and c) being relatively successful in that struggle.

One important factor in this context was the absence of a strong countermovement, in particular of a strong anti-abortion movement. In Germany, abortion is "illegal but not subject to prosecution" under certain conditions. This so-called abortion compromise is widely accepted and unchallenged. The absence of a strong anti-abortion movement allowed feminists to critique reproductive technologies from a gender perspective without immediately jeopardizing the right to abortion.

THE POLICY ENVIRONMENT

During the hot stage of the debate, Social Democrats and Greens together held the majority in Parliament and formed the executive. The 1998 coalition contract determined that human genetics and reproductive medicine were under the responsibility of the Ministry of Health. The final decision on a potential new act would have to be made by the Parliament as mandated by the constitution. These were the fixed elements of the policy subsystem structure.

On the other hand for the first time the Greens formed part of the federal government. As the Green minister of health, Andrea Fischer had a great impact on the bioethics debate; this was clearly a factor that contributed to the opening of the policy environment. Additionally, there was a conflict about whether a new act was needed at all or whether the existing ESchG would allow PGD and the import of human embryonic stem cells. Therefore, it was unclear who was to decide. If PGD was considered to be allowed by the act, it could have been, for instance, the Chamber of Doctors who decided about its application. If no act was considered necessary for importing human embryonic stem cells then the decision about importation could legitimately be made by researchers and research associations. Thus, it was a matter of conflict whether the state or societal institutions were to have the power to decide.

Furthermore, the constellation of actors changed insofar as new types of experts, such as sociologists, political scientists, midwifes, social workers, or psychologists, entered the scene, many of whom were women. Additionally, from May 2000 the debate extended to a broader public. The media became engaged, and conferences and workshops were organized by numerous civil society organizations. The absence of pre-set or clear rules for this type of debate may also encourage a more open policy environment.

Although it became ever more clear that existing law was not considered sufficient and hence decision making would be up to the legislature, it was not at all clear how decision making was to proceed. At least three of the party factions in Parliament—the SPD, the CDU/CSU, and the PDS—were deeply divided on the issue. There was a cleavage in Parliament as well as in government not along party lines but between two issue-specific camps. Another peculiar feature indicating an openness of the policy environment was the fact that the final law was not drafted by the Ministry of Health, which would have been the usual procedure, but by an inter-factional alliance of MPs. In short, this stage of the bioethics debate was characterized by a complex, untypical, and relatively open policy environment.

The frames used by both "camps", that is the "good society frame" on the one hand and the "autonomy frame" on the other, were both compatible with women's movement's goals, referring to women's individual right to self-determination on the one hand and to non-discrimination, social equality, and social support on the other. Even though it was mainly women who gendered these arguments, the issue frame fit was compatible in both camps.

CONCLUSION

The German bioethics debate shows us that changes in state-society relations towards deregulation, downsizing of government, or shifting responsibilities from state to society do not always occur smoothly. While the debate had clearly been initiated by attempts to deregulate the issue area of biomedicine and to shift responsibilities from the state to the medical community, and respectively, the research community, these attempts did not fully succeed. Nevertheless, in the end, we do observe some changes in policymaking, such as the increasing role of ethics committees. Here, we find the generation of new institutions as the state's response to technology conflicts.

Women played an important part in the debate, as policymakers, experts, and civil society actors. Governmental organs such as the Health Ministry, under Andrea Fischer, and the *Bundestag* created different opportunities for women's participation and for gendering the issue. However, this was not a result of the activities of women's policy agencies. The federal minster for women was completely absent in this debate and had no impact on the policy process whatsoever.

We can conclude, rather, that it was the openness and complexity of the policy environment in combination with an unusual alliance of women's movement actors with people from the disability rights movement and pro-lifers that generated the opportunity for gendering the issue. Furthermore, the dominant issue frame, the autonomy-versus-the-good-society frame, was wholly compatible with WMA's ideas and aspirations. However, towards the end of the debate, when the dominant issue frame shifted and the debate on embryo rights tended to supersede the topic of the good society, the space for gendering narrowed down again.

Nevertheless, women were accepted as legitimate actors and women's movement actors managed to introduce a series of gender-related arguments that were taken up by certain governmental bodies. We may therefore conclude that the bioethics debate represented a dual response to women's movement ideas.

The bioethics debate in Germany cooled down considerably after the decision to establish a new Stem Cell Act in January 2002. Since then, no major policy changes have occurred. Together with the enactment of the Stem Cell

Act, the new Central Ethics Commission for Stem Cell Research at the Robert Koch Institute in Berlin was founded. The Robert Koch Institute started assessing and licensing research projects involving human embryonic stem cells, taking into account the opinion of its Central Ethics Commission. Between July 2002 and December 2005, it approved twelve such research projects. The Stem Cell Act did not undergo any changes since 2002.

PGD is still considered illegal and the Embryo Protection Act is still in place. The October 2005 general elections led to the replacement of the SPD/Greens coalition by a "grand" coalition between the Christian Democrats and Social Democrats. As the Christian Democratic Party announced their decision not to vote for a legalization of PGD, and MPs in other factions are opposed to it too, policy change is highly unlikely here.

Concerning abortion law, Christian Democratic MPs recently (December 2005) have announced to strive for a more restrictive regulation on abortions occurring after the twenty-third week of pregnancy. However, they also said that revising the existing abortion law was politically unfeasible and new regulations would rather refer to extended psychological counseling and inhibiting so-called wrongful birth rulings, which in their view indirectly promote abortions after PND.

Thus, the outcomes of the bioethics debate are currently still in place.

REFERENCES

ASF 2001: Arbeitsgemeinschaft Sozialdemokratischer Frauen (ASF), Presseerklärung: PID löst Grundkonflikt nicht, 31.05.2001, Berlin.

BÄK 2001: Der Diskussionsentwurf der Bundesärztekammer zu einer Richtlinie zur Präimplantationsdiagnostik. In: Graumann 2001, pp. 157–168.

Berg, Giselind 2001: Eizellspende—Eine notwendige Alternative? In: BMG 2001, pp. 143–152.

BMG 2001: Fortpflanzungsmedizin in Deutschland. Fortpflanzungsmedizin in Deutschland. Wissenschaftliches Symposium des Bundesministeriums für Gesundheit in Zusammenarbeit mit dem Robert Koch-Institut vom 24.–26. Mai 2000 in Berlin. Schriftenreihe des Bundesministeriums für Gesundheit, Bd. 132. Baden-Baden: Nomos.

BMI 2001: Bundesministerium des Innern, Bericht der Unabhängigen Kommission Zuwanderung, Berlin, 4 July 2001, www.bmi.bund.de/dokumente/Artikel/ix_46877.htm, 15.8.2003.

Bürgerkonferenz 2001: www.buergerkonferenz.de, 5.9.2003.

Coester-Waltjen, Dagmar 2001: Elternschaft außerhalb der Ehe-Sechs juristische Prämissen und Folgerungen für die künstliche Befruchtung. In: BMG 2001, pp. 158–162.

Das Parlament 2001: Zu dieser Ausgabe. In: Das Parlament, ed. by the Bundeszentrale für Politische Bildung, No. 11, 9 March 2001, www.das-parlament.de/2001/11/thema/2001_11_004_4828, 5.6.2003.

Deutscher Ärztinnenbund 2001: Dammbruch-Effekt befürchtet: Ärztinnenbund lehnt in Ethik-Stellungnahme Präimplantationsdiagnostik ab. Köln, 21.01.2001, www.aerztinnenbund.de/Homepage/Presse/PID.html, 28.9.2002.

Deutscher Bundestag (2001): Plenarprotokoll 14/173, Deutscher Bundestag, Stenographischer Bericht, 173. Sitzung, Berlin, Donnerstag, den 31. May 2001.

DFG 2002: Deutsche Forschungsgemeinschaft, Entscheidungen und Initiativen der DFG zum Thema Stammzellforschung 1997–2002, www.dfg.de/aktuelles_presse/themen_dokumentationen/stammzellen/entscheidungen_zur_stammzellforschung.html, 4.9.2002.

Dryzek, John, et al. 2003: *Green States and Social Movements: Environmentalism in the United States, United Kingdom, Norway, and Germany*. Oxford: Oxford University Press.

EK REM 2002a: Deutscher Bundestag, Referat Öffentlichkeitsarbeit (Hg.), Enquete-Kommission Recht und Ethik der modernen Medizin, Stammzellforschung und die Debatte des Deutschen Bundestages zum Import von menschlichen embryonalen Stammzellen, Zur Sache 1/2002. Berlin 2002.

EK REM 2002b: Deutscher Bundestag, Referat Öffentlichkeitsarbeit (Hg.), Enquete-Kommission Recht und Ethik der modernen Medizin. Schlussbericht, Zur Sache 2/2002. Berlin 2002.

Fränznick, Monika 2001: Statement. In: BMG 2001, pp. 385–386.

Frommel, Monika 2001: Status des Embryos: Juristische Aspekte. In: BMG 2001, pp. 67–75.

Gerhard, Ute 2000: Atempause: Die aktuelle Bedeutung der Frauenbewegung für eine zivile Gesellschaft. In: Kathrin Braun/Gesine Fuchs/Christiane Lemke/Katrin Töns (eds.), Feministische Perspektiven der Politikwissenschaft. Tübingen: Oldenbourg, pp. 293–314.

Geyer, Christian (ed.) 2001: Biopolitik. Die Positionen. Frankfurt a.M.: Suhrkamp.

Graumann, Sigrid 2000: PID: Gen-Check vor der Schwangerschaft. In: GID 139, 13–16.

Graumann, Sigrid (ed.) 2001a: Die Genkontroverse. Grundpositionen. Mit der Rede von Johannes Rau. Freiburg, Basel, Wien: Herder.

Graumann, Sigrid 2001b: Gesellschaftliche Folgen der Präimplantationsdiagnostik. In: BMG 2001, pp. 215–220.

Graumann, Sigrid 2002: Situation der Medienberichterstattung zu den aktuellen Entwicklungen in der Biomedizin und ihren ethischen Fragen. Gutachten für die AG "Bioethik und Wissenschaftskommunikation" am Max-Delbrück-Centrum für Molekulare Medizin. Berlin.

Hagel, Antje/Antje Schuhmann 1994: Aufstieg und Fall der Frauenbewegung. In: Cornelia Eichhorn/Sabine Grimm (eds.), Gender Killer. Texte zu Feminismus und Politik. Berlin/Amsterdam: Edition ID-Archiv, pp. 69–75.

Hauffe, Ulrike 2001: Statement. In: BMG 2001, pp. 382–383.

Hennig, Eike 1999: Die wichtigsten Probleme und die Parteieigung in der Bundesrepublik, http://www.uni-kassel.de/fb5/Politikwissenschaft/Demokratietheorie/wi_prob.html, 30.6.2003.

Hochgeschurz, Marianne 1998: Zwischen Autonomie und Integration. Die neue (west-)deutsche Frauenbewegung. In: Florence Hervé (ed.), Geschichte der deutschen Frauenbewegung. Köln: PapyRossa Verlag, pp. 155–184.

Hofmann, Heidi 1998: Die feministischen Diskurse über Reproduktionstechnologien. Positionen und Kontroversen in der BRD und den USA. Frankfurt/New York: Campus.

Holland-Cunz, Barbara 2000: Wo steht die Frauenbewegung? In: Elke Begander (ed.), Was uns bewegt. Beiträge aus der Frauenforschung. Bielefeld: Kleine, pp. 24–48.

Jansen, Mechthild 1998: Was wird aus der Gleichheit der Geschlechter in einer ungleichen Gesellschaft? Perspektiven der Frauenbewegung. In: Ingeborg Mues, Was Frauen bewegt und was sie bewegen. Frankfurt a.M.: Fischer, pp. 212–228.

Kollek, Regine 1999: "Wegen der ethischen Brisanz nicht akzeptabel." In: GID 131, 14–16.

Kollek, Regine 2000: Präimplantationsdiagnostik. Embryonenselektion, weibliche Autonomie und Recht. Tübingen.

Lenz, Ilse 2001: Bewegungen und Veränderungen. Frauenforschung und neue Frauenbewegungen in Deutschland. In: Ursula Hornung/Sedef Gümen/Sabine Weilandt (eds.), Zwischen Emanzipationsvision und Gesellschaftskritik. (Re)Konstruktion der Geschlechterordnung. Münster: Westfälisches Dampfboot.

NER 2001: German National Ethics Council, Opinion on the import of human embryonic stem cells. December 2001 (Document 001/01), www.ethikrat.org/_english/publications/opinions.html, 5.9.2003.

Nida-Rümelin, Julian 2001: Bioethik. Wo die Menschenwürde beginnt. In: Tagesspiegel Berlin 3.1.2001.

Nüsslein-Vollhard, Christine 2001: Wann ist ein Tier ein Tier, ein Mensch Mensch? In: FAZ 2.10.2001.

Rau, Johannes 2001: Wird alles gut? Für einen Fortschritt nach menschlichem Maß. In: Graumann 2001, pp. 14–29.

Reprokult 2002: Women's Forum for Reproductive Medicine, Reproductive Medicine and Genetic Engineering. Women between Self-Determination and Societal Standardisation. Proceedings of the conference held in Berlin from 15 to 17 November 2001.

Rucht, Dieter (ed.) 2001: Protest in der Bundesrepublik: Strukturen und Entwicklungen, Frankfurt/Main: Campus.Schäuble, Wolfgang 2001: Vergeßt die Mutter nicht. In: FR 21.5.2001

Schneider, Ingrid 2001: Embryonale Stammzellforschung. In: BMG 2001, pp. 248–254.

Tolmein, Oliver 1998: Ein Recht auf fehlerfreie Babys? In: GID 125/126, 57–58.

Weiss, Magdalene 2001: Statement. In: BMG 2001, pp. 383–385.

Zumstein, Monika 2001: Keimzellspende—Juristische Thesen. In: BMG 2001, pp. 134–142.

NOTES

1. See Geyer 2001, Graumann 2001a, and InteressenGemeinschaften Kritische Bioethik Deutschland 2003, www.kritischebioethik.de/deutschland_presse.html, 5.9.2003.

2. Pre-implantation genetic diagnosis (PGD) serves to detect genetic and chromosomal deviations before an embryo is implanted into a woman's womb (Kollek 2000).

3. Stem cells are so-called pluripotent cells that are capable of self-renewal and differentiation into a wide variety of cell types.

4. The *Hartz-Kommission*, named after its chair, Peter Hartz, was an expert commission established by the German government in 2002 in order to develop recommendations for restructuring the German labor market

5. German source translated by author into English.

6. The priorities of the contemporary Women's Ministry can be found under www.bmfsfj.de, 26.5.2003. They did not change compared to the administration period 1998–2002 (Interview Icken 26.5.2003).

9

The Reform of the State in Italy

Marila Guadagnini

This chapter examines the debate about decentralization and the reorganization of local government in Italy. This reorganization has involved different apportioning of administrative, legislative, and fiscal powers between the state and the local authorities. The pace of the debate was stepped up and it became part of the political agenda as one of the top-priority issues in the nineties for a number of reasons.

As was the case in other European countries, the factors that affected the reorganization of local governments were, on the one hand, the crisis in the welfare state and, on the other, the demands made by pro-autonomy forces (Bobbio, 2002). Central governments had played an absolute lead role in the development of Keynesian policies and of the welfare state. Only at the national level was it possible to manage macroeconomic policies able to satisfy demand, achieve full employment, and support large-scale public investments. Neocorporative agreements between the government, trade unions, and employers were reached at the national level, with a high degree of centralization. The crisis of the welfare state, the assertion of neoliberal ideologies, and the inability to cope with problems such as inflation, the public debt (which reached abnormal proportions in Italy in the 1980s), and high levels of taxation forced central government to downsize. Local authorities found themselves in dire financial straits: to balance their budgets, they could only count on their own efforts. They demanded greater autonomy in terms of taxation.

Social and economic imbalances between different regions also tended to produce a shift towards decentralization. As in Spain, in Italy too it is the richer regions that lead the struggle for greater autonomy, stressing real or supposed ethnic/national differences. Their economic power and threats of secession have induced national governments to rethink the setup of the state.

In Italy too, the drive towards decentralization has been encouraged by the process of European integration. The EU has adopted policies aimed at overcoming the imbalances within member countries by implementing development funds, whose beneficiaries are the regional or local governments (Bobbio, 2002). It has created a European space in which sub-national states are free to set up alliances with other sub-national entities; it has provided a protective umbrella and a means for local elites to bypass the state (idem).

In addition, as happened in other countries, the issue of decentralization became part of the political agenda when the rift between center and periphery had been advocated by strong regional parties: in Italy, without the electoral success of the Northern League (Diamanti 1996), the question of federalism would never have formed such an important part of the political agenda.

Finally, the issue of an overall reconfiguration of the state as a process of political restructuring and relocation of power became a priority in the political agenda in the 1990s due to the crisis that shook the Italian political system (Ginsborg 1996). The collapse of the traditional parties, the emergence of new political forces, and the loss of legitimacy of the political elite and institutions opened up a wide-ranging debate on the need to reform the overall architecture of the state.

As part of the institutional reform, the debate on decentralization from the national to local levels, which this chapter analyses, provides an interesting viewpoint for understanding the tensions between the need for renewal and resistance by a political system that, in the case of Italy, had been highly centralized, hyper-bureaucratic, and inefficient.

This chapter examines the debate that preceded the reform of Section 5 of the second part of the constitution, concerning the relocation of power between the national state and local authorities (Constitutional Law no. 3, 2001).[1]

SELECTION OF THE DEBATE

The debate taken into consideration in this chapter was not the only priority issue in Italian national politics in the 1990s. Other top-priority debates can be identified during the decade according to the criteria of scope, degree of conflict, range of public attention, and interest of major policy actors. A review of the parliamentary activities, political parties' programs, and opinion polls provided a list of hot issues in the 1990s. The top five that compose the universe of hot issues were the institutional reforms, the adoption of the euro, the reform of the labor market, the reform of pensions, and immigration.

The institutional reforms designed to modify the workings of the political system were at the center of the political agenda throughout the 1990s. Some of them, such as the reform of the judicial system, of the relationship between Parliament and government, and of the powers of the head of state and of the prime minister, are still being discussed. Others which have been adopted include the reform of the electoral systems for local and national assemblies, with a change from a proportional to a mainly majority system. The reforms were presented as being necessary for modernizing the state, but caused deep conflict among the political parties and were given considerable media coverage, involving the entire population, who in some cases were called upon to express their opinion by means of referendums.

Another question which was at the center of the political debate concerned the entry of Italy into the single European currency. The debate concerned not so much monetary union (as a founding member of the Common Market in 1957, Italy has a long-standing political commitment to Europe) but concerned more the type of economic policy measures to adopt in order to put public finances into order and reduce inflation and the national debt according to the parameters established at the European level. Political parties were divided between those who maintained that participation should not involve excessive reductions of public spending on pensions, social welfare, and health care and those that maintained the need to make considerable cuts in the welfare state, reducing taxation. Measures to reduce the deficit were adopted by the five-party government headed by Giuliano Amato (June 1992–April 1993) and by the "technical" government led by Carlo Azeglio Ciampi (April 1993–May 1994), which reduced public spending in a number of areas, including health and social security. They also introduced new taxes (on property and independent workers): a series of agreements on the cost of labor was signed by both sides of industry. These decisions were given considerable media coverage, in order to justify these restrictive measures in the eyes of the public. During the Prodi government (May 1996–October 1998), a special tax, referred to as the "tax for Europe", was adopted. Thanks to the economic policies adopted Italy became part of the euro zone.

A highly controversial matter that occupied the political agenda was that of the reform of the welfare state and in particular the reform of pensions. In Italy, the welfare model has long been based on the figure of the male worker as the only source of income for the family, and as a person with a permanent job. As a result, social policies have mainly focused on short-term support in the case of temporary wage losses during the person's working life, and on forms of long-term support for retirement. Lower than in other EU countries, the cost of welfare in Italy is tipped in favor of older people, with insufficient resources for social assistance, education, training, and the jobs market. In the nineties, a series of reforms (adopted between 1992 and 1997) established new rules for calculating pensions, increases in the age of retirement, stricter criteria for eligibility, and greater contributions (D'Ercole and Terribile, 1998). A more radical attempt at reform put forward by the Berslusconi government was contested by street demonstration. The debate is currently under way.

Another issue that was at the center of a heated debate concerned the labor market. Accelerated by the economic crisis that affected Italy in the early nineties and by the rising rate of unemployment, which according to all opinion polls was considered the most serious problem in the eyes of the public, the labor market reform introduced elements of deregulation by means of a series of laws approved by Parliament and agreed upon by both sides of industry (Guadagnini, 2001). The dominant issue was that only by introducing greater elements of flexibility would it become easier to create new jobs. Also in Italy, during the Center Left governments (1996–2001) there was a discussion about reducing the working week to thirty-five hours, but this did not lead to the results obtained in France.[2]

The second Berlusconi's government (created in 2001) tried to abolish some guarantees provided for by the workers' statute, such as dismissal with just cause (Accornero and Como 2003). It was highly opposed by mass mobilization; the debate divided the political parties not only into Left and Right, but also divided the various parties on the Left.

Finally, one issue that was at the center of political debate and that radically divided public opinion was that of immigration. Throughout the nineties, Italy—a country with a history of emigration rather than immigration—found itself facing waves of immigrants.[3] The debate was about how to regulate the influx, how to deal with illegal immigration, and, more in general, how to deal with the matter of giving immigrants civil and political rights, as well as the problem of coexistence and cultural integration.

The debate divided the political parties with on the one hand the extreme right-wing parties, such as the Northern League, associating immigration with a problem of security and joining the bandwagon of intolerance and, on the other, those attempting to find a means of integration. A reform adopted during the Center-Left governments (40/1998, the so-called Turco-Napolitano Law) (Koff, 2001) provided for detailed rules on the problem of regulating the flow of immigrants and of controlling and preventing illegal immigration. It introduced harsher sentences both for trafficking in women for prostitution and for those who employ illegal immigrants, establishing regulations for the expulsion of irregular immigrants and, on the other hand, defining the objectives of integration, delegating the authority for implementing integration programs to regional, provincial, and municipal administrations. The subject of immigration associated with crime and urban blight was widely used by the parties on the Right (in particular by the Northern League) in election campaigns during the 1990s (Colombo and Sciortino 2003). During the second Berlusconi government (2001–2006) a more restrictive immigration law was approved (189/2002). Among other regulations, it provided for stricter planning of immigration and reduced the duration of residence permits (idem).

Any one of these debates would be an interesting case to study in order to ascertain the impact of women's policy agencies and the women's movement on hot issues in the 1990s. However, we have decided to select the debate prior to the adoption of Constitutional Law no. 3 of 2001 for a number of reasons. The law had considerable scope: the reform of the state. It gave constitutional coverage to a number of provisions adopted in the 1990s concerning the decentralization of policy power from the national to the local level. A high number of people would be potentially affected by this reform. The debate about the decentralization and reorganization of local government caused considerable conflict between political parties, between the political elites in national government, and between political elites elected at the local level. Public opinion was divided between the rich north, which favored a form of devolution that might lead to financial autonomy and the possibility of adopting neoliberal policies, and the south, which feared it might lose the benefits it received through the national state (Lupo 1996). The debate was given much coverage in newspapers and high priority in the political agenda of the parties. Citizens were involved in the debate because the matter entered the electoral program of the parties and because they were called upon to confirm the above-mentioned law by means of a referendum.

THE WOMEN'S MOVEMENT IN THE 1990s

In the 1990s, the Italian women's movement was characterized by a multitude of groups with different goals and areas of operation. There are no systematic studies on the numbers, resources, activities, and operational models adopted by the numerous women's associations, centers, and groups. The lack of a complete picture of the activism and participation of women has helped create an idea of a crisis, if not the disappearance, of the women's movement. In actual fact, the number of associations—particular those that are small in size and that are active at local levels—seems to have increased. Various components of the movement can be seen. A vast group, which was clearly visible not only at the local but also at the national level, was that of the movement for equal gender representation in electoral posts and in the institutions. It included women in the political parties (mainly of the center-left-wing parties),

in the public administration, femocrats, women in the women's policy agencies at the local and national level, women elected at all levels, and women in
the trade unions.

Another part of the movement comprised associations for the promotion of
equal opportunities in the world of employment at all levels and in all jobs
(*Fidapa*/The Italian Federation of Women in Arts, Professions and Business,
Donne in carriera, *AIDDA*, the Association of Women Entrepreneurs and
Managers) and national associations such as *UDI*, *Arcidonna*, numerous *Casa
delle Donne* (House of Women), and collectives of women in various cities,
which supported the battles on issues promoted by female left-wing party
members and trade unions. Then there was the cultural part of the movement
which worked on women's identity and difference and consisted of the
groups set up in the 1970s and 1980s (such as the *Libreria delle
donne*/Women's Bookshop, the *Orlando* association, the *Libera Università
delle donne*, the *Società delle storiche*, etc.) and groups that brought women's
points of view inside other movements of so-called libertarian left-wing
movements (for peace, for the ecology, or against racism and globalization)
(Della Porta 2003, p. 60).

Finally, a vast component of the movement was that of associations and
groups acting at the local level. Many of them were institutionalized not-for-
profit associations which had a certain degree of professionalization. They
worked in the field of social services and in a number of policy areas:
women's health and culture, women's labor, violence against women, etc.
(Della Porta 2003). Many groups provided social services, particularly in the
field of maternity, women's diseases, and violence against women. For example, in the city of Turin alone, in the late 1990s there were no fewer than
twenty associations that worked on the issue of violence against women.
Many associations organized courses of a cultural or professional nature,
guidance courses for family problems, legal consultation, homeopathic med-
icines, music, and so on. They provided intercultural mediation services (such
as the association *Alma Mater*) and help lines on violence against women
(*Telefono Rosa*).

Compared with the 1970s, there was less ideological conflict, a more pragmatic approach, a positive attitude to the pluralism of groups and associations
and to alliances, and networking on practical objectives. The attitude towards
the institutions had changed: in the 1990s it was open to cooperation in an increasingly close relationship with local authorities. The fact that in most cases
women's organizations required public funding had increased awareness of
the importance of having women in political decision-making posts both at
local and at national levels.

Those who took part in the debate on the reform of the state were women
in the institutions and parties, women and associations who identified with

the movement for equal gender representation and, more in general, with the movement for promoting equal opportunities between men and women in social, economic, and political life. Grassroots groups did not take part directly, even though they were by no means hostile to the movement for a balanced gender representation within the institutions.

DEBATE: CONSTITUTIONAL REFORM NO. 3 OF OCTOBER 18, 2001: MODIFICATION TO SECTION V OF THE SECOND PART OF THE CONSTITUTION,[4] 1992–2001

How the Debate Came to the Public Agenda

The road to decentralization in Italy has been and still is anything but straightforward: It is a story of resistance, changes of mind, and about-turns. The constitution adopted in 1948 set up the Italian Republic as a central and unified state. Even though it provided for the creation of local governments at municipal, provincial, and regional levels, it was only in the late 1960s that the regions were actually set up.[5] The transfer of legislative and administrative functions to them did not substantially modify the traditionally centralized system.

The reform of the state had been on the agenda since the 1980s. The debate outlined the need to make the regional authorities, and the state mechanisms in general, more efficient. Even though a Bicameral Commission for Reforms (*Commissione bicamerale per le riforme*), chaired by Aldo Bozzi (1983–1985), was set up to implement the reform, no provisions were adopted (Fusaro, 1998).

In the 1990s, the overall reorganization of the state became a priority issue in the political agenda for the reasons we have mentioned above. There were a series of phases in the debate:

1. After the 1992 elections, in which the majority parties were defeated and the Northern League moved forward, a second Bicameral Commission for Reforms (September 1992–January 1994) took up the issue of decentralization. In this period, mention was not yet being made of federalism but of a "strong" regionalism, which would have given the regions the power of choosing their own form of government and their own electoral laws. The commission failed in its task due to lack of agreement between the parties.

   In March 1993, at the time of greatest crisis in the political parties, a significant reform was adopted (Law 81/1993). This provided for the direct election of mayors and presidents of the provincial governments (together with new regulations for the election of municipal and provincial councils). The debate outlined the need to strengthen the legitimacy, as well as the stability, of local government in order to achieve efficiency.

2. After the general elections of 1994 and the constitution of the Center Right government headed by Berlusconi, the revision of Part 2 of the constitution was entrusted to a committee chaired by Speroni (Northern League), the minister for institutional reforms. The committee put forward a proposal more oriented towards federalism, which granted the regions exclusive policymaking powers in a number of areas and provided for the creation of a second chamber, a senate representative of the regions. The project was neither discussed nor approved by the Parliament as it was submitted on December 21, 1994, just before Berlusconi's government resigned.

3. The 1996 elections brought good results for the Northern League (11 percent of the votes), victory to the Olive Tree Coalition (Ulivo, made up by Center Left parties) and the creation of a Center Left government: the reform on decentralization was one of the priorities to be tackled.

The debate outlined the need to decentralize and to simplify administrative and policymaking functions in order to make the state more efficient and citizen-friendly.

In 1997–1998, a series of reforms (referred to as the "Bassanini reforms" after the minister for the civil service) provided for the devolution of administrative functions from the center to the periphery in a number of policy-making areas including economic development and production, the labor market, the territory, environment and infrastructures, services for the person and for the community, and administration police (Ventura, 2002; Gilbert, 1999).[6]

In the same years (1997–1998), the constitutional reform of the state was included in the third Bicameral Commission for Constitutional Reforms presided over by Massimo D'Alema, leader of the Democratic Party of the Left (Vassallo, 1998). The project put forward by the commission was never approved by the Parliament due to disagreements between the political parties.

A few months after the failure of the D'Alema commission, new initiatives got under way. In 1999, Constitutional Law no. 1 of November 22 established the direct election of the president of the region and gave regional governments the power to adopt their own statutes. Regional governments were given the power to decide themselves—in accordance with the constitution but within their own statutes—the form of government and the fundamental principles for their organization and operations (Baldini and Vassallo, 2001).

In 2000, a decree law (Dds 56/00) abolished the transfer of funds from the state to the regions: these were to be replaced by funds raised through local taxation. All finance for health care was to be provided by regional funds. That same year, the so-called Stability Pact approved by the government obliged the regional and local governments to reduce their deficits: this had a considerable impact on health care, which constitutes 75 percent of regional spending (Maino, 2000).

Dominant Frame of the Debate

In the debate, "decentralization" was interpreted in different ways, ranging from a simple form of "advanced decentralization", more administrative than legislative, simply a method for bringing about reorganization of the public and administrative system, to a concept of a "competitive federalism" based on the political and legislative autonomy of the communities. It can be seen that there was a shift in topic in the various phases of the debate referred to above. In the first phase, the emphasis was on the need to implement "strong regionalism" in order to make the state more efficient and citizen-friendly. In the same years, the Northern League was gathering growing consent in the north, proposing a reform based on federalism justified by the argument that not only was the state inefficient and overextended, but it was also corrosive of market-based efficiency because it existed to redistribute resources from the "productive" north to the dependent south.

In the second phase (1994), which coincided with the first Berlusconi government and the presence of the League in the government, explicit reference was made to a federalism-based reform. In the third phase—that of the Center Left governments (1996–2001)—the adoption of the reforms mentioned to decentralize the administrative functions was motivated by the need to make the state not only more efficient but also more transparent and responsible towards the citizens. In the discussion on constitutional reform that took place in the third bicameral commission (1997–1998), explicit mention was made of a "federal organization" of the republic, even though the content of the project did not provide for a reorganization in a federal sense. The term appeared to be used to satisfy the electorate in the north of Italy, and the League voters who had achieved a very satisfactory result in the 1996 elections.

The highly controversial debate in Parliament that preceded the adoption of the constitutional reform (1999–2001) clearly reflected different political stances: that of the Center Right parties (*Forza Italia* and the Northern League), which held power in all the northern regions and were more oriented towards authorizing private institutions to provide services and towards full competition between service providers, and that of the Center Left parties, which were oriented towards strengthening the power of the regions, but coordinated centrally both in term of access to funds and in control of expenses. Center Left parties favored a form of decentralization that would not accentuate the imbalance between the regions: they stressed the need for cooperation and economic solidarity, uniformity, and standardization in order to guarantee minimum levels of services in all areas of the country.

The right-wing parties opposed the constitutional reform because it was not considered to be devolutionary enough: it gave too few exclusive legislative powers to the regions and it did not provide for a second chamber representative of the regions.

GENDERING THE DEBATE

Gender considerations were barely mentioned in the formal debate prior to the 1990s. At the beginning of the 1990s a number of actors (women in Center Left political parties, women members of Parliament, and femocrats of Center Left parties) succeeded in gendering the debate on the reform of the electoral system for the election of the mayor, the president of provinces, municipal and provincial councils (1993), and regional councils (1995). They asked for quotas to be adopted in the electoral laws in order to achieve a more balanced gender representation in decision-making bodies: Italy had one of the lowest percentages of women present in elective posts as compared to other European countries. The quota proposal gave rise to a lively debate that divided not only the right-wing parties from those of the Center Left but also the women's movement: cultural-centers-of-difference feminism opposed quotas in the electoral laws, as they regarded them as a measure to accept women's weakness. Quotas for candidates were finally adopted by the Parliament, but they were then abolished by the Constitutional Court in 1995 (Guadagnini 2005).

Gender issues were mentioned in the debates in the third Bicameral Commission for Constitutional Reforms (1997–1998) and on the "Bassanini reforms". The need for women to be involved in drafting the reform, both in the case of the constitution and in that of ordinary laws, was outlined by a number of actors, including the president of the third bicameral commission and secretary of the Democratic Party of the Left (PDS), Massimo D'Alema, who emphasized how there were too few women in the commission and how this showed the "insufficient attention paid by political parties to the political and civic participation of women". D'Alema outlined the need for consultation with women representatives and with women in Parliament, so that the reform could be drafted with "the objective of obtaining a more open state, closer to its citizens, able to better respond to the needs of a society in the process of change".[7]

Among the women who took part in the debate in the commission (the president of the National Commission for Equal Opportunities and women members of Parliament) the dominant issue was that the constitutional reform had to enclose amendments aimed at ensuring women's descriptive and substantial representation at all levels. Mentions were often made of the programs and documents adopted by the UN, the Council of Europe, and the European Union. Only if the reform provided for the principle of gender-balanced participation would the new institutional setup have a more solid democratic foundation, regaining the trust of citizens in the institutions and making them "more open and authoritative through the participation of all".[8] An amendment was finally included in the document adopted by the commission stating that regional laws should promote equal opportunities in the access to elective posts. The amendment proved to be an important precedent since it was included in the constitutional reform adopted in 2001.

In the debate on the reforms involving administrative decentralization, Minister Bassanini also stressed the need to involve women in the process of reform. He declared that the reform "needs women, their creativity and everyday experience, their ability to evaluate and monitor the process of change that the reforms introduce" (Commissione Nazionale per la parità e le pari opportunità, 1999, p. 27). According to the women who took part in the debate on the Bassanini reforms (women members of the Parliament of Center Left political parties, femocrats) since the reform was designed to reorganize and modernize the country, it had to enclose the principles of gender mainstreaming and empowerment of women as elements of authentic democracy. Women involved in the debate managed to obtain a series of amendments in the "Bassanini laws" concerning the promotion of equal opportunities in the policy areas assigned by the laws to the regions (labor market, economic development, etc.).[9]

Following on from the 1999 law that established that the regional governments could adopt their own statutes, women's movement advocates (women elected at the local level, women of political parties both of the Center Left and the Center Right, femocrats, experts) required that the new regional statutes should enclose, among their objectives, the achievement of gender equal opportunities in social, economic, and political life and in access to regional elective posts. The advocacy capacity of the women who took part in the debates on decentralization, in the different arenas, set an important precedent in the discussion in Parliament prior to the adoption of the constitutional reform of 2001.

POLICY OUTCOME

In March 2001, the constitutional law revising Section 5 of the second part of the constitution was passed. Fiercely challenged by the Center Right, it was approved under the Giuliano Amato's Center Left government, obtaining no more than the votes of the Center Left (which was then defeated in the elections shortly afterwards). The reform was later submitted to a constitutional referendum held on October 7, 2001, which had a positive outcome.[10] Even though it did not provided for a federalist reconfiguration of the state, it made important steps towards a stronger decentralization. In the new text for the constitution, regional legislation was placed on the same level as state legislation: the law clearly states that "legislative power is exercised *by the state and by* the regions in accordance with the Constitution". Regional laws are no longer submitted for government control although, should a regional law be considered contrary to the constitution, it can be contested before the Constitutional Court (Ventura 2002).

The law establishes that the state has exclusive legislative powers in the matters listed in detail: the list includes a regulation that gives the state the power to "establish the basic levels of service in terms of civil and social rights that must be guaranteed throughout the country". About thirty policy areas (including legislation concerning work and safety, education, pensions, health, and commerce) are subject to "concurrent legislation" by which the central state establishes the general principles of a given law, and the regions legislate within the established limits, although there is no list of issues on which the regions enjoy "exclusive" legislative powers (Cento Bull 2002). The law also contains reference to taxation federalism, including a commitment to economic solidarity for weaker regions that are at an economic disadvantage.

Administrative functions are entrusted to the municipalities, except in the case of metropolitan cities, provinces, and regions when it is necessary to ensure consistent exercise of these functions, in line with the principle of subsidiarity. The financial autonomy of local authorities is more pronounced. They are assigned not simply "their own taxation rights and revenues" for now "they have their own autonomous resources" and "establish and apply their own taxes and revenues" as well as taking their share of "the income from taxation from their own territory". The law has a clear limitation: no representation of the regions is foreseen at the parliamentary level through an upper chamber. The constitutional reform as well as the Bassanini reforms encountered a number of difficulties in their implementation due to the resistance of the central state's attempting to shed as few as possible of its functions and powers, while some regional governments attempted to secure as much power and resources—but not functions and tasks—as they could (Pasquino 2002)

A clause concerning equal opportunities in terms of access to electoral posts was included. Indeed, Article 3 of the law (which replaces the text of Article 117 of the constitution), clause 1, paragraph 7, states that "regional laws shall remove all obstacles to equal opportunities between men and women in social, cultural, and economic life, and promote equal opportunities for the access of women and men to electoral posts."

Even though the constitutional reform was an important step forward on the road to greater decentralization, it cannot be considered an end point in the debate on this issue. After the victory of the Center Right coalition in 2001, during the second Berlusconi government (2001–2006) a new constitutional reform to amend the reform discussed in this chapter was approved only with the votes of the Center Right majority. The law provided for the establishment of a "federal senate" for the representation of the regions, to replace today's higher chamber and for *exclusive* powers of legislation to be assigned to the regions, on matters of health assistance and organization, local police, school organization, and the drafting of school programs of specific regional interest (Cento Bull 2002). The law also introduced modifications to the powers of the prime minister and those of the president of the republic. The reform was not approved by the popular referendum held in June 2006.

MOVEMENT IMPACT

Women's movement actors saw the policy outcome as a victory for two reasons: the law establishes that there is a constitutional obligation for the regions to remove all obstacles to equal opportunities and makes it possible to adopt quotas in regional electoral laws. Approval of the amendment came about thanks to the capacity for advocacy of women in the various arenas of debate on decentralization from the third bicameral commission to the laws on the administrative decentralization (Bassanini laws). Within the third bicameral commission, women of the center left-wing parties managed to get the support of the president of the commission, Massimo D'Alema.

In the discussion in Parliament prior to the constitutional reform, it was mainly women members of Parliament in the Center Left parties, together with their party members, who supported the adoption of the amendment on equal opportunities, mentioned above. In the parliamentary vote on the reform, the Center Right women voted against the law, not because they were against the paragraph on equal opportunities, but for reasons of party discipline: indeed, the Center Right parties voted against the entire law.

According to the RNGS model, the impact of the movement can be defined as dual response: women were involved in the policymaking process and they obtained a favorable outcome. The paragraph enclosed in the constitutional law had significant effects. The statute passed by the Valle d'Aosta region had established that the lists of candidates should include representatives of both sexes. The statute was contested by the Berlusconi government, but was judged to be admissible by the Constitutional Court. In addition, the success achieved gave further impetus to the effort to modify Article 51 of the constitution, approved in February 2003, which established the constitutional obligation to promote equal access to elective posts in all elections (Guadagnini 2005).

WOMEN'S POLICY AGENCY ACTIVITIES

In the 1990s, women's policy agencies were more consolidated than in the previous decade. At the national level there were two national commissions. The National Committee for Implementation of the Principles of Equal Treatment and Opportunities between Workers of Both Sexes (*Comitato nazionale per l'attuazione dei principi di parità di trattamento e uguaglianza di opportunità tra lavoratori e lavoratrici*), created in 1983 at the Ministry of Labor, had the task of monitoring the implementation of the law on equality (Law 903/1977) and of promoting affirmative actions (Law 125/1991) (Guadagnini 1995). It consisted of representatives of the trade unions and employers and women's associations and movements. It had no mandate to intervene in the debate taken into consideration in this chapter.

The second commission, the National Commission for Equality and Equal Opportunities (NC), set up in 1984, attached to the Prime Minister's Office consisted of representatives of the political parties, both sides of industry, the most representative women's associations in the country, and other members of society. It had little funding, a modest staff, and a purely advisory mandate for all issues that did not concern employment, as these were seen to by the committee in the Ministry of Labour: it had a cross-sectional scope as the commission was involved in a wide range of issues pertaining to the social, economic, and political interests of women. The NC had made the advancement of women in decision-making arenas one of its most important objectives.

In addition to the two national commissions, in 1996, during the Center Left government, headed by Romano Prodi, a new agency was created—this was the Ministry for Equal Opportunities (without portfolio). It was given the tasks of preparing and developing governmental gender equality policies and of implementing the gender-mainstreaming strategy. It had limited economic means and resources. In 1997 a DPO (Department for Equal Opportunities) was also set up to provide support for the minister's activities.

At local levels, during the 1990s, commissions for equal opportunities were created in most of the regions, provinces, and municipalities.

The national commission took an active part in the debate. A work group on institutional reforms was set up within the commission. The minister for equal opportunities firmly supported and cooperated with the NC. In 1996, Minister Anna Finocchiaro (PDS-Democratic Party of the Left) adopted a directive approved by the government, which stated that the principles of gender mainstreaming and the empowerment of women should be applied in all policies. These were the key words used by the women's policy agencies to influence the debate. Since the discussion concerned one of the most important reforms concerning the transfer of policymaking and administrative powers to the local level, women's policy agencies demanded that not only should they be involved in the decision-making process but also that women's presence should be increased in local administrations.

A representative of the NC, Laura Cima, was nominated in the Technical Commission set up by Minister Bassanini for the reform of the public administration and for the decentralization of administrative and policymaking functions. A number of proposals were put forward: training programs for developing gender culture in the public administration, affirmative action to give women access to senior management positions, respect for the principle of equal opportunities in the new areas of responsibility attributed by the law to the local level (economic development, employment market), the creation in local governments of equal opportunities departments, and policies for reconciling work and family life. The president of the NC, Silvia Costa, took part in a hearing during the third bicameral commission (chaired by D'Alema), and obtained an amendment on equal opportunities to be included in the final document adopted by the commission. Women members of Parliament of all parties supported the amendment. The document was never approved by the Parliament, due to disagreements between political parties; nevertheless, the amendment was maintained in the debate in Parliament that preceded the adoption of the constitutional law and was finally approved.

After approval of the 1999 law, which gave the regional governments the right to adopt their own statutes, a network was set up between the national and the regional commissions for equal opportunities. This network came up with a series of proposals: the regional statutes were to include among their objectives that of promoting equal opportunities, the principle of gender-balanced representation was to be included in the electoral laws, and the role of the regional commissions for equal opportunities was to be reinforced.[11]

The national commission drew up a proposal that was discussed in a meeting with the regional commissions for equal opportunities (April 22, 2002) and that provided for the new regional electoral laws to include suitable mechanisms to ensure equal access and equal presence of the two sexes in the lists of candidates. It also stated that the regional statutes should include programs and initiatives to ensure a balanced presence of women and men at work, in caretaking activities, and in participation in social and cultural life. At the moment, most regional governments have not yet definitively adopted their statutes (Guadagnini 2003).

Women's policy agencies played a role which can be classified as insider because they incorporated the goals of the women's movement involved in the debate and they were successful in obtaining a favorable outcome.

WOMEN'S MOVEMENT CHARACTERISTICS

By the end of the 1990s, what I have called the movement for a gender-balanced representation in decision-making posts was in growth and close to the left. The movement's activists were to be found in the political parties, particularly those of the Left, in elective posts at national and local levels, and in the women's policy agencies. This movement gave rise to many initiatives. In Piedmont, the *Consulta delle Elette* was set up in 1996: this is a coordination and support organization for women of all parties elected in local administrations with the aim of increasing descriptive and substantial representation. An association called *Emily-Italia* made up by women of Center Left parties was also created.

One place where the women's movement was especially active was inside the Democratic Party of the Left (PDS). Thanks to a quota system adopted since the birth of the party (1991), at the end of the 1990s women achieved greater weight inside decision-making posts. The promotion of equal opportunities between men and women in all areas (in social, cultural, economic and political life) was included in the party's program.

Even though the women members of Parliament, femocrats at local and national levels, and experts who played an active role in the Bassanini reforms debate were mainly from the left-wing parties, women members of Parliament of all the parties supported the adoption of the amendment concerning equal opportunities in the third bicameral commission: there was no counter-movement on the issue. Women members of the Parliament of the Center Right party opposed the constitutional law adopted in 2001 not because of the paragraph concerning equal opportunities but to be loyal to their parties. The empowerment of women and gender mainstreaming in all policies were a high-priority issue for the movement.

POLICY ENVIRONMENT

Constitutional laws have to be approved twice by both branches of the Parliament (the Chamber of Deputies and the Senate). Since the third bicameral commission made up by members of the two chambers failed in achieving an agreement on the reform, the text of the law to be discussed and approved in Parliament was prepared by the *Commissione affari istituzionali* (Commission for Institutional Affairs) of the Chamber of Deputies and of the Senate.

Even though specific proposals on various aspects of the reform came from various actors, for instance the presidents of regions, the *Conferenza Stato Regioni* (Conference State-Regions), and the ANCI (*Associazione Comuni Italiani:* Association of Italian Municipalities) and the debate was open to different ideas, the final process was controlled by the majority in Parliament. The policy environment may be referred to as moderately closed.

A Center Left government led by Giuliano Amato (April 2000–April 2001) was in power. The constitutional law was voted on by the Chamber of Deputies on September 26 and by the Senate on November 17, 2000, and was approved again by the Chamber of Deputies on February 28 and by the Senate on March 8, 2001, just before the general political election of 2001, with the votes only of the Center Left parties and strong opposition from the Center Right coalition. Through this reform, the Center Left coalition hoped to regain the consent of that part of the electorate, especially in the north of Italy, that was in favor of a federalist reform of the state.

While the number of women in Parliament remained low (11 percent in 1996 elections), continuing internal party pressure from women of the left-wing parties and the advocacy capacity of the women's policy agencies all contributed to the creation of some channels through which women's issues could be raised and promoted.

The dominant frame of the public actors that mobilized around the issue stressed the need to make the decision-making process more efficient and to democratize public policy, bringing it closer to the citizenry through greater autonomy of local powers. The dominant frame of the debate matched women's demands for increasing representation, both descriptive and substantial, as a matter of democracy.

The debate took hold during the Center Left governments that came after the 1996 elections. The Center Left governments were characterized by some of the highest levels of female participation: three women ministers out of twenty-two in the Prodi government (May 1996–October 1998), six women ministers out of twenty-five in the D'Alema I and II governments (October 1998–April 2000), four out of twenty-four in the Amato government (May 2000–June 2001).

CONCLUSION

Notwithstanding a conventional opinion that the Italian women's movement is weak, fragmented, and divided, the movement that mobilized around the issue demonstrated a certain degree of cohesion and capacity for advocacy. The outcome of the debate was considered a success given the long-standing tradition of Italian policymakers' being resistant to gendering their approaches and mainstreaming women's rights. EU legislation and programs on gender equality, gender mainstreaming, and women's empowerment were widely mentioned and used by women's activists to support their claims and they may have been an important source of pressure on policymakers.

A number of reasons might explain the success. First of all the issue of increasing women's descriptive and substantial representation was a high priority for the movement due to the decrease in the number of women elected at all levels in the second half of the 1990s. Secondly, Center Left women members of Parliament succeeded in mobilizing support not only among party colleagues but also among women in other parties, at least during one phase of the debate: in the third bicameral commission, there was a cross-party agreement to introduce an amendment on equal opportunities of access to elective posts. In the final discussion and vote in Parliament (1999–2001), the women in the Center Right parties opposed the reform not because it contained an article that favored women, but because they had to vote in line with their parties. Thirdly, there was a synergy of action between the Center Left women in Parliament, the National Commission for Equal Opportunities, and the minister for equal opportunities. Fourth, the policy subsystem that adopted the law was controlled by a Center Left majority, making it possible for women's movement activists to get support for their claims.

Finally, one of the reasons that might explain the success is that the law was permissive: it simply stated a general principle that regional laws should remove all obstacles to equal opportunities between men and women in all fields and promote equal opportunities for access of women and men to electoral posts. It would then be up to regional legislators to adopt precise measures to implement the new terms of the constitution. In fact, the implementation of the law has been limited. In the regional elections held in April 2005, only five regions adopted a quota system which established that no more than two-thirds of candidates in the lists may be of the same gender. Only 11.49 percent of candidates elected to regional councils were women — a disappointing result.

We can conclude that if, on the one hand, the approval, within the constitutional reform discussed in this chapter, of an amendment on gender equal opportunities has to be considered a success, on the other hand, only the degree to which the reform will be implemented in the next years will give a measure of its effectiveness.

NOTES

1. Constitutional Law no. 3, 2001, concerned the fifteen ordinary regions (see note 5). In fact the reform of Section 5 of the second part of the Constitution involved also the five regions with special statutes (Constitutional Law no. 2, 2001). In the chapter we take into consideration the Constitutional Law no. 3, 2001, because it affected a greater number of regions.

2. See the chapter concerning France in this volume.

3. The number of immigrants doubled in Italy, passing from 1.1 percent of the population in 1993 to 2.2 percent in 2000 (Koff 2001, p. 187).

4. Published in the *Gazzetta Ufficiale* no. 248, October 24, 2001.

5. The constitution established the creation of five regions with special statutes giving them ample legislative and administrative autonomy, and fifteen ordinary regions with fewer legislative and administrative powers. Laws promulgated by ordinary regions were to concern only strictly established areas and they were to be subject to control not only by the government, but also by the national parliament.

6. See law no. 59/97, "Delega al Governo per il conferimento di funzioni e compiti alle regioni e agli enti locali" and the decree no. 112/98, "Conferimento di funzioni e compiti amministrativi dello Stato alle regioni e agli enti locali in attuazione della legge 15 marzo 1997, no 59".

7. See *Resoconto stenografico*, seduta n. 16, www.camera.t/bicam/rifcost/ressten/sed016rt.htm, p. 482.

8. See "Audizione della Presidente della Commissione Nazionale per le Pari Opportunità, Silvia Costa", www.camera.it/parlam/bicam/rifcost/ressten/sed016rt.htm, p. 483.

9. For example, in referring to the training activities assigned to the regional governments, decree 80/98 mentioned the "enhancement of women's specific qualities and the implementation of a gender culture". One article provided for the awarding of special facilitations, grants, incentives, etc., to businesses set up by women. As concerns regional labor policies, one amendment provided for initiatives to be planned to support equal opportunities policies, in particular the promotion of projects and incentives for new business activities set up by women. *Sportelli Donna*—women's bureaus—were provided to assist women wishing to set up businesses.

10. Thirty-four percent of eligible voters turned out for the referendum and 64.2 percent of these approved the motion to change the constitution, while 35.8 percent rejected it (Cento Bull, 2002, p. 219).

11. The proposal establishes that the equal opportunities commissions shall not be merely consultative organs, but shall have the power to intervene with a binding opinion at least as far as regional budgets are concerned and to monitor and report any discrimination to the council.

10

Electoral Reform in Mid-1990s Japan

Misako Iwamoto

The 1990s has been called both the age of reform and the lost decade in Japan. Social and political shifts in Japan in the late 1980s offered policy-makers an important opportunity to dislodge the conservative oligarchy that had ruled Japan since the Second World War. Many debates in the 1990s were concerned with the devolution from the state bureaucracy to the Diet members, the NPOs, businesses, and local governments. However, the most significant with respect to state change were proposals to replace the single non-transferable vote (SNTV) multiple district electoral system with a combination of single member districts and proportional representation. This reform promised to open up the system to more competition, and to represent groups that had previously been shut out from power. One of these "groups" was Japanese women. This policy debate occurred during a window of opportunity that briefly dislodged the power structure from its monopoly. At the same time, it reveals the adroitness of the conservative Japanese male hierarchy to regroup and adapt to protect their power.

JAPANESE POLITICS IN THE 1990s

From the late 1940s until 1990, Japanese politics had three major characteristics. First, male bureaucrats took charge of modernizing the state after the Meiji Restoration in 1868, importing institutions to catch up with the Western countries. The Japanese people, in accord with the Confucian idea that male bureaucrats should govern, regarded them as unselfish and superior. Second, from 1947 on a domestic "cold war" raged between conservatives and progressives. The Liberal Democratic Party (LDP) dominated the conservative arena and was steadfastly pro-American. The so-called progressive parties, such as the Socialist Party of Japan (SPJ) and the Japan Communist Party (JCP), were considered pro-Soviet or pro-China, objecting to the Japan-U.S. Security Treaty and to the reform of article 9 of the constitution of 1946—the peace clause which prohibits any armament. Third, the LDP, rallying supporters from the ultra-Right to the Center-Right, held executive power from 1955 to 1993 and had a monopoly on the distribution of state favors to maintain their power. The male LDP politicians indulged in pork barrel politics on a huge scale. At the same time, the party was composed of several factions which competed for dominance. I would like to add a fourth characteristic of the pre-1990 period: the exclusion of women from all political power (Iwamoto 1997, 2003).

Although women's suffrage was guaranteed by the 1946 constitution, Japanese women remained outsiders in politics. It was only in the latter half of the 1980s that women, led by Takako Doi, then female chair of the SPJ, burst onto the political scene in significant numbers, a change called the "Madonna Boom" (Iwamoto 2001b).[1] Women voters mobilized to challenge the introduction of a consumption tax, the inadequate welfare policy for the aged people tied to women's unpaid work, and widespread political corruption.

Although there were five factions in the LDP,[2] the faction of Kakuei Tanaka, the former prime minister, dominated the LDP after 1972. When Takeshita became leader of the faction in 1985, it became known as the *Keisei-Kai* faction. As the key negotiators in Japanese pork barrel politics this faction was blamed for the extensive corruption in Japanese politics. Nevertheless, Takeshita dominated the Keisei-Kai and the LDP even after his prime ministership, from his resignation in 1989 until his death in 2000. The Keisei-Kai continues to dominate prime ministers, who come from other small factions (Uno, Kaifu, Miyazawa, and Mori), giving them support and then manipulating them from behind the scenes.

A split in 1992 between the dominant Obuchi and smaller Hata subfactions in the Keisei-Kai led to the rare loss of power for the LPD from August 1993 to June 1994 (see table 10.1). The Hata faction, led by Ozawa, left the LDP in the dispute over political reform in July 1993. Under the new name of the Shinsei-to Party, it formed a non-LDP coalition government with six other parties including the SPJ. However, Ozawa quarreled with the SPJ, because, while he is neoconservative, the SPJ insisted on both the "welfare state" line and on remaining neutral in any international conflict. The Keisei-Kai tried to join hands with the SPJ and succeeded. The LDP, the SPJ, and the small Sakigake Party (the Forerunner) formed coalition governments from June 1994 to

Table 10.1.   Japanese Governments, 1989–2005

TERM	PRIME MINISTER	GOVERNING PARTIES	KEISEI-KAI DOMINANCE
1989 Aug–1991 Oct	KAIFU	LDP	STRONG
1991 Oct–1993 July	MIYAZAWA	LDP	STRONG
1993 Aug–1994 April	HOSOKAWA	NIHON-SHINTO; SPJ; KOMEITO; JDS; SAKIGAKE; SHINSEI-TO	—
1994 April–1994 June	HATA	NIHON-SHINTO; SHINSEI-TO; KOMEITO; JDS	—
1994 June–1996 Jan	MURAYAMA	SPJ; LDP; SAKIGAKE	WEAK
1996 Jan–1998 Aug	HASHIMOTO	LDP; SPJ; SAKIGAKE	MODERATE
1998 Sept–2000 May	OBUCHI	LDP; LIBERAL; KOMEITO	STRONG
2000 May–2001 March	MORI	LDP; KOMEITO; CONSERVATIVE	STRONG
2001 April–2006 Sept	KOIZUMI	LDP; KOMEITO	DECLINING

August 1998 (the SPJ's Murayama government and the LDP's Hashimoto government). Some structural reforms started under the LDP-SPJ-Sakigake coalition, for example the Non-Profit Organization Act, which provided for non-profit organizations' corporate rights, decentralization, long term care insurance, and the legal establishment of the women's political machinery.

After the LDP's defeat in the upper house election in July 1998, Hashimoto, a subleader of the Keisei-Kai, resigned as the prime minister and Obuchi, the successor as boss of Takeshita faction, became the president of the LDP. Obuchi chose the Komei-to Party,[3] which is supported by a Buddhist sect Soka-Gakkai, as his coalition partner, after he had already hooked Ozawa's Liberal Party. Obuchi suffered a stroke in May 2000 and Mori, who was the leader of a small faction,[4] became the prime minister. The Obuchi government collapsed after Ozawa left the coalition because Obuchi (and Mori) were not able to implement neoconservative reforms. As a prime minister, Mori, considered a puppet of the Keisei-Kai, was very unpopular, especially among women.

Koizumi, the subleader of the Mori faction, became president of the LDP in March 2001. He proved popular due to his distance from the Keisei-Kai. And at last at the snapshot dissolution in August 2005, Koizumi ran some "assassin" candidates against the boss politicians who voted against the post privatization bill and who all but one belong to other factions than Koizumi's. He stumped all over Japan for the assassins, one-third of whom are women, and won with all twenty-six women candidates including no assassins, giving him a new hero image. He as a successor of Fukuda faction, the biggest rival against Tanaka and Takeshita, defeated Keisei-Kai.

This brief review of the politics of coalitions in Japan in the 1990s shows that Japanese politics developed around the fortunes of Keisei-Kai. The dynamics set the stage for a struggle over the survival of Keisei-Kai's corrupt pork barrel politics.

SELECTION OF THE DEBATE

Identifying the Universe of Hot Issues

The top priority issues in 1990s Japan were the electoral reform, decentralization, the long-term care insurance, the fiscal crisis, and the Anti–Domestic Violence Act. I shall now examine these issues in turn showing their scope, degree of conflict, range of public attention, and policy actor agenda.

All the turmoil over the corruption based on LDP's monopoly in power (led by the Keisei-Kai faction) led to defections of LDP politicians to protest the corruption. This set the stage for consideration of a reform of the SNTV (single non-transferable vote) system for the powerful lower house of the Parliament.[5] The old system was based on mid-sized districts (three-five seats) and each voter had just one vote, and the winners were taken from the top vote getters. This meant that the LDP candidates often competed with each other, stimulating even more corruption through distribution of lucrative public construction projects and gifts of money at funerals and weddings. The reform proposal was to adopt a combination of single member seats and proportional representation. In addition, political subsidies were introduced with a view to ending the cozy relationship between political and business circles. After the departure of the LDP from power in August 1993, the bill for a system based on a combination of single seats and proportional representation was finally introduced. There was significant public attention to this issue because of the corruption, and the reform gave the voters a dream to finish all the illness in politics and money.

Decentralization policy abolished the notorious "organ delegation" system where ministries ordered prefectural governors from above in complete disregard of the arguments of local politicians. As for gubernatorial responsibility, self-government of the prefecture was only 30 percent of the job; the other 70 percent was essentially administration as an organ branch of the ministries. The abolishment of "organ delegation" and the reinforcement of the autonomy of local and prefectural governments in 2000 had the potential to be a revolutionary change (Nishio 1999). But the budgetary financial system remains centralized. It was a big mistake not to touch the financial system because one of the objectives of decentralization was to reduce the heavy national debt. This issue had less public attention than some of the others, but some members of coalition governments who were former governors and mayors took initiative of this reform.

The third issue was the introduction of the public long-term care insurance system in 1997, which began work in 2000. The new system ended the bureaucratic power to decide who should live in nursing homes. Aged people who need care became able to contract with companies and the NGOs, which offer care according to the degree of need, and the insurance pays 90 percent of the cost. However, the system doesn't work well. Because of low profits, the service supply falls short. Moreover, the 10 percent expense is sometimes prohibitively expensive for aged people. The sacrifice of the daughter-in-laws continues, as they are expected to take care of their aging families. This issue affected many families. It was considered as a serious culture crisis for some senior male politicians to end the Japanese virtue of taking care of aged people inside the same family, but many Japanese women welcomed the insurance.

The fourth major development was the fiscal crisis, which came as a result of economic stagnation since 1990. The public debt amounted to 700 trillion yen. Prime Minister Hashimoto kept close to the Ministry of Finance's balanced budget line. He raised consumption tax from 3 to 5 percent, and the patients' charge in public health insurance from 10 to 20 percent. However, his policy worsened the recession, and after losing the election of the House of Councilors in July 1998, he resigned. His successor, Obuchi, took the route of increasing public spending, especially in big construction. But his policy did not boost the economy either because the construction companies wasted vast amounts of money and did not stimulate general consumption. One of the main purposes of political reform was to abolish the iron triangle of the LDP politicians, the bureaucrats, and the old-fashioned kind of industries such as construction companies, but it failed. Prime Minister Koizumi was crying out for structural reform, including the reorganization of the construction companies and government spending. He faced big resistance from inside the LDP especially on the highway construction and the post privatization. His future is in doubt, and he may yet repeat the failure of Hashimoto. This is a high conflict issue and the stakes affect many politicians. It also has widespread impact, and has potential to attract public attention.

Finally, the Anti–Domestic Violence Act was proposed by the women members of the Research Committee of the Diverse Society, one of the standing committees in the upper house in 2000 (Fukushima, 2001). In such a bureaucratized society as Japan, private members' bills are very exceptional but are the primary way to bring women's and feminists' issues to the public agenda, because the male bureaucrats were never able to and still cannot propose or establish effective women's policies (Iwamoto 1997 pp. 28–35).

At the beginning of the 1990s, the term "domestic violence" in Japan meant that of children against parents. The dominance of the husband/father accorded with the traditional Japanese conception that the family composed an organic body and could not be separated. As a result, violence of the husband to the wife was not recognized as a social problem. Japanese feminists made a concerted effort to place the problem in the public sector as had been done in Western countries. The members of the Research Committee, a standing committee of the upper house, fought against conservative judicial bureaucrats to establish the protection order for victims of domestic violence (Iwamoto 2005). Ordinary Japanese women do not know much about the law. Although the survivors and the members of the private shelters were invited to testify, women senators did not receive enough support from women for their struggle, so the instituted protection order has many weak points and is hard to use.[6] This issue attracted attention of the small feminist community and the shelter movement, but did not have a high priority for the policymakers nor attract much public attention.

Identifying the Debate for Study

I have selected the electoral reform as the priority issue to analyze because it had the potential to have the biggest impact on state-society relations. Indeed, at the beginning of the 1990s, the mass media and male political scientists claimed that electoral reform would be an almighty magic wand, which would stop all the pork barrel politics, make politicians devote themselves to policy competition, and end the domination of the policymaking process by arrogant bureaucrats in Kasumigaseki, Tokyo. It meant the end of the dominance of the state over the society and an end to the fiscal crisis because conservative politicians would stop wasting public funds on favors to their clients.

In order to understand how these attempts at devolution never reach the goal, we must inspect the politics of the reform process. Despite a change to a mixed system, pork barrel politics survives and politicians remain service brokers in tight networks; bureaucrats remain unaccountable for using their autonomous power. But the change in the electoral system strengthens the power of the LDP president against faction bosses. Koizumi succeeded in cutting the public construction budget by half. NGOs, including the women's associations such as private shelters, the businesses, and the citizens can only partially share in "the public domain". The politicians don't become a liaison between the state and wider civil society of both sexes.

THE WOMEN'S MOVEMENT IN THE 1990s

Women's political activism in Japan has developed slowly, especially in comparison with movements in the Western democracies. Whereas much of the energy behind movement activism in the 1960s and 1970s in the U.S., for example, came from married women not content to limit their lives to home and family, at the same time, the baby boom mothers in Japan were the first generation of middle-class housewives. They admired the status and role of the housewife very much, seeing it in contrast to their own their mothers who were the weak and overworked daughter-in-laws of farmers' or merchants' families. These baby boom mothers focused on ensuring that their children were prepared for difficult and very competitive entrance examinations for higher education.

Moreover, in the early 1970s, the Japanese women hated "the political". For them politics meant one of two choices: either the corrupt conspiracy between the LDP male politicians and the male bureaucrats, or supporting a communist revolution more radical than the Soviet case. The male leaders of the radical communists ordered the women members not to follow the feminist cause but the cause of class (Iwamoto 2001c).[7] Unlike in Western countries, Japanese feminists were too weak to promote the feminist mantra "The Personal Is Political" to counter the domination of the male radical communists. In any event, almost all radical movements were bankrupted after the Asama incident in March 1972, where one radical communist group barricaded themselves in the mountains and killed each other in the name of the revolution. When it was discovered that one of the leader communists was a woman, then "revolutionary women" came to mean "mad killers". It took another fifteen years for Japanese women to reenter into politics, not by means of violence, but by means of elections. This was the "Madonna Boom".

In the latter half of the 1980s, after the end of their children's high school or university entrance examinations, the first generation of housewife mothers faced an identity crisis like the Western women of 1960s. In the 1970s–1980s, awakened housewives took part in citizens' movements in areas such as welfare, education, and the environment. Working women began to support feminist movements. These two groups at times have worked together, for example, in order to keep abortion legal in 1972–1974 and 1982–1983. However, because of the tough division of labor between men and women and the long working hours of male workers, it is very hard for mothers to stay in the workforce. The feminist culture of single working women is alien to many housewives who are totally dependent on their husbands' wages. Housewives as well as feminists were excited by the Madonna Boom of the latter half of the 1980s. But new women members of the Diet

sometimes lacked the specialized training of law, negotiation, or management, and failed to meet their responsibilities. The higher ambitions brought
the bigger disappointment.

At the beginning of the 1990s, Japanese women were disappointed by a series of events: the end of the Madonna Boom, the bursting of the economy
bubble (which gave women many work opportunities), and the fall of the Soviet Union. Till then, Japanese women's and feminist movements were close
to the Left, i.e., the SPJ and the JCP, but these left-wing parties could not adjust to the post-Soviet era and proceeded to lose women's support.

In the mid-1990s, Japanese women awoke to problems such as domestic
violence and the scarcity of women politicians especially at the local level.
They were much influenced by the UN conference in Vienna in 1993 on human rights and the UN women's conference in Beijing in 1995. The women's
movement, like other citizens' movements in Japan, shifted from protesting
against the establishment to developing their own alternative proposals at this
time. In the latter half of the 1990s, women's groups proposed the drafts of
the Anti–Domestic Violence Act and developed many training classes for
women candidates, as well as providing funds for them. These movement activists have a strong feminist orientation, but are not a united movement on
the national level; there are no strong lobbying organizations in Tokyo working to influence legislators in the Diet and the bureaucrats. Rather, they are
loose federations of the local movements here and there.

DEBATE ON ELECTORAL REFORM 1991–1994

How the Debate Came to the Public Agenda

The growing scandals over corruption in the government brought an electoral
reform plan to policy arenas in the legislature. For example, in 1988, it was
revealed that the real estate company Recruit-Cosmos had sent investment
letter stock to the LDP faction leaders, and lent 500 million yen to the prime
minister of the time, Takeshita. In December of the same year, a group of
young Diet members introduced "The Proposal for Political Reform". In November 1988 the LDP Political Reform Committee was established and it released "The Political Reform Program", which included electoral reforms, in
May 1989 to dodge the critique against the LDP as a system of corruption. In
the elections of the upper house in June 1989, the LDP was defeated. The
LDP and the Keisei-Kai then rallied with the puppet prime minister Kaifu,
who was then a subleader of a small Miki faction. He declared he would reform the mid-sized district SNTV electoral system of the lower house. The
government advisory committee on the electoral system suggested the com-

bined system of single seats and proportional representation. Kaifu added a measure providing for public subsidies to the political parties and proposed this package of political reforms to the Diet in August 1991. Nevertheless, when the LDP factions resisted, the proposal failed and Kaifu resigned as prime minister in October 1991.

The mass media, however, liked the claim that the mid-sized district SNTV system was the root of all evil in Japanese politics and supported the idea of combined single member seats with proportional representation. This combination provided for a closer relationship between voters and their representatives with single member districts as well as preserving the survival of the small opposition parties through proportional representation. The Socialists and the Komei-to Party proposed a German-style combination, and in April 1993, the *Minkan-Seiji-Rincho* (Private and Provisional Council of Political Reform),[8] organized by business, labor, and male opinion leaders, proposed a similar combined system (Minkan-Seji-Rincho 1993).

Dominant Frame of the Debate

The frame of the debate began by posing "the innovators versus the old reactionaries". Those who called themselves innovators were the Ozawa group, the Nihon-Shinto Party, the Sakigake, and those who wanted the reform both in the LDP and the SPJ. Some male political scientists said that the change of the electoral system was indispensable for the power shift (Horie 1993, Sasaki 1989, 1991, 1992a, 1992b, 1995, Yamaguchi 1993).[9] The term "old reactionaries" was applied to all those who objected to political reform.

The next prime minister, Miyazawa, obstructed by LDP leaders, was unable to move further to promote electoral reform. The debate at this time focused on the particular type of electoral system to put in place. The dominant Keisei-Kai faction supported an all single-seat system, which was damned by both the opposition parties and public opinion and was impossible to pass through the Diet. By taking this stand, which they no doubt knew would never pass, the LDP male senior politicians hoped to keep the old system and the advantages they derived from the local support clubs, formed through exchanges of votes for budgetary appropriations.

In early 1992, the debate shifted to focus more directly on corruption. Before the election of the upper house in June 1992, several amateur politicians and Hosokawa, a former LDP politician and former governor of Kumamoto prefecture, organized the Nihon-Shinto Party. They demanded political reform and succeeded in winning four seats. In the latter half of 1992 and in the first half of 1993, Japanese politics was boiling over the issue of political reform especially after it was revealed that Kanamaru, the godfather of the Keisei-Kai, had violated the regulations of political finance and evaded being taxed.

In June 1993, the opposition parties brought forth a resolution of no confidence. One faction-crossing group (later to become the Sakigake Party) led by Takemura, abstained. The Hata faction (later to become the Shinsei-to Party), led by Ozawa, voted no confidence. Miyazawa did not resign, but did dissolve the lower house. The Sakigake group withdrew from the LDP and banded with the Nihon-Shinto Party. They were now to get the deciding vote on whether the LDP kept power or not. At the same time, the Hata faction left the LDP, too. In the election of the lower house in July 1993 it was said that even a monkey running as the candidate of the Nihon-Shinto Party would have won, and it got thirty-five seats while the LDP had lost its single majority. The opposition parties including the Shinsei-to Party and the SPJ (excluding the JCP) decided to agree with the Nihon-Shinto Party and the Sakigake in accepting their proposal of a combination of single seats and the proportional representation; half the seats were to be elected by national proportional representation and the other half were to be occupied by the winners of single seats. The LDP also decided to accept the offer of the new parties, but it was too late to save their government.

In September 1993, the frame came to focus on the particular balance of single-member seats versus proportional representation seats. The Hosokawa government advanced a political reform package with 250 single seats and national proportional representation of 250 seats in September 1993. In fact an amendment proposing 274 single seats with national proportional representation for 226 seats was proposed in October 1993 after negotiation under the table with the opposition LDP. For the LDP senior members, more single seats were better to keep their support club system alive. On the other hand, anti-LDP politicians thought that to widen proportional representation was more democratic. And some radical Socialist politicians thought that even combined with proportional representation, single seats might allow too much power for the LDP and enable the abolishment of the peace clause of the constitution. They said it was the destruction of Japanese democracy. Hosokawa had to negotiate with the LDP because these radicals in the SPJ might have voted against the government's proposal.

Gendering the Debate

Mariko Mitsui was one of the few women who participated in the political reform debate. A former member of the Tokyo Metropolitan Assembly elected in 1988, she introduced the Nordic Quota into Japan (Mitsui 1992). It was difficult to gain support for such a reform. Elite women, who love the idea of self-help, and common women not sensitive to the feminist cause had little knowledge of the idea of quotas. In fact, words such as "underrepresentation"

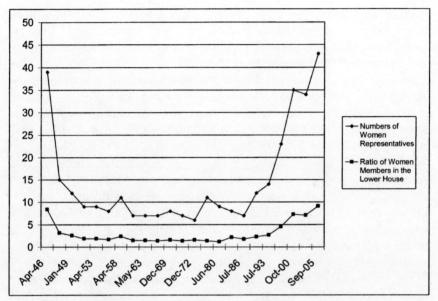

Figure 10.1. The Number and Ratio of Women Representatives of the Lower House

and "overrepresentation" were seldom found in Japanese political science textbooks, whose only exception was referring to the overrepresentation of the rural area. Since 1947 to 1993 with the mid-sized SNTV, Japan recorded a lower ratio of women representatives than the countries where the lower house members are elected through single seats such as UK, France and USA.

Because of the mid-sized SNTV in each district, every faction of the LDP and every opposition party wanted to run one candidate, the selection of the candidates was a zero sum situation, so the faction bosses and the opposition leaders strongly preferred male to female candidates. For example, in the three-seat constituency, Party A may run one or two candidates. By running two candidates, Party A risks splitting its vote, because the three other party candidates could win more votes than Party A's two candidates. However, if Party A runs only one candidate, it risks loosing the seat it could have gained through a better division of votes. So how many candidates to nominate was a top strategic secret of the LDP and sometimes of the SPJ. No transparency in nominating candidates prevented women from being selected. Before 1996, only the 1946 election was held with a plural ballot, when thirty-nine women representatives were elected, and it kept the record until Koizumi won with women assassins in 2005.

There were no textbooks which noted the underrepresentation of women before 1996 (Abe 1996), let alone such concepts as "critical mass". Even after the Madonna Boom of the SPJ, politics was a "men's matter" conforming to the stereotype of Confucianism. At the beginning of the 1990s when the election reform was the biggest issue, Japanese women did not have the capability to suggest any idea of the quota as a realistic alternative, nor the idea of linking the political subsidy with increasing the number of women candidates, like France. The movements to train the women candidates had only just gotten under way in 1993. The first of them is the Political School for Women by the Nihon-Shinto Party.[10] The second, which started in 1994, is the Political Participating School of Ichikawa Fusae by the Memorial Association for Fusae Ichikawa, a late prominent Japanese woman suffragist. And the training classes for women candidates of local assemblies, so-called backup schools, started after UN Beijing Women's Conference in 1995 across the country. But these movements were motivated by disappointment that almost all women were excluded from the debate of the election reform.

The theorem that the proportional representation system promotes more women in politics than the single-seat system was popular among Japanese women. They did not know, however, that even with the single-seat system, the party can promote more women candidates by the national coordination of the party executive (similar to the British Labor Party after 1992). Some of so-called Madonnas shared the opposition to the single-seat system, and voted against the Political Reform Package proposed by the Hosokawa cabinet on January 21, 1994.

Policy Outcome

The bill passed the lower house in November but in the upper house seventeen Socialists opposed, and the bill was rejected on January 21, 1994.[11] Hosokawa had to negotiate with the LDP openly, and they came to an agreement at the end of January. The combination of three hundred single seats and proportional representation of two hundred seats[12] through eleven regional blocs passed the Diet on March 4, 1994. It meant that as a consequence of the radicals' own objections, the number of single seats increased. Among them there were some women Socialists who had been elected in 1989 and were known as Madonnas.

After the return to power of the LDP with SPJ and Sakigake, the male politicians of the LDP, including the Keisei-Kai, reconstructed their support club system with minor changes to fit the new electoral system. The old parts of the mid-sized districts were treated as if they had been the fiefs of the incumbents of the LDP. For example, old mid-sized District A was divided into three new single-seat districts: A, B, and C. When the Incumbent A decided to run from the new District A, he gave the list of his supporters of the new District B to the Incumbent B, who decided to run from the new District B, instead of the list of D's supporters in the District A. And E also gave the possible candidate F, who decided to run from the new District C, the list of E's supporters of the District C, instead of the list of G's (late representative and F's father-in-law) supporters in the new District A.

In October 1996 the first election under the combination of single seats and proportional representation was held. The LDP got 239 seats out of 500. It could not recover its single majority but it kept forming the coalition with the SPJ and the Sakigake. The Keisei-Kai-dominated support club system survived through this electoral success. After the election, the party went to work on independent members and the members of the other parties to join the LDP in order to recover the single majority.

Some male political scientists argue that if the LDP had been out of office for more than two years, the support club system would have ended. Being an opposition party meant it could not touch the national budget or receive political money from business interests; Japanese political money prefers the governing party or parties very much. The change of the electoral system was not a panacea. The behavior of the SPJ, which allowed the LDP to return power after eleven months' absence, was fatal. It ensured the survival of the triangle consisting of LDP politicians, bureaucrats, and such kind of industries which depend on the subsidy of the state. This triangle resists any devolution from state bureaucracy.

The combination of single seats and proportional representation did succeed in pushing more women into the lower house. Although there were only fourteen women members of the lower house in 1993, and even fewer before that, this number rose to twenty-three in 1996, thirty-five in 2000, thirty-four in 2003, and forty-three in 2005 (9 percent). Feminist criticism against the new system was revealed as a mistake. After the Madonna Boom, women were able to run more easily, but without any affirmative action, it is difficult to make a dramatic increase in the representation of women.

Women's Movement Impact

Women's movement actors wanted electoral reform, but they failed to articulate a claim for using the electoral reform to improve the representation of women in the legislature. In fact, this failure stimulated some activities after the reform passed to train women and demand quotas. The electoral reform which abolished the old electoral system coincided with the general goals of women's movement activists; however, the debate was not gendered and there was no attention to the issues of women's representation in the debate or the outcome. In fact without any affirmative action, the political reform package was not attractive for women. Further, some feminists objected to the reform because it promoted the single-seat system. Women's movement activists were present in the policy debate, but only a few articulated women's movement goals of quotas. Still, their presence is sufficient to classify this debate as an example of *co-optation*—women' movement actors obtained procedural access through their representation in the legislature (a result of the Madonna Boom) but they did not obtain a policy that coincided with their demands.

Women's Policy Agencies and Characteristics

At the time of the debate there were two women's policy agencies (WPAs). The Section on Gender Equality in the Prime Minister's Office was established in 1975 by an agreement of the Miki cabinet. It was charged with concern for all women's issues; like other Japanese bureaus and sections it was exclusively made up of permanent bureaucrats. Certain high-spending ministries and the Ministry of Finance hold a great deal of power and interest. Other coordinating ministries like the Ministry of Environment have very little power and almost no interest. The Section of Gender Equality is of the latter type. According to the Confucian way of thinking, the officials charged with particular tasks may not make any mistakes, and the rivalry over territory is very strong. The section employees continue to feel ill at ease among the more powerful ministries. The women/feminist issues are inter-ministerial in nature. In the bureaucratic culture, where no (male) bureaucrat is willing to change his original ideas, women's political machinery cannot challenge the decision of any other ministry. Moreover, administrative bodies are not supposed to intervene in legislative matters, thus the section has no opinion about political reform (Nuita 2002) and is *symbolic*. The section has given no money to women's groups.

The second WPA is the Advisory Committee on Gender Equality, which reports to the prime minister. However, until 1997 it had no legal basis nor was it permanent. In 1997 under the Hashimoto (LDP), Doi (SPJ), and Domoto (Sakigake) coalition (the latter two are women), it was finally established by law. At this point it began pushing for the basic law on gender equality, and new measures against domestic violence. However, it remains very modest about political representation. Therefore during the debate on electoral reform, this WPA, too, was *symbolic*.

Women's Movement Characteristics

Although there was some interest from the women's movement activists in the electoral reform debate, they were not well organized to promote a campaign. Nor did they agree on the particular reform they preferred. The priorities of the feminist movement at the beginning of the 1990s were in reducing job entrance barriers for female students graduating from university, and forcing the Japanese government to accept blame for the sexual slavery at the time of the Asian and Pacific War (W.W. II). Women's initiatives in politics had cooled by the end of the Madonna Boom. Many women were not interested in the discussion of electoral reform, thinking that it was a "men's matter". A few women, including Diet members, moved against the introduction of the single seats. No party linked the discussion of the electoral system with women's progress into politics.

Around 1994 another issue was on their agenda—a proposal to reform the civil code to afford women the ability to keep their maiden names (the "family part" of Japanese civil code was reformed drastically by the General Headquarters of the occupying army just after World War II. The new spouses can choose either family name, though they choose the husband's family name in 97 percent of legal marriages) (Nihon 1994). The advisory committee of the Ministry of Law reported the reform of the code to afford both spouses to keep their family names; it meant that the bureaucrats of the ministry accepted the change. But the reform failed because of the strong opposition of the male senior Diet members of the LDP before the reform bill was proposed to the Diet.

It is clear at this time that the movement was in an emerging stage, and was just finding its way in the complicated maze of Japanese policy processes. The leaders of the Japanese women's movement believed naively that "our propose should and could be realized because it is right", at the time. They didn't understand the necessity of tactics both in the Diet session and in the pre-decision process of the Diet. The movement of the 1990s maintained its distance from the Left. SPJ remained an ideological rather than a pragmatic party, and it never really opened up to common people of both sexes. It continued to be an organization of the male trade unionists, especially from the public sector.

The strongest resistance to the women's movement and their effort to push more women candidates was not a counter-movement. Elections of local assemblies are held by mid-sized or big-sized districts (maximum 120 seats) with one-vote electoral systems. Male notables in the community select a male candidate (supposedly independent) in each smaller area of the district and the inhabitants are quietly encouraged to vote for him "in order to keep the harmony of the community". To be selected as the candidate of a small area means almost certain victory, and he proceeds to work for the local branch of the LDP at the time of national elections. In the local assemblies, the ratio of women representatives was less than that of national Diet till 2003. This exclusion of women's political initiatives at the local level and the rule of the LDP in general are stronger in more rural regions.

One part of the reason is that before the popularization of Windows 95, journalists, professors, and bureaucrats, over 90 percent of whom were men, monopolized the import of foreign information. An issue like the women's quota, which doesn't fit the interests of these people, was not selected as the matter to be imported and discussed. The indifference of the political parties led to independent female candidates running at the local level after the mid-1990s. Some of them now condemn not "the political", but "the political parties" (Teramachi 2002).

Policy Environment

After the revelations about the Recruitment scandal in the mass media, the public opinion turned against the corruptive tendencies of the LDP. In order to dodge the critique against it, LDP managed the discourse strategy to characterize not the LDP but the mid-sized district as the root of all evil. Soon, the attention of the mass media was channeled toward the electoral reform. The Keisei-Kai was split into those who would like to champion the interests consolidated under the mid-sized district (Obuchi faction) and those who supported the political reform (Hata faction). The Shinsei-to Party, former Hata faction of the LDP, was welcomed as one of the new parties like Sakigake and Nihon-Shinto Party. They became very popular in the mass media instead of Doi at the time of the Madonna Boom. The governing coalition of the center was composed of Nihon-Shinto, SPJ, Komei-to, JDS, Sakigake, and Shinsei-to parties, which were in power during the debate.

This fragmentation of the factions in the LDP dislodged, for a time, the monopoly on power exercised by the conservatives. Thus, there was a window for political reform. The policy subsystem in the Diet and the Senate was opened to influence from mass media and public opinion. The eighth Governmental Advisory Committee of the Election System suggested a combination system of the single seats and the proportional representation. Almost all party politicians took part in the debate. They included both the reformers and the opponents of the LDP, reformers and opponents of SPJ, Komei-to Party, which joined with the reformers of the SPJ to suggest a combined system, JCP (opposition), the Nihon-Shinto Party, Sakigake and Hata faction of the LDP, which became Shinsei-to Party. Outside the Diet there were the Minkan-Seiji-Rincho, male political scientists (many reformers and a few opponents), and the National Federation of Feminist Representatives including Mitsui. The Political School for Women of the Nihon-Shinto Party and the Political School of Ichikawa Fusae were not involved in the debate of the election reform.

We can conclude that the policy subsystem was moderately closed, in that the old chain of command (politicians, bureaucrats, and local supporters) had broken down briefly and the new one had not yet been established. Common Japanese people could declare their opinion whether for or against the election reform by faxes to the political parties and to the mass media. In Japan, alphabet typing had not been used; usually, the facsimile, which can send the written letters, was very popular. Before popularization of multipurpose computers connected to the Internet in the latter half of the 1990s, the Japanese word processor was very popular. In 1993 people sent both the written letters and typed letters of the word processor by the facsimile to the parties and the TV show among the party leaders.

Despite this openness, negotiations inside the legislature were necessary to enact the final legislation. After establishment of the Hosokawa government, dealing with the Socialist radicals safely became the biggest puzzling problem. In order to pass the Election Reform Package through the Diet, the leaders of the non-LDP coalition negotiated under the table with Kohno, the then president of the LDP. After the package was introduced into the Diet, the tension among the mainstream of the coalition, the Socialist radicals, and certain members of LDP who might vote for the package contrary to the party discipline of the LDP was reinforced. After it passed the lower house, the special committee of upper house became the heated arena. Because of the opposition of seventeen of the Socialist senators, the package failed. Then the negotiation between Prime Minister Hosokawa and the LDP president Kohno became the real arena and this arena was closed. Hosokawa compromised and increased the ratio of the single seats and divided the national proportional representation into eleven regional blocs, which favors the large parties. And the revised package was approved.

CONCLUSION

The year 1990 was an important turning point in Japanese politics. About this time, the catch-up-style modernization of Japan succeeded and finished. It meant the end of policy leadership by the senior male bureaucrats and the need for a new type of leadership with its roots in civil society. From 1986 to 1990, women politicians led by Doi seemed to fit the bill for this new type of leadership. However, lacking training in management skills, some new women politicians suffered from their professional shortcomings and have failed to be reelected.

In 1990 as well, the cold war ended. It then seemed logical to overhaul the electoral system, which had been introduced in 1947 to exclude Socialists and Communists from power.[13] Many hoped that competition by ideology and clientelism would give way to the competition by party policies and programs. If this had occurred, it might have paved the way for devolution reforms. However, the rapid comeback of the LDP to power in July 1994 allowed traditional pork barrel politics and autonomous bureaucratic power to continue.

The policy debate on electoral reform found women's movement actors with some presence in the legislative policy arena; however they found limited opportunity to promote their ideas for positive action to promote women's representation in the new system. Despite the Madonna Boom of the late 1980s, women's representation in elected office was one of the lowest among postindustrial democracies. The content of the reform—a mixed single seat/proportional representation system—appeared to respond to the factional politics of Japanese legislative parties and leaders. But Koizumi, lacking the sympathy for the electoral reform in 1993–1994 because the new system would make the party executive more powerful than the faction bosses, dissolved the lower house in August 2005 with tough nomination of "assassin" candidates over the faction bosses. He utilized at most the new electoral system. He ran twenty-six women, the record for the LDP, to the single seat with the safe seats of the upper rank in the bound lists of the proportional representation through eleven blocs. So he proved that the new system is not per se anti-women.

Concerning the electoral reform, the state response was co-optation and the women's policy agencies were symbolic, having been restricted from getting involved in such policy proposals. The movement, in the growth stage, stayed distant from the Left. The actors were not cohesive in their demands nor did they consider electoral reform to be a top priority despite widespread support among women's public opinion for change. The JCP, one of the Left parties, objected to the political reform and its influence was weak. The SPJ, the other Left party and one party of the Hosokawa coalition government, was split into the reformers and the objectors, so the influence of the party was not strong. The Hosokawa coalition, the center government, was able to get the reform through. The policy subsystem, because of the defection of LDP factions from their party, was moderately closed during the debate.

Despite what appeared to be a major change in the electoral system, LDP-centered coalitions continue to this day. In 2004, it is said that Koizumi compromised with the upper house Keisei-Kai, but he blew off almost all of the power of Keisei-Kai by the dissolution of the lower house in August 2005.

At the September election Koizumi ran the "assassins" against the broker politicians who voted against the post privatization bill and were supported by the local male notables including the half-official half-private small post office masters. These notables have been the key members of "the harmony of the community". After the "assassin" election, the continued rule of male senior notables as clients of state favors faces a big crisis. Koizumi wanted to shift the base of the LDP from the declining local notables to the urban independent voters including young and middle-aged women. In the urban regions, voters began to complain about budget distribution in favor of the rural regions, in the form of wasteful public construction projects. So some governors began to challenge the pork barrel of the LDP dominating system. In 2000 for the first time in Japanese history two women won elections for governor. Today, women governors comprise five out of forty-seven prefectures. And one of them, Domoto, is on the line of these "new governors".

Koizumi tried to show himself as woman-friendly, for example with five women ministers in his first cabinet. But his woman-friendly style appears to be a sham, as he does not connect to women's grassroots initiatives. Some of his women "assassin" candidates are famous for their anti-gender-equality policies. On the other hand, he set a fresh woman representative on the newly established Ministry of Gender Equality. Japanese women are now watching which of the women LDP representatives are woman-friendly or others are neoconservative or neoliberal.

At the local level, women began training female candidates and raising funds for them after the mid-1990s (Iwamoto 2001a). This is, in effect, a rebellion against the rule by the grassroots patriarchy, the suffocating aspect of the Keisei-Kai dominance. Women's initiatives face the mid-sized or big-sized one-vote system in local elections, which makes the coordination among women candidates difficult at the same time as the selection of the male candidate by the male notables. Changing the electoral system of local assemblies, for example, by the introduction of the plural vote, may yet dramatically favor women candidates.[14] In addition, after Koizumi's assassin election in 2005, Japanese women should study the electoral system, the party quota, and the quota by law around the world to utilize the electoral systems of both houses and to offer a new electoral system of the local assemblies.

NOTES

1.

Table 10.2. Women's Political Representation, 1986–1998

Women Politicians	1986	1989	1998	2005
Upper House	8.8%	13.1%	17.1%	13.6%
Lower House	1.4%	2.4%	7.3%	9.0%
	1987	1991	1999	2005
Local Assemblies	2.3%	3.1%	5.9%	8.0%

2. The LPD in the 1980s was composed of five big fractions, i. e., the rightist and militarist Nakasone faction (pursued the neoliberal policy in the early half of the 1980s and got off it because of the recession), also rightist Fukuda faction, Tanaka-Takeshita faction (favors the huge public construction and the spending to support weak business), Ohira-Miyazawa faction (prefers economy to military and favors the balanced budget), and Miki faction (the most liberal in the LDP and the most critical of the political corruption).

3. Though from 1964–1970, the Komei-to Party tried to make their Buddhism the state religion; after the criticism regarding the separation between religion and government, it changed to say that it is a secular and centrist party.

4. Sintaro Abe (the late father of Shinzo Abe, the prime minister since September 2006) took over the Fukuda faction, but died of illness before he became the prime minister. Mori took over that faction, and Koizumi and Shinzo Abe were its subleaders.

5. The power of the upper house is strong. If it decides other than the lower house, the lower house can revise the decision only with a two-thirds majority. Such a case has never occurred.

6. The domestic violence act was reformed by the women senators of the Research Committee in 2004 to lengthen the term of protection order and so on.

7. In Japan, fewer women had higher education than in Western countries. So women participants of the youth protests were rarer. The middle-class women who graduated the senior high school entered into the junior colleges as finishing schools, where such protests seldom occurred.

8. "Rincho" was used as the nickname of the official provisional council of administrative reform in the first half of 1980s, which aimed for a neoconservative reduction in bureaucracy.

9. Promoting the election reform, Fujimoto et al. (1992) introduced many foreign cases without commenting on the women's quota or positive actions. Yoshiaki Kobayashi, one of the popular political scientists, opposed the reform because it tended to exclude other parties than the big two.

10. The power of the upper house is relatively strong. If it decides other than the lower house, the lower house can revise it only with a two-thirds majority. Such a case has never occurred.

11. It shifted to Shinshin-to Party when Senator Yoriko Madoka entered into this party after the dissolution of Nihon-Shinto Party, and now is attached to the Democratic Party not as the party project but as her personal action.

12. The lower house members elected through the proportional representation were decreased to 180 in 2000.

13. At the same time the Communist parties were excluded from French and Italian coalition governments.

14. It is not realistic to claim the introduction of the proportional representation, because the majority of the members of local assemblies name themselves "independent".

11

The "Home Care Gap": Neoliberalism, Feminism, and the State in the Netherlands

Jantine Oldersma and Joyce Outshoorn

Home care became a "hot issue" when the Dutch welfare state was downsized in the 1980s. Worries about the "demographic shift" and the increasing number of elderly have kept the issue alive since then. More recently, it is becoming apparent that the segment of the workforce from which home care workers were traditionally recruited—housewives—is disappearing fast as a result of the changing position of women. Welfare states differ as to who provides care for those not able to care for themselves, such as many of the elderly and people with a chronic disease or handicap. The Netherlands acts like a conservative corporatist welfare state, operating on the principle of subsidiarity; the state only steps in when the "family" cannot provide the necessary care (Kremer 2000).

Home care is part of health care provision, which in the Netherlands was, and is, largely in the hands of private organizations. A national health insurance system for all employees below a certain yearly income was introduced in 1964 (*Ziekenfondswet*) and in 1968 the AWBZ (*Algemene Wet Bijzondere Ziektekosten*, General Law on Special Medical Costs), a program designed to cover medical risks that are considered to be "not insurable", became effective. During the 1970s policies were mainly aimed at providing equal access to health care, but in the 1980s cutting costs became a dominant concern. The costs of health care, though privately administered, were regarded as "public" spending, and keeping them within limits was important in keeping down the costs of labor. The Ministry of Public Health, Welfare, and Sports[1] used to be a typically corporatist policy unit; for implementing policies it was dependent on negotiations with the organizations of private care providers. The influence of the major players in the field, however, was curbed severely when a general reshuffling of all corporatist bodies in the 1990s made the policy network of public health care, like all others, more technocratic (Maessen 1989; Oldersma et al. 1999).

Since 1989, home care has been financed by the taxpayer under the AWBZ. As an issue, it intersects between government policies designed to cut costs, women's attempts to enter the labor market and consequently spending less time in the home taking care of relatives and friends, and demographic developments, leading to fewer young and more old people in the population.

SELECTION OF DEBATE

During the 1990s, the four most important political debates were social security, the crime rate, immigration, and health care. All of these debates took place in public arenas and have resulted in a series of formal decisions of consecutive cabinets (Website NKO). During this period the Netherlands had a women's policy agency, the *Directie Coordinatie Emancipatiebeleid* (DCE, Department for the Coordination of Equality Policy), established in 1978 and surviving to this day.

In terms of degree of conflict, there is little difference between the four issues; all are highly contested. Attempts to reduce disability benefits in the early 1990s mobilized trade union membership and cost the Social Democrat Party a large part of its electorate in the 1994 elections. Attempts to curtail entitlements in health care insurance have been resisted throughout the whole period; evidences of malfunctioning in the provision of care, such as waiting lists, cause vehement protest. Immigration and the crime rate became the main issues towards the end of the decade, giving rise to the populist party of Fortuyn. All issues became top priorities of the major actors involved (cabinet, political parties, the social partners, the insurance sector) during the 1990s. The range of public attention has been, witnessing media attention and the huge amount of material produced by interest groups involved in the issues, very high.

Health care has the widest scope. It touches on everybody's daily lives, both in the sense that everybody is liable to illness and has to pay the costs somehow. Moreover, the public at large is very concerned about health care, and is willing to pay more for improved quality and provision of care (SCP 1994: 502–505; SCP 2000: 262–263).[2]

Of these issues, two issues, the crime rate and immigration, do not touch the restructuring of the state along neoliberal lines, although public debate has linked some aspects of these issues to the welfare state. The debates on health care and on social security issues clearly fall within the universe of debates around the neoliberal paradigm. At the heart of these debates is the matter of state responsibility and the introduction of market principles into the system of benefits and health care. We have chosen health care as our case.

The health care issue in fact contains sub-issues. It is about the organization and provision of health care, the costs, insurance schemes, the labor market for health care workers, their training, and so forth. It was therefore necessary to choose. We have decided to select the issue of home care. In the Netherlands, home care is a mainstay in the system of the provision of health care, increasingly so when hospitals are discharging patients sooner, when helping patients on a day care basis becomes more common, and old age homes and nursing homes are reduced in numbers. Moreover, the greying of society is increasing demand for home care. Home care is partly provided by state-financed agencies (through the AWBZ), which provide professional (or formal) care, and partly by informal care provided by family members, neighbors, and friends. The AWBZ is deemed too expensive by many politicians and cabinets, and therefore targeted for reform. Home care has become also highly debated because of increasing demand and the chronic shortage of care workers leading to long waiting lists. In attempts to cope, the sector has been in a continual rash of reorganization.

WOMEN'S MOVEMENT IN THE 1990s

During the high point of the second wave of feminism in the late 1970s, the Netherlands had a large and lively women's movement that addressed a huge variety of issues, ranging from abortion and equal pay to the critique of patriarchal religion and women's internalized oppression (Vries 1981; Kaplan 1992). The autonomous movement consisted both of socialist and radical feminists, and its growth rejuvenated the women's sections of the political parties. This led to a broad range of the repertoire of action: consciousness raising, demonstrations, and lobbying, especially during the highly successful abortion campaign organized by the platform of *Wij Vrouwen Eisen* (We Women Demand) (Outshoorn 2001).

By the time the political mood swung to the right in the 1980s, with eight years of Christian Democrat/Liberal cabinets, the women's movement was entrenched in a number of professional institutions and specialized networks. Many of these were subsidised by various levels of government. In the same period, the large traditional women's organizations adapted to feminism, leading to national alliances on economic independence and the combination of family and work. There were numerous cultural activities, meeting places, and a lively "service" sector on issues ranging from rape to women's health issues. On the whole, the movement was relatively successful, achieving policy satisfaction on important issues as abortion, equal pay, education, and sexual violence (Outshoorn 1995). However, by the mid-1980s the autonomous movement submerged in the institutionalized part of the movement and in work organizations. The central movement organization, Man-Women-Society (*Man-Vrouw-Maatschappij*—MVM), was dissolved in 1987. Lobbying and taking part in the corporatist networks of the consensus democracy of the Netherlands became the major operative mode of the various branches of the movement.

In the 1990s the movement went into decline. The network between the women's policy agency and the movement was broken down, while many subsidized service organizations were forced to merge into mainstream institutions and subsidies supporting important groups were cut. What remained were the traditional women's organizations, united in the *Nederlandse Vrouwenraad* (Netherlands Women's Council), still uniting nearly a million women (Oldersma 1999: 418). In 1994 the *Breed Platform voor Economische Zelfstandigheid* (Platform for Economic Independence) merged with the *Associatie voor Herverdeling van Betaalde en Onbetaalde arbeid* (Association for Redistribution of Paid and Unpaid Labor) to form the *Vrouwen Alliantie* (Women's Alliance) as a defensive move against the cuts and declining membership rates. The active and feminist women's section of the Labor Party was abolished in 1995, but the women's section of the Christian Democrats increased its influence on the party program.

Many networks remained, however, and proved able to mobilize when necessary (Outshoorn 2000). Women's presence in trade unions has remained strong, as in many work-related organizations and in the universities. Feminist lawyers are well organized and monitor CEDAW as well as supporting women taking their cases to European courts. Women's studies have survived many reorganizations within academe, and the major feminist magazine, *Opzij*, still has about forty thousand subscribers and sales often reach over eighty thousand copies per issue. There are numerous websites and a major portal for women's affairs (www.emancipatie.nl). A new feature is the mobilization of minority women. Surinam, Turkish, and Moroccan women have had women's organizations since the 1980s, but permanent organization has proved difficult, and at the local level groups come and go. The cut in subsidies hit these especially hard.

THE DEBATE

How the Issue Came to the Public Agenda

Home care has been an issue since the 1970s, when the incumbent cabinet changed its policy on the elderly in an attempt to curb state expenditure.

While previously residential care had been the major goal of policy after the Second World War, the elderly were now encouraged to stay in their homes as long as possible. Home care was to provide the services to facilitate this, but over the years it neither expanded nor modernized to accommodate the new demand. Instead, a new type of home care worker was introduced in the mid 1970s, the so-called alpha workers, who work on twelve-hour contracts for their clients, so that they could be excluded from social security and thus were cheaper to employ (Maessen 1989). The idea was to recruit married women, who were thought not to need social benefits, as they had a bread-winner entitled to social security. This made the work unattractive, so that even with the high unemployment of the 1980s, shortages of home care workers occurred. To make up for the lack of care, successive cabinets then started to promote informal care, to be provided by family members and neighbors. Formal care became redefined as supplementary to informal care. The move was ideologically legitimated in terms of informal care being more humane and "warmer" than professional care (Lyke 2000; Potting 2001).

The demographic shift and the increasing number of elderly people started to cause concern in policy circles in the mid-1980s: a plethora of official reports ensued. Their recommendations included substituting intra-mural care for extra-mural care, to be supplied by "self-care", professionalization of care work, more efficiency, and cutting of costs. In 1991 a cabinet policy paper *Ouderen in tel* (The Elderly Count) addressed the matter of the supply of carers for the first time. Under the label of the need to "participate more fully in society", middle-aged women were encouraged to take on more informal care work—although it emerged they were already providing the lion's share.

By the early 1990s policymakers tried to expand services by a number of reorganizations of the care work sector to improve performance and efficiency. Different types of home care were centralized into larger territorial organizations. Under influence of the new management ideology, these were quite hierarchical, with financial-economic experts (mainly men) moving in for the top positions, leaving the middle level of management to the original directors with their field knowledge (mainly women) (Meloen 2000). The alpha workers continued to do the fieldwork, but were now faced with increasing taylorization of their work, leading to dissatisfied clients, high turnover and absenteeism, and problems in recruiting new workers (Vulto and Morée 1996). There was an increasing amount of studies and reports describing the situation in home care, and workers' and clients' complaints received wide coverage in the media.

The first major paper on home care by the Christian Democrat–Social Democrat cabinet Lubbers III (1989–1994) was published in 1991: *Thuiszorg in de jaren negentig* (Home Care in the 1990s; Thuiszorg 1991) placed home care firmly on the political agenda. Its successor, the two cabinets of the "Purple Coalition" (Liberal-Social Liberal, Social Democrats 1994–1998; 1998–2002) produced a paper specifically on this issue: *Home Care and Care at Home* (Thuiszorg en zorg thuis 1997) and the *Policy Paper on Care 2001* (Zorgnota 2001) that paid ample attention to home care. All three were debated in Parliament, and all three received widespread publicity and criticism. As the 2001 paper hardly mentioned the issue of informal care, several MPs forced the cabinet to produce a separate paper on home care that same year (*Zorg Nabij*—Care at Hand), just before the cabinet resigned in April 2002.[3] Today home care is still high on the cabinet agenda.

Dominant Frame of the Debate

Central to discussions about care in the Netherlands from the 1970s onwards is the conviction of all political parties that the costs of health care should be controlled. The dominant frame in the 1990s can be characterized as economic: budgetary problems were the center of attention and the driving force behind policy. The demographic shift and the emancipation of "citizens" (read: women) were portrayed as the main threat to budget control. Underlying the discussions is the fear that "citizens" will shirk their responsibility for giving care, thus adding to the financial burdens of the state. In the 1980s, the exploitation of married women as cheap labor was introduced as a remedy for the lack of formal care. In the 1990s "rationalization" by merging care organizations was one major answer to the problems. When this did not help, stricter bureaucratic rules to ration care were introduced to prevent families from unnecessarily seeking state help to take care of their elderly relatives.

In the 1990s policymakers realized that the demographic shift would lead to permanent demand for home care institutions. The cabinet's (Lubbers III) solution to this problem was the introduction of market-type relations. Because home care was part of the AWBZ, financing was heavily dominated by government rules, intent on keeping costs low, which obstructed flexibility and coordination within the system. According to the cabinet, the main actors in the care system—insurers, care suppliers, and consumers/clients—would be able to switch to a more demand-oriented and efficient mode, if they were given space to "take their responsibility". Allowing commercial organizations into the field would promote competition and thus efficiency. For home care, a limited number of clients could apply for a personal budget, to hire carers themselves.

In 1997 the first Purple cabinet (Kok I) published *Home Care and Care at Home,* in which the problem definition was very much the same. This cabinet, however, was forced to freeze the introduction of market-type relations because of perverse effects: the entrance of twenty-five commercial organizations into the home care market led to selection of clients, leaving the less attractive ones for the other organizations, and to undercutting of union pay rates. To cut costs, more bureaucratic rules were introduced. The cabinet relied on its vision of extra-muralization and informal care as the prime source of help for the elderly for the long term.

At the end of the 1990s, budgetary restrictions on health care were lifted. The discussions illuminated the fact that there was no consensus in the coalition about the way forward: Social Democrats disagreed with both liberal parties about the way to finance care: insurance-based versus state-induced "solidarity". This disagreement also informed their immediate remedies. More market stands for "freedom of choice" in the liberal perception; less market stands for "solidarity" in the view of left-wing spokespersons. (Handelingen Tweede Kamer, zittingsjaar 2000–2001, 27401, nr. 8. Verslag van de Vaste Kamercommissie voor VWS, 13 November 2000, 24; Zorgnota 2001).

Gendering the Debate

At the beginning of the 1990s, the debate was gendered to a certain extent. Although the 1991 cabinet paper chose informal care as the fundament of home care and defined professional formal care as supplementary, it did acknowledge that informal care was mainly performed by women. They are the main providers of home care, and the increasing labor market participation of women will therefore affect the availability of informal care. Policy should aim at maintaining the current level of informal care and streamlining the existing professional care services. Informal carers were to be trained and supervized by the professional home carers. To ensure labor supply for formal care, the 1991 paper targeted women returners to the labor market as the most promising reserve of labor.

This solution was accepted by the major actors in the arena, save for a rising feminist lobby of women's studies scholars, two new trade unions for health care workers (*Stichting Network Gezinsverzorging*–STING—Foundation of the Network for Family Care; and *Nu 91*—Now 91), the *Vrouwenalliantie,* and two interest groups of older women (*Landelijk Platform Vrouwen 50+*—National Platform of Women, and the *Wijze Oude Wijvennetwerk*—WOUW—Network of Wise Old Women). They all pointed to the necessity of increasing formal care services and decreasing the burden of informal care by women. The official advisory body to the government on the status of women, the *Emancipatieraad* (Emancipation Council), which included a high percentage of feminists, also took up the issue of home care in its several reports to the cabinet. As the major tenet of the council's philosophy was that labor market participation is fundamental to women's emancipation, it emphasized the necessity of providing sufficient professional care, so that women could participate in the labor market. It held that child care and informal care of others was a major reason for women not to go out to work or to only work part-time. It therefore reversed the government's policy aim: informal care was seen as supplementary to professional care, preferably to be supplied by government services (Emancipatieraad 1993). In subsequent reports the council stuck to this position (Emancipatieraad 1995, 1996). From these it emerged that the very old are mainly women, often surviving their husbands, and therefore dependent on formal care. Government measures to ration the amount of formal care according to strict criteria of need turns out to advantage men: they are more likely to receive help, despite the fact that older men are usually healthier than their female contemporaries. These older generations of men never learned to do the household work, so they are perceived to be more needy than women. The council stressed that informal carers were overwhelmingly women, and that the "sandwich generation", women between forty and sixty who still have children to look after but also aging parents, was becoming overburdened. It therefore maintained that the limits of informal care have long been reached and that formal care should increase at least 1.5 percent per annum to keep pace with the demographic shift (Emancipatieraad 1996).

The position of the council involved a difficult balancing act. It supported professionalizing home care and criticized the alpha helpers' construction, as their wages would never bring them economic independence. At the same time it was aware that professionalization would also make home care too expensive for clients with limited budgets (mainly women) and thus be priced off the market. The position of the Council was informed by *STING*, the organization of home care workers (Interview Betsy Albers, 4-10-02) and feminist scholars who researched the issue. However, the 1997 cabinet paper lost the gender analysis of its predecessor. It was completely written in gender-neutral language, taking the existing gender order as given and assuming women's traditional identity of carers that would ensure they would continue to produce the bulk of care.

The parliamentary debate on the government paper focused mainly on the issue of privatizing home care and the structure and costs of the national health insurance system (Handelingen Tweede Kamer, 19 June 1997). No party attacked the basic philosophy of seeing formal care as supplementary to informal carers. Several of the opposition pointed out that informal carers were already overburdened, but these carers had no gender.[4] The poor working conditions for care workers was a concern for the Left, who were in favor of improving their social security status, but this clashed with the approach of Liberals and Social Liberals to introduce the personal clients' budgets, which would enable clients to buy their own care either from the regular formal care institutions or private services on the market. The Left was worried this would lead to lower wages, loss of job security, and no entitlements to social security benefits for care workers. The loss of a gender perspective can be attributed to the general approach of the cabinet to scrap policy for "specific groups". Women's issues were being integrated in "general policy", obscuring the fact that, despite improvements in women's position, inequality still remains, especially among the older generation of women. There is also a general tendency to think that equality between women and men has already been achieved, no longer making it necessary to distinguish between women and men. Moreover, many thought that to "single out" women would be discriminatory to men, the more so since consecutive cabinet papers on the status of women stressed that men also had to alter their attitudes towards family responsibilities and care.

After 1997 the Emancipation Council disappeared from the policy arena. Its gender perspective, however, had slipped into the Council for Social Development, the new major advisory body to the Ministry of Health, Welfare, and Sports after 1999. (Raad voor Maatschappelijke Ontwikkeling 1999). There was also some support for a gendered frame from the *Wetenschappelijke Raad voor het Regeringsbeleid* (Netherlands Scientific Council for Government Policy, WRR) in its major report on aging (WRR 1999). It was a partial gendering, as women only appeared as workers having to enter the labor market to earn and maintain the collective costs of the welfare state in the future (Outshoorn 2002). This was also the dominant framing of its 2000 report on labor market trends (WRR 2000).

The second Purple cabinet (1998–2002) produced a *Zorgnota 2001* (Policy Paper on Care) (2000), which sticks to a gender-neutral frame and analysis. The only reference to gender is that the policy paper notes that 78 percent of workers in the health care sector are women, and that 73 percent of all jobs there are part-time ones (as compared to 44 percent of all jobs in the Netherlands; ibid. 175). Even returners to the labor market are not gendered, but if one looks at the measures for recruiting them, a woman-mother is obviously in mind: jobs should be close to home, with suitable hours, and a limit on the number of hours (ibid. 187).

As to home care, the basic philosophy about the mix of formal and informal care remained untouched. The cabinet notes that elderly people are staying at home much longer out of choice, but also because there are waiting lists for residential care. This leads to higher work pressure for both home carers and carers in residential care. The paper proposes a number of measures to increase efficiency and improve the system of indication for formal care. The alpha workers are now offered the choice to become employees of care work organizations or retain their old status. Informal care is not discussed.

The policy paper had its first reading in November 2000. During the debate no party challenged the basic philosophy on the mix of home care; the only gendering came from the Social Democrat spokesperson who pointed to a labor reserve of migrant woman returners who can be recruited into care (Handelingen Tweede Kamer, 13 November 2000, 10). The minister did not mention informal care at all, but after pressure by several women MPs, (Liberal and Social Democrat), the cabinet produced the 2001 paper *Zorg Nabij* (Care Close to Home).

This paper praised the informal carer for contributing to social solidarity, and acknowledged that long-term carers are threatened by social isolation and overload. An informal carer should be able to participate in social life normally; the professional home care institutions should not limit the amount of formal care at the maximum an informal carer can provide (Zorg Nabij 2001: 9, 22). The informal care worker, however, appears in the paper as male, as it stubbornly uses the Dutch masculine nouns and pronouns to denote the home carer, despite the fact that the paper notes that twice as many women as men provide informal care, and do so for many more hours (the paper does not specify the exact amount; ibid. 10). The paper still banks on women's traditional roles, with their obligation to take care, and women's identities in the provision of care. All proposed measures—more volunteers, advice centers for informal carers, weekend takeover when things become a bit much, and "respite" leave—are all aimed at preventing the informal carer from calling in the professionals. It is noted that labor market participation of women still needs to increase, but a more generous future system of paid care leave will enable "working people to take on informal care, and informal carers to work" (ibid. 17).

Policy Outcome

The most important policy outcome of the discussions and protests about waiting lists in home care at the end of the 1990s was an increase in the budget. Attempts to oust home care from state-funded social security arrangements were not successful. Most attempts at commercialization were also frozen in a nascent stage, with the exception of personal budgets for clients, which have increased considerably. After the mergers of organizations at the beginning of the decade, most attempts at structural change seem to have died an early death. Informal care is still the cornerstone of the home care system; despite numerous attempts at recruiting more care workers, there are still shortages in nursing and home care, with policies to make the work attractive mainly targeting working conditions, flexible hours, leave, and child care. Pay is seen as a matter of the social partners, but the cabinet is not in favor of higher wages because of the consequences for labor costs and the competitiveness of the Dutch economy in the international market.

Women's Movement Impact

Attempts at gendering the discourse on home care have not been successful: the interrelatedness of formal and informal care, the necessity to address the poor working conditions of care workers, the limits to increasing efficiency, and the impossibility of providing more care if budgets do not increase have not been addressed adequately by policymakers. Even if references to gender did enter the discourse at certain points, it did not impact the framing of the debates. At the same time we do see that women abounded in the policy process. Feminist movement actors were active in several of the advisory councils and in Parliament, and even within the Ministry of Health, Welfare, and Sports. In the public debate feminist scholars and women's movement groups were involved, raising awareness of the issue. This therefore is the case of no policy satisfaction alongside representation of women advancing feminist ideas: *the case of co-optation*.

The structure and the priorities of the women's movement should be taken into account to explain this. Women's organizations as well as feminist groups drew their support mainly from middle- and higher-class women. Interest in the conditions of low-paid workers in the care sector was not missing, but it was a typical "issue caretaker" activity by academics and later on by professional women. Care workers themselves are not very well organized and the organizations that were formed in 1991 cannot be designated either as feminist or as women's movement organizations, although their insistence on the worth of the caring professions is in alignment with feminist ideals. The Women's Alliance, the platform of traditional women's organizations and feminist groups dealing with balancing work and care responsibilities, is mainly concerned with the interests of informal carers.

Feminist professionals and intellectuals active on the issue did advance an integrated vision of the importance of care work, but were not able to decisively influence policy. This integrated vision was put forward by the Emancipation Council, stressing the inter-relatedness of economic independence for women and demographic shifts, working conditions in care and the quality of care, and, above all, the need to provide budgets if taking care of the elderly is indeed a serious concern. This concern was taken over by "mainstream" advisory boards after 1997, but not by consecutive cabinets.

Women's Policy Agency Activities

Since 1978 the women's policy agency has been the DCE, which is a regular section of the Ministry of Social Affairs and Employment. During the cabinet of Lubbers III, its political head was a socialist junior minister, Elske ter Veld, a feminist who was primarily interested in women's employment and social security. With the onset of the Purple Coalition in 1994, women's public policy became the concern of the minister, the Social Democrat Ad Melkert, who continued to give women's employment priority. The agency always had a cross-sectional scope, enabling it to intervene in the affairs of other ministries, but this became a less powerful instrument when mainstreaming came *en vogue*, shifting responsibilities and control to these other departments. Its administrative resources during the 1990s remained fairly stable.[5]

The earlier directors of the DCE, all regular civil servants, had been sympathetic towards feminism, as were most of the civil servants at the beginning of the 1990s, but after 1996 the unusual move of a political appointment took place: a former communist MP became the new director. She had no prior experience in either feminism or the civil service, and under her directorship many of the feminist civil servants resigned. Furthermore, the position of the DCE was weakened by the policy of mainstreaming, which left the agency with few specific issues in its portfolio. The DCE's relationship with the women's movement reached an all-time low when the new head reorganized the traditionally strong structure of relationships between movement groups and the agency, with the intention of building alliances with mainstream players such as employers and linking women's issues to mainstream concerns. With the arrival of the second Purple cabinet in 1998, women's policy again acquired its own junior minister, the Social Liberal (D66) Annelies Verstand, who also had no previous ties to the women's movement. She ridded the DCE of its unpopular director, but provided little stimulus for women's issues save the usual 1990s emphasis on employment and child care. The succeeding director was an outside appointee from local government, with no record in the women's movement.

In the period of the 1990s the DCE's priorities were women's employment and facilitation of the combination of employment with family care.[6] Care was mainly thought of in terms of child care and housework (Sevenhuijsen 2001) and since the mid-1990s, when a major policy goal became the redistribution of paid and unpaid work between the sexes, men were also encouraged to take on more family responsibilities. Home care was not one of the agency's priorities or interests in any of its mid-1990s policy papers. The issue was seen to fall under the mandate of the Ministry of Health, Welfare, and Sports, headed by the Social Liberal Els Borst, who had two consecutive female junior ministers on the home care issue. The DCE started to take an interest in the issue of home care at the end of the 1990s. The *Commissie Dagin-deling* (Commission Dayplanning), set up by the cabinet to further the combination of work and family life in 1996, and its successor, *The Stuurgroep Dagindeling* (Steering Committee Dayplanning), had a budget of nearly 30 million euro to spend.[7] It did take up the issue of informal care, but when the DCE followed its lead, in its new policy paper, the *Meerjarennota 2000*, it still accepted earlier analyses of Dutch culture uncritically, which held that the Dutch prefer informal care to state care, both in the areas of child care and home care: people have "more time to look after children, kin, and their living environment themselves, which proves to be an essential part of Dutch culture, and is highly valued by women as well as men" (Meerjarennota 2000: 12). The policy paper did recommend long-term care leave and the extension of home and residential care provision. The DCE also published a yearbook on care (Handboek 1999) and organized several debates on care provision.

Despite these activities, the women's policy agency's role has to be classified as *symbolic* in this debate. It did not articulate movement goals and it was not active on the issue, despite the fact that home care had a prominent place on the political agenda and had been gendered by a variety of women's movement activists. This is partly due to the policy of mainstreaming, but also to divisions within the agency and the movement on the place of care and work for women's emancipation. Often criticized for its hard line on women's work as a prerequisite for women's emancipation, the DCE only became more responsive to those rethinking the issue of care after 2000 and even to those feminists who wanted women to remain at home and look after their family as a valid life choice.

Women's Movement Characteristics

In the nineties the women's movement was in a state of undeniable decline. After its high profile during the 1970s and its firm consolidation in the 1980s, activities declined and organizations declined. The movement had also lost its strong ties to the Left, and had not forged new ties to other political parties.

In previous sections, it has been noted that home care is an issue where different types of women's interests are at stake. Informal carers in the home have an interest in adequate provision of formal care, to prevent burnout and to enable women to work in the labor market. This interest is well represented by the Women's Alliance, who organized a *Nationaal Zorgdebat* (National Debate on Care) in the early 1990s. Women working in home care provision are not very well represented, however, in feminist organizations or in labor unions because they tend to be more oriented to the family than most feminists. As a result of their lack of organization, the unions were not very active in defending their interests. During the 1990s this has changed for the better, but protests against the alpha help contracts have not been pursued vigorously by either feminist groups or labor unions.

In 1991, nurses organized strikes and demanded better wages and working conditions. They formed an independent organization, Nu'91, because the established unions were seen as too complacent and little inclined to support action on their behalf. Home care workers, however, were expelled from *Nu 91* and formed an organization of their own, STING (Goelabdien 1995). To avoid problems with the unions, STING concentrates on home care work as such and is careful not too pay too much attention to working conditions and wages, as this is regarded by the unions as their turf (Interview Betsy Albers, 4-10-02). STING clearly incorporates feminist ideas and cooperates with feminist researchers, but cannot be regarded as a "women's movement" actor. Feminist researchers have shown an interest in home care (Herik 1991; Gremmen 1995; Vulto and Morée 1996; Lyke 2000; Kremer 2000) and have participated in many advisory committees. Their work provided ammunition for the Emancipation Council. STING also lobbied the DCE on the position of the alpha workers, but the DCE did not see it as a priority. STING has also lobbied the health ministry on the home care issue (Interview Betsy Albers, 4-10-02).

The conclusion must be that the issue of home care had a low priority for the women's movement in the Netherlands in the 1990s. Issues that occupied center stage were the combination of work and family, child care, and workfare for welfare mothers. There were no groups or organizations, with the exception of STING, for whom home care was the central issue. Moreover, the interests of informal carers and the interests of providers of home care clearly do not coincide. There was therefore little cohesion around this issue. Despite the fact that the Netherlands always lacked a counter-movement actively opposing the women's movement, it needs to be stressed that when it comes to care, it is still a highly conservative society tending to view women as natural carers. As many as a third of Dutch women want to be full-time mothers; in 2000, 70 percent of all women worked part-time, not only because of the lack of child care but also as they want to mother themselves, and care is still valued very strongly as both women's fulfilment and obligation (Portegijs et al. 2002: 91). Among the religious parties this ideology informs the party platforms, and the language of choice (to be a full-time or part-time mother) abounds.

Policy Environment

The policy environment was moderately open during the 1990s: the Department of Health, Welfare, and Sport had a corporatist tradition, dominated by organizations of medical specialists. In the restructuring of the advisory boards, organizations of clients and more women than before gained access in the policy process. Increasing the number of women in advisory bodies was an official goal of the major restructuring of the advisory bodies to government in 1997. Organizations of care workers also achieved entry.

However, the discourse of the segments of the women's movement engaged in trying to gender the discourse on care and care work was highly incompatible with the dominant issue frame. The abstractions that abounded in policy papers in the 1990s were "budget control", "competition", "market", and "efficiency", and these abstractions served very well to waive all direct responsibility for what happened in the institutions delivering care. An integrated vision on work and care and a concern for the quality of care did not fit in. The notion that care budgets would necessarily have to expand, given the rising numbers of elderly people, the influx of women in the labor market, and the higher demands of workers, ran contrary to the dominant issue frame.

As to the composition of government, the Social Democrats had a central position governing coalitions during the entire decade. From 1989 until 1994 they formed a cabinet with the Christian Democrats (Lubbers III) in which Junior Minister Hans Simons (PvdA) was responsible for health care under Minister Hedy D'Ancona (also PvdA). From 1994–2002 the Purple Coalition formed by Liberals, Social Liberals, and Social Democrats (VVD, D66, PvdA) was in power. During the entire period Els Borst (D66) led the Ministry of Health, Erica Terpstra (VVD) was responsible for home care from 1994–1998, and Margot Vliegenthart (PvdA), who had been the spokesperson for this subject for her party from 1994–1998, became junior minister between 1998 and 2002. Home care was also part of her portfolio.

CONCLUSION

Women's movement groups were not able to gender the debate on home care in new ways in the Netherlands, although the overwhelming burden of this care rests on women's shoulders, whether provided as informal care or by professionals either at home or in state-run or -funded institutions. The policy outcome was not in line with the demands of important movement groups: informal care remains the fundament of the home care system and the various cabinets have resisted increasing the availability of professional care (increase in spending on the sector not withstanding). Nor were wages increased—the government insisted that extra budget was only justified if it generated extra "output"—even though some attempts have been made to improve the working conditions of professional carers. Despite the presence of feminist actors in several parts of the policy arena, most of the policy discourse was in gender-neutral terms, while still implicitly resting on the assumption of the availability of informal carers whose identities incorporate the obligations of taking care of their kin. A major reason for this failure lies in the incompatibility of the dominant framing, with its emphasis on budget control, efficiency, and faith in work, with feminist framings, pointing out the poor working conditions and low pay of the professional carers and the overload of the informal carers. Moreover, women's movement actors are not unified on the issue, nor does it have high priority. The feminist movement at large is divided on the basic and underlying issue of women's participation in the labor market: informal care is at odds with the demand for economic independence. The debate on home care in the Netherlands has been classified as the case of co-optation: women are represented in the policy process, but did not receive policy satisfaction.

The conflict about women's role returns at the level of government itself. Consecutive cabinets have placed increasing women's participation in the labor market as a top priority on their agenda, to be able to finance the welfare state of the future, especially old age pensions. At the same time they still predicate their policies on home care on the existence and willingness of women informal carers and, when confronted with contradictions, stick to the idea that in the future there still will be enough informal care to go round. In this predicament, the DCE, the women's policy agency, has not been of great help. It did not back the varied demands of the women's movement during the crucial period of the debate and did not regard home care as one its priorities. Overall, the agency appears to have toed the line of the cabinets: no increase in wages and only a slight increase of professional care to meet the growing number of old age people. Its role can therefore be seen as a symbolic one.

The issue of home care shows the dynamics of neoliberal policies. The focus on budget control forces governments, whether Center Left or Center Right, to shift costs to other parties. Meanwhile demographic changes and women's changing roles in the labor market all work to make care a scarce resource. Families (read: women) are in the middle of this squeeze: the responsibility for the elderly and the disabled is put on their shoulders again. The interests of—mostly female—care workers and—often female—elderly people in need of care conflict squarely with the interests of the government in need of a balanced budget to meet the terms of the Stability and Growth Pact of the European Union.

Despite two recent major reforms in health care provisions, the new Health Insurance Act (*Zorgverzekeringswet*) and the Act on Social Support (*Wet Maatschappelijke Ondersteuning*—WMO), the basic philosophy underlying home care policy remains intact. The Health Insurance Act does away with the distinction between the *Ziekenfonds* and private insurance, offering all citizens a downsized basic health care insurance. It also incorporates parts of the AWBZ, leaving long-term residential health care in the latter. The WMO regulates home care provision, removing it form the AWBZ and decentralizing it to the local community. The act, formulated in strictly gender-neutral terms, stresses that primary care is first and foremost the responsibility of "citizens". Women's movement organizations and feminist MPs have pointed out that this act will increase the burden on women providing informal care, but the act passed both houses of Parliament in 2005.

NOTES

1. The Ministry of Public Health, Welfare, and Culture was renamed Public Health, Welfare, and Sports in 1994.

2. When asked what they value most in life, Dutch respondents consistently prioritize: a harmonious family life, good health, and enough money to live comfortably. Between 1966 and 1992 health became the most important of these; mentioned in 1992 by 67 percent as first priority (SCP 1994: 504). In a Eurostat survey in 1996 more than 50 percent of Dutch respondents gave as their opinion that government should spend more on health care (SCP 2000: 263).

3. Ms. Jet Bussemaker and Ms. Kadijha Arib, both from the Labor party published a manifesto for informal carers; Ms. Stephanie van Vliet (D66) put the decisive motion to the floor (Handelingen Tweede Kamer, 2000–2001, 27401, nr 37H., and Ms. Nancy Dankers (CDA) asked parliamentary questions on the issue.

4. The two senior citizens' parties, and the Christian Democrats.

5. At the beginning of the 1990s the budget was approximately 13 million euros a year (on a total government budget of 86 billion euros). The agency employed around 28 full-time equivalent staff. During the 1990s the total budget plummeted to 7 million euros (on a total budget of around 100 billion) mainly because the responsibility for subsidies was shifted to other ministries. Staff was reduced to about twenty-four full-time employees in 1993, but at the end of the decade the volume had risen again to around thirty-four full-time employees. The total amount of subsidies was also back to its 1990 volume as the mid-1990s loss was compensated by a new subsidy for *Dagindeling* (Dayplanning).

6. For this analysis, the following policy documents were read: *Met het oog op 1995* (Handelingen Tweede Kamer 1992–1993, 22913, nr 2, 19-11-1992), *Emancipatie in uitvoering* (Handelingen Tweede Kamer 1995–1996, 24406, nr 6, November 1995); Beleidsbrief Emancipatiebeleid 1997; Voortgangsbrief Emancipatiebeleid 1997–1998; Meerjarenprogramma emancipatiebeleid *Van vrouwenstrijd naar vanzelfsprekendheid* (Handelingen Tweede Kamer 1999–2000, 27061, nr. 1–2 (March); Meerjarenbeleidsplan, November 2000.

7. Personal communication Eelco Wierda of the DCE, 31-1-02.

12

The Women's Movement, State Feminism, and Unemployment Reform in Spain, 2002–2003

Celia Valiente

This chapter examines the role of the women's movement and the main central-state women's policy machinery (the Women's Institute, WI) in the debate on the 2002–2003 reform of the unemployment protection system in Spain. The WI did not participate in the aforementioned debate. Subsequently, agents from the office could neither represent women's movement goals nor gender the frame of the debate. The state response to women's movement claims in this debate was pre-emption, since the policy content coincided with movement goals (the maintenance of the unemployment protection system existing before 2002) but women were hardly involved in the policy process.

The *symbolic women's policy activities* and the pre-emptive state response to the women's movement occurred under a conservative government with an absolute majority in both chambers of Parliament, and a women's movement in a stage of consolidation. The lack of impact of the women's movement and the WI on the 2002–2003 unemployment reform, this chapter argues, was mainly (but not exclusively) a result of the nature of the policy subsystem. The constellation of major actors that participated in the 2002–2003 unemployment reform formation was firmly closed to policy actors outside the government, organized labor and management, and political parties with parliamentary representation. The women's movement and the WI did not stake out any strong position known by the mass public around the specific problems that the debate on unemployment reform addressed.

SELECTION OF DEBATE

In the 1990s and onwards, opinion polls showed that the topics that the majority of the population regularly considers hot issues in Spain have been unemployment and terrorism. Other concerns have also been recognized by Spaniards as hot topics (but to a lesser extent than unemployment and terrorism) including drugs, crime, housing, and immigration. Still other matters have been regarded as hot concerns too, although only for a short period of time, such as the mad cow disease in the early 2000s.[1] For instance, in July 2004, a representative sample of the Spanish adult population was asked what were the three most pressing problems in current Spain (up to three answers were allowed). Unemployment, terrorism, lack of safety on our streets, housing, and immigration were chosen by 61 percent, 47 percent, 20 percent, 20 percent, and 17 percent, respectively (Centro de Investigaciones Sociológicas 2004).

Since the aforementioned issues are highly contested topics, many debates developed around them since the 1990s. The list of all deliberations on these matters is extremely long. In order to avoid such a long list, in this chapter I only focus on unemployment. The unemployment rate has hovered above 11 percent between 1981 and 2003.[2] Given the double-digit rates of unemployment that have permanently characterized the Spanish economy in the last three decades, the debate about the best system of income maintenance for unemployed individuals has always been present in the political discussion.[3]

The early 1990s was a period of change in the system of unemployment protection. The major (restrictive) reform took place in 1992 (Royal Decree Law 1/1992 of April 3, and Act 22/1992 of July 30). The minimum period of contribution to be entitled to contributory unemployment benefits was raised from six to twelve months. The period of perception of contributory unemployment benefits was shortened from half to a third of the period contributed. The amount of contributory benefits was reduced. The 1992 reform also tightened the conditions to reject job offers for recipients of non-contributory unemployment benefits. The debate previous to the 1992 reform is the first deliberation of the universe of important policy discussions on unemployment since 1990.

Another restrictive measure was introduced in December 1993 (Act 22/1993 of December 29). The minimum amount for contributory and non-contributory unemployment benefits was cut down. A reduction of the income threshold to receive non-contributory unemployment subsidies was established. The definition of "family responsibilities" to be entitled to non-contributory unemployment benefits became more restrictive. Since 1994, contributory unemployment benefits are subject to taxation, and recipients have to pay a part of the contributions to the social security system, a duty from which they had been exempted in the past. The debate that took place before the 1993 reform is the second policy deliberation in the universe of the main policy discussions on unemployment since 1990.[4]

In spring 2002, the conservative People's Party (*Partido Popular*, PP), which was in government since 1996, announced that at least four aspects of the unemployment protection system would be reformed in a restrictive way: the circumstances under which unemployed individuals receiving unemployment benefits could reject job offers; non-contributory means-tested unemployment benefits for short-term agrarian workers living in Andalusia and Estremadura; income protection for dismissed workers who sue their employers on the grounds of illegal dismissal (*salarios de tramitación*); and income protection for people who work discontinuously for the same employer under permanent contracts (*trabajadores fijos discontinuos*). Opposing the 2002 reform project, unions called a general strike on June 20, 2002. Then, the governmental proposal was reflected in Royal Decree Law 5/2002 of May 24 (hereafter "Royal Decree Law 5/2002"). Some months after the partially successful general strike, the government gave in. Act 45/2002 of December 12 and Royal Decree Law 426/2003 of April 11 (hereafter "Act 45/2002" and "Royal Decree Law 426/2003" respectively) reestablished a system of unemployment protection very similar to that existing prior to the 2002 bill. The debate that took place around the 2002–2003 reform is the third major deliberation on unemployment protection since 1990.

The three debates mentioned in this section fulfill the RNGS criteria of top-priority deliberations since 1990. A *major scope* characterizes the policies enacted after the three discussions, since these measures could potentially affect a large sector of society: most participants in the labor market. A *high degree of conflict* defines the three deliberations, because major political actors participated in the debates advancing very different and contrasting views and defending them vehemently. The three discussions attracted a *wide range of public attention*, since the three of them generated the interest of the public as demonstrated through public opinion polls, demonstrations, strikes, public conferences, media coverage, and the like. The policies adopted after the three deliberations were a *top priority of major policy actors*, because these policies were high on the agendas of the political executive, leaders of labor unions, and employers' organizations, and political party leaders.

The discussion selected for close investigation in this chapter is the deliberation previous to the 2002–2003 reform on unemployment protection. The 2002–2003 unemployment policy involved a major change in state-society relations, because the implementation of Royal Decree Law 5/2002 for a long period of time would have meant that considerably less unemployed people would have been covered by unemployment protection than in the past, and that some of the unemployed individuals still covered would have been protected with a more modest level of benefits than before. In other words, if implemented during a long time, Royal Decree Law 5/2002 would have implied a selective downsizing of government towards the income protection of unemployed people, or a devolution of social responsibilities (unemployment protection) from the state to civil society and individuals. The 2002–2003 unemployment measures had a *major scope*, since these could affect not only unemployed individuals, but also all people who at any moment in time risk becoming unemployed, that is, most individuals who participate in the labor market. The policymaking process has generated a *high degree of conflict* that included a call to a general strike that was followed by an important proportion of workers on June 20, 2002 (see below). The policy debate attracted a *wide range of public attention*. The majority of the population knew about the existence of the discussion and had an opinion on it. Mass demonstrations punctuated the policymaking process. The deliberation was very often covered by major newspapers on their front page. Other mass media referred to the debate usually in prime time. The 2002–2003 unemployment reform was a *top priority of major policy actors*, since it was high on the agendas of the government, political parties, and organized labor and management.

The sources of this chapter include legislation, the parliamentary debate prior to the enactment of Act 45/2002, and published and unpublished documents from the women's movement and the WI. I have also used the coverage of the debate in the daily edition of *El País*, which is the main national newspaper. The first piece of news studied was published in *El País* on April 12, 2002 (the announcement by the government that it would reform the unemployment protection system). The last piece of news studied was published on April 12, 2003 (the approval by the cabinet of the Royal Decree Law 426/2003).

THE SPANISH WOMEN'S MOVEMENT

The women's movement in Spain is internally very heterogeneous. Groups and individuals who consider themselves feminists form the feminist branch of the Spanish women's movement (hereafter "the feminist movement"). It has been amply researched.[5] In comparison with other Western countries, the feminist movement in Spain, while not negligible, has been historically weak, its activities involving only a minority of women. The movement has occasionally shown some signs of strength, however. For example, it has organized national feminist conferences regularly attended by between three thousand and five thousand women. Nevertheless, the movement has not achieved high visibility in the mass media or initiated many public debates.

The political environment influenced the feminist movement regarding its political allies, its goals, its organizational structures, and its activities. From the mid-1930s to 1975, Spain was governed by a right-wing authoritarian regime headed by Franco, which severely eroded women's rights and status. The second wave of feminist collective activism appeared around the 1960s and 1970s in opposition to the authoritarian regime, where it encountered mainly (illegal) left-wing political parties and trade unions. These have been the political allies of the feminist movement ever since. An important proportion of the goals of the feminist movement has been instrumental (as opposed to expressive). The feminist movement has pursued political objectives (among other aims): the democratization of the country and an equal presence of women in political institutions (parity democracy). The movement has been unable to establish strong and long-lasting umbrella organizations in part because of the close links of feminist groups with parties. The fact that the state did not provide women with some services that they needed, such as sexual information, contraceptives, and legal advice, made Spanish feminists willing to invest considerable energy in service provision since the 1970s. Service provision by feminists has been further accentuated since the 1980s (to the detriment of identity-oriented activities), when the state started giving subsidies for women's organizations which provide services.

We know much less about the non-feminist branch of the women's movement, which is formed by housewives' organizations, widows' associations, mothers' groups, and cultural and religious associations, among others (but see Oleaga 1990; Ortbals 2004; Radcliff 2002, 2; Valiente 2003a). Therefore, this chapter focuses chiefly on the feminist branch of the women's movement.

In the 1990s, both the feminist and non-feminist branches of the movement were in a stage of consolidation. Groups proliferated, many of which were single-issue organizations. Many associations continued to focus on service provision. Protest activities have been increasingly rare, and have focused on the demand of the liberalization of abortion (advanced by the feminist branch) and the fight against violence against women (advanced by both the feminist and the non-feminist branches).

Since the transition to democracy a process of political decentralization has taken place, when many powers of the central state have been transferred to the regions. Spain became a member of the European Union (EU) in 1986. Since then, some responsibilities of the central state have also been shifted to the EU. Both branches of the women's movement have responded to this central state responsibilities off-loading (down to the regions and up to the EU) by increasing their activities at both the regional and the European level (Jenson and Valiente 2003; Valiente 2003b).

DEBATE ON THE 2002–2003
REFORM OF UNEMPLOYMENT PROTECTION

On April 11, 2002, the Ministry of Labor and Social Affairs of the conservative government, through Juan Carlos Aparicio Pérez, announced that the government was preparing a reform in the unemployment protection system (*El País* 12 April 2002, 68). The main details of the reform were known in the following days. The reform would change the unemployment protection system in four regards. First, conditions to reject job offers by unemployed individuals would be tightened. Before the reform, the unemployed person decided which job offers were adequate to him/her (*colocación adecuada*). The reform would transfer the responsibility of this decision to employment services after unemployed people have received unemployment benefits for a year. A new definition of adequate job offers would be established. Before the reform, an adequate job offer was one corresponding to the job or profession usually performed by the unemployed person. The reform would establish that an adequate job offer would be any offer corresponding to any job or profession that could be performed by the unemployed person given his/her education level and his/her physical condition; was paid above the minimum wage; was available at a distance from the home of the unemployed person equal or shorter than fifty kilometers, provided that the unemployed individual needed no longer than three hours a day to go to and return from work and needed to spend on transportation less than 20 percent of the monthly net salary; and was regulated by any type of work contract (whether temporary or permanent, part-time or full-time). If the unemployed person rejected an adequate job offer, s/he would be penalized with a reduction of three months of the period of entitlement to unemployment benefits. If s/he rejected a second adequate job offer, this reduction would be of six months. If s/he rejected a third adequate job offer, s/he would no longer be entitled to unemployment benefits.

Second, the scheme of non-contributory means-tested unemployment benefits for short-term agrarian workers living in the regions of Andalusia and Estremadura and included in the special social security scheme for agrarian workers (*Subsidio para trabajadores eventuales incluidos en el régimen especial agrario de la Seguridad Social*) would cease to exist in the midterm.[6] The scheme would remain in place for current beneficiaries, but new entrants would not be permitted. Instead of this scheme, a new scheme of unemployment benefits for agrarian workers active in the whole of Spain would be established. These benefits would be given to unemployed agrarian workers who have contributed to the system for at least twelve months. These contributions could correspond to agricultural and non-agricultural work. The proportion between the period of reception of this benefit and the period of contribution to the system would be one to four.

Third, the reform would propose a sharp reduction of the payment that an unemployed person receives when s/he sues her/his employer on the grounds of illegal dismissal (*salario de tramitación*). Before the 2002 reform project, up to the decision of the court (if it were favorable to the worker), the employer had to pay up to sixty days of salary, while the state paid the salary during the remaining period. The reform would abolish these employers' and state payments altogether except in the minority of cases in which the court decided that the dismissal was not illegal but void (*nulo*), and therefore the worker had to be reinstated into her/his job.

Fourth, the government would tighten the conditions under which some permanent workers could claim unemployment benefits. Discontinuous permanent workers (*trabajadores fijos discontinuos*) are workers who work for the same employer for interrupted periods. Before the 2002 reform project, these workers received unemployment benefits when they did not work. For instance, a waitress working in the cafeteria of a school worked during the school year on a full-time basis, and did not work but received unemployment benefits during the school breaks. The 2002 reform project defined these workers as part-time workers and therefore did not allow them to claim unemployment benefits.

DOMINANT FRAME OF DEBATE

Unemployment protection debates in Spain contain general statements about the following broad questions. Why are individuals unemployed? Which is the most effective and fair unemployment policy? Who should maintain the income of unemployed individuals (the state, the market, or unemployed people themselves)? These types of wide issues constitute what social scientists usually study when they analyze the "frames" of debates. But unemployment protection debates in Spain are also composed of discussions on very detailed and at times technical questions related to the system of income maintenance for unemployed individuals. These specific deliberations are inextricably linked to broader discussions, so both are reviewed in this section on frames. First, I present the arguments advanced by the initiator of the reform, the conservative party. Second, I summarize the views of the opponents of the reform.

The conservative government affirmed that during the period of perception of unemployment benefits, the current system of unemployment protection gives people strong incentives not to look for work and even to reject job offers. This system then nurtures a culture of dependence on state payments.

This system of perverse incentives has to be changed in order to encourage people to actively look for jobs and take them after finding them. Currently, there is a mismatch between labor supply and demand. The Spanish rate of unemployment is very high. Nevertheless, a relevant number of unemployed individuals are rejecting job offers in part because some of them receive unemployment benefits, and employers have to rely on immigrant workers. An efficient system of unemployment protection has to maintain the income only of those who try hard to find work but cannot find it. A well-designed system nourishes a culture which values independence and autonomy derived from income earned in the labor market. The current system fosters the underground economy. In order to retain the entitlement to unemployment benefits, some unemployed people cheat the system by rejecting job offers in the formal economy while simultaneously taking jobs in the shadow economy.

While referring to the suppression in the midterm of the scheme of non-contributory means-tested unemployment benefits for short-term workers living in Andalusia and Estremadura, the government thought that fraud was present in this scheme. The existence of these benefits has had the non-intended effect of artificially fixing a significant proportion of the rural population to the countryside and to non-skilled work. If market forces had not been distorted by the scheme, part of the rural population would have migrated to the cities years ago, or would have acquired the qualifications necessary to perform some skilled jobs in the agrarian sector, where labor demand exceeds labor supply.

The social and political actors that opposed the governmental reform were labor unions and left-wing parties. The main labor unions in Spain are the Workers' General Union (*Unión General de Trabajadores*, UGT) and the Workers' Commissions (*Comisiones Obreras*, CCOO). The main left-wing political forces are the Spanish Socialist Workers' Party (*Partido Socialista Obrero Español*, PSOE) and the electoral coalition to the left of the PSOE, the United Left (*Izquierda Unida*, IU). The PSOE was in power between 1982 and 1996 and since spring 2004. The PSOE was the main party in opposition between 1996 and 2004. Labor unions and left-wing political forces reminded the government that most recipients of unemployment benefits receive contributory benefits. These recipients have already contributed (together with their employers) to finance the system, and then have already earned their entitlement to unemployment benefits. Around 40 percent of unemployed individuals do not receive any benefits. Therefore, one of the problems of the Spanish system of unemployment protection is that it does not protect at all a high proportion of involuntary unemployed Spaniards.

Labor unions and left-wing political forces also affirmed that one of the main problems of the Spanish labor market is job scarcity. Most unemployed people do not work because they cannot find work, not because they systematically reject job offers while living on unemployment benefits, as the government proposed. It is absurd and economically inefficient to try to force unemployed people to accept almost any job offer. An efficient and fair system of unemployment protection is a system that provides people with the necessary time, information, and income to find the best possible available job.

The conservative government was also reminded that the National Employment Institute (*Instituto Nacional de Empleo*, INEM) was created in 1978 with three main functions: administer unemployment benefits, place individuals in jobs, and manage training courses. The INEM did take on the enormous task of managing unemployment subsidies, enormous due to double-digit rates of unemployment in Spain. It incompletely carried out its other two responsibilities mainly due to staff shortages. For instance, it is calculated that the INEM only administers around 15 percent of all job offers. Then, it is nonsensical to give the INEM the additional task of deciding which job offers are adequate to unemployed individuals and penalize them if they reject these offers. What the government should do is to increase the resources of the INEM for it to adequately perform its responsibility of placing individuals in jobs.

Regarding the scheme of non-contributory means-tested unemployment benefits for short-term agrarian workers living in Andalusia and Estremadura, opponents to the governmental proposal brought to the attention of the government, that they have also helped to denounce and identify fraud in the scheme, but argued that fraud is not systematic but sporadic. This scheme for Andalusia and Estremadura has contributed to the valuable objective of making life in the countryside attractive to young people and encouraging them to stay in their places of origin instead of migrating to the city where there are no jobs for them.

Left-wing parties and unions also criticize vehemently the governmental plan of drastically diminishing the number of cases in which workers receive payments from their employers and later the state if they have sued their employers on the grounds of unlawful dismissal until courts make a decision. Opponents to the governmental proposal interpreted this part of the reform as an attempt to erode the difference between unlawful and lawful dismissals, make dismissals much cheaper to employers, increase the number of circumstances in which employers could freely dismiss workers, and encourage workers to negotiate with employers cheaper dismissals instead of suing them for unlawful sacking.

Finally, opponents to the governmental project criticized the government for attempting to reform the unemployment protection system when its situation was one of surplus (not of deficit). The government was also severely reprimanded for trying to undertake this reform unilaterally instead of attempting to negotiate it with the social partners.

GENDERING THE DEBATE

The debate on the 2002–2003 unemployment reform was framed in very gender-neutral terms. Participants in this deliberation did not refer explicitly to women or men except in a negligible number of moments, nor did they refer to the possibility that the governmental reform could affect women and men differently. This gender-neutral frame is surprising, given the fact that women are disproportionately hit by unemployment: the female unemployment rate is two times the male unemployment rate (in 2002, 16 percent and 8 percent respectively; Franco and Jouhette 2003, 4, 6).

In order to illustrate the gender neutrality of the debate, let me point to the very few explicit references to gender made by *El País* while reporting on this deliberation. In general terms, *El País* has a reputation of gender awareness, because it usually includes articles on gender issues or articles on other issues but written from a gender-sensitive point of view. However, as shown next, *El País* used a very gender-neutral tone while covering the 2002–2003 unemployment reform. This gender-neutral tone in a usually gender-sensitive newspaper reflects the fact that the debate was non-gendered.

The first group of references to gender made by *El País* were mentions of women's programs. One of the versions of the governmental project included the establishment of some (very minor) non-contributory programs (*Renta Activa de Inserción*) directed to people with special difficulties to participate in the labor market, such as women. *El País* referred to mentions made to these programs by the Minister of Labor and Social Affairs (May 2, 2002, 48), and the regional Minister of Employment in Catalonia (May 21, 2002, 52). *El País* itself referred to these programs directed to women while explaining to its readers the content of the governmental reform (May 25, 2002, 44). The subsequent version of the governmental proposal included another measure targeted at women: a one-year exemption of employers' contribution to the social security system while hiring a female worker in the two years after delivery. *El País* documented a mention of this program made by the president of government José María Aznar (May 26, 2002, 23). *El País* also reported that in reaction to the government proposal, the Socialist Party prepared an alternative proposal that included special provisions for unemployed women who were victims of domestic violence or found a job in sectors where women were underrepresented (September 8, 2002, 16).

The second group of references to gender made by *El País* were very generic mentions made by conservative policymakers about women as specially benefitted by the governmental reform (June 14, 2002, 15). *El País* also reported that unions had denied that women would benefit from the 2002–2003 unemployment reform (25 July 2002, 21), and that unions had claimed that the modification of the unemployment benefit for agrarian workers should take in mind the special situation of women, youngsters, and elderly workers (January 4, 2003, 44; January 6, 2003, 1; January 19, 2003, 57). None of the declarations made by conservative politicians or trade union leaders specified in which regard women would benefit (or not) from the reform, or were special in comparison with men.

The last group of references to gender made by *El País* includes very critical statements against women. For example, *El País* reported that the general secretary of employment, Juan Chozas, illustrated the fraud on the scheme of non-contributory means-tested unemployment benefits for short-term agrarian workers living in Andalusia and Estremadura by affirming that "it is documented that since 1996, 75 percent of the new entrants in the scheme are middle-aged women older than 40 years."[7] The general secretary of the Agrarian Workers' Union (*Sindicato de Obreros del Campo*), Diego Cañamero, replied: "It is true that there are women who have not seen the countryside even in television but receive the unemployment benefit (for short-term agrarian workers). We call them 'those of the long nails'. But the dimension of this problem has been overestimated. The majority of the people try hard to work" (*El País* May 5, 2002, 57). While explaining the main restrictive aspects of the governmental proposal to its readers, *El País* itself referred to the fraud perpetrated by these women as one of the problems that the government wanted to solve (June 3, 2002, 18).

In sum, the debate on the 2002–2003 reform of the unemployment system reflected in *El País* hardly contained any notion of gender. The whole discussion was described in highly gender-neutral terms. The extremely few references made to women in this policy deliberation were mentions to programs targeted at women, very vague remarks to women as individuals specially benefitted by the governmental reform, or images of women as cheaters of the unemployment protection system.

POLICY OUTCOME

As said, unions asked the government to withdraw the whole project under the threat to call a general strike. A spiral of conflict between the government and the unions progressively developed. Unions were supported by left-wing political forces. In reaction to the threat of the general strike, the government converted by surprise its reform project into Royal Decree Law 5/2002 modifying only slightly its original proposal. For instance, the original proposal stated that some unemployed individuals must accept any job offer up to fifty kilometers away from home, while Royal Decree Law 5/2002 lowered this maximum distance from fifty to thirty kilometers.

On the whole, the main employers' organizations, the Spanish Confederation of Employers' Organizations (*Confederación Española de Organizaciones Empresariales*, CEOE), and the Spanish Confederation of Small and Medium Enterprise (*Confederación Española de la Pequeña y Mediana Empresa*, CEPYME), were in favor of the governmental proposal. However, employers asked the government to reduce employers' contributions to social security, and differentiate the financing of contributory and non-contributory unemployment benefits (*El País* April 18, 2002, 49; May 14, 2002, 50). Contributory unemployment benefits should be financed by employers' and workers' contributions to the social security system, while non-contributory unemployment benefits should be financed through taxes. In the current system, contributions are used to finance all types of benefits. The government did not satisfy either of these two employers' demands.

As for the June 20, 2002, strike, unions and the government gave citizens very different data about the proportion of workers on strike: 84 percent and 17 percent, respectively. The number of workers on strike was higher in industry, transportation, and the building sector than in the remaining sectors of the economy. The support of the strike was geographically uneven, with a peak of support in the region of Andalusia. Mass demonstrations against the reform took place in some of the main cities and towns. Unions and the government also provided very different data on the number of demonstrators (*El País* June 21, 2002, 1, 18).

In fall 2002, parliamentary work took place to convert Royal Decree Law 5/2002 into an act. Although the conservative party controlled an absolute majority of votes in the two chambers, the conservative party gave in. Act 45/2002 and Royal Decree Law 426/2003 reinstated a system of unemployment protection very similar to the system which existed prior to the reform.[8]

MOVEMENT IMPACT

El País did not report any participation at all of the feminist movement in the policymaking process of the unemployment reform or the discussion previous to it. Evidence gathered for the preparation of this chapter suggests that generally speaking the feminist movement has joined forces with labor unions and left-wing political forces in their demand of the whole withdrawal of the governmental project rather than advancing their own requests. For instance, on June 17, 2002, the UGT and the CCOO convoked an act in Madrid where the women's secretariat of both unions and other labor representatives explained to the public that "women have reasons to take part in the general strike."[9] On June 4, 2002, the women's secretary of the UGT made public a document titled "The Impact on Women's Employment of Royal Decree Law 5/2002" (available on August 30, 2002 at www.ugt.es/Mujer/mujeres.htm). The main argument of this document is that women would be particularly worst hit by the governmental reform because they comprise (together with young people, immigrants, disabled individuals, and other citizens) the sector of the labor force in the weakest position. This document rejects the governmental proposal but does not explicitly identify concrete policy goals regarding women. By explaining the different effects that the governmental reform would have on women and men, documents of the movement contain a gendered frame.

At least one female trade unionist with a high feminist profile participated in the meetings of organized labor and government representatives: general secretary of employment of the CCOO, Dolores Liceras. However, *El País* did not report that she tried to advance specific feminist claims in the negotiations with governmental policymakers. Thus, I conclude that the state reacted to the claims of the women's movement with *pre-emption*. The organizations of the movement did not energetically push forward specific women's demands. The government satisfied the main objective of the movement (and of the unions and left-wing parties): the complete withdrawal of the project of unemployment reform. It is true that state authorities interacted with a team of opponents of the governmental proposal that included Dolores Liceras, but she was probably not there representing gender interests.

WOMEN'S POLICY AGENCY ACTIVITIES

The WI is the main national-level women's policy office in Spain. The WI was officially created in 1983 (Act 16 of October 24). The WI has been the main central state women's policy agency since its establishment. The scope of the WI is very broad, because the WI has five comprehensive goals: to promote policy initiatives for women through formal enactment of policy statements; to study all aspects of women's situation in Spain; to oversee the implementation of women's policy; to receive and handle women's discrimination complaints; and to increase women's knowledge of their rights. The WI is a permanent bureaucratic agency and not a political appointment. Up to 1988 the WI was a part of the Ministry of Culture and between 1988 and 1996 a part of the Ministry of Social Affairs. These ministries are two of the ministries considered less important in the Spanish state.[10]

Since the WI is not a ministry but a unit within a ministry, it is generally distant from major power centers. In 2002, the WI had already acquired an extensive staff and budget.

During the debate (April 2002–April 2003) the leadership of the WI was weak and non-feminist, because there were three different WI directors and the three of them lack a marked feminist profile. In 2000, the PP appointed Pilar Dávila del Cerro as the WI director. She was a former civil servant. To my knowledge, she had no ties with the feminist movement. She had a previous significant experience in the policy area of women's rights because she had been the sub-director of the WI between 1996 and 2000. Between September 2002 and March 2003 the WI director was Carmen de Miguel y García. She was a civil servant with expertise in trade issues. On March 7, 2003, Miriam Tey de Salvador was appointed WI director. She had a professional career in the publishing sector.[11]

Since the establishment of the WI in 1983, WI officials have always been worried about the modest rate of female paid employment and the highest rate of female unemployment. The WI has always stated that access to paid employment is a necessary step towards the advancement of women as a group. However, the WI did not take any position publicly known on the 2002–2003 unemployment protection reform, and remained silent during the whole policymaking process. The Third and Fourth Equality Plans and the WI web page did not say anything on the modification of the system of unemployment protection.[12] *El País* did not document any WI activities regarding the 2002 unemployment reform. Given the WI's general high interest in unemployment and the lack of WI's position on the unemployment reform, it is reasonable to affirm that unemployment was an issue of moderate priority for the WI. Given the WI's non-participation in the discussion on the 2002–2003 unemployment reform, the WI could not advocate women's movement goals in this debate nor gender this deliberation. The WI's activities were then mainly *symbolic*.

WOMEN'S MOVEMENT CHARACTERISTICS

As noted above, most of the feminist groups have been very close to the Left, but this is not the case of the non-feminist branch of the women's movement. This branch is composed of groups that are close to the Left, to the Right, and to no party at all. Therefore, the women's movement as a whole is close to the Left.

Unemployment is an issue of moderate priority for the feminist movement in its entirety. This statement requires an explanation. Given the comparatively low proportions of women participating in the Spanish labor market, the overwhelming majority of Spanish feminists since the 1970s have thought that access to employment is a basic ingredient in the receipt of women's liberation. Most Spanish feminist documents of the last decades contain the demand that women should be treated equally in employment. However, if we leave the realm of the general principles and declarations and examine the mobilization (or the absence of activity) of the feminist movement in the concrete moments of the elaboration of employment and unemployment reforms in the last decade, we see that in general the movement has not been a main policy actor, for instance, regarding chief job-training policies (Valiente 2001a).

As for the *cohesion* of movement organizations, I have not found any evidence that the movement was divided around unemployment. Then, the movement was cohesive (but also quite inactive) around the 2002–2003 unemployment reform. To my knowledge, no *counter-movement* to the feminist movement was active around the issue of unemployment. The *location* of the most visible movement actors regarding unemployment reform was mainly that of labor unions, but not so much autonomous groups and established interest organizations. Regarding the degree of *feminist activism* of women's movement actors in the debate, I have not found any evidence of non-feminist mobilization.

POLICY ENVIRONMENT

In post-authoritarian Spain, generally speaking the employment (and unemployment) policy system has operated as a "closed" system: in Anderson's terms, "with its limited participation, resistance to external influences, and preoccupation with material interests" (1994, 75). The main actors in the policy area on unemployment protection include the government, the main trade unions, and the chief employers' organizations. When unemployment policies take the form of acts, members of Parliament of all political parties with parliamentary representation may take part in the parliamentary debates that precede decisions, since acts require parliamentary processing. Nevertheless, many decisions in the policy area of unemployment protection do not take the form of parliamentary acts, but of other types of laws (such as royal decree laws), which do not require parliamentary processing.

The dominant frame in which major policy actors discussed the 2002–2003 unemployment reform was compatible with the frame elaborated by the feminist movement and the WI but both frames did not match, since the former was not gendered at all while the latter was gendered. In 1996, the conservative party came into power, where it remained until 2004. Between 2000 and 2004, the conservative party controlled the absolute majority of seats in both chambers of Parliament.

CONCLUSION

This chapter has shown that the feminist movement and the WI did not directly participate in the policy debate that preceded the most important political decision on unemployment since 1994: the discussion around the 2002–2003 reform of the system of income protection of unemployed individuals. The WI did not take any position on the reform, while the feminist movement mainly joined forces with unions and left-wing parties pursuing the reestablishment of the income protection system for unemployed individuals that existed before the reform. The absence of the movement and the WI in this 2002–2003 mainstream deliberation occurred while both have traditionally had an interest in employment and unemployment. The closed nature of the employment and unemployment policy subsystem, with its fixed line-up of participants—government, organized labor and management, and political parties with parliamentary representation—appeared to be a major (but not the only) factor in the lack of influence and presence of the WI and of women's movement actors, and feminist approaches to the problem of unemployment more generally.

NOTES

1. In order to identify the main hot issues in Spain since the 1990s, I have analyzed the so-called Barometer surveys undertaken by the governmental Center for Sociological Research (*Centro de Investigaciones Sociológicas*). These surveys periodically asked Spaniards to identified the main troubles of the country.

2. The unemployment rate is the proportion of registered unemployment in the active population (employed and registered unemployed individuals).

3. The most important part of the Spanish income maintenance system is composed by several compulsory contributory professional programs, among them retirement, disability, unemployment, family allowances, and maternity/paternity. Employed individuals are mandatorily covered. The self-employed are also obligatory covered except in the unemployment scheme. The system is financed mainly (although not entirely) by the contributions of employers and employees. People who are not engaged in waged work (for instance, housewives/husbands) do not have direct access to the system. Regarding the income protection of unemployed individuals, there are two types of unemployment benefits: contributory unemployment benefits and non-contributory (means-tested) benefits. A description of the system of

income protection in general and income protection for unemployed individuals in particular in Spain can be consulted in Guillén (1996).

4. The debates on income protection benefits for unemployed individuals in democratic Spain including the aforementioned 1992 and 1993 discussions have been already described in academic works (Guillén and Matsaganis 2000; Gutiérrez and Guillén 2000).

5. For English accounts of the Spanish feminist movement, see Durán and Gallego 1986; Jenson and Valiente 2003; Kaplan 1992; Sundman 1999; Threlfall 1985, 1996; Valiente 2003b.

6. In the Spanish income maintenance system, different schemes exist for different types of workers. A general scheme covers dependent workers. Five special regimes cover agrarian workers, domestic servants, coal miners, self-employed individuals, and sea workers. Public servants are insured in a separate scheme. All these schemes are different with regard to conditions of access, contributions to be paid, and benefits. Andalusia and Estremadura are two of the poorest regions in Spain. Seasonal unemployment of temporary agrarian workers is higher than in other regions.

7. In this chapter, all translations from Spanish to English are made by Celia Valiente.

8. The parliamentary debate previous to the approval of Act 45/2002 is available at the web pages of the low chamber of Parliament, the Congress of Deputies (*Congreso de los Diputados*; www.congreso.es), and the upper chamber, the Senate (*Senado*; www.senado.es). This parliamentary debate contains very similar arguments to the debate described above that developed before fall 2002 and was also very gender-neutral. The parliamentary debate has been analyzed in depth by Celia Valiente in preparation for this chapter but is not described here due to the limitations of space.

9. The announcement of this act was available on August 30, 2002, at www.ugt.es/Mujer. A caveat is necessary at this point. Since the appearance of the second wave of feminist activism in Spain, an important number of activists have acted as feminists within labor unions. I then consider as part of the feminist branch of the women's movement the women working in women's departments of unions.

10. In 1996, the Ministry of Labor and Social Security and the Ministry of Social Affairs were merged into the Ministry of Labor and Social Affairs.

11. For more on the WI, see Threlfall (1996; 1998); Valiente (1995; 1997; 2001a; 2001b; 2004).

12. A gender equality plan is a policy instrument. It contains gender equality measures to be applied during a given period by some ministries. The Spanish central state has had four gender equality plans to be applied in 1988–1990, 1993–1995, 1997–2000, and 2003–2006 (Instituto de la Mujer 1988; 1993; 1997; 2003). Gender equality plans are prepared by the WI in collaboration with the ministries that are going to put in practice the measures included in the plans. When the period of implementation of the plans ends, the application of them is evaluated (Instituto de la Mujer 1990; 1996).

13

The Debate about Care Allowance in Light of Welfare State Reconfiguration

Christina Bergqvist

In the light of welfare state reconfiguration in the 1990s the Swedish family policy model came under threat. In Sweden family policies have primarily been identified as issues about child care in a broad sense, like paid parental leave, day care centers, and direct financial support to families (usually paid to the mother). During the 1970s Sweden had established, for the time being, a very radical family policy model based on the assumption that both parents should have the same rights and obligations in all spheres of life. In the 1960s there had been considerable political conflict around the issue whether to strengthening the male breadwinner model by introducing a care allowance paid to mothers caring for their children at home or whether to promote a dual breadwinner model by expanding publicly provided child care. Initially there was a strong support for a care allowance not only among parties to the Right, but also among Social Democrats and members of the National Federation of Social Democratic Women.[1] Since the 1970s the Swedish concept of family policy (*familjepolitik*) resembles what is today called reconciliation policy in the EU, thus government "action that explicitly addresses the relationship between work and family to improve women's situation" (Mazur 2002: 102).

Feminist and social movement actors, researchers, and insiders in the policy process played a crucial role for the shift towards a new family policy model. Gradually the Social Democrats came to unite around the dual breadwinner model, which also got support from the Liberal Party. During the mid-1970s and 1980s the principle of the dual breadwinner family became the public norm and gender equality was a key concept in public policies concerning families. The norm of individuality and gender equality was institutionalized in policies like separate taxation, expansion of public child care, and a transformation of the maternal leave legislation into a *parental* leave legislation allowing the mother and the father to share the leave if they so wished. Solo-parent families (mostly headed by a woman) were eligible for extra support, like for example a housing allowance, to be able to combine work and family. During the years to come this model has been strengthened and has had political support from a broad political spectrum. The more conservative political forces have been rather passive. Also when non-Social Democratic (so called bourgeois) government coalitions have been in power during the late 1970s and early 1980s the basic principles of the model were kept or even strengthened (see Bergqvist 1999; Sainsbury 1996, 1999). In sum, family policies have been a well-integrated and substantial part of the Swedish welfare state known to be universal, generous, and egalitarian. However, it has to be remembered that the universality is mainly based on employment status. Thus, labor market participation is crucial for the eligibility for the generous income-related benefits.

It was not until the early 1990s that the principles of the family policy model were challenged. The conservatives and the neoliberals opposed the established model that in their eyes did not give the families sufficient freedom of choice concerning the care of children. The model did not give enough space for private solutions and market forces, they said. In their view the prevailing public policies favored institutional care rather than family care and the expansion of public child care services had gone too far. A nostalgic longing for the traditional housewives could be discerned in the debate.

In 1991 a right-wing-led coalition government took over after almost ten years of Social Democratic governments. One of its ambitions was to engineer a "system shift" in the public sector allowing a higher degree of decentralization, deregulation, and privatization. They aimed at implementing a "revolution of choice" (Blomqvist and Rothstein 2001:9). During the time in government they introduced a home care allowance (*vårdnadsbidrag*), which would make it possible for one of the parents (usually the mother) to stay at home for more than around the one to one and a half years that the prevailing parental leave legislation allowed. The home care allowance was a means to privatize child care responsibilities back to the families. In the long run the purpose of the "system shift" was of course a way to downsize public spending and public institutions. In the short run the home care allowance would, however, be a rather expensive reform and its main purpose was rather a way to shift family policies in a new direction (Bergqvist and Nyberg 2002).

It is also important to mention some other reforms undertaken in the area of family policy. The Social Democratic government had opened up the possibility for public support to child care centers not run by the municipalities (the local government), but they had continued to exclude private for-profit child care. The new government changed this and today commercial child care centers can get public funding if they follow the public regulations. The bourgeois government also introduced some improvements in the availability of child care places, at the same time as the state assumed a new role. Authority and responsibilities were decentralized and, at the local level, the provision of child care became more diversified. To some extent the changes in the area of family policies followed the logic of a neoliberal restructuring of the welfare state. However, the legacy of strong public responsibility and generous public spending was not overthrown. This can be seen in measures like a child care law and the introduction of a so-called daddy month, that would encourage more fathers to take parental leave (Bergqvist and Nyberg 2002). The debate about the care allowance will be the focus of this chapter, because it clearly shows the conflict between different principles of family policy in a phase of welfare state restructuring.

WOMEN'S MOVEMENTS IN THE 1990s

Background

A large part of the Swedish women's movement in the 1960s and 1970s had its roots in the first wave of the women's movement and was in general rather pragmatic and state-oriented. Women's organizing in general was high and often took place in unions and women's political party organizations. The division in the women's movement has to a high degree followed party lines. The movement was in general oriented towards issues of work and family and was highly involved in public debates about issues like whether to encourage women's paid work or not, whether to expand public child care or promote a home care allowance, and whether individual or joint taxation was in women's interest. The Social Democratic Party had dominated the political scene for several decades. Despite their identification with the "male worker" and the close cooperation with LO, the blue-collar union, there was some space for women's views and the women's movement to have an impact on several of the welfare reforms that took place in the 1970s. However, the new Left and the feminist movement won terrain also in Sweden. The influence of the new women's movement and the foundation of the feminist organization Group 8 radicalized the debate and put pressure on the established women's organizations as well as the political parties (Jenson and Mahon 1993; Sörensen and Bergqvist 2002).

In the 1980s the most radical movement languished away or changed in nature. On one hand it moved into the universities and public administration and feminist activities became less visible in society. On the other hand feminists and women in general became more engaged in informal women networks related to their professional role and in their neighborhood (Gustafsson, Eduards, and Rönnblom 1997). During the 1980s many of the issues from the 1970s around child care and the right and possibilities for women to participate in all spheres of society seemed to have found a fairly satisfactory solution. Feminist attention turned to issues about representation, power and women's bodily rights, violence against women, sexual harassment, etc.

Women's Movement Resurgence in the 1990s

During the beginning of the 1990s there was a resurgence of a more visible feminist movement. Neoliberal ideas about the welfare state had won ground in public debates and retrenchment and restructuring of the welfare state was undertaken by Social Democratic as well as bourgeois governments. The discontent with the situation peaked after the elections in 1991 when women's representation in Parliament decreased from 38 to 34 percent and a bourgeois government coalition took over after the Social Democrats. For the first time the Christian Democratic Party was included in a Swedish government coalition and a populist party, New Democracy, had managed to enter the Parliament. Many women feared that the gains won earlier were in danger.

A new feminist network called the Support Stockings (*Stödstrumporna*) stood in the forefront for the mobilization of women. The Support Stockings with the well-known journalist Maria-Pia Boëthius and researchers Agneta Stark and Ebba Witt-Brattström managed to reach out to the general public with their forceful slogan give women "half the power and full pay". They got a lot of attention in mass media and the political debate, but disappeared from the political scene after the elections in 1994 when one of their goals was more or less fulfilled. The 1994 Parliament consisted of 40 percent women and in the new Social Democratic government the number of women and men were equal. (See Sainsbury 2005 about the role of the Support Stockings for the increase of women's representation.)

The trend towards engaging in networks rather than in more traditional organizations became widespread during the 1990s. Other examples, not as visible as the Support Stockings, were Tjejligan of LO (The Gals' Team of the Swedish TUC) and several local networks. At the same time the traditional women's federations of the political parties were encouraged by the feminist discourse suddenly on everybody's lips.

A new umbrella organization was established in 1997, the non-partisan Swedish Women's Lobby (SWL earlier SAMS), which organizes around forty organizations, groups, and networks that work for women's rights and gender equality. The lobby is represented in European Women's Lobby

(EWL) and the possibility to be represented in the EWL was one of the reasons behind the creation of SWL. On their home page they claim that they "bring together 1.4 million Swedish women".[2] However they do not organize individuals but organizations like some of the traditional women's organizations, some of the women's party federations, professional networks like for example female medical doctors, different regional and local groups and network, groups for immigrant women, etc. The number 1.4 million women is probably an exaggeration (Rönnblom 2002:74; www.sverigeskvinnolobby .se). Another new trait, so far overlooked in the literature, is the rather long history of immigrant women's organizing and the more recent mobilization around issues of the rights of young immigrant women.

SELECTION OF THE POLICY DEBATE

Identifying the Universe of Hot Issues

Economic crisis and unemployment marked the 1990s in Sweden. This of course influenced several of the debates. There are four debates that I have found to have a high degree of "hotness". They all fit the criteria for a hot debate when it comes to scope, degree of conflict, range of public attention, and interest of major policy actors. The debates are about the economic crisis (1990–1995), unemployment (1990–1997), EU membership (1990–1994), and care allowance (1991–1995).[3]

The economic crisis emerged in the early 1990s, but is said to have its roots in the 1980s. During the first years GDP declined and the government budget showed a deficit. In 1990 there was a surplus of almost 19 billion SEK, while in 1993 the deficit amounted to almost 210 billion and in 1994 to almost 200 billions SEK (SOU 2000:3, 40). After having tried to fight the crisis by different so-called austerity packages, including such things as strike ban, pay freeze, and reduced replacement for sick pay, the Social Democrats made huge losses in the general elections in September 1991. During the new bourgeois coalition led by the Moderate Party (right-wing) the economy continued to worsen. New "crisis packages" were agreed upon with the Social Democrats. During 1994 the economy again noted positive growth and public deficits were shrinking and then turned into a surplus again. The debate about the fight against the economic crisis could be a strong candidate as a hot issue. However, it seems that the issue of interest is not the economic crisis in itself, but the debate about what to do about it and the effects of it. I think it is fair to say that many experts, economists, and some politicians debated the pure economic measurements. For a more general public they were often seen as too "technical" and the debates did not have as high scope as issues more directly related to everyday life like for example unemployment and sick pay.

The 1990s also saw an increase in unemployment and a decrease in total employment. The unemployment rate rose to historically very high levels and although a decrease has occurred since 1997 the unemployment rate is still higher than in the beginning of the period. This of course led to debates about how to fight unemployment. As with the economic crisis some of the debates as well as the substantial measurements were related to the welfare state. Everybody agreed that something had to be done. The debate about unemployment drew a lot of public attention and was given high priority by the policy actors. Even though the scope of the debate was high, the degree of conflict was fairly low, which makes this debate less suitable as a candidate for the "hottest" issue.

Another hot issue was the debate about EU membership. During the early 1990s the Swedish political leadership rather suddenly started a process towards EU membership. The debate had great scope and high conflict. For example it divided the political parties into yes and no camps and women were more critical than men were. A referendum was decided for 1994, which of course led to an intensive debate about the pros and cons of EU membership. With a small majority the yes to membership alternative won and already in 1995 Sweden became a member of the EU. Since then the issue of joining the EU or not has lost its topicality.

During the 1990s there were several debates related to the superior issue of welfare state reconfiguration and family policies. The debates concerned for example how to make fathers take more parental leave and different issues related to the child care system. There is no doubt that in this universe of debates the debate about the care allowance was the "hottest". The debate about care allowance illustrates several interesting problems related to the general debate about the reconfiguration of the welfare state and the relationship with civil society (including the family). It also relates to the topical debates in Europe about the demographic challenge (low birthrates and an aging population), women's labor market participation, and the discussion about how to reconcile work and family. The scope of family policy is wide as its immediate effects concern everybody who has or who wants to have children. The scope could also be widened to include all taxpayers and children, and family policies make up a rather large share of the public budget. Both public attention and public priority is high. There is a clear conflict between a Left/liberal bloc and a conservative bloc and the issue of care allowance is very ideological. At the time it even led to a government crisis as the bourgeois minority coalition were, as we will see below, highly divided over the issue.

DEBATE: THE CHILD CARE ALLOWANCE 1991–1995

How the Issue Came to the Public Agenda

The debate about a care allowance reappeared on the public agenda in the beginning of the 1990s. The term "care allowance" (*vårdnadsbidrag*) originally had a resemblance with a mother's wage and the purpose was to support a traditional family with a male breadwinner and give housewives some economic support. The bourgeois party bloc in Sweden had in principle continued to support a care allowance since the 1960s and 1970s. The Center Party, the Moderate Party (right-wing), and the Christian Democratic Party strongly supported a care allowance, while the Liberal Party was more ambivalent. Despite this support, bourgeois government coalitions in power during the late 1970s and early 1980s did not change the direction of the established family and child care policies.

However, during the end of 1980s and early 1990s the political climate changed and neoliberal as well as conservative ideas were more pronounced. During the campaigns for the general elections in 1991 the issue of a care allowance was again a highly contested issue. After the 1991 elections a bourgeois minority coalition took over after almost ten years of Social Democratic minority governments. For the first time the Christian Democratic Party was included in a government coalition together with the three other bourgeois parties, the Moderates, the Liberals, and the Center Party. For the Christian Democrats a care allowance had been one of their top priorities in the election campaign. Also for the former farmer's party, the Center Party, the introduction of a care allowance has been seen as the most important way to support families outside the urban regions. A change of the prevailing family policy model and the introduction of a care allowance now came high on the political agenda and the heated debates about the issue continued in Parliament where the Social Democrats and Left were strong opponents to the care allowance.

Dominant Frame of the Debate

The differing opinions inside the bourgeois government led to several rounds of negotiations before they could unite around the bill on a care allowance. The government was a minority coalition and the government's parliamentary base included the right-wing populist New Democrats. Any proposal from the government to the Parliament was dependent on support from that party or any of the two parties in opposition, the Social Democrats and the Left Party. At last, the compromise agreed upon contained something that could suit all the parties in government. The Moderates, the Christian Democrats, and the Center Party got the care allowance and a lowering of the replacement level in the parental leave benefit from 90 to 80 percent. The lowering was supposed to finance the care allowance. The Liberal Party had already managed to get support for the introduction of a child care law to secure working parents' rights to public child care and a so-called daddy-month, which would encourage more fathers to take more time for parental leave than they usually do.[4] The other coalition parties were initially against this, but they accepted it in exchange for the Liberals' support for the care allowance. The government negotiations had taken around two years and their bill on the care allowance was presented in February 1994 (Prop. 1993/94:148). The bill led to two large debates in Parliament (Parliamentary minutes 1993/945:106 and 108). The context and the two debates that finally led to the introduction of a care allowance are analyzed in this section.

Initially the dominant frame of the debates was about the principles of the welfare state and the direction of the Swedish family policy model. How much and what kind of responsibility should the state take for family policies? In general the new bourgeois government wanted to see a shift in the welfare state towards more decentralization, deregulation, privatization, and choice. However, the four parties in government had different views on how to transfer these general goals into the area of family policies.

As we have seen there was a strong tension inside the cabinet between, on one hand, the three parties in favor of a care allowance, the Moderates, the Christian Democrats, and the Center Party, and on the other hand, the Liberal Party, who did not see a care allowance as an attractive reform. The Liberal Party defended strong public support for child care institutions and stressed the importance of an equal sharing of care responsibilities between women and men. The Liberals saw the care allowance as a risky project, but as the other parties they were in favor of more deregulation and marketization inside a framework of publicly financed child care. The care allowance could be seen as a way to privatize more of care responsibilities back to the family, which was not in line with the Liberal vision. The Liberal Party leader and minister of social affairs and gender equality, Bengt Westerberg, has been described as a social liberal and his vision was to combine a strong political responsibility for a publicly financed child care system with neoliberal reform. In the parliamentary debates the Liberal Party had to defend the agreement about the care allowance, but they tried to diminish the negative effects that they used to point at. They chose a rather passive role in the debates.

The three other bourgeois parties were generally more supportive of traditional family values and more critical towards the former development of family policies than the liberals. The Moderates were promoting the most far-reaching neoliberal ideas and were eager to downsize the public sector and introduce what they see as more "choice" for the families. Other themes in the debate were about justice between different families and about how a care allowance would affect the personal development of children. One favorite argument from the advocates of a care allowance was that so far the state had subsidized only those families who used the public child care system, while parents who care for their children at home got nothing. The Christian Democrats, who were the most eager promoters of a care allowance, pictured the world without a care allowance as cold and unsafe for children.

In sum the spokespersons in favor of a care allowance claimed that the introduction of a care allowance was a step towards a new family policy model, which would increase the possibilities for families in their choice of type of child care. The care allowance would make it economically possible for one of the parents to take care of their small children in their own home. Under prevailing circumstances, they claimed, families with small children did not have a real choice of freedom. They carefully avoided talking about women and mothers, but rather talked about parents and the family.

In the parliamentary debates the Social Democrats and the Left Party strongly opposed a care allowance. They stressed that under the current economic crisis and the large budget deficit it was irresponsible of the government to introduce new expensive reforms. Some also considered a care allowance as a bonus for the already well off and said that the amount of the care allowance was too low to be of any help for low-income families and single parents. For them there would not be any real choice between paid work and staying at home to care.

The new populist party, New Democracy, who held the balance between government parties and the opponents in Parliament oscillated between being in favor and being against the care allowance. Their reason to be against was mainly economical. On one hand they said a care allowance would be a heavy burden for the public budget; on the other hand they liked the ideology behind the care allowance. They of course used their position to gain influence and they were very active in the debate. The government and especially the minister of social affairs and gender equality, Bengt Westerberg, were very annoyed by their moves.

All along the opponents of the care allowance tried to gender the debate and the issue of gender equality was brought up in all phases of the debate. In the end, when the care allowance was about to be introduced, the dominant frame of the debate was highly gendered. As the next section shows there were some very strong feminist voices participating in the parliamentary debate.

Gendering the Debate

In comparison to the debates about care allowance versus expansion of public child care in the 1960s and early 1970s the debate in the 1990s was often held in a gender-neutral language. Especially the spokespersons in favor of a care allowance were careful about talking about "the parent who wants to stay at home" or "the freedom of choice for the parents". This was a way to give the illusion that the care allowance did not threaten gender equality. As will be expanded on below the opponents did, however, not frame their arguments in a gender-neutral language. On the contrary they stressed that given the prevalent gender order they expected very few men to use the allowance. Women's movement actors, outside Parliament as well as inside Parliament, were far from united on the issue. There were feminist actors to the Left who strongly opposed the care allowance and there were proponents of more traditional and conservative women who saw the care allowance as very important as a tool to increase the "value" of housework.

For the opponents of a care allowance gender equality was one of the most important themes in the debate. The feminist movement on the Left was thus very critical to the care allowance, which generally was seen as a "women's trap" (*kvinnofälla*), a trap that would lock women inside the home and restrict their autonomy. This was also an important theme for the Social Democratic and Left debaters in Parliament irrespective of their gender. However, the strongest emphasis on gender equality came from women MPs like Maj-Inger Klingvall and Margareta Winberg, who were affiliated with the National Federation of Social Democratic Women.[5] They were engaged in the parliamentary debates as well as in media debates and argued that the care allowance was a threat to women's rights on the labor market and to gender equality, because in the long run it would hollow out the public support for child care centers. In their view gender equality is to a large degree about being able to reconcile work and family and this is only possible if women and men share responsibilities at home and if public policy encourages this. The problem, for them, was not about more possibilities to stay at home. This they claimed was already possible under the parental leave legislation; the problem was rather about more child care places and more engagement from the fathers. Another Social Democrat, Mona Sahlin, promised to take away the care allowance as soon as the party was back in government.

The proponents answered the critique that the care allowance was incompatible with gender equality with the argument that women today are independent individuals who know what they want. A care allowance is not a trap, but a possibility for "parents" to choose the child care form they like best. In their view it is even possible to see the care allowance as a reform that improves gender equality, because it is a means to upgrade care work done in the home.

The debate about the care allowance was part of a bigger debate about the principles of the Swedish welfare state in general and more specifically what kind of family policy model to promote. As we have seen different opponents gendered the debate from a feminist perspective. However, as mentioned earlier also agents inside and close to the government were skeptical towards the care allowance and did not want to see the care allowance as a substitute to generous public spending on other child care facilities. Many of these agents were found in the Liberal Party and they were also eager to promote the role of fathers as carers and gender equality. In some respects the minister of social affairs and gender equality, Bengt Westerberg, and many other Liberals were closer to the Left Party and the Social Democrats. The role of the liberals in the parliamentary debates therefore becomes a bit peculiar. They had to defend the care allowance because it was a part of the deal they had negotiated, even though their party leader, Bengt Westerberg, had been very critical of the allowance. The few Liberal MPs that participated in the debates tried to diminish the significance of the care allowance and the consequences for gender equality.

SHIFT IN GOVERNMENT AND NEW DEBATE

The care allowance was finally introduced in July 1994 and then abolished in December the same year. In between these two dates the Social Democrats had come back in power and formed a minority government. They soon enough presented a bill on the abolition of the care allowance (Prop. 1994/95:61). Thus, there was another parliamentary debate about the care allowance. This time the four bourgeois opposition parties defended the allowance with almost the same arguments as before. Last time the bill on care allowance had passed with the help of the populist party, New Democracy (ND). This time ND had not secured enough votes for a parliamentary mandate. However, the Green Party was back in Parliament, and with the help of them and the Left Party the Social Democratic government won enough support in Parliament for the abolition bill.

It is interesting to note that in the previous two parliamentary debates under the bourgeois government there were thirteen men MPs and ten women MPs participating in the chamber. This time eleven out of sixteen participating MPs were women and the dominant frame of the debate was highly gendered from the start.

Policy Outcome

The bill about the care allowance proposed by the government (Prop. 1993/94:148) and finally accepted by the Parliament in July 1994 was given a neoliberal and modern touch. It was designed more as a child care check than as a mother's wage. The allowance could either make it possible for one of the parents to stay at home for a longer period than the regular parental leave period, or be used to "purchase" public or private forms of child care. The care allowance was given to all families with children between ages one and three. The amount was far from sufficient to be able to support oneself (2,000 Skr/month).[6] A lowering of the replacement level in the parental leave benefit would partly cover the cost for the reform.

The care allowance was introduced in July 1994, just as new general elections were approaching. The Social Democrats had, as we have seen, promised to abolish it if they won the coming elections. The new Social Democratic government thus took away the care allowance, but in order to save money they decided to keep and even decrease the replacement level for parental leave. They also kept the Act on Child Care and some other reforms that had been introduced by the former government. On one hand the Act on Child Care made publicly financed child care more universal, but on the other hand the other reforms led to more decentralization and deregulation. The Social Democratic government has thus accepted the trend towards privatization of child care providers, but the Act on Child Care guarantees that it is publicly regulated and publicly financed. Also the so-called daddy month was left untouched and today has become two months.

Movement Impact

Here we will look at the impact of women's movement on the debates and the policy outcome. The Swedish women's movement is often described as weak. In a comparative study Joyce Gelb claimed that "Swedish women . . . appear to have many of the demands of their feminist sisters elsewhere taken care of by the state and political system, yet their concerns seem to be almost obscured by the efforts to reach equality that are, in the main, not the result of their own efforts" (Gelb 1989: 173). In this kind of description women's party organizations are usually overlooked as well as the fact that women representing the women's movement for a long time have been rather integrated into the political system. Contrary to the picture of Sweden as a country with feminist policies without feminists the analysis of the debates has shown women and movement actors to be very active and forceful participants in the policy debates.

In Sweden as in most places there is, as we have seen, no unified women's movement, but a wide range of organizations, groups, networks, etc. Some (I guess most) of them were against the care allowance, while some were in favor of it. For example the feminist network the Support Stockings, who were very active during the time, saw the care allowance as a threat to the achievements women had gained so far. In general they opposed and actively acted against a rollback of the public sector (Ulmanen 1998).

Left and Liberal feminists outside as well as inside Parliament were in agreement over the importance of high-quality and publicly financed child care facilities for children's well-being and possibilities for their parents to combine family and employment. The goal of Left and Liberal feminists was to secure this by increasing the places in child care facilities outside the home for children from the age around twelve to fifteen months. The universal right to parental leave is usually used until the children are at least fifteen months, but due to its flexibility it can be stretched out for a longer time. Thus there are very few children below the age of one and a half years old in day care institutions. The existing income-related parental leave legislation was thus seen as an economically more attractive and flexible measure for parents with small children. In their view the parental leave legislation has many advantages for the possibilities to reconcile work and family and it also makes parental sharing possible. However, the low uptake of parental leave by fathers was considered a problem. Many feminists are therefore in favor of a more individualized parental leave system, which does not make it possible for fathers to transfer the whole period of leave to the mothers. The Left feminists and most of the liberal feminists strongly opposed a care allowance.

Conservative and neoliberal women in general and particularly women from the Center Party and Christian women's organizations were engaged in the debate in favor of a care allowance. Here I will not define them as feminist, but recently some of them and their organizations and parties define themselves as Center feminists and Christian feminists. Their arguments followed the line of their parties and in their view a care allowance would favor ordinary women, who wanted to stay at home with their children. The introduction of the care allowance was thus a victory for these women, but not for the Left feminist movement.

In sum, women and women's movement actors have had a high impact on family policy in Sweden. In both the case of the care allowance reform and in the case of its abolition, women and women's movement actors were important participants in the policy process and they managed to gender the debates in a way that had an impact on the outcome. In both cases women movement actors were represented in government and Parliament. The introduction of the care allowance was of course a failure for the Left and Liberal feminists, a failure that soon was turned into a victory. In the end the outcome of the debates was more in accordance with their ideas and goals. The reactions during the debates from feminist organizations and actors were strong signals to the politicians that conservative or neoliberal ideas about the family and the relationship between the state and family were not accepted. During the campaign for the general elections in 1994 issues about gender equality, family policy, and social policy were high on the agenda. The attempt by the bourgeois government to turn the "Swedish (Social Democratic) model" into a neoliberal model was not popular and the Social Democrats won the election. With the return of the new Social Democratic government with 50 percent women ministers the "system shift" in the family policy sector was stopped.

Given that the feminist standpoint here is defined as being against the care allowance, the introduction of the same implies that at first it was a case of co-optation. In the governmental negotiations the Liberals and Bengt Westerberg had to accept the care allowance and a lower replacement level in the parental leave, in exchange for a compulsory "daddy month" and a child care act. However, just a few months after the implementation of the care allowance the new Social Democratic government abolished the allowance, which then turned the issue into a case of *dual response.* The outcome was thus in accordance with Left feminist goals.

Women's Policy Agency Activities

In the Swedish case it is more accurate to talk about gender equality agencies as this is the term used in Sweden. Often gender equality agents have been women, but not always. The most important bodies belonging to the "gender equality machinery" are the Division for Gender Equality under the minister for gender equality and the equal opportunities ombudsman (*JämO*) and since a few years back there are twenty-one regional experts for gender equality, one in each county administrative board.

The most relevant body in this case is the Division for Gender Equality, at the time located in the Ministry of Social Affairs. The head of the division was the minister of social affairs and gender equality and leader of the Liberal Party, Bengt Westerberg, who as we know initially opposed the care allowance. The Division for Gender Equality can therefore be categorized as an *insider.* When the minister of gender equality realized that he had to accept the care allowance he managed to frame the debate in terms of gender equality. By bringing the issues of child care law and parental sharing, which are more in line with feminist views, to the forefront he tried to restrict the negative effects on gender equality.

Women's Movement Characteristics

The women's movement engaged in the issue of reconfiguration of the welfare state and family policy was in a *consolidation* period except for the Support Stockings, which at the time being perhaps was in a growth period, but has since faded away. There was no *cohesion* of the movement. The feminists acted against the care allowance and were affiliated with the Left or the Liberals. The more conservative women's movement actors were in favor of the care allowance.

Policy Environment

The family policy subsystem (especially issues of parental leave and child care) has since the 1960s involved social and women's movement actors, intellectuals, and experts (pedagogues, psychologists, child care workers, etc.) in different working groups and public investigations. They have also been included in the Swedish referral system (*remisssystem*), which means that government authorities, institutions, advocacy groups, and other organizations that could be affected by the issue at hand may be given an opportunity to submit their views before the government makes a decision. The subsystem is thus in general fairly open. However, in this case there was a rather restricted use of public investigations and of the referral system. The primary participants were the political parties and women's movement actors. It is thus classified as *moderately closed.*

CONCLUSION

Women's movement groups and representatives have been active in gendering the debate on family policies in general and also the debate about the home care allowance. Since the 1960s the left wing and liberals have always been able to stop different initiatives to introduce a care allowance for parents (mothers) who take care of their children at home. However, during the early 1990s the feminist movement was for the first time in several years surprised by initiatives from neoliberal and conservative women promoting the old model of home care allowance as a new model for the future. For socialist and liberal feminists this was old wine in new bottles. The policy outcome of the first round of debates, a home care allowance, was not in line with the feminist defense of a gender-equality-friendly state supporting policies to promote parental sharing, high-quality and publicly funded child care, etc. Despite the fact that the debate was gendered and that the feminist arguments were well represented in the debates, the neoliberal and conservative discourse about choice and traditional values had won ground. The neoliberal and conservative discourse was not about dismantling the child care system, but to complement it with the care allowance.

The bourgeois government, with the exception of the Liberals, seems to have made the home care allowance as a symbol for a shift in the hegemony of the Social Democratic family policy model. However, their situation was not easy when their own minister of social affairs and gender equality was going against them with the same arguments used by feminists from the Left. To solve this divergence inside the government the decision about the care allowance was supplemented with a decision about a "daddy month" and a child care law. Although the debate about the care allowance at the time was a hot issue of principal interest, it did not have a long-lasting impact. With the return of a Social Democratic government it was soon abolished. The outcome of the debates is thus in accordance with the goals of the women's movement to the Left.

EPILOGUE: SHIFT IN GOVERNMENT AND A NEW DEBATE

The child care allowance introduced in July 1994 was abolished in December the same year. In between these two dates, the Social Democrats had returned to power and formed a minority government. Almost immediately, they presented a bill to abolish the child care allowance (Prop. 1994/95:61), resulting in another parliamentary debate about the child care allowance. This time the four bourgeois opposition parties defended the allowance with almost the same arguments as before. In July the bill on child care allowances had passed with the help of the populist party, New Democracy, but ND did not win enough votes in the 1994 election for a parliamentary mandate. Instead the Green Party was back in Parliament; and with the Greens and the Left Party the Social Democratic government had sufficient support in Parliament to pass the bill abolishing child care allowances.

Although the new Social Democratic government eliminated the child care allowance, they decided to keep the reduction of the replacement rate for parental leave benefit and even decreased it in order to save money. They also kept the Act on Child Care and some other reforms introduced by the former government. The Act on Child Care made publicly financed child care more universal, but the other reforms led to more decentralization and deregulation. The Social Democratic government thus accepted the trend towards privatization of child care providers, but the Act on Child Care guarantees that it is publicly regulated and financed. The "daddy month" was left intact and increased to two months 2002.

Feminist organizations and actors during the debate sent a strong signal to the politicians that neither conservative nor neoliberal ideas about the family and the relationship between the state and family were accepted. During the 1994 general election gender equality, family policy, and social policy were major campaign issues. The attempt of the bourgeois government to turn the "Swedish (Social Democratic) model" into a neoliberal model was not popular, and the Social Democrats won the election. With the return of the new Social Democratic government with 50 percent women ministers, the "system shift" in the family policy sector was stopped.

Since the abolishment of the child care allowance there has not been any serious attempts to reintroduce it. The model with a generous parental leave and publicly financed child care outside the home has rather been strengthened and more universal. During recent years there has been a shift from a focus on child care as a service for mainly working parents to a right for all children to attend a child care center/pre-school.

DATABASE AND ARCHIVES

Rixlex. Database from the Swedish Parliament
Pressarkivet. Archive for press material. Uppsala University.

NOTES

1. Initially the Moderate Party considered a care allowance as too much state interference in the family. A care allowance was even seen as connected with "the communist ideology", but in the beginning of the 1970s the party had changed its standpoint and came out in favor of a care allowance (Hinnfors 1992:5, 99).

2. The mission is based on the Convention for the Elimination of All Forms of Discrimination against Women (CEDAW), and the action plan that was adopted in 1995 at the United Nations Fourth World Conference on Women, held in Beijing.

3. I have used information from a database from the Riksdag (the Swedish parliament) called Rixlex and from the Swedish government as well as research reports about political opinions and the election campaigns in 1991, 1994, and 1998. Also the Press Archive (*Pressarkivet*) at Uppsala University has been used. The result is that the debates listed above all could qualify as hot issues, but I do not think it is possible to rank them.

4. The parental leave legislation in Sweden is gender-neutral and the parents have the right to sixty-four weeks of paid leave (three months with low flat rate and the rest is income-related). All weeks used to be transferable between the parents with the result that mothers used almost 90 percent of the time. The introduction of a "daddy month" and a "mummy month" meant that these two months were not transferable.

Either the father or mother had to use it and stay at home or the family would lose one month of leave. This is thus a kind of individualization of the parental leave. Many feminists argue that the leave should be fully individualized and thus give mothers and fathers the right to have for example eight months each.

5. Winberg was the chair and Klingvall sat on the board of the federation.

6. The parental leave was 450 days, whereof 360 days were income-related and for 90 days the parent was given a flat rate. In practice the reform meant that the 90 flat-rate days were replaced with a care allowance lasting until the child was three (Lag 1994:553 om rätt till vårdnadsbidrag).

14

The UK: Reforming the House of Lords

Joni Lovenduski

The UK constitution is frequently described as unwritten. There is no single document that sets out the operation of the system and the rights and duties of its citizens and leaders. In fact it is uncodified; its provisions are written down but in a number of places, variously based on royal prerogative, statute, common law, conventions, and authoritative opinion. These sources support a system of government so powerful and so centralized that it has famously been referred to as an elected dictatorship. Until 1998, when the European Convention on Human Rights was incorporated into British law, there was no constitutionally entrenched bill of rights. The architecture of the system is grounded in principles of parliamentary sovereignty according to which no areas of the law are beyond Parliament's reach. Constitutionally the people of the UK are not citizens at all; instead they are subjects of the reigning monarch. The system is animated by party government whereby the majority party in the House of Commons determines the political composition of the cabinet and the prime minster is the leader of the majority party. The combination of large parliamentary majorities with regimes of strict party discipline ensures that the cabinet dominates Parliament in a highly centralized system of national government in which the center has also long dominated the periphery. In this system the boundaries of the constitution are difficult to specify, a matter of convention and agreement. For the purposes of this essay I will assume that issues to do with the nature of political representation and the architecture of political institutions are constitutional matters.

In the early twentieth century constitutional issues such as reform of the first-past-the-post electoral system for the House of Commons frequently dominated the UK political agenda, but after 1945, when Labor won a landslide victory and decided it no longer favored reform of the first-past-the-post simple majority electoral system, the issue faded. It reemerged in the late 1980s, partly in response to worries about a system in which small electoral majorities generated by a minority of voters were translated by the electoral system into huge parliamentary majorities. Thus powerful and overcentralized governments were repeatedly elected by only a small proportion of the electorate. Moreover, unrest in Northern Ireland and demands for devolution in Scotland and Wales called the union into question.

At the end of the 1980s Charter 88 was set up to campaign for constitutional reform. This group was able to mobilize informed opinion and create coalitions of the various groups wanting change. Coincidental with the politicization of the second wave of feminism in the UK, the constitutional reform movement brought together a range of oppositional opinion in politics including Labor and Liberal Democrat parties, the trade unions, and civil rights organizations such as Liberty. However, with the exception of local government reform aimed at reducing the powers of elected local councils, the Conservative governments of the 1980s were not interested in tinkering with the constitution. Hence reform mobilizations were ineffective until New Labor adopted some of the Charter 88 program in the mid-1990s.

Constitutional reform movement demands included the establishment of Scottish and Welsh parliaments with powers to tax, directly elected by some form of proportional representation; devolution of power to the English regions; proportional representation for parliamentary (Westminster), local, and European elections; the reform of the House of Lords to an elected second chamber with the abolition of its hereditary principles; a freedom of information act to reduce secrecy in government; a bill of rights to be accomplished by incorporating the European Convention on Human Rights into UK law; and, finally, a written constitution and the establishment of a constitutionalist culture. At least in theory the demands for more democratic arrangements for political representation offered opportunities for intervention by women's advocates and women's policy agencies because by participating in the associated debates they could argue for their preferred policies.

In 1997 the Labor Party was elected on a platform that included support for many of these changes. In government Labor quickly introduced reforms including devolution in Wales and Scotland and made clear its intention to proceed to other areas of the constitutional reform agenda. Their proposals attracted considerable support in Scotland and Wales where Labor was competing not with the Conservatives for votes but with the nationalist parties. However in England voters continued to be motivated largely by bread and butter issues. There constitutional reform had numerous supporters with numerous interests. If it was not a popular issue, it was not unpopular, and because it was important to informed opinion it generated widespread and heated debate. Some reforms proved very controversial to sections of the political elite, hence parliamentary and press debates were protracted and management of the issue in the Houses of Commons and Lords was difficult. This is one of the senses in which the reform was a "hot issue".

The Labor Party electoral victory in 1997 came after four successive Conservative governments, lasting from 1979 until 1997. Those Conservative governments implemented a new Right political agenda. During the 1980s there was active public debate about the nature of Thatcherism and the failure of socialism. Debates covered the various issues of the new Right agenda including the implementation of monetarism (introduced and soon abandoned by Margaret Thatcher), competition policy, privatization of publicly owned utilities, the marketization of government and public services, the control of trade union power, the downsizing and restriction of the independence of local government, the reduction of direct taxation in favor of indirect taxation, and the privatization of social policy. These issues were largely resolved by the end of the 1980s. Meanwhile the Labor Party was reforming and modernizing its organization and agenda under successive leaders. By the mid-1980s the Labor Party had determined to maximize its vote share by courting voters at the center of the political spectrum. Gradually party leaders accepted elements of the new Right agenda. By the time of the 1997 general election the Labor Party had dropped promises to reverse Thatcher's reforms.

Beyond the overheated world of internal party politics, other issues percolated into the 1990s. Most important were the perceived erosion of democracy as government became more centralized and mechanisms of accountability eroded, the structure of the UK in terms of the relationship between England, Scotland, Wales, and Northern Ireland, and Britain's place in the European Union. These became the new "hot issues". Each of the issues had constitutional implications; hence constitutional matters were at the root of the "hot issues" of the 1990s.

The cumulative effect on the political agenda was significant. The consensus in favor of the welfare state established between Labor and Conservative parties after the Second World War appeared to have broken. The political landscape changed as nationalized industries and numerous state functions were privatized, devolved to agencies, or artificially marketized. A system of performance targets was established throughout the public sector. The targets were monitored by a regime of inspection that reduced professional autonomy and increased central control. The welfare state was rolled back and the political consensus shifted to the Right taking the party system with it. To win election in 1997 the Labor Party demonstrated acceptance of Conservative policies in its manifesto and promised to adhere to Conservative spending policies during first two years of office. The low financial costs of constitutional reform made it an attractive manifesto item for a party that had left itself little room for electoral maneuver.

The Conservative reforms were unpopular with a large section of the electorate who hoped that Labor would improve public services and restore the welfare state. They were disappointed. Indeed, many commentators claimed that the Blair government adopted its constitutional agenda to distract attention from its failure to deal with issues of public service reform. They reasoned that constitutional reform was relatively costless whilst the improvement of public services would mean commitment to already ruled-out increases in public spending. However, in practice Labor made some substantial changes to social policies. Benefit regimes were overhauled and the elimination of child poverty became a central goal. A national minimum wage was instituted as was the New Deal for Lone Parents and a national child care strategy. After the two-year deadline, public spending increased and plans for further increases in spending on health and education were announced. Except for the railways however, privatization and agencification of the civil service continued under the Blair governments, which broadly accepted the state reconfiguration of the 1980s and 1990s.

Labor's political achievements were marred by accusations of non-accountability, of spin, of excessive secrecy, all issues that touch on the constitutional reform agenda and highlight the importance of proper arrangements to ensure transparency, accountability, and democratic representation. It is difficult to avoid the conclusion that the key political debates in the 1990s were about the constitution. Constitutional reform is central not only to the traditional considerations of democratic theory but also to the effective functioning of democratic politics.

SELECTION OF THE ISSUE

None of the 1990s debates fully meet the "hot issue" selection criteria. However I have shown above that constitutional reform debates meet some of all of the criteria and all of some of the criteria. They also frame the major issues of the period. Thus the selection of constitutional reform as the UK hot issue can be justified on the grounds of its major scope, its attendant conflict, its priority for political leaders, and the amount of public attention it generated. In terms of scope, the debates about constitutional reform have been radical and far-reaching. They resulted in important changes in the rules about elected office including the introduction of new elected bodies at the regional level whose members are elected by a variety of electoral systems, reform of the structure of local councils, and changes in the system of elections to the European parliament to a party list system. Debates about descriptive and substantive representation intertwined bringing issues of identity, representation, and accountability into the forefront of public discussion. Another sense in which the scope is major was that the rights of all citizens to participate in, to scrutinize, and to control their government at various levels were at stake. The constitutional reform proposals involved a high degree of conflict both within and across parties, between northern and southern MPs, between new and experienced MPs, and between the cabinet and the legislature. The media were consistently interested in the debates and elite public opinion coalesced around various issues as advocacy organizations and constitutional watchdogs such as the Democratic Audit and Charter 88 convened conferences, produced reports, informed the press, and lobbied government.

The main problem of debate selection is whether to regard constitutional reform as a single, continuing debate, to consider each debate separately, or to cluster certain debates that have a core objective. For example parliamentary reform encompassed changes in the procedures of the House of Commons and changes in the composition of the House of Lords. Devolution brought new assemblies to Scotland and Wales, a new assembly and mayor for London, referenda on elected mayors, and promises for referenda on regional reform in England. Moreover developments in the European Union continued to have substantial effects on parliamentary sovereignty and state competence.

Each of these clusters of issues affects the structure of the state and each potentially affects the democratic citizenship of each member of the population. The devolution acts of the 1990s in which Wales and Scotland both got new legislatures have been widely discussed as bringing major changes to the structure of the UK state. However, I have not chosen them for exploration here. Although devolution opens the possibilities for further substantial change across the UK, it directly affected and engaged only the people of Scotland, Wales, and Northern Ireland who are fewer than 15 percent of the population. The devolution debates generated little interest in England where regional reform attracted little support. Hence they do not meet the RNGS hot issue election criteria that the selected debate must directly affect a large proportion of the population. European Union debates are disqualified on different grounds. Although EU debates are about issues that affect the whole of the population, they did not generate widespread public interest and mobilization during the 1990s. Nor did political leaders give them high priority. Leaders of neither major party wished to draw attention to division in their parties about continued integration and especially over Britain's possible inclusion in the Eurozone. The issue warmed up considerably in the next decade, and will undoubtedly get hotter as politicians find it increasingly difficult to manage, but it was not "hot" in the 1990s.

I have decided therefore to concentrate on the reform of Parliament. This array of change debates about the reform of Parliament best fits the RNGS criteria, albeit imperfectly. Parliamentary sovereignty remains the lynchpin of the British constitution. Neither its erosion by membership in the European Union nor the changes in its lawmaking powers portended by the Human Rights Act have yet altered its centrality to the architecture of the political system. It is the party majority in Parliament that determines the considerable powers of successive prime ministers. Hence parliamentary reform portends a significant change in the workings of the state and in particular a reorganization of the relationship between government and legislature. Reform of Parliament directly addresses the nature of democracy, hence has a determining effect on the nature of the political system. The parliamentary debates exposed to public view show the inadequacies of British democracy, bringing into sharp relief the lack of accountability of its system of party government.

The main themes of the debates were the modernization and democratization of Parliament in the sense of its ability to scrutinize government and hold it to account. There is therefore a "sub" universe of debates about the reform of Parliament that took place at the end of the 1990s and the early years of the twenty-first century including the modernization of the House of Commons and reform of the House of Lords. I have selected the debates on reform of the House of Lords. Because the House of Lords has relatively little legislative power this selection may seem perverse; hence more explanation is necessary.

The House of Lords is the UK's "second chamber". Although less amenable to strict party discipline than the House of Commons, it is historically dominated by the Conservative members who occupy the majority of its seats. It has long been something of an anachronism. Until 1998 most Lords inherited their seats. It is a weak institution. Its powers to reject legislation passed by the Commons were dramatically reduced in 1911 and further reduced in 1949; hence the current House of Lords has only delaying power and some capacity to revise government legislation. However democrats were concerned that a weak second chamber reduced the legislature's capacity to hold government to account. This concern became more pressing as executive dominance of the House of Commons increased over the decades after World War II. Some reforms of the House of Lords were made in the ensuing decades. In 1958 the Life Peerages Act made two reforms. First, the heredity principle was broken by a provision for the establishment of life peerages. Life peers would be appointed by the government of the day on advice from the civil service and opposition parties. Second, women were admitted to the House of Lords. After 1958 only a handful of hereditary peerages were created. New members of the House of Lords were appointed by the government of the day, a process that successive governments set about with some enthusiasm. The privileges and political responsibilities of hereditary peers continued.

In this form the House of Lords presented a number of problems. First the option to establish an adequately democratic second chamber was effectively closed. The limited functions of the normally compliant House of Lords were very convenient for successive governments, which were appreciative of the status quo of executive domination. Second, its composition did not result from democratic elections. It reflected neither the characteristics of the population nor that of the political class. By October 1996 there were 626 hereditary peers and 401 appointed peers in a house of 1,053 members that also included 26 Church of England bishops. Only 7 percent were women (Bogdanor 1997, 118). Third, the presence of the bishops was one of the symbols of the fusion of church and state. Such fusion breaches a principle held by many democrats that church and state should be separate. Fourth, with the presence of 12 law lords, the senior judiciary of the UK breached the principle of separation of powers, another widely held democratic principle. Fifth, many life peers were appointed for patronage reasons (for example as a reward for contributions to political party funds). Sixth, the hereditary peers were also the country's aristocracy, their privileged position a powerful symbol of the class-ridden British social structure. In short the House of Lords lacked legitimacy; it was undemocratic and unrepresentative, a waste of a second chamber and a symbol of inequality.

By the middle of the twentieth century all agreed that the Lords needed to be reformed, but there was little agreement about what sort of reform there should be. Between 1958 and 1997 only minor reforms were attempted. One of these was an effort to increase the number of women peers. Although the Life Peerage Act of 1958 enabled women to become peers, women hereditary peers were not admitted until 1963. The provision allowing women to succeed was permissive. Each hereditary peerage had its own rules about succession. Because only a minority of hereditary peerages provided for women to succeed, there were by 1996 only 16 women among 767 hereditary peers (Women were then 67 of 382 life peers). In March 1994 Lord Diamond proposed a bill whereby the firstborn would inherit whether male or female. His proposal was rejected in the House by 74 to 39 votes. In this debate Lord Mowbray and Stourton expressed fears that the eldest daughter of an ancient house "might marry, shall we say, an American film star from Hollywood". Even more "appalling" would be "if a daughter of an ancient house were to marry a Frenchman and the family become French" (Bogdanor 1997, 117–118). Undoubtedly the House of Lords was long overdue for reform.

Parliamentary sovereignty is the central principle of the British unwritten constitution. There is a tension here. In this political system the government has most of the initiative in legislation. The essence of UK democracy is party government. Accountability operates through the party system via the House of Commons. It is a system of elected party government in which the majority party forms the government; its leader becomes the prime minister, who appoints leading party figures to his or her cabinet. The larger a government's majority, the more autonomy it has. Ironically large electoral majorities also afford governments considerable autonomy from their parties because they need to pay less attention to building support for legislative proposals in the House of Commons. There are connections between electoral processes and what governments do. Political parties are elected on the basis of the manifestos they put before the electorate, those manifestos are developed in political party decision-making fora and are the subject of intervention, bargaining, mediation, and negotiation by interest groups, think tanks, special advisers, social movements, experts, and the media. In general governments implement the policies pledged in their election manifesto. In practice there are differences between governing and opposition parties and between those with large and small majorities in the way that policies are agreed. For obvious reasons governments with large majorities and strong leads in opinion polls rely less on party decision-making processes to determine their legislative agenda than those with small majorities. Incumbent parties have better access to policy advice than opposition parties. Once devised, governments present their legislative program to Parliament where both Houses must agree on bills. Normally the government's majority assures passage of its legislative proposals in the House of Commons. But the legislative timetable tends to be crowded, which gives the less reliable House of Lords the ability to use its delaying powers to frustrate government policies, particularly on complex constitutional matters and especially on proposals to reform Parliament. Historically the Conservative-dominated House of Lords is more likely to refuse Labor than Conservative governments. Indeed one of Labor's many political problems was that of how to get a majority in the House of Lords. Ultimately Parliament decides about its own reform, which means that it must also be on the government's agenda as the government controls the parliamentary schedule. Even then reform is not assured. In 1967 the Wilson government attempted a major House of Lords reform, which got consent in the Lords but failed to achieve a majority in the House of Commons. Of course the incoming Labor government of 1997 with its large majority faced better prospects for reform than Wilson had.

WOMEN'S MOVEMENTS SINCE THE 1990S

By the early 1990s the UK women's movement was active in the political parties, professional associations, and most major interest organizations. The movement was characterized by a functional division of labor in which integrated feminists campaigned around a fairly standard issue agenda including equal pay and opportunities, reproductive rights, women's shelter and freedom from violence, prostitution and traffic in women and children, gay rights, and equality of political representation. Many feminists, especially those located in mobilizing organizations such as trade unions and political parties, campaigned on a number of different issues. The independent women's advocacy organization, the Fawcett Society, brought women from various organizations together in campaigns for equality of political representation. The most directly relevant feminist concern was the issue of equality of women's representation. Feminist claims for equal representation predated the parliamentary reform and modernization movements by many years (Lovenduski and Randall 1993; Lovenduski 1997, 2001).

At the 1997 general election a record number of women MPs were elected to the House of Commons. Following that success activists were able to ensure a substantial presence of women in the newly formed Scottish parliament and Welsh assembly. They were immediately engaged in improving women's share of seats in the European parliament, in local government, and in publicly appointed bodies. Prior to 1997 much of the activity over women's representation took place within the political parties, especially the Labor Party, in the trade unions, and in women's advocacy organizations, many of which were ad hoc and short-lived. After 1997 women and some male supporters in Parliament and in government set about mobilizing support for and sensitizing opinion to the need for special measures to achieve equality of representation. When the general election of 2001 returned fewer women than in 1997, government acceded to demands for changes in the law so that there would be no legal obstacles to parties wishing to introduce quotas of women candidates. The Sex Discrimination Electoral Candidates Act received Royal Assent in 2002.

HOW THE DEBATE CAME TO THE PUBLIC AGENDA

Parliamentary reform received a fair amount of public attention from the 1980s until the present. Reform of both Houses was discussed in the press in articles, editorials, and letters to the editor from private citizens. The regular public opinion polls by MORI, Gallup, and NOP normally included items on reform. Civic organizations and the business community were very active in lobbying government on reform. During the 1990s there was a widespread acceptance of the need for parliamentary reform.

Campaigns were mostly elite-led affairs that sought to influence "informed" opinion. Thus Charter 88, the leading constitutional reform group, did not have members; rather its leaders recruited supporters. Supporters were mainly expected to contribute cash and, less frequently, numbers, but not to intervene in decision making. Charter 88's efforts to influence operated according to the main conventions of British politics. Pressure was placed on government in various ways. Interventions made at the times of the annual party conferences, during election campaigns, and in the run-up to scheduled parliamentary debates. Campaigners established themselves as experts by issuing reports and press releases, organizing conferences, submitting advice to commissions and committees of enquiry, briefing sympathetic MPs and peers, and so forth. Some experts, including a number of academics, found their way into the heart of the reform process. Conflict mainly occurred over what sort of reforms were necessary and how they would be implemented. For example there was disagreement about the abolition of hereditary positions in the House of Lords.

Such debates are often opportunities for feminist advocates, who must be well placed in government, parties, advocacy organizations, and the media if they are to take advantage of them. Feminist advocates played a major role in Scotland. Meg Russell, a leading feminist advocate of increased women's representation, became special adviser on Lords reform to Leader of the House of Commons Robin Cook from 2001 until he resigned in 2003.

THE DOMINANT FRAME OF DEBATE

Attempts at Lords reform tend to get mired in disagreements about the details. The 1997 Labor government decided to break the logjam by undertaking reform in two stages. Stage 1 was the removal of the right of hereditary peers to sit in the Lords. Stage two concerned the definition of the powers and membership of the new second chamber. Stage 1 was almost completed after a compromise to allow the retention of 92 hereditary peers in the House enabled the passage of the House of Lords Act 1999. Preparations for stage two began with the establishment of a royal commission to consider the form the reformed House would take (Gamble 2003). This was the Wakeham Commission chaired by Conservative peer Lord Wakeham, a former Conservative leader of both the House of Commons and the House of Lords. It consisted of twelve members, of whom four were women. It worked diligently to collect evidence, consulting expert and popular opinion. Six thousand consultation papers were sent out to forty-five thousand individuals. Some 1,734 pieces of written evidence were received, mainly from individuals, but also from groups, parliamentarians, and former peers. Twenty-one public hearings were held (Wakeham 2000).

The Wakeham Report, *A House for the Future*, was published on January 20, 2000. The report recommended changes to make the House of Lords more representative of the British public and more effective as a governing body. Its recommendations were a partially appointed and elected upper house of around 550 members; an appointments commission; appointments that reflect a variety of interests including, gender, ethnicity, religion, region, nations, and professions, 30 percent of members to be women, and 20 percent of members to be non-partisan cross-benchers. Wakeham recommended that the House of Lords should have increased power.

The Wakeham Report marked not only an end point, but also the beginning of new debates that have continued to the time of writing in 2004. The issue is how members of the House of Lords should be recruited, whether they should be appointed or elected. Wakeham recommended a largely appointed chamber with a small elected element, offering a range of between 12 and 35 percent elected members. Supporters of an appointed or largely appointed second chamber argued that an elected second chamber would undermine the authority of the House of Commons. However, the proposal was heavily criticized and found little support either in the House of Commons, the political parties, or the reform movement. The response to Wakeham revealed cynicism and disillusion with the Blair government, and suggested exasperation with the "inexhaustible courtesies and illusions of participatory democracy . . . when all that matters from first to last is what Tony wants" (Vincent 2000).

Wakeham's recommendations were incorporated into the government's white paper *The House of Lords: Completing the Reform*, published in November 2001. *Completing the Reform* followed only some of the Wakeham blueprint. It proposed a 600-member house of 120 elected peers, 120 cross-bench (i.e., non-party) to be appointed by a statutory appointments commission, 12 law lords, 16 bishops, and 330 nominees of political parties. The undemocratic proposals of the white paper were derided by the press and by MPs. It had no chance of getting through the House of Commons. According to Andrew Gamble (2003) no Labor MP could be found to support the white paper; most of the Labor party wanted an elected second chamber. The Public Administration Committee of the House of Commons made various counter-proposals. In 2002 Robin Cook, leader of the House of Commons, proposed a joint all-party committee of both Houses. This committee was charged with bringing a set of options to be voted on by both Houses of Parliament. The core disagreement was over the proportion of the chamber that would be elected. Various alternatives were proposed ranging from 100 percent elected to 100 percent appointed. On February 6, 2003, the Commons voted on the proposals and rejected every one of them, marking the end point of this debate (Gamble 2003: 28–31; Cook 2003, 279). The wider debate continues. In the summer of 2003 the government announced plans to abolish the law lords and create instead a separate supreme court. In July 2003 the government tabled another set of proposals about House of Lords reform, the core provision of which was to remove the remaining "hereditaries".

The debate was framed by advocates of reform in terms of modernization and democracy. The problem to be solved was a classic issue of democratic representation, that of who should be present in a representative assembly. The role of the House of Lords is to approve and where appropriate to revise government legislation and act as a non-partisan "watchdog". But because most of its positions were hereditary, and the remainder were appointed rather than elected, its democratic legitimacy was questionable. The House of Lords was not representative of the British public. Thus the recommendation for a partially elected and partially appointed House that would reflect a cross-section of society was central. Hence descriptive representation was explicitly considered in the wider debate and the discourse frame fit was compatible with feminist goals of equal political representation.

GENDERING THE DEBATE

Women's representation was part of the wider vision of Wakeham of a House of Lords that looked like Britain. Within the royal commission the pressure to take account of diversity came from Bill Morris, leader of the T and G, a powerful trade union with a strong equalities section. Morris was and is known to be a strong advocate of provision for the representation of diversity. His presence as a member of the Wakeham Commission was important to ensuring that the report advocated provision for adequate representation of women and of previously underrepresented ethnic and religious groups.

The Wakeham argument for women's representation did not adequately reflect feminist concerns. In some respects it contradicted them. The desirability of the presence of women in the House of Lords was invoked to counter arguments that the whole reformed chamber should be elected. It was said that only with an appointed house would there be adequate women's presence. Baroness Jay, leader of the House of Lords and minister for women between 1998 and 2001, argued that only recruitment by appointment could secure a fair presence of women. Her views were incorporated into the report. Ignoring the experience in the devolved assemblies of Scotland and Wales where women were 36 and 38 percent, respectively, of returned members, the Wakeham Report stated that "direct election delivers results that may be geographically representative but which are seldom gender balanced" (Wakeham 2000). In other words the criterion of gender balance was advanced in support of an undemocratic proposal.

Three women's organizations were expert witnesses to the Wakeham Commission—the National Board of Catholic Women, Wales Assembly of Women and the National Federation of Women's Institutes. Evidence was also submitted by the Democratic Audit Task Force that included feminist members and made the case for increased women's presence (Democratic Audit 1999). Similar evidence was offered by Mary Ann Stephenson, Director of the Fawcett Society, an organization that dates to the suffrage movement and is the main advocacy group on women's representation in the UK.

The report discussed women as a distinct but seemingly uniform group within society. Nowhere in the report is there a mention of divisions among women, or that women are members of ethnic and religious groups even though multiple identities and multiple interests are discussed. The media paid little attention to any debates about gender, except to mention the fact that women's representation was an issue. In the *Times,* among articles, letters to the editor, and lead articles, no article specifically addressed women and the House of Lords. The inclusion of religious representatives featured more prominently in the media, perhaps because, as Vincent (2000) notes, the churches were prominent in the Wakeham consultation process.

MOVEMENT IMPACT

Although women's substantive interests were not addressed, women's presence in the reformed House was discussed. Feminist observers suspected that the Wakeham Report's gender balance requirement was a cynical device to assure women's movement support for its recommendations. Arguably the debate was not gendered, although some women's advocates attempted to intervene. Nevertheless Wakeham did propose an improved presence of women, along with ethnic and religious groups in the reformed House of Lords. The report proposed an Appointments Commission with a statutory duty to ensure that at least 30 percent of new members of the House of Lords would be women and that steady progress of a balanced presence of both sexes was made. The Appointments Commission was to "use its best endeavours to see that minority ethnic groups are represented in proportion to their presence in the population as a whole" (Vincent 2000). However, Wakeham also opined that the representation of specific interests was not desirable (Wakeham 2000, Section 11.22). Moreover, although the Wakeham Report stated that women would not achieve equality of representation through an election process, it does not consider why elections might not deliver parity of representation. Hence an opportunity to address issues of women's representation in the context of an important constitutional reform was not taken despite the efforts of the Fawcett Society and the exhortations of some feminist activists. The Wakeham Report was criticized for this failure by a number of constitutional watchdog organizations including the Constitution Unit, the Democratic Audit, and Charter 88.

Women's interests were not regarded as central by the Wakeham Commission. Few women's organizations were consulted; there is no paper or analysis of women's issues listed as part of the commissioned papers. However, evidence was received from a few women MPs and peers who were advocates of women's representation. The Fawcett Society made a submission that called for a 40 percent minimum quota of women. This submission disputed the contention that appointment rather than election would guarantee women's presence. The Fawcett Society also argued on gender grounds that service in the reformed House of Lords should be paid. Their case was that women were less likely to have the financial resources necessary to serve on an unpaid basis. During the drafting stage of the government's post-Wakeham white paper the commitment to a minimum proportion of women was omitted. It was reinstated only after Meg Russell, by then special advisor on House of Lords reform to Robin Cook, the leader of the House of Commons, (see above), noticed the omission and redrafted the relevant passage. The impact of the movement is difficult to classify. The women's movement participated in the debate but did not prioritize the issue, perhaps because it was preoccupied with the renewed campaign to increase women's representation in the House of Commons. On the one hand a recommendation was made for a minimum proportion of women in the House of Lords; on the other, the recommendation was based on arguments that were not supported by the women's movement. At the end of the debate all the proposals were defeated. No one, except the Blair government, got what they wanted. Hence movement impact in this debate is *co-opted*.

CHARACTERISTICS AND ACTIVITIES
OF THE WOMEN'S POLICY AGENCY

The WPAs in existence during the time period—the Equal Opportunities Commission (EOC), the Women's National Commission (WNC), the Ministry for Women, the Cabinet Office Women's Unit, and the Cabinet Committee on Women—became marginally more powerful. Following reorganization after 1997 when the new women's unit was established in the Cabinet Office both the EOC and the WNC interpreted their mandates to include activity about women's representation.[1] Christine Crawley, a Labor-appointed member of the House of Lords and reliable advocate of women's representation, was a member of the WNC during the period of the debate. For most of the period WPA priorities were elsewhere. They did not give expert advice to the Wakeham Commission and they did not attempt to publicize the issue. The minister for women, Baroness Jay, who had overall responsibility for the rest of the WPA between 1998 and 2001, was a political appointee, a cabinet member, and, more importantly, leader of the House of Lords. However as a proudly self-declared anti-feminist, for most of her tenure she was clearly irritated by her role as a spokesperson on women's issues. A loyal member of the cabinet from the House of Lords she had no independent political base. Her loyalties were to the prime minister and her priority was House of Lords reform. Her leadership is best described as non-feminist and the WPA activities as *symbolic*. The WPA were, however, more extensive, better funded, and closer to the center of power than they had been in the 1970s and 1980s.

It is worth noting that the first Blair government (1997–2001) only grudgingly honored its pledge to put women's issues at the heart of government (Lovenduski 2005). Tony Blair and his advisers believed that special measures to ensure sex equality in politics were vote losers, a stance that was encouraged by the press. During the first part of the second Blair government, between 2001 and 2003, when the vote on the method of selecting members of the House of Lords was taken, some of the personnel of the women's policy agencies changed. Another member of the House of Lords, Sally Morgan, briefly became minister for women. When Morgan left the government to become political adviser to Tony Blair, she was succeeded by Patricia Hewitt, the minister for trade and industry, who continued in both posts at the time of writing in summer 2004. During the second Blair government more attention was paid to WPAs, which became marginally more powerful and competent. However the WPA did not intervene in the Lords reform debates in that period; hence the classification of its activities on this issue as symbolic describes the entire debate.

WOMEN'S MOVEMENT CHARACTERISTICS

The movement was fragmented but the part of the movement interested in political representation issues was at a stage of *consolidation*. Support for such issues had grown as had movement capacity. However, advocates were naturally more interested in increasing women's representation in the House of Commons. Hence the issue was, for those who were interested, of *moderate priority*. This part of the movement was close to the left of the political spectrum, especially to the Labor Party but also to the Liberal Democratic Party who by then were thought by many political scientists to have outflanked Labor on the left (Webb 2000). At the end of the 1990s feminism benefited from high-capacity advocacy organisations such as the Fawcett Society and well-established channels of access to the government. The movement was fairly *cohesive* and the counter-movement *weak* on women's representation aspects of House of Lords reform.

THE POLICY ENVIRONMENT

After Labor came into power in 1997 the Blair leadership quickly established a highly centralized mode of government that privileged loyalty and unity within the governing party. Decision-making remained highly centralized. A regime of special advisers, appointed gatekeepers, and leadership by spin and focus group soon attracted criticism. The royal commission had only advisory capacity. To get its recommendations implemented government agreement was required. Although government was minded to agree, widespread disagreements over how members of the reformed House of Lords should be selected cooled its immediate enthusiasm. Eventually the prime minister prevailed. On the face of it, the access of women's advocates to the policy environment improved during the long period of the debate. Reorganization and expansion of the WPA, the historic election of 101 Labor women to the House of Commons, the appointment of record numbers of women to government, continuing internal party pressure from Labor women, and the growing capacity of advocacy organizations such as the Fawcett Society all contributed to the establishment of some channels through which women's issues could be raised and promoted. However on this debate the policy subsystem and the policy system coincided. The prime minister preferred an appointed House of Lords and Parliament itself was divided. Ultimately the policy subsystem was the policy system in the sense that the whole government decision-making system was in play. Whilst interventions could be made by advocates and agencies, their voices could not be decisive without government support. Hence the policy environment may be characterized as *moderately closed.*

CONCLUSION

Debate about the reform of the House of Lords continues. It has only ever been minimally gendered. Although it is not a priority, feminist advocates continue to keep their eyes on the issue. Largely because of developments in EU treaty obligations, WPA mandates now include political representation and the government is alert to the need to appoint women. What is striking about the debate between 1997 and 2001 is that not only was it not gendered, but also the issue of gender may have been cynically used and WPAs were not engaged. Between 2001 and 2003 there was little evidence that anyone was attempting to gender this debate.

Acknowledgements: Alison Warner of Nuffield College Oxford conducted some of the research for this essay. Meg Russell, Deborah Lincoln, and Mary Ann Stephenson all supplied important information.

NOTES

1. The mandate change also reflected the EU policy to increase the proportions of women in decision making.

15

Welfare Reform: America's Hot Issue

Dorothy E. McBride

In the U.S., with its federal system, limited state, and entrenched culture of liberal political thought, any change resembling neoliberalism, it seems, might be hardly noticed, let alone "significant." Nevertheless there is at least one policy debate that offers a magnificent struggle among a wide range of policy actors over whether even America's comparatively meager commitment to state responsibility should continue in the context of a devolution of powers to state and local government. This is the four-year struggle that resulted in the Personal Responsibility and Work Opportunity Reconciliation Act (PRWORA) of 1996—the "end of welfare as we know it."[1]

In the 1970s, neoliberalism's most powerful advocate, Ronald Reagan, mounted a campaign to move the Republican Party dramatically to the right; a central feature of this campaign was to get "gov'ment" (as he called it) off the backs of private citizens. In this, Reagan meant the central government in Washington, and, as president from 1981–1988, he furthered a plan for devolution of central-state relations through his *New Federalism*. Reagan's approach proved to be successful for Republicans, whose election fortunes gradually improved through the 1980s. It appeared that bashing the government was popular with the voters, while appeals from Democrats to government's responsibility to deal with social problems met with dwindling support. Soon the New Democrats appeared, led by Governor Bill Clinton, and put together a successful campaign for the presidency based on appropriating many of the neoliberal issues raised by the Republicans. One of these was the promise of a drastic overhaul of the major national social welfare program that had survived since the 1930s: Aid to Families with Dependent Children (AFDC). This promised to be a popular move because the vast majority of Americans hated welfare and disapproved of those entitled to receive its cash payments.

SELECTION OF THE DEBATE

The debate leading up to the adoption of major welfare reform legislation—Personal Responsibility and Work Opportunity Reconciliaiton Act—in 1996 was not the only priority issue in U.S. national politics in the 1990s. This section presents the evidence that justifies the composition of the universe of hot issues and the ultimate choice of welfare reform as the hottest RNGS issue.

Identifying the Universe of Hot Issues

The first step was to determine the universe of top-priority debates during the decade according to the criteria of scope, degree of conflict, range of public attention, and interest of major policy actors. A review of the *Congressional Quarterly Reports* provided an initial list of issues that occupied the U.S. Congress from 1990–2001. Then evidence of scope, conflict, public attention and policy actor interest was gathered for each issue. The top five compose the universe of hot issues in the 1990s: health care reform, 1992–1994; crime/gun control, 1990–1994; welfare reform, 1992–1996; partial-birth abortion ban, 1995–2000; the North American Free Trade Agreement, 1990–1993.

According to the criteria, the hottest issue of the 1990s was health care reform. It came to the public agenda at the top of President Clinton's first-term agenda. The goal of his proposal was to expand insurance coverage for medical and hospital expenses to all Americans, including 35 million uninsured. Reaching this ambitious objective would have required an overhaul of the entire health insurance system in the U.S. and affected every person living in the United States. The proposal was very controversial, made even more so by the prominent role played by First Lady Hillary Rodham Clinton in the preparation stages of the bill and in testifying before Congress. This led to extensive media coverage. The public debate played out in massive advertising campaigns by the protagonists (Kolbert 1993). By some accounts (Lewis 1994), "health care reform has become the most heavily lobbied legislative initiative in United States history." The debate had great scope and high conflict. Nevertheless, although many voters thought it important, prosecution and prevention of crime was more important to them. At the same time, policy actors, other than the president and his supporters in labor unions, were not especially keen on overhauling the health care system. The policy proposal gradually lost support in Congress and never came up for a final vote.

Because of citizens' concerns, the crime bill/gun control issue was the second hottest issue of the 1990s according to the criteria (Jaroslovsky 1993). By affecting police protection and safety of communities throughout the country it had scope second only to health reform. The most heavily lobbied issue involved a ban on nineteen semi-automatic assault weapons and on larger capacity ammunition clips, higher standards for gun dealers, and restrictions on juveniles' owning guns and those under restraining orders connected with domestic violence. Although pro-gun lobbyists sought to soften the gun restrictions, they were unsuccessful when the Republican leadership learned that bans on assault weapons had strong public support (Clymer 1996). The issue was on the Clinton administration's agenda, but the president merely reacted to congressional initiatives on gun control while taking the leadership role on health care. The Republican leaders were especially receptive to the gun lobby. While the conflict was intense on the gun issue, the rest of the bill was not as discordant as the Clinton health care reform proposal.

Welfare reform stands as the third hottest policy issue of the 1990s using the criteria outlined above. It was the issue that was the top priority of the major policy elites in both parties (Weaver 2000). Clinton included the famous phrase "to end welfare as we know it" in his campaign platform in 1992. Gingrich and the Republicans made it a cornerstone of their Contract with America in 1994. [2] There was strong public support for a major overhaul of the welfare system, which was established in the 1930s, although there was not the extensive media coverage dedicated to health care reform. With widespread agreement on the need for reform, the conflict developed over different solutions offered by the major parties. It was fairly contentious; after the Republicans won the majority in Congress in 1994, President Clinton vetoed their welfare proposals three times before finally signing PRWORA in 1996. The scope of the policy was limited to the poor—mostly women and children and disproportionately the minority—not the entire population.

While welfare reform was the issue that policy actors in both parties agreed was a top priority, NAFTA was next most important across the political spectrum. NAFTA was also of great significance to the business community. At the same time, the public was not much engaged in the issue. Opposition arose from labor, farm, and environmental interests, but the policy process also revealed divisions within the parties over the proposal, muting the cleavages in Congress. By affecting various sectors, rather than the entire economy, NAFTA ranks as the fourth highest priority issue in the 1990s.

The abortion issue has been extremely controversial since the 1970s and the conflict over the Partial-Birth Abortion Ban Act was no exception. And, although it was supported by the Republican majority, the issue was certainly not high on either party's agenda. The public, while aware of the issue, was not particularly affected by it and it had the least scope of all the issues considered, applying only to very few women seeking late-term abortions, although the moral and human rights implications of the abortion issue always pertained to a much larger population than women with problem pregnancies.

Thus although for a minority of advocates the partial-birth abortion ban was a major life/death issue, it is the lowest priority among the universe of issues.

Identifying the Debate for Study

Any one of these debates, because of their scope, degree of conflict, public engagement, and elite support, would be an appropriate case to study the effect of women's policy offices on hot issues in the 1990s. However, to enhance the potential of comparative analysis, we are to select the debate that would involve major changes in state-society relations. In examining the proposals for change at stake in these five policy debates, it was clear that welfare reform involved the greatest change in state-society relations. Through the radical devolution of funds and policy leadership on the welfare issue from the national federal government to the states, PRWORA constituted an extensive policy reorganization of the U.S. federal system. In addition, the focus of the policy shifted from ending poverty toward moving people off welfare rolls, shifting responsibility for the well-being of the poor to groups, such as churches, in the non-profit sector. The idea behind reform was to turn poor mothers into workers seeking economic self-sufficiency and largely fending for themselves in getting help from the government. None of the other debates in the universe of hot issues in the US could be linked to as many indicators of changes in state-society relations.

WOMEN'S MOVEMENT IN THE NINETIES

The U.S. women's movement that contended with the welfare reform issue in the 1990s had changed significantly from earlier decades. In the 1960s and early 1970s actors had brought two different feminist discourses to the public arena. Liberal feminism envisioned the full and equal integration of women and men in all aspects of society. Radical feminism, or women's liberation, focused on the defeat of male domination, thus remaking personal relations between the sexes. Activists representing these discourses favored different organizational forms and strategies: the liberals through mainstream interest organizations and policy campaigns and the radicals through autonomous egalitarian organizations and direct action. By the 1990s, radical feminist activism had seemed to disappear and the visibility of the women's movement generally had declined. Was feminism dead?[3]

The feminist discourse in the 1990s reflected that change had certainly occurred. As opposed to community and social solidarity, individual initiative and work had a central place. At the same time, priorities for movement activism reflected the integration of the radical feminist perspective into the movement: sexuality issues such as lesbian concerns, sexual abuse, date rape, violence and woman battery, reproductive rights, and sexual harassment. In fact, diversity was the hallmark of the nineties movement ideologies. While the pitch at the national arena appeared to become moderate and the activists feared marginalization, radical feminist goals were the province of countless grassroots efforts (Whittier 1995).

Diversity in organization and strategies in the nineties mirrored the diversity in goals and a rather neat division of movement labor. Nationally, a large number of organizations were well established in Washington, D.C. Many had large staffs with fund-raising mechanisms built in. Their leaders composed the ninety-plus Council of Presidents, which met monthly to share information and take positions on issues. Together they were part of a complex women's policy network linking with traditional women's organizations, media, other movements, and even government officials to work on specific campaigns on issues such as education policy, women's health, and, as it turned out, welfare reform (Boles 1993).

Women's movement actors and especially feminist activists were busy at the state and local levels of American politics as well. Networks and coalitions worked on state government issues while local women's policy networks joined together a large number of grassroots feminist groups. Local networking was especially a feature of African American women's movement activism. The local level remained a place where radical feminist ideas and tactics could be found. In fact, on the welfare issue, JEDI Women (Justice, Economic Dignity and Independence for Women) mobilized women in speakouts, demonstrations, and marches to protest proposals for drastic cutbacks.

If one could put the movements in the 1970s and the 1990s side by side, what would be different? What would be the same? Outwardly, there were many differences. In the 1970s, movement discourse was new, revolutionary, and dynamic; in the 1990s, it was familiar, centrist, and often invisible. In the 1970s, the dominant tendency was radical; in the 1990s, it was moderate. In the 1970s, the movement claimed to speak for all women in a unity of interest; in the 1990s, the movement claimed to speak for no one group, and fragmented through a politics of racial, gender, and class identities. In the 1970s, the movement activists were outside the policy arenas, trying to gain access. In the 1990s, movement activists were inside, through institutionalized representation in policy networks and government agencies, and especially through a growing representation of women in Congress.

The differences in these two periods are understood by the events of the 1980s, when radical and revolutionary energies waned and the right wing gained more power through election and appointment. Movement strategies shifted from "pushing the envelope" toward protecting the gains made in abortion, equal pay, and equal education. What Tobias (1997) calls "Third Generation Issues"—women in combat, pornography, comparable worth, and motherhood—of the 1990s sparked conflict and controversy among feminist activists, making it increasingly difficult for organizations to present a united front, much less represent *women* to policymakers. Still, it was clear by the beginning of the 1990s that the terms of debate on many national questions had permanently changed as if women mattered: abortion, work and pay, work and family, education, family law, and sexuality. However, in other areas there was less success in gendering the national debate. One of these pertained to gaining economic justice for the poor.

During the 1980s there was a shift in feminist thinking about poverty that affected activists' role in the welfare reform debate. A growing body of research documented the dreary economic status of women, despite gains in legal rights. The *feminization of poverty* was a concept intended to shift policymakers' conception of the poor and solutions to poverty (Pearce 1967; Sidel 1986). It was well documented that the majority of the poor were women, either elderly women (considered by policymakers as *deserving* poor) or young single mothers (considered by many policymakers as *undeserving*). Evidence of the rapid increase in the number of female-headed families, the realization that many of these were very poor and black, and the social pathologies that resulted led to a shift in some feminist thinking. Whereas in the 1970s, feminists defended a woman's right to form a family without a man as a social improvement,[4] by the 1980s, they were less optimistic, looking to ways to alleviate the economic burdens of single parenthood for women through increased child support, increased child care, and improved job opportunities. For many feminists, jobs were seen as a way to emancipate women from dependency on the government and on abusive men.

At the same time, other feminists retained a maternalist perspective and continued to view the mother-only family as legitimate and deserving of support. They viewed financial aid to single mothers as a way to allow them the choice to be caregivers, the way that middle-class mothers with breadwinner husbands did. To deprive poor women, who were mostly black, of this option was both racist and classist, they argued. These different perspectives affected the strategies of those feminist organizations active during the welfare reform proposals in the 1980s. While Tobias (1997) and O'Connor (2001) attribute the split to different understandings of the plight of single mothers, Mink (2000) blames class and race biases of active feminists, especially the feminists in Congress who overwhelmingly voted for punitive welfare reform provisions. It is not the case that feminists abandoned coalitions opposing the cutbacks in welfare support. NOW (National Organization of Women), NOW LDEF (Now Legal Defense and Education Fund), and others joined with the

National Welfare Rights Union in the campaign "Up and Out of Poverty, Now," and NOW LDEF helped organize eighty groups into the Child Exclusion Coalition (Abramovitz 1996). And most movement groups favored retaining the federal welfare entitlement. What separated the two feminist factions was the issue of jobs. Groups such as the Institute for Women's Policy Research, Wider Opportunities for Women, and the National Black Women's Health Project accepted the notion that paid work for welfare mothers was a top goal. The feminist minority, represented by the Women's Committee of 100, was nearly alone in claiming the right of welfare mothers not to work and be supported by government programs.[5]

DEBATE: PERSONAL RESPONSIBILITY AND WORK OPPORTUNITY RECONCILIATION ACT, 1992–1996

How the Debate Came to the Public Agenda

In the 1960s, welfare reform meant efforts to expand support for the poor, while helping them to work. Typically, however, work programs exempted women with children under six years of age, the majority of AFDC recipients. By the 1980s, welfare reform had come to mean proposals to move people off welfare and reduce costs. The 1988 Family Support Act (FSA) had bipartisan support to allow states to experiment with programs to move welfare clients into jobs. One of the chief advocates and beneficiaries of the FSA was Governor Bill Clinton of Arkansas. According to Naples (1997), FSA marked a new consensus between the Left and Right that the poor should work. Many concepts, such as *self-sufficiency* and *parental responsibility* that were later to become entrenched in the 1990s, were first introduced in the hearings in 1988. Between 1988 and 1992, reports showed increases of 30 percent in AFDC cases as well as more and more out-of-wedlock births. There were declining rates of AFDC recipients getting work and evidence of generations of grandmothers, mothers, and daughters on welfare. The concept of *dependency* was increasingly used to describe this particular pathology (O'Connor 2001). In addition, there were many studies that claimed to document the negative effect on children of growing up in families headed by single, never-married mothers. For many, these data documented the failures of social programs under the War on Poverty of the 1960s as well as giving credibility to works by Charles Murray that it was the welfare program itself that caused poverty.[6] Both Democrats and Republicans were receptive to this shift in knowledge about welfare. The program had few supporters Left or Right; President Clinton gave it the necessary push to the congressional agenda during his campaign and in his first few months in office.

Dominant Frame of the Debate

1992

The dominant frame of the 1990s welfare reform debate had been established with the enactment of the Family Support Act in 1988. All agreed that welfare rolls must be reduced and that the recipients should take jobs. By 1992, the Democrats controlled the definition of the issue of welfare reform when the Committee on Hunger of the House of Representatives first held hearings. The problem of welfare was depicted as the failure of AFDC, unchanged since its establishment in 1935. Recognizing that the public resented cash assistance to the idle poor, the Democrats felt some urgency to provide tools for people to get off welfare and into work. FSA provided the starting point, and many looked for ways to expand its provisions, specifically by giving people education and training, along with needed supports of child care, child support, and health insurance. With the twin goals of poverty reduction and self-sufficiency, the government would take the lead in developing this new approach that, Democrats hoped, would bring about public support for assisting the poor.

House Republicans claimed that the welfare system perpetuated dependency and poverty and individual members suggested a variety of solutions such as allowing asset accumulation, enterprise zones, more educational choice, health care, and job training. But they were not in a position to make a specific proposal. The committee did give opportunities to the conservatives to testify, bringing Robert Rector of the Heritage Foundation to make what would become a regular appearance before a variety of congressional committees considering the welfare issue. Rector's "world of welfare" was quite different from that portrayed by the majority. Instead of the earnest poor needing help to get a job, he saw a system which rewarded "behavioral" poverty—the poverty of idleness and immorality, which he said was much more serious than material poverty of housing, food, and medical care. He argued for an end to the "bad incentives" that perpetuated his version of poverty, that is, an end to the free ride from the government. The poor would respond, he maintained, to disincentives such as work requirements, lifetime limits on assistance, and reduced support for single mothers and would be more likely to limit the size of their families and choose marriage.

Clinton's Initiative, 1994

In 1994, Secretary of Health and Human Services Donna Shalala appeared before the House Committee on Education and Labor to explain the Clinton administration's Work and Responsibility Act, the first stab at a comprehensive change in the law. It left the federal entitlement of AFDC intact and focused on getting welfare recipients into jobs. The administration considered that the federal government would invest in training, employment, child care, and medical assistance and would help enforce child support orders, all to achieve the primary goal: "Make Work Pay." With references to the need for child support and prevention of out-of-wedlock teenage pregnancy, the keystone of the Clinton reform was to make mothers economically self-sufficient.

In these waning days of the Democratic Party's (congressional) dominance, advocates for welfare recipients were allowed to present their views. Insisting on presenting the welfare mothers' point of view, these advocates gave tacit support for training, child care, and transportation as helping them prepare for jobs. But their primary argument was that poor mothers should have the option, with state support, to devote themselves to caregiving, just as some middle class women were able to do with their husbands' breadwinner income (Mink 1998).

Laced among the witnesses were leaders of the Congressional Caucus for Women's Issues (CCWI). One of several legislative service organizations (LSO), the CCWI included nearly all women members of Congress and even more male members as associates. The co-chairs were from the two major parties. In these early hearings, Marge Roukema (Republican) focused on the need for better child support as a solution to the poverty faced by single mothers. This pertained to welfare in two important ways. First of all, AFDC recipients qualified because they were in charge of children who did not receive adequate financial support from their parents (usually, fathers). Improving enforcement of fathers' responsibilities for support would improve situations for these children and perhaps remove the mothers from dependence on welfare. Secondly, she argued that the government should take an active role in establishing paternity of children born out of wedlock, rather than automatically enrolling these children and their mothers in AFDC.

Thus, in the first two years of the Clinton administration with the Democrats still in the majority in the Congress, the dominant frame of the welfare reform debate maintained a national cash entitlement for poor families (mostly single mothers and children) and a strong role for the federal government in moving these welfare mothers toward jobs. There were modest time limits on the table but few punitive measures for those who did not comply with the dominant work ethic. In addition, the frame presented the federal government with responsibility for funding the support for bringing poor mothers into work. Necessary job training, child care, and medical assistance promised, if successful, to be costly or, if unsuccessful, a continuation of past failures to put welfare mothers to work.

Contract with America, 1995

The Gingrich Republicans were serious, and they were not going to take the Clinton bill as a template. They provided their own Personal Responsibility Act in 1995 to represent their reframing of the dominant discourse on welfare. Their plan was based on assumptions echoing Murray's argument: the poor rise to the expectations you have of them (Murray 1984). The approach placed morality and behavior at the center of the discussion. Specifically, poverty and a number of other social ills were blamed on increases in illegitimacy and families headed by single mothers. Otherwise their goal was to decrease welfare rolls and reduce federal expenditures for the poor. They would stamp out immorality and require responsibility and work through federal regulations; they would save funds through block grants to the states—a fixed fund that states could use to accomplish the goals.

The Right included all federal social programs in their definition of *welfare*, not just AFDC, which the earlier frames had done. Taking all the money spent on these programs together they presented evidence that welfare programs increased poverty; they expected the poor to be lazy and immoral and as a result they were. They used Murray's and other conservative intellectuals' writings to show that children were in the best condition in two-parent (married and raising biological children) families, and in dire condition (low education levels, juvenile delinquency, drugs) in families of never-married mothers. Government should encourage marriage or require work, they argued, by whatever means possible, and liberate these poor women and children from the bondage of the federal dole. They tended to scoff at job training as a waste of money, opting for more regulatory policy tools:

1. family caps: no additional financial support for children born while parents are on welfare
2. require welfare recipients to work
3. provide no benefits for unmarried mothers under eighteen. (A typical comment: "If they can't live with parents, then they should be in group homes or put their children in orphanages or up for adoption.")
4. require welfare recipients to name fathers of out-of-wedlock children to get payments
5. force fathers to pay support or participate in work programs
6. enact lifetime limits on welfare eligibility
7. deny assistance to both legal and illegal immigrants (as in, "We don't want people coming to the U.S. to get on our welfare rolls.")

While the Gingrich Republicans and their intellectual allies on the Right supported decentralizing block grants instead of earmarked funds for federal programs, they did want a strong role for the federal government in regulating the morality of the poor. In this, they tended to run counter to a very strong actor in the welfare debates: the National Governor's Association (NGA).

The NGA wanted to turn welfare, lock, stock, and barrel, over to the states, all except for the funding responsibility, which they wanted to keep in the federal treasury. They promised that the states would be more capable of enforcing child support, paternity establishment, and work requirements. They would also encourage marriage and cure dependency. They noted that states like Wisconsin had already taken the lead in bringing welfare mothers into the workforce. The NGA worked closely with Republican congressional leaders and were able to temper some of the federal regulations in favor of more state flexibility.

President Clinton and the Democrats were, in 1995, in the unfamiliar position of reacting to the Republicans' lead on the issue. Shalala came before the House Committee on Ways and Means and tried to soften some of the punitive approaches in the Republican bill. Democrats attempted to bring back the old issue frames of helping children and reducing poverty to divert attention from talk of orphanages. They opposed denying benefits to mothers under eighteen because it would hurt children, and were critical of the low priority given to child support enforcement. They argued that pushing people off welfare will not necessarily put them into jobs, but rather would increase their suffering.

Summary of Dominant Issue Frame

From 1988 on, actors in the policy process agreed that the problem with welfare was the welfare program itself, specifically AFDC. It was too costly. They agreed that its primary purpose should be temporary assistance with provisions that aimed to move people off welfare and into work. They also agreed that responding to the problem of poverty pertained to the individual needs and demands of single mothers, rather than confronting structural deficiencies in the economy.

Within this frame were three major points of conflict. First, there were two schools of thought with respect to the reasons single mothers needed government support. Some, mostly moderate Democrats, looked to the lack of skills, education, and experience, compounded by bad luck; others, mostly on the Right, blamed immorality exacerbated by dependency on government handouts. Depending on the view of the reasons single mothers were on welfare, there was debate over the government policies to move them off the rolls. One approach was to increase training, education, child care, and other supports to enable mothers to find jobs. The other approach used regulations, such as family caps, lifetime caps, and exclusion of teen mothers. Regardless of which approach they took, policy actors agreed on the need to increase child support from absent fathers. The third point of contention was the role of the federal government in welfare policy. The federal role would be nearly eliminated by those favoring block grants and state regulations. Others favored the retention of the federal entitlement to provide a basic safety net for the poor. The right wing wanted a federal role to enforce regulations on the poor.

Gendering the Debate

Between 1992 and 1995, there was little explicit gendering of the debate over welfare reform. Democrats and Republicans had the habit of referring to welfare recipients as *mothers* because in the AFDC program, single mothers were the primary clients. But these references carried few explicit gender references or analysis with them. Implicitly, however, they were packed with race and gender meaning. Experts advising both parties referred to the studies that showed that the long-term, dependent welfare clients were never married and were mostly black. Their children were raised in homes without fathers. Democrats charged that Republicans tended to blame women for their poverty, and called in experts claiming that most women on welfare were not lazy but work, at least part-time, and move off of welfare before the end of five years. Republicans and the Right envisioned (mostly black) teenage girls getting pregnant and expecting to be supported, while their children grew up to be juvenile delinquents. Democrats were more likely to consider the structural explanations for poverty—lack of jobs, education, or recession—while the Republicans focused on character inadequacies and immoral behavior. The consequences of illegitimacy were seen as catastrophic. Single mothers were incapable of raising their sons, leaving poor areas with young men ". . . not civilized in a family context who perpetuate a reign of terror of drugs and crime. Both mother and father have responsibility for raising and supporting children."

During the 1995 hearings, Clinton administration officials and their Democratic allies in the Congress declined to gender their presentations. However, with the extensive hearings on the reform, advocates for women's groups made their way to testify—usually in five-minute blocks, submitting written testimony for the record. Mink (1998) accused middle-class feminists of acquiescence or silence about the effects of the right-wing plan for welfare reform on poor women. It is true that they were for the most part reactive, denying the claims of the Republicans that welfare mothers were lazy teenagers watching television all day on the government dole. They tended to support jobs and education for women to break the cycle of poverty and improve self-esteem. Kate Michelman of the National Abortion and Reproductive Rights Action League (NARAL) viewed reform as a way to help women make responsible decisions about childbearing and encourage self-sufficiency. She argued that the purpose of government policy should be to give women dignity and opportunity, not punishment.

Right-wing advocates for women's interests also participated in the hearings. They saw welfare mothers and their children as victims of welfare, and criticized the fact that with welfare women can bear children with men they know they would or could never marry. Not every family should be preserved, said Catherine Young of the Women's Freedom Network, referring to single teenage mothers. In fact, to her, group homes were not a bad idea.

Advocates for fathers' rights also contributed to the gendering of the debate. They portrayed fathers as being driven away from their children by welfare policies that focused on mothers. Fathers should be an alternative, not just to be "forced" to pay child support, but to have a chance to gain custody or extensive visitation with their children. Fatherhood rights groups tended to link providing financial support with access to their children, a position that many advocates for women opposed. As this debate unfolded it became clear that those in charge—the Republicans of the Contract with America—and the right-wing intellectual community did not want a society where poor women had the option to form families independent of the fathers of their children unless they could, by some miracle, become economically self-sufficient.

Policy Outcome: PRWORA, 1996

The act reflected the Republican proposal, eliminating the federal entitlement AFDC and establishing Temporary Assistance to Needy Families (TANF), funded through block grants to the states (these were capped grants, meaning the amount of money allocated to each state was fixed for five years). The policy outcome represented a paradigm shift in welfare policy holding the poor, individually, responsible for their poverty and for ending it. The new policy required welfare recipients to get jobs within two years of receiving benefits and take community service jobs before that. No more lifelong dependency, the act imposed a lifetime limit of welfare eligibility of five years and denied support altogether for legal immigrants not yet citizens. The act did not guarantee child care although it provided funds for that purpose. To promote child support, welfare recipients were required to name fathers of out-of-wedlock children to get payment. Failure to cooperate would reduce benefits at least 25 percent and maybe eliminate them altogether.

Republicans did not win federal controls over the most punitive proposals, however, since the act gave states wide discretion over a variety of restrictions.

For example, states could impose family caps, that is, provide no additional financial support for children born while parents are on welfare or whose children don't attend school regularly. They were authorized to deny benefits for unmarried mothers under eighteen unless they live with an adult relative and attend school. To reduce illegitimacy, there were financial incentives to states to reduce out-of-wedlock births without increasing abortion. States had the option of eliminating the $50 child support pass-through to TANF recipients.[7] Child care funding was included under the capped block grant; any additional funds would be available only if the state matched them. It was not all the Republicans wanted: Medicaid, the health care provision, was preserved for poor women and their children. In addition, states had some discretion to exempt some mothers from the work requirements and more punitive requirements. For example, the Family Violence Option allowed states to waive time limits, child support/paternity establishment cooperation requirements, and family cap provisions where it would "make it more difficult for individuals receiving assistance to escape domestic violence," defined as "battered or subjected to extreme cruelty."

Movement Impact

Women's movement actors could claim only a few victories in this outcome. They were happiest about the Family Violence Option, which had been drafted by Martha Davis of NOW LDEF and introduced by Democratic Senator Paul Wellstone. There was no denial of health care for welfare recipients, and efforts to drastically reduce child care funds had been stymied. They were relieved there was no national family cap. These were, however, small victories in the face of great defeats, especially the elimination of AFDC financial and child care entitlements, a provision opposed by all women's movement actors. They also lost on paternity establishment, the child support pass-through, and the denial of assistance to teen mothers. Of the thirteen major provisions of the act, four coincided with women's movement actors' goals, six did not coincide, and on three the actors did not take a public stand.

Although female members of Congress were successful in a few areas, overall the women's movement actors saw the policy outcome as a failure. Thus this case demonstrates movement impact of *co-optation*. Individual women and organizations advocating women's interests participated in the welfare debate. As members of Congress, Republican women were key players on committees, shaping child care and child protection provisions and adding provisions to increase child support. Women's movement organizations presented testimony at congressional committees, although they were not particularly active in this regard in the later stages of the debate. They were, however, active in lobbying efforts and NOW and NOW LDEF leaders spoke of new alliances made during the course of the debate. NOW capped its activism with a publicized hunger strike to protest President Clinton's signing of the bill.

Women's Policy Agency Activities

The Women's Bureau was *symbolic* in the welfare reform debate. Although issues of job training and work are in its mandate, the Department of Labor, where it is housed, was not involved in the welfare reform.[8] The Congressional Caucus for Women's Issues was an *insider* in the policy debate. Established in 1977, CCWI was a group of legislators committed to improving the status of women. It was not, however, the product of a formal government decree, and thus is classified as a quasi-women's policy agency (QUAWPA). All women in the House and the Senate were members and paid dues, while male members could join as associates. Women legislators formed the caucus in response to a request by women's movement organizations, such as NOW, the National Women's Political Caucus, and the Federation of Business and Professional Women's Clubs. They saw the CCWI as a conduit to enable them to communicate their objectives directly to the congressional agenda, providing them with a formal entree into policy agendas. It received offices and expenses from the Congress and had a $240,000 operating budget derived from members' dues. In 1995, however, the Newt Gingrich Republicans ended administrative support for all such legislative interest organizations. The CCWI then became an all-women's organization of legislators and formed a nongovernmental organization, Women's Policy, Inc., to provide support through fund-raising from private sources. The scope was cross-sectional, as CCWI involved itself with a wide range of issues pertaining to economic, social, and political interests of women and their families. As a legislative organization, its members were close to the power centers as policymakers and members of committees and policy subsystems. CCWI was a bipartisan organization led by elected co-chairs (one Democrat and one Republican) and an executive committee. In the 1995–1996 period, the co-chairs were Constance Morella and Nita Lowey. Both were feminist advocates for women's rights. Policy priorities were developed by the executive committee and assigned to task forces. However, its bi-partisan nature and the desire to advocate positions unanimously approved by the members limited the CCWI's mandate on welfare. It did, however, decide to focus on issues pertaining to children in the welfare debate especially child support enforcement and child care provisions. Connie Morella organized bi-partisan efforts to maintain child care provisions and Nancy Johnson, well placed on the Ways and Means Committee, presented CCWI's child support and child care proposals (Casey & Carroll 2001). These were two of the three provisions of PRWORA which coincided with women's movement goals.

The Women's Bureau was the other women's policy agency with a mandate related to the issues raised by the welfare reform debate. As the oldest agency, established by statute in 1920, the bureau is charged with promoting the interests of working women (Stetson 1995). Its director, which, by statute, must be a woman, is appointed by the president although the agency itself is a bureaucratic office located in the office of the secretary of the Department of Labor; thus the director is close to a member of the president's cabinet. In the 1970s, the secretary decreed that the bureau would review any programs under consideration or administered within the department that have an impact on women. Bill Clinton appointed Karen Nussbaum as director, an active feminist in union politics, especially recognized for her role in establishing 9-to-5, a union promoting the rights of working women. She had an annual budget of around $7 million and supervised ten regional offices. The staff was organized into three policy teams: training and employment; work and family; and women and the global economy.

The welfare program itself was not within the mandate of the Women's Bureau; rather, it was the responsibility of the Department of Health and Human Services. Thus, the bureau took no position on the issue or sought to participate in the debate (Interview with Karen Nussbaum 4/14/03). However, the agency was involved later in setting up regulations relating to the Welfare to Work program for welfare recipients that was administered by the Employment and Training Administration of the Department of Labor.

Women's Movement Characteristics

By the 1990s, women's movement actors at the national level were found in well-organized interest groups and inside government institutions; as a result of the 1992 election there was a significant increase in the number of women's advocates in the Congress itself. In contrast to the 1970s, the movement discourse was diverse and the organizations complex. One place where women's movement actors were especially active was inside the Democratic Party. At the 1992 Democratic convention, feminists were everywhere and feminist values taken for granted in the party culture (Freeman 1992). Feminist concerns were in the party platform in sections covering abortion and family. In 1996, the feminists remained inside the party and sex and gender issues were pervasive in the 1996 platform (Freeman 1997).[9]

Despite efforts of some activists, however, welfare reform was not a high priority on the women's movement agenda. Reproductive rights, domestic violence, and sexual harassment garnered more attention. Mink (1998) claims that this was due to class interests of most feminists. But the lack of cohesion on the issue may explain this situation better. On those issues where there was agreement, such as improving child support, women's movement organizations came together. And, while they agreed that AFDC and its federal entitlement for poor mothers should be retained, they disagreed on the work issues. Some organizations argued that work leading to self-sufficiency would improve women's status and focused on getting more job training and child care support in the welfare bill. Others, a minority, fought for the right of poor mothers to be supported by the government to take care of their children (Kornbluh 1996).

Whatever their priorities in the welfare reform debate, women's movement actors faced a strong counter-movement in the Republican Party's Contract with America. This conservative approach focused on women's behavior and values, not the economy. Poor women and girls were blamed for their own poverty. According to Orloff, analysts consider that the "end of AFDC entitlements reflects the culmination of a long standing series of racist and misogynist campaigns against welfare on the part of conservative political forces" (Orloff 2001: 8).

Policy Environment

The policy subsystem occupied with welfare programs is centered in Congress—including several major committees of both houses and invited witnesses at their hearings—in interaction with the governors of the states on the one hand and the president and the Department of Health and Human Services (DHHS) on the other. This subsystem has been debating various aspects of welfare reform for over forty years. In the 1990s, the issue came to the national agenda through feedback from those states experimenting with provisions of the 1988 Family Support Act. Also, there was the perception of a crisis in welfare spending that prompted legislative action. Specific proposals on various aspects of the reform came from the governors, the Republican Contract with America, and the administration, specifically Clinton's task force on welfare reform. With all these actors widely distributed throughout the federal system the debate is open to many ideas, but the final process is controlled by the majority in the Congress, whose members command the activities of the vital legislative committees which resolve conflicts into law. Thus the policy process was moderately closed.

The issue frame that dominated the policy subsystem had shifted in the 1980s from an ideology to use welfare policy to fight poverty to an ideology that welfare assistance promoted poverty. This frame portrayed single mothers as responsible for their own poverty through their immoral behavior and laziness. The dominant goal was to end welfare and move people off the rolls. Some of the policy proposals in this frame appeared to promote women's status, such as improved enforcement of child support and child care policy, but there was no attention to the fate of women in their new roles as workers. The micro-frames of the women's movement actors emphasized fighting women's poverty. Although movement actors disagreed on the means, none blamed women for their poverty nor sought to end entitlements. The dominant subsystem issue frame was mixed: some aspects were compatible but more were threatening to women's movement aims.

Finally, welfare reform was closely tied up with party politics. The outcome was affected by the victory of the Republican majority in Congress in the 1994 elections energized by their anti-welfare and anti-feminist Contract with America. While Democrats had the White House and the Congress at the beginning of the debate (1992–1994), Republicans ruled Congress when the debate concluded with the end of welfare entitlements and the Personal Responsibility and Work Opportunity Reconciliation Act.

CONCLUSION

In the 1990s, women's movement organizations were well entrenched in many of the policy arenas in national politics. Not only were they experienced in forming lobbying coalitions to launch policy campaigns, but they had, since the 1970s, a direct line to women's movement actors inside the Congress through the Congressional Caucus on Women's Issues. A recent study concludes: "Feminist organizations have had readier access to Congress than they had before 1977, and congresswomen have been better able to take advantage of the systematic support and reinforcement of groups such as NOW, AAUW and the Older Women's League—in much the same way as Agriculture Committee members, for example, have relied on leaders of the country's farm organizations"(Gertzog 1995: 237–38). On one of the hottest issues of the 1990s, welfare reform, which affected millions of poor women and their children, however, they were able to use these resources only to make modest amendments to what they considered a punitive policy for poor women. They were unable to affect the dominant frame of the issue centered on the agreement that federal entitlements should end and the poor, mostly women, should be required to work with no other options. Throughout, rather than moving toward their own goals, women's movement actors and women's policy agencies fought to make the developing policy less harsh to single mothers.

Using the RNGS framework, there are four reasons for this situation. First of all the issue of welfare reform was not a high priority for the movement constituencies, although some organizations considered it a major concern. Secondly, while all women's movement activists sought to retain federal entitlements through AFDC, they were not united on the issue of work for welfare mothers. Some sought ways to provide support for women to enter the workforce while others campaigned to maintain a maternalist policy of support for poor mothers and children. Third, the dominant issue frame that AFDC perpetuated poverty and immoral behavior by poor women threatened the micro-frames of both the majority and the minority of women's movement actors. Finally, the policy subsystem was controlled by right-wing Republicans, making it impossible for feminists to form alliances with the Clinton administration or gain access to the central arenas of the debate. Both the movement and the active women's policy agency had to work on the margins to gain minor concessions in the bill.

Despite the requirement that Congress reauthorize PRWORA in 2000, the 1996 statute remains the last substantive policy outcome relating to national welfare reform. Since 2000, the Congress has temporarily extended the act ten times. The right-wing Republicans have demanded that any reauthorization strengthen work requirements and cut more people from welfare rolls altogether; the moderates and feminists demand increased funding for child care. Republicans had some success by inserting stricter goals for states in meeting their obligations under TANF into the Deficit Reduction Act of 2005. After October 2006, the law requires states to get 50 percent of single-parent families and 90 percent of two-parent families into work or lose welfare funds. The act authorized DHHS to issue a uniform list of activities that qualify as "work," which will restrict educational and job training opportunities for welfare recipients. The act authorized $200 million more per year for child care (total of $5 billion) until 2010. This response, however, still means a continuing decline in child care funds given inflation.

Women's movement actors have a larger agenda for making welfare policy more supportive of economic self-sufficiency and reducing female poverty, but the dominant frame of debate limits their access to voicing support for more child care funding. The results of the welfare reform debate are in line with studies of the US women's movement in the late twentieth century (e.g., Tobias 1997). The movement actors have been remarkably successful in gaining both substantive and descriptive representation and have changed the frame of debate on a number of issues: abortion, sexuality, work and pay, work and family, and violence against women. They have not been successful, however, in gaining such representation on issues of economic justice for poor women. Despite naming the problem—feminization of poverty—in the

1970s, U.S. feminism, in comparison with its counterparts in other postin-dustrial democracies, has shown little interest or attention to formulating a discourse to address that poverty. Reasons are likely to be many, but investi-gations of this anomaly must focus on the confounding problems of race, class, and gender among women's movement thinkers.

Acknowledgments: Research for this chapter was made possible by a grant from the National Science Foundation (SES 008450). I am grateful to Lind-say Walker for her work in collecting information on hot issues, women's movement actors and women's policy agencies.

NOTES

1. President Clinton used this phrase in his campaign of 1992, and it has come to be a vastly overused and oversimplified way of describing what happened in the wel-fare reform process.

2. The Contract with America was the name for the platform of the Republicans running for Congress in 1994. It was heavily influenced by right-wing ideology.

3. This was a question that periodically attracted media attention. In response, a number of authors have provided evidence that the movement remains alive, if in a different, less visible form (Epstein, Barbara 2001; Epstein) Cynthia Fuchs 1999; To-bias 1997; Whittier 1995; Rosen 2000; Freeman 1995).

4. In this they were critics of Daniel Patrick Moynihan's (1967) claim that the black community was kept in poverty due to the increase in female-headed families, what he called a "destruction."

5. Even they were not in full agreement on that point. See Kornbluh 1996.

6. Charles Murray's book *Losing Ground* (1984) argued that the poor responded to *perverse* incentives from the government; AFDC rewarded them for having babies, not working, and not being married. According to Murray, the welfare programs of the 1960s created the culture of poverty and dependence.

7. When the federal government or the state collects child support payments from non-custodial parents (usually fathers), most of the money remains with the govern-ment while the mother received welfare payments. The pass-through is the amount the mother can receive from the child support paid by the father.

8. Several other agencies were in existence, but far removed from this hot issue: Office of Women's Health in the Department of Health and Human Services; DACOWITS (Defense Advisory Committee on Women in the Services); and the White House Office for Women's Initiatives and Outreach established in 1995.

9. Freeman notes what may be an effect of the welfare reform debate on the party platform. In 1996 the rhetoric linked women to families and children, undermining thirty years of feminist education maintaining that women have status in their own right.

16

Conclusion: State Feminism and State Restructuring since the 1990s

Birgit Sauer, Melissa Haussman, and Dorothy E. McBride

The previous chapters have described the fate of a remarkable array of major policy debates in postindustrial democracies. The goal of the comparative analysis of these debates is first to explain variations in the impact of women's movements on these debates and second to determine to what extent women's policy agencies were allies of movement activists in the policymaking process. Following a common framework, each country study has described the trajectory of a top-priority debate, the involvement of women's movement activists, the role of women's policy agencies, the policy outcome, and characteristics of the movement and the policy environment. When faced with policy debates launched by state restructuring, have women's movement actors been effective in gaining descriptive and substantive responses from the government? Have women's policy agencies been able to assist movements by inserting women's interests into the political agenda? This concluding chapter combines and compares the results of the fourteen country case studies to answer these main questions. The comparative analysis is based on the RNGS model, which is presented and described in chapter 1.

Policy debates on issues of top national priority differ in several ways from those usually associated with feminist comparative policy, women's movement activism, and state feminism (Mazur 2001, Stetson and Mazur 1995). First, these issues are not, at first glance, associated with women as a group when they arrive on the policy agenda. Therefore, they are unlikely to be explicitly gendered by the main policy actors or by the media. Like all issues, however, they have gendered implications. Second, since they have been selected according to their importance on the national policy agenda, they are characterized by a large scope, by high political conflict, and by the involvement of the major policy actors in a country. These "hot topics" are often connected to discourses about the fate of a country—either in debates about the fiscal crisis, about economic recession, or about the demographic development. Third, these priority issues provoke significant partisan differences and reveal significant social divisions other than gender, such as class, age, and ethnicity. Given these differences, it is likely that the movement and women's policy agency would be both less interested and less successful in influencing the debates and their outcomes on these priority issues than on women's concerns. At the same time, any success would show the expanding importance of these actors in the policy-making processes of postindustrial democracies.

The case studies provide an excellent opportunity to describe and assess the state of the second-wave women's movements more than twenty years after they first appeared. In seven overall sections, this conclusion assesses the development of state feminism since the 1990s in the context of restructuring states in postindustrial democracies. The *first section* focuses on general patterns of change of the women's movements in the 1990s, while also noting similarities in these patterns. The chapter's *second section* describes the universe of policy issues with high national priority and classifies them according to the type of state restructuring they represent. The *third section* then describes the clusters of policy debates on state restructuring and how these issues arrived on the public agenda. The *fourth section* analyzes and compares the dominant definitions and frames used during the policy process and the attempts of gendering and degendering these issues with top priority. The *fifth section* gives an overview over the characteristics and activities of women's policy agencies in the 1990s, and the *sixth section* presents the results of the analysis and gives answers to the hypotheses formulated in chapter 1. *Section seven* of this chapter portrays the contributions that the RNGS model of state feminism has made to understanding the patterns of state restructuring revealed in the fourteen countries.

1. WOMEN'S MOVEMENTS DURING THE 1990s

By the 1990s, all the movements had changed significantly from earlier decades. In some of the fourteen countries, in the 1970s and 1980s the movements were divided, for example, between a more liberal women's rights approach and a more radical or identity-based branch, in Australia and the US, or between socialist and radical feminists in the Netherlands. In only a few countries were movements close to power, for instance in Canada and Finland, while in the other countries movement activists remained distant from state institutions at the beginning of the mobilization and only moved towards the centers of power during the 1990s.

At the beginning of the 1990s, women's movements in Western postindustrial democracies were consolidated (eleven out of fourteen); some of them were institutionalized in political parties, in professional associations, in interest organizations, and in elected bodies, as for instance the movements in the UK, Austria, Germany, and the Netherlands. Moreover the movement was institutionalized in state bureaucracies, significantly in Austria, Germany, Netherlands, Sweden, Finland, and the US.

Only in one country—in Japan—was the movement in the stage of growth, namely after the UN conferences in Vienna (1993) and in Beijing (1995). In two of our countries, the movement was in decline already, in the Netherlands and in the US. In three countries, the movement was reemerging during the 1990s and it became newly visibility in public. This occurred in Austria and Sweden as a reaction to austerity politics and cuts in state budgets. In France younger women and women from ethnic minorities became involved in feminist activities.

The women's movements in all of the countries show a broadened focus by the 1990s. Consolidated movements are characterized by diversification of issues, approaches, and projects, by professionalization of services, and by institutionalization of organizational structures and cooperation with state institutions. Women's movements moved from "the streets" to offices, institutions, and organizations.

Overall, in countries with consolidated movements the ties between movement activists and political and state institutions were strong at the beginning of the 1990s. Movement activism was state-oriented in Austria, Finland, Italy, and the US. Lobbying for legal equity and cooperation with political and state institutions was a characteristic of movements in Australia, Finland, and France, and in some of these countries, movement actors were running for political office.

Movement activism became a "profession" and feminist groups for instance in Austria, Canada, Germany, Italy, and Spain were providing specific services in education, health, and culture for women. While some "old" movement issues such as bodily integrity, gender equality policies, and reconciliation of family and work stayed on the agenda, new issues moved in to the top of the priorities for movement activists in the 1990s, as for instance domestic violence (Austria, Finland, and Japan), sexual harassment (France), and measures for the political representation of women (Austria, France).

In most of the countries forms of actions were transformed during the 1990s and the movements were less visible in public—for instance in Belgium, Finland, and Germany the movements did not mobilize for spectacular street demonstration, but new forms of activism have been developed, such as lobbying or organization besides formal associations, namely in networks (Finland).

In most of the countries, movement activism was state-funded during the 1980s; when a great number of our countries came under fiscal pressure—for instance Austria, Belgium, Canada, and the Netherlands—funds and space for activism tightened. This occurred especially where conservative governments came to power as in Australia in 1996, in Austria in 2000, and in Sweden in 1991. While in Australia and Austria women's issues were disarticulated and the movement was delegitimized, the conservative change in Sweden led to a reemergence of the women's movement.

Still there existed different branches of movement organizations, some of them with more autonomous or radical feminist approaches, others with more equal rights orientations. And in European countries party feminism was still strong. But the former bipolar ideological divisions disappeared and the movements became more fragmented—over issues, forms of organizations, and mobilization. For instance, in the US the movement was characterized by rather different claims of diverse groups. In Canada and Belgium the movements were more representative of different national identities. In other countries the diversification of issues and movement groups did not lead to division of the movement but to a multitude of women's groups and a division of labor between different branches and orientations, like in Australia, Austria, Finland, Italy, Spain, and Germany. Diversification can also be understood as regionalization and localization: in Austria, Germany, and Italy the national movements spread to regional and community levels.

During the 1990s in some countries the movement had strong links with leftist parties and unions (Austria, Belgium, Germany, Spain, UK). In Germany, the movement also had ties with Christian-conservative party members. Some national movements or movement organizations—for instance in Austria, France, and Sweden—actively took part in transnational women's networks at the EU and UN level.

2. POLICY DEBATES WITH HIGH NATIONAL PRIORITY

Which have been the issues of top political priority since 1990 in postindustrial societies? According to the research design of this study, each author selected the policy debate for analysis using a set of criteria to ensure comparability across the cases. The first criterion was that the debate would be selected from a list of the four or five issues that were at the top of the national agenda according to scope, degree of conflict, public attention, and agenda of major policy actors. The second criterion was that each researcher would select from the list of top priorities the one debate that involved the greatest degree of state restructuring. As a result of these steps, the country

Table 16.1. Clusters of Issues with High Priority in the 1990s

	Fiscal/economic structure	Deregulation/privatization
Australia	Tax reform	Tariffs, banking, labor market
Austria	Budget cuts	Privatization of state-owned industry
Belgium		Divestment of state-owned companies
Canada		
Finland	Economic crisis	
France		Privatization of national industry
Germany	Unemployment	
Italy	Labor market reform	
Japan	Fiscal crisis	
Netherlands		
Spain	Unemployment	
Sweden	Economic crisis, unemployment	
UK		
US		

	Welfare state reorganization	EU/NAFTA/NATO	Immigration asylum Indigenous rights
Australia			Asian immigrants, Indigenous rights
Austria	Family support	EU accession	Migrants, asylum seekers
Belgium			Immigration, citizenship
Canada	Health insurance	NAFTA	Aboriginal rights
Finland	Day care	EU membership, membership in EU monetary union, NATO	
France			Citizenship and immigration
Germany			Asylum, migration
Italy	Welfare state reform	Single European currency	Immigration
Japan	Long-term care insurance		
Netherlands	Social security, health care, home care		Immigration
Spain			Immigration
Sweden	Child care allowance	EU membership	
UK			
US	Health care reform, welfare reform	NAFTA	

	New areas of state regulation	State apparatus
Australia		Monarchy-republic
Austria		
Belgium	Food, farming, pig and chicken disease	Federalization, reform of police and justice system

Table 16.1.   *(continued)*

	New areas of state regulation	State apparatus
Canada		Constitutional reform Charlottetown
Finland	Nuclear plant, homosexual partnership	
France	School subsidies, thirty-five-hour workweek	
Germany	Biotechnology	German Unification
Italy		State institutional reforms
Japan	Domestic violence	Electoral reform, decentralization of state
Netherlands	Crime rate	
Spain	Terrorism, public security, housing	
Sweden		
UK		Constitutional reforms (devolution Wales and Scotland, electoral system, reform of Parliament)
US	Crime bill/gun control, partial-birth abortion ban	

studies provide a picture of the similarities and differences in the issues that preoccupied policymakers from 1990 to the early 2000s.

Many of the more than fifty "hotly debated" issues reflect the pressures coming from economic globalization on national policymaking agendas. Seventy percent of our countries have contended with the need to reorganize the welfare states, brought about through problems with costs of health care and pension systems, child care, support for the poor, and housing problems (in ten countries: Austria, Canada, Finland, France, Italy, Japan, Netherlands, Spain, Sweden, and the US). In six countries, the issues of economic and fiscal crisis, for instance unemployment and tax reform, were high on the national agenda (Australia, Finland, Germany, Japan, Spain, and Sweden). Connected to these issues were the deregulation of industry and public service, the privatization of state-owned business, or the reregulation of labor (Australia, Austria, Belgium, France, and UK).

Globalization has brought the issues of immigration and naturalization, asylum, citizenship, and Indigenous rights to the top of agendas over national debates in nine countries (Australia, Austria, Belgium, Canada, France, Germany, Italy, Netherlands, and Spain). The reinvigoration of regional integration had an effect on seven countries as they struggled with the implications of joining the European Union, NAFTA, or NATO (Austria, Canada, Finland,

Italy, Sweden, UK, and US). Another cluster of issues was reconfiguring the national state apparatus—for instance constitutional, police, and judicial system reform, devolution and decentralization of public schools, had top priority in seven countries (Belgium, Canada, France, Italy, Japan, UK, and US). Debates about the expansion of the state into new policy fields and the regulation of new societal issues have emerged at the top of national consciousness as well. In seven countries, new regulation was at stake in the field of biotechnology (Germany), crime (Netherlands, Spain, and US), homosexual rights (Finland), animal diseases (Belgium), domestic violence (Japan), and partial-birth abortion regulation (US). The remainder of the issues cannot be traced directly to influences of globalization and occurred, rather, due to matters unique to the events in the country, for instance German reunification and terrorism of ETA in Spain.

3. RESTRUCTURING STATES SINCE 1990—POLICY DEBATES OF CHANGING STATE-SOCIETY RELATIONS

The fourteen policy debates, which have been selected according to the project criteria described in this study, cluster along three major dimensions of state restructuring: (1) the downsizing of state responsibility and activities, (2) the fiscal expansion of the state and expansion into new policy areas, and (3) the transformation of the state structure itself. The reform of the Canadian health care system and US reforms of welfare, the reorganization of the Dutch home care system and of the Finnish day care provision, and unemployment policies in Spain are examples for *shrinking states*, mainly in the fiscal realm.

The *expansion of the state* into new policy areas is found in the debate on biotechnology in Germany and the French debate over the thirty-five-hour workweek. Also, the Austrian and Swedish debates on child care subsidies and family allowances involve budget increases and fiscal expansion of states.

The third dimension of state restructuring includes *transformations in the constitutional organization of states*—the decentralization of the nation-state in Italy, changes in the electoral system in Japan, the reorganization of the House of Lords in the United Kingdom. Another field of changes in constitutional arrangements is the redefinition of citizenship rights, analyzed in Australia and Belgium.

Extremely interesting is the fact that we have no case in which the women's movement or the women's policy agencies actively took part in putting the issue on the national agenda. Along all three issue sets, government invoked the sudden, pressing need to pass the reform, justifying this action by

Table 16.2.   Hot Issues in State Restructuring

Downsizing of state	Expansion of state	Transformation of state structures
Canada (heath care)	Austria (child care	Australia (Indigenous rights)
Finland (day care)	allowance)	Belgium (citizenship)
Netherlands (home care)	France (thirty-five-hour	Italy (devolution)
Spain (unemployment)	work week)	Japan (electoral system)
US (welfare)	Germany (biotechnology)	UK (House of Lords)
	Sweden (child care	
	allowance)	

referring to external factors, such as vague references to economic and political pressures accompanying the rise of the global marketplace. This approach was used to justify reforms in Belgian immigration policy, the length of the French workweek, reduction of unemployment benefits in Spain, and a delay in expanding universal access to child care in Finland. While not an economic issue, Italy's devolution policies were portrayed as necessary compliance with the Maastricht treaty. For other issues, policy leaders suggested a need to reinscribe a traditionalist view of the family, either by emphasizing male responsibility for parenthood, such as in Austria and Sweden, or making it more difficult for single mothers to access and keep welfare benefits, as in the US. Germany's hot issue of broadening the grounds for stem cell research was grounded in the traditional debate about control over the reproductive process. In Canada and the Netherlands, health care downsizing had simmered on the back burner for decades and was finally brought in during the 1990s, portrayed as a large "budget buster" which had to be fixed. In Australia, Japan, and the UK, governments somehow amassed the political will to pass constitutional changes, which had been discussed for at least ten years.

4. FRAMING AND GENDERING TOP-PRIORITY ISSUES

Information about the problem definition and suggested solutions on the hot issues is essential to understand the influence of women's movements inside and outside governments and decision-making bodies. Framing and shaping issue definitions are important strategies for all policy actors to influence policy solutions. Women's movement actors attempt to insert their ideas and frames into dominant discourses in order to change policy frames. One assumption of movement activists and of researchers is that gendering issues are more likely to result in procedural and policy successes. Gendering in the issues of high national priority may mean, for instance, sensitizing policymakers about gender differences in policy outputs and showing that a policy might affect women differently than men. On the other hand, degendering—explicitly shifting the emphasis away from gender difference toward gender-neutral terms—can also be a women's movement strategy for achieving procedural and policy success (Marx Ferree et al. 2002). Both strategies of framing are present in the policy debates analyzed in this study. Dominant frames—frames that most policymakers share—in hot issues define a new national situation that needs attention. All issues in one way or the other refer to the future of the nation under new conditions—due to economic globalization and economic restructuring, due to demographic situation or to migration and to the accession of transnational organizations like NAFTA or the EU.

Other questions that are present in deciding the "dominant frame" of debates are whether and in which ways women's movement actors and women's policy agencies gendered the debate. Was the issue "about women" or about gender relations and men? Did gendering open up the policy debates to women's participation and to meeting women's movement goals? In other words, did adding gender lead to a substantial and procedural success?

The findings in the chapters show that the gendering of policy frames may be one factor for dual success of women's movements. In three out of four cases, where the movement had procedural and substantial success, the

Table 16.3. Gendered Debates and Policy Outcomes

Country	Debate	Gendering of Frames	Policy Outcome
Australia	State structures	Not gendered (certainty to land use)	Co-optation
Austria	Expansion	Gendered (women's choice)	Co-optation
Belgium	State structures	Not gendered (integration of migrants)	Dual response
Canada	Downsizing	Not gendered (decrease costs)	Co-optation
Finland	Downsizing	Gendered (care as men's concern)	Dual response
France	Expansion	Gendered (gender equality of work)	Pre-emption
Germany	Expansion	Gendered (women's health and autonomy)	Dual response
Italy	State structure	Gendered (women's equal opportunity)	Dual response
Japan	State structure	Not gendered (proportional representation is democratic)	Co-optation
Netherlands	Downsizing	Not gendered (more market)	Co-optation
Spain	Downsizing	Not gendered (incentives for work)	Pre-emption
Sweden	Expansion	Gendered (gender equality in care work)	Co-optation
UK	State structure	Gendered (adequate representation of women)	Co-optation
USA	Downsizing	Gendered (single mothers)	Co-optation

policy frames were gendered at the end of the policy debate: in the Finnish day care debate, the German biotechnology debate, and the Italian discussion about decentralization. In the fourth case, in Belgium, the degendering of the issue—claiming that it is not only about women—was a successful strategy to gain a dual state response.

However, there were cases where gendering did not lead to success. In eight of the fourteen debates the policy frames were gendered at the end of the debate (57 percent). In most of the cases, women's politicians or movement activists were able to bring in women's—only in some cases men's— issues into the policy discussion. Two debates of transforming state structures were gendered, while only one was fully successful (Italy). Three of the transformation of state policies were not gendered, and only the Belgian case gained dual response.

5. WOMEN'S POLICY MACHINERIES SINCE THE 1990s

We find that state feminism still exists in the early twenty-first century, but having suffered blows to its status and esteem, it has become "older and wiser" than its 1970s and 1980s counterpart. Thus, overall, women's policy agencies since the 1990s have often looked and acted differently from their earlier counterparts. The positive and negative aspects of these changes will be outlined.

In more than half of the fourteen countries studied, the women's policy agency structure suffered some type of retrenchment during the 1990s. Retrenchment often involved shuffling the women's policy agencies to places more remote from power centers, many times as a result of a change in government. Some were demoted from the status of strong, independent agencies with their own budget lines to being subsidiary offices located within other departments.

In terms of the party composition of government, while we would generally expect to find leftist governments promoting women's policy agencies and rightist ones cutting them, the fourteen chapters in this volume present a much more complicated picture. There are three examples where the election of a Labor (UK), Socialist (France), nor Social Democratic (Germany) government helped women's policy agencies to have influence upon the "hot issue". However, these leftist governments usually helped to preserve or expand the actual women's policy agency structures and/or funding levels. The paradox rests in the fact that these governments tended to bypass the traditional agency structures when getting policy advice on the "hot issues". On the other hand, there are three clear examples where right-wing governments ignored or actively destroyed women's policy agencies, as in Austria, Australia, and Japan.

The Dutch case shows how a Liberal–Social Democratic governing coalition used the mainstreaming argument to weaken the historically strong women's agency, while the Canadian case confirms centrist governments' ambivalence about women's policy agencies. While femocrat ministers are useful to the maintenance of political support for women's policy agencies, it has been shown in France, for example, that they can be bypassed when debate on the hot issue takes place. Different from this case, the Belgian issue shows many positive actions of those appointed, confirming a national government commitment to the survival of the agency.

Two countries where the change to a Center Right government did not seem to affect the capacity of the women's policy agencies in either a negative or positive way were Finland and Italy. In Finland, despite a change to a Center Right government coalition the capacity and funding of the agency remained consistent. In Italy state feminist processes have been responsible for including draft language in sub-national statutes for equal representation in political, economic, social, and cultural life.

6. STATE FEMINISM AND STATE RESTRUCTURING IN THE 1990s: THE FINDINGS

Using cross-tabulations we here summarize the findings for hypotheses with respect to high-priority debates of the 1990s, the "hot issues". Then, using qualitative comparative analysis (QCA) the section concludes by uncovering causal configurations that explain women's movement successes.

When we started our analysis we expected to find that women's movement activists had more difficulties in gaining substantial and procedural representation in the policy process in highly debated issues of the 1990s than they did in policy debates on other issues in the RNGS project (Hypothesis 1). What we found is that women's movements achieved dual success in only four of the fourteen hot issue debates (28 percent). That is, in four debates descriptive representation was accompanied by policy content that coincided with the perspectives of the women's movements. "Hot issues" show much more difficulty than abortion (53 percent), prostitution (53 percent), and political representation (54 percent) debates. These results are, however, identical to the results on the job training debates, which also had only 28 percent of dual response.

On the other hand, movements had less complete failure or *no response* (0 percent) on hot issue debates than on job-training debates (50 percent).

Table 16.4.   Women's Movement and State Responses in Fourteen Debates

Dual response	Co-optation	Pre-emption	No response
Belgium	Australia	France	
Finland	Austria	Spain	
Germany	Canada		
Italy	Japan		
	Netherlands		
	Sweden		
	UK		
	USA		

Actors have had the most success in gaining procedural access to the policy subsystems and less in policy success in priority issues. This access occurred in twelve of fourteen or 86 percent of the cases (cases of dual response and co-optation). Cases of co-optation were 57 percent (eight cases) compared to 18 percent for the job-training debates. Rarest were instances where the policymakers preempted movements by changing policy without giving them access (two cases, that is 14 percent).

Moreover we can conclude that there is no relation between type of hot issue and the states' responses. The four dual response cases include cuts in welfare provision in Finland, expansion of state services in Belgium and Germany, and constitutional reform in Italy. Similarly the co-optation cases are distributed across the issue types with five in welfare state shrinking—Canada, US, Netherlands, Austria, and Sweden—Australia among the state expansion debates, and UK and Japan debates on constitutional reform. Preemption was the state response in the unemployment debate in Spain and the thirty-five-hour-workweek debate in France.

These results testify to the progress women as individuals and in organizations have made in penetrating policy subsystems even in policy debates that are not considered women's issues or explicitly gendered. Procedural representation of women in policy processes, the right to take voice is one of the successes of the women's movement. In none of the analyzed issues were women denied access to the universe of political discourse. On the other hand, they cannot expect that presence will yield substantive representation: dual response—that is women's access and integration of women's movements goals—is still quite rare (four cases). Both of the results have to be explained—on the one hand the success in bringing women into policy processes of top national priority and on the other hand the failure to gender the issue frames and achieve substantive policy content that takes women and gender concerns into account.

Women's Movement Allies? The Role of
Women's Policy Machineries in Hot Issues

Hypothesis 2 asserts that women's movements are likely to be more success-ful where women's policy agencies have acted as insiders in the process of policymaking. The RNGS state feminism framework indicates that women's policy agencies can become allies of movement actors gaining them both pro-cedural access as well as policy content by stepping from their positions in-side the state to gender debates. We have found that the women's policy agen-cies have had little or no effect as allies or adversaries of movement actors in debates of high national priority. For the most part they were out of the de-bates altogether. One outcome of the studies is that in debates of high national priority women's policy agencies do not actively promote women's move-ment goals and they do not gender the debate. State feminism is rather weak or absent in these policy issues.

First of all, it is evident that while women's policy agencies have been very important as allies for women's movement in policy debates on abortion, pros-titution, and representation, they are mostly window dressing when policy-makers consider the issues of top national priority in the 1990s and early 2000s. In only three debates, in Italy, Sweden, and the US, did the machinery act as an *insider* by gendering the debate and representing women's movement goals (the US agency was a quasi women's policy agency in the legislature). In France the women's minister acted marginally, taking a position on the de-bate that coincided with the movement position, but did not gender the issue. In ten out of fourteen cases (71 percent) the women's policy machineries were *symbolic*; they neither advocated feminist goals nor did they gender the debate.

Table 16.5. Women's Policy Agencies and Movement Impact

	Insider	Marginal	Symbolic	Non-feminist
Dual response	Italy		Belgium Finland Germany	
Co-optation	Sweden USA		Australia Austria Canada Japan Netherlands UK	
Pre-emption		France	Spain	
No response				

To sum up, we found in the hot issue cases that there was no association between the activity of the agency and the outcome of the debate.[1] While in three cases of dual response—in Belgium, Finland, and Germany—the women's policy machineries were symbolic, only in one case—in the Italian debate on state reform—it acted as insider. Two out of three cases where the agency acted as insider (family allowance in Sweden, and in the US debate on welfare reform) led to co-optation, which means to the involvement of women in the debate but not the substantial success of bringing women's movement goals into the policy. This leads to the conclusion that in cases where the agency acted as insiders, dual response was not more frequent than in cases where it acted merely symbolically. In the eight cases of co-optation— when women took part in the debates, but could not bring in women's movement goals—the women's policy agency was also symbolic. In two out of three debates, in which the agency acted as insider, women were accepted in the policy process but women's movement goals were not reflected in the policy outcome.

Even if the women's policy agency acted only symbolically, women were able to have a voice in the debates (six debates). There was also one case of pre-emption in France, where women were not accepted in the policy discourse but the policy outcome coincided with the aims of the French move-

Table 16.6.   Results for Fourteen Hot Issue Debates

Insider/Dual Response		
ITA Constitutional Reform	1997–2001	**1 Case**
Insider/Co-optation		**2 Cases**
SWE Child Care Allowance	1991–1995	
*USA Welfare Reform	1992–1996	
Symbolic/Dual		**9 Cases**
BEL National Law	1999–2000	
FIN Day Care	1993–1994	
GER Biotech	2000–2002	
Symbolic/Co-optation		
AUSTRAL Indigenous Rights		
AUST Family Policy	1999–2001	
CAN Health Care	1993–1994	
GBR Constitutional Change	1997–2000	
JAP Election Reform		
NLD Home Care	2001–2002	
Symbolic/Pre-emption		
SPA Unemployment Insurance	2000	**1 Case**
Marginal/Pre-emption		**1 Case**
FRA 35-hour workweek	1997–2000	

*=QUAWPA (Quasi Women's Policy Agency)

ment. Finally, there were three cases of dual response, despite a symbolic agency.

We can thus conclude that there is no clear role of the women's policy agencies and of state feminism in debates of high national priority since the 1990s. In these debates the alliances between women's policy agencies and women's movement actors are not very important for movement success or failure.

Characteristics of Women's Policy Agencies and Movement Success

Hypothesis 3 states that women's policy agencies with greater administrative capacities are more effective than those with lesser administrative capacities in building linkage between the movement and policymakers. If we look at allies within governments (three cases of insiders) we see that the resources of these agencies were not high. The amount of money or staff does not seem to be important for agencies to become allies of the women's movement. But another characteristic might be significant—the closeness of the agencies to power (all three cases) as well as feminist leadership (all three cases).

The symbolic agencies varied in both resources and form. Half of them were bureaucratic agencies inside ministries without a specific gender portfolio (such as the Ministry of Labor or Social Affairs). As such they were likely to be removed from the debates on top-priority issues. In addition, over half of the symbolic agencies had non-feminist leadership (five out of eight), while all the insider agencies benefited from leaders with experience and contacts with feminist politics. There were only three insider agencies among the hot issue debates. While they were closer to power and had feminist leaders, they did not have the greatest administrative resources in terms of budget and staff.

The results for the hot issues concerning the activities of the women's policy agencies are similar to the job-training debates. Agencies acted symbolically in most of the cases and therefore had difficulties in helping the movements to realize their aims. RNGS research has found state feminism—that is women's policy agencies acting as insiders—most important on abortion, prostitution, and, especially, political representation issues.

Movement Characteristics, Policy Environment, and Policy Success

The RNGS framework suggests that variations in state responses may be linked to variations in characteristics of movement actors and aspects of the policy environment (Hypothesis 4). Our findings indicate that elements of movement characteristics and the policy environment are associated with

Table 16.7. Women's Policy Agency Characteristics and Impact

		WPA					
	Type	Proximity	Leadership	Resources	Scope	Mandate in Issue	Impact
Australia							
Office of the Status of Women	bureaucratic	close	feminist	medium	cross-sectional	no	co-optation
Austria							
Ministry for Health and Women	bureaucratic	close	non-feminist	low fiscal, bit of staff	cross-sectional	no family policy	co-optation
Belgium							
Minister for Labor and Equality of Opportunity	political and bureaucratic	close	feminist	medium	cross-sectional	no	dual response
Canada							
QUAWPAs on women's health	political (and bureaucratic)	close	non-feminist	medium	cross-sectional	yes (indirect)	co-optation
Finland							
Council for Equality Equality Ombudsman	political-administrative	close close	non-feminist non-feminist	limited small	cross-sectional	yes	dual response
France							
Ministry of Women's Rights and Job Training	political	distant	non-feminist	high	cross-sectional	yes	pre-emption
Germany							
Ministry for Family, Seniors, Women, and Youth	political	distant	feminist	low resources, some staff, medium	cross-sectional	no	dual response

Italy

1) National Committee for Equal Opportunities	1) political	1) close	1) feminist	1) limited resources	1) cross-sectional	1) no	dual response
2) National Committee Min. of Labor	2) political	2) distant	2) non-feminist	2) little funds, modest staff	2) single issue	2) no	
3) Ministry for Equal Opportunities	3) political	3) close	3) feminist	3) limited resources	3) multi-issue	3) yes	
Netherlands							
DCE	administrative	distant	non-feminist	medium	cross-sectional	no	co-optation
Spain							
Women's Institute	bureaucratic	distant	non-feminist	extensive staff + budget	cross-sectional	yes	pre-emption
Sweden							
Ministry for Gender Equality	bureaucratic	close	feminist	low	cross-sectional	yes	co-optation
UK							
Ministry for Women	political	close	non-feminist	well	cross-sectional	no	co-optation
USA							
Congress Caucus	political	close	feminist	low	cross-sectional	yes	co-optation
Women's Bureau	bureaucratic	close	feminist	medium	single issue	no	

Table 16.8.   Women's Policy Agency Activity

Symbolic	Marginal	Non-feminist	Insider
Australia	France		Italy
Austria			Sweden
Belgium			USA
Canada			
Finland			
Germany			
Italy			
Netherlands			
Spain			
UK			
USA			

success in gaining procedural and policy responses from the state. The best path to success found by QCA is when the issue has high priority on the women's movement agenda and the dominant issue frame is compatible with movement discourse. Facing a policy subsystem that is not completely closed to access is another important condition for success.

The cases give information on stage of the movement, its closeness to the Left, cohesiveness around, and priority of the issue. On stage and closeness to the Left, there is not much variation among the fourteen cases. Nearly all movements were classified as *consolidated*. Only two cases (Germany and Netherlands) found the movement in decline, while it was in the stage of growth in Japan. There was even less variation in the closeness to the Left. In all but Japan, the researchers classified the movements in the 1990s as close or moderately close to the Left. With so little variation, these characteristics are not useful to explain the variations in the state responses.

The priority of the issue to the movement is much more promising. In all the cases of dual response the issue being debated was a top priority for the movement: these issues were child care in Finland, immigration and citizenship in Belgium, biomedical technologies in Germany, and constitutional reform in Italy. In the eight cases of co-optation, however, only one found the movement placing the issue as a top priority (Sweden). In the others, the issue was of moderate or low priority. The cases also vary with respect to the cohesiveness of the movement actors in presenting their positions at the time of the debate. However, there is no pattern associated with cohesiveness of the movement and state co-optation and dual responses. For the two cases of pre-emption, the movement actors were both cohesive in their view—which did not get them access to the policymaking process, however.

Table 16.9.   Women's Movement Characteristics and Women's Movement Impact

	Women's Movement				
	Stage	Closeness to left	Issue priority	Cohesiveness	Impact
Australia 1997–1998	consolidation	close	low	cohesive	co-optation
Austria 2001	consolidation	close	low	not cohesive	co-optation
Belgium 1999–2000	consolidated	moderately	medium	medium coh.	dual response
Canada 1993–2004	consolidated	moderately	moderate	cohesive	co-optation
Finland 1993–1994	consolidation	close	high	cohesive	dual response
France 1997–2000	consolidation	close	high	high	pre-emption
Germany 2000–2002	decline	close	high	not cohesive	dual response
Italy 1997–2001	consolidated	close	high	cohesive	dual response
Netherlands 2001–2002	decline	close	moderate	low cohesion	co-optation
Spain 2002–2003	consolidated	close	moderate	cohesive	pre-emption
Sweden 1991–1995	consolidation	close	moderate	not cohesive	co-optation
UK/GB 1997–2003	consolidated	close	moderate	cohesive	co-optation
USA 1992–1996	consolidated	close	not high	not cohesive	co-optation

Researchers presented information on four features of the policy environment for each debate: the openness of the policy subsystem, the party in power, the compatibility of the movement frame with the dominant frame of the subsystem at the beginning and end of the debate, and the existence of a countermovement. The results indicate that the policy environment is a more promising explanation for movement success than movement characteristics. In all four of the dual response successes, the movement actors faced a policy subsystem that was not firmly closed (either moderately closed or open) and their issue definitions were compatible with the subsystem frame at the beginning of the debate. In three of the four cases, in addition, Left parties were in power.

In the six cases of co-optation, on the other hand, the policy environments lacked one or more of these successful conditions: the subsystem was closed (Austria, Australia), the Left was not in power (Canada, Austria, Sweden, Australia), or the issue frame was incompatible (US, Netherlands, Austria, Sweden, Australia). In the UK and Japan the policy environments had all three successful characteristics, but women's movement actors gained only procedural representation in the policy debates. We could conclude that facing an incompatible or threatening issue frame is the most significant obstacle for women's movement actors. Coupled with that is the failure of movement actors to place the issue as a top priority.

The existence of a counter-movement is not significant for a movement success or failure: While in Belgium we found a moderate counter-movement and in Finland a strong opposition, the debates in Germany and Italy, both also with dual response, didn't have a counter-movement. In the cases of co-optation we have three debates where a counter-movement existed and five cases where no or only weak counter-movements operated. We could conclude that counter-movements are not that important for women's movement actors be present in policy debates or even gain substantial policy success.

Women's Movements and Policy Environments in "Hot Issues"

Hypothesis 5 posits that women's movement characteristics and policy environment characteristics in the hot issue cases are likely to differ from other issues, thus explaining the greater expected incidence of movement failure. The findings do not support the hypothesis that women's movement characteristics and policy environment characteristics differ from other issues. And, contrary to expectations, there is not a greater incidence of failure in the cases in this book than all other issues of the RNGS project. The greater consolidation of the movement actors inside policymaking arenas in the 1990s might explain these results.

Table 16.10. Policy Environment and Movement Impact

| | Policy Environment | | | | |
	Open/closed	Left in power	Issue frame fit	Counter movement	Impact
Australia 1997–1998	closed	no	incompatible	strong	co-optation
Austria 2001	closed	no	incompatible	counter	co-optation
Belgium 1999–2000	moderately c.	coalition	compatible	moderate	dual response
Canada 1993–2004	open	no	compatible	weak	co-optation
Finland 1993–1994	moderately c.	no	compatible	strong	dual response
France 1997–2000	closed	no	incompatible	no	pre-emption
Germany 2000–2002	moderately o.	yes	compatible	no	dual response
Italy 1997–2001	moderately c.	yes	matching	no	dual response
Netherlands 2001–2002	moderately c.	yes	incompatible	no	co-optation
Spain 2002–2003	closed	no	compatible	no	pre-emption
Sweden 1991–1995	moderately c.	yes	incompatible	no	co-optation
UK/GB 1997–2003	moderately c.	yes	compatible	weak	co-optation
USA 1992–1996	moderately c.	executive	threatening	strong	co-optation

Allies within State Apparatus?

If women's policy agencies are effective links between movement activism and state substantive and procedural response, then variation in movement and policy environment characteristics will have no independent relation to state response, but are mediated by the women's policy agency (Hypothesis 6). The women's policy agencies are not effective linkages for either substantive or procedural response in the hot issue debates. There is only one case where an insider agency obtained a dual response for movement actors. For the most part, these studies found symbolic agencies. Therefore the characteristics of the movement (cohesiveness) and the policy environment (compatibility of frames) are the most important factors for women's movement success.

Movement Impact and Issue Area

Hypothesis 7 states that women's movement actors are more successful on issues that expand state action and they are least successful in policy debates that involve reducing the range and scope of national institutions. There seems to be slightly more success on the expansion issues with 50 percent of them dual responses and 25 percent pre-emption and 25 percent co-optation. The three constitutional debates, which do not involve spending, show one dual response and two co-optation results. These results are far from robust and do not lend much support to the hypothesis. It is the case that only 12 percent of the debates on proposals to limit the range and scope of the state in welfare issues (or one debate) achieved a dual response.

Explaining Movement Success—Qualitative Comparative Analysis (QCA)

Another approach to finding explanations for movement success or failure is qualitative comparative analysis, or QCA (Ragin 1987, 2000). The central goal and biggest challenge of QCA is finding the conditions that combine to lead to the outcome of interest, in this case, movement success: procedural, policy, or dual response. The method uncovers the causal configurations— that is, the combinations of movement and policy environment characteristics —that lead to success. The fewer contradictory configurations found— combinations of conditions that lead sometimes to procedural response and other times to some other outcome—the more powerful the results.

With the cross-tabulations of the findings we examined the explanatory factors one at a time. With QCA we were able to look at combinations or typologies. We were especially interested to see whether the combinations of women's movement resources and the policy environments in which they

Table 16.11. Explaining Women's Movement Success (1 = Dual Response)*

Typology	Truth Table Properties	Crisp Set Solutions	Comments
Women's Movement Resources	1/8 (12.5%) Hypothetical 14.3% contradictory configurations	WMPRIORITY* COMPATIBLE Cohesiveness of actor doesn't matter in dual response	Low percentage of hypothetical contradictory configures shows confidence in these results.
WM Resources/ Access	6/16 (37.5) hypothetical 10% contradictory configurations	WMPRIORITY* COMPATIBLE *NOT CLOSED	Very low percentage of contradictory configurations shows confidence in the results; however 37% hypothetical shows need for more cases to confirm.

Women's Movement: A = Issue is high priority (WMPRIORITY)
                    B = Movement actors cohesive (WMUNITY)
                    C = Compatible frames (COMPATIBLE)

Resources/Environment: A = Issue is high priority (WMPRIORITY)
                        B = Movement actors cohesive (WMUNITY)
                        C = Compatible frames (COMPATIBLE)
                        D = Policy subsystem not closed (NOT CLOSED)

**We ran other combinations including conditions of the Left in power, counter-movement strength, and closeness to the Left without uncovering any patterns.

worked would show a path to dual response from the state. We examined a number of typologies and found two that reveal causal configurations for dual response.[2] These findings (see table 16.11) are consistent with the cross-tab descriptions.

The best recipe for success (*Women's movement resources* typology) is when women's movements place a high priority on the issue, and their framing in the debate is compatible with the dominant issue frame in the policy subsystem. Most of the dual response cases fit this pattern. The *resources/access* typology also reveals a path to success, a configuration combining the high-priority, compatible frames with policy subsystems that are not closed to outside participants. However, with nearly 40 percent of the configurations hypothetical—that is, there were no examples of these found in the data—we would need to examine more cases to show that access to the subsystem adds an important condition for success. The cohesiveness of the actors does not matter in obtaining a dual response in either solution.

7. STATE FEMINISM AND STATE RESTRUCTURING: TOWARDS A THEORY OF STATE FEMINISM IN THE AGE OF GLOBALIZATION

What we may sum up as knowledge from these case studies includes the following: Right-wing parties cut back the scope and resources of women's policy agencies and typically ignore their attempts to influence policymaking (Austria, Japan, Australia). The cases do not provide a strong case for the reverse, however—that leftist governments are always supportive. The German, French, and UK cases demonstrate that in the 1990s, femocrats faced a chilly climate from left-wing governments as well. There are also instances where centrist governments may actively hurt the women's policy agencies in terms of their resources, such as was found in Canada and the Netherlands.

This decline of women's policy machinery in the 1990s coincides with, and perhaps explains, the low incidence of state feminism. In only three cases did agencies act as insiders and only one of these achieved a dual response. With women's policy agencies moved farther from power and their policy "teeth" removed under the aegis of gender mainstreaming, as in the Netherlands, Canada, and Austria, these results are understandable. Only in Italy has gender mainstreaming seemed to work to expand the status and influence of the women's policy agencies as allies for movement actors.

At the same time, the 28 percent success rate for the movement in these top-priority debates shows that there is a potential for activists to gender issues that have, at first glance, little to do with women as a group or gender differences. Thus, our conclusion is that to the extent that women's movement actors had any impact at all in making the public or legislature aware of gendered implications of the "hot issue" policy, these could count as successes, not just in policy impact but also in the learning curve by women's movement and policy agency actors in terms of how to get things done since the 1990s.

NOTES

1. This observation is confirmed by the QCA analysis. None of the typologies that included insider agencies show results that explain women's movement success.

2. Following QCA methods, the typologies were based on theoretical foundations for the RNGS research project.

Appendix A

WORKSHEET 1: SELECTION OF POLICY DEBATES FOR STUDY

STEP 1: Issue Area Universe of Top-priority Policy Debates

BASE CRITERIA: (1) debates take place in public arenas such as the legislature, courts, news media, policy party conferences, or electoral campaigns; (2) debates occur when a women's policy agency is in existence; (3) debates end with an official state decision, including, for instance, legislation, an executive order, a court ruling, or a government policy proposal.

List universe of at least four policy debates that meet all the following criteria:

Major scope: A large portion of society could be affected by the proposed policy change.

High degree of conflict: The policy debate engages the major socio-political actors (political elites, political parties, social partners, interest groups, movements).

Wide range of public attention: The policy debate generates public interest as demonstrated through public opinion polls, demonstrations, strikes, public conferences, media coverage and the like.

Top priority of major policy actors: The proposed policy is high on the agendas of the political executive and political party leaders.

Universe of Top-priority Debates Listed:

1.
2.
3.
4.

STEP 2: Selection of debate

Select one debate from the top-priority universe that involves major changes to state/society relations, such as:

Selective down sizing government?
Devolution of policy to regional/local governments?
Devolution of social responsibilities from state to civil society?
Marketization of state policies?
Shifting of policymaking to new networks?
Expansion of state activities in response to technological change?

Debate selected _____

For debate selected, give evidence of the following:

SCOPE

CONFLICT

PUBLIC ATTENTION

PRIORITY

WORKSHEET 2: POLICY DEBATE INFORMATION

1. Policy Debate

2. Appeared on Public Agenda

3. Endpoint Government Decision

4. WPA(s) in Existence Over Period of Time

5. Debate Sites: Organizations/Level of Government

6. Documents and Other Sources Used

7. Describe Policy Debate in Three Stages
   - Dominant frame at the beginning of debate
   - How frame changes
   - frame at the end of debate

   What is the problem? What is it that needs fixing? (wrong; injustice; threat; situation that needs corrective action, etc.)

   Who is to blame for the problem?

   What should be done? Corrective Action

   Content of Gendered Debate:
   a. Images of women and what they are like.
   b. How men and women are different from each other. How men and women are NOT different.
   c. The ways gender systems shape situations/identities.
   d. How to correct? Challenges to male domination? Challenges to traditional gender roles? Is gendered debate feminist?

8. Gendering and Policy Debate
   a. Who presented gendered issues? (groups, individuals, networks, publics, WPAs, women's movement, trade unions, etc.)
   b. Centrality of gendering to the debate?
   c. Effect on law and legislation?
   d. What was the position of the women's movement on this policy debate?

9. Women's Participation (How did women participate in this policy debate—not necessarily feminist women—and did they advocate some aspect of women's interests in the debate?)
   Individuals
   Groups
   Networks
   Publics

WORKSHEET 3: VALUES FOR MODEL VARIABLES

Policy Debate Name and Dates

Endpoint Government Decision

1. IVI-WM Women's Movement
   Mapping the WM: What are the major organizations, movements, individuals, and the major ideas espoused by this constellation of actors? The following information should be gathered as well:

   a. Stage (emerging/re-emerging, growth, consolidaton , decline/abeyance)
   b. Closeness of WMO to the left and/or political parties/groups that espouse social equality
   c. Strength of counter-movement
   d. Priority of issue to movement agenda
   e. Cohesion of movement

2. IVII-PE Policy Environment
   Policy subsystem:

   a. Structure: Who are the major actors, dominant structures, and patterns of interaction? (open, moderatley closed, closed)
   b. Dominant Discourse Fit: What is the dominant discourse used by the policy actors in the subsystem? To what degree does it fit with the positions of the women's movement and WPAs? (Matching, compatible, incompatible)
   c. Party in Power/Coalition

3. INTERVENING VARIABLE:
   Women's Policy Agency Characteristics (if more than one WPA, information should be gathered on each):

   Scope (single issue, cross-sectional, other?):

   Type (political, administrative, other?):

   Proximity (position in government hierarchy):

   Administrative Capacity (budget, staff, administrative divisions, field offices, women's group subsidies, etc.):

Individual Leadership (feminist, political, bureaucratic, etc.):

Policy Mandate (major policy orientations):

Women's Policy Agency Activities (Insider, Marginal, Non-Feminist, Symbolic)

WPA-Gendered Policy Debate?

WPA-Promoted Women's Movement Goals?

4. DEPENDENT VARIABLE
Women's Movement Impact (Dual Response, Co-optation, Pre-emption, No Response)

Were women (individuals, group networks, constituencies) advanced? Was some aspect of women's interests accepted in the policymaking process?

Policy action achieved women's movement goals or not?

Bibliography

BIBLIOGRAPHY

"247,000 nieuwe Belgen," *De Standaard*, 15 June 2005, p. 5.

Aalto, Terhi. "Kuka vie? Naiset, politiikka ja päivähoitolainsäädäntö. Tapaukset päivähoidon subjektiivinen oikeus 1994 ja kotihoidon tuen leikkaus 1995." Master's thesis, University of Helsinki, 2003.

Abe, Hitoshi. *Seijigaku Nyumon*. Tokyo: Iwanami Shoten, 1996.

Abramovitz, Mimi. *Regulating the Lives of Women: Social Welfare Policy from Colonial Times to the Present*. Boston: South End Press, 1988.

Abramovitz, Mimi. *Under Attack, Fighting Back: Women and Welfare in the United States*. New York: Monthly Review Press, 1996.

Accornero, Aris, and Como Eliana. "La (mancata) riforma dell'art.18." Pp. 239–62 in *Politica in Italia. I fatti dell'anno e le interpretazioni. Edizione 2003*, edited by Jean Blondel and Paolo Segatti. Bologna: Il Mulino, 2003.

Ackers, H. Louise. *Shifting Spaces: Women, Citizenship and Migration within the European Union*. Bristol: Policy Press, 1997.

Alanen, Riitta. "Päivähoidon yhteyksistä naisten asemaan ja perheeseen. Päivähoitokeskustelun piirteitä 1970-luvun Suomessa." Master's thesis, University of Helsinki, 1981.

Algemene Directie Werkgelegenheid en Arbeidsmarkt. *De Immigratie in België Aantallen, Stromen En Arbeidsmarkt: Rapport 2001*. Brussel: Algemene Directie Werkgelegenheid en Arbeidsmarkt, 2003.

Algemene Rekenkamer. *Zorgen voor toegankelijkheid in de ouderen- en gehandicaptenzorg*. Den Haag: Algemene Rekenkamer, 2002.

Allwood, Gill, and Kursheed Wadia. "French Feminisms: National and International Perspectives." *Modern and Contemporary France* 10, no. 2 (2002): 211–23.

Allwood, Gill, and Kursheed Wadia. *Women and Politics in France*. London: Routledge, 2000.

Amazone, Nederlandstalige Vrouwenraad, Sophia and Vrouwen Overleg Komitee. *De toekomst begint vandaag Perspectieven voor de vrouwenbeweging* (based on database of survey of women's organizations) Referaten/Rapport Brussel: Amazone, 2002.

Ambler, John. "Conflict and Consensus in French Education." Pp. 199–230 in *Chirac's Challenge: Liberalization, Europeanization, and Malaise in France,* edited by John T.S. Keeler and Martin Schain. New York: St. Martin's Press, 1996.

Anderson, James E. *Public Policymaking: An Introduction.* Boston: Houghton Mifflin, 1994.

Anfrage der Abgeordneten. "Anfrage der Abgeordneten Barbara Prammer et al. zur Kinderbetreuung." 25.5.2000. www.parlament.gv.at (August 2003).

Anttonen, Anneli. *Lasten kotihoidon tuki suomalaisessa perhepolitiikassa.* Sosiaali- ja terveysturvan tutkimuksia. Kansaneläkelaitos, Helsinki, 1999.

Appleton, Andrew. "The Limits of the Maastricht Referendum and the Party System." Pp. 301–24 in *Chirac's Challenge: Liberalization, Europeanization, and Malaise in France,* edited by John T.S. Keeler and Martin Schain. New York: St. Martin's Press, 1996.

Arbeitsgemeinschaft Sozialdemokratischer Frauen (ASF). *Presseerklärung: PID löst Grundkonflikt nicht.* Berlin, 31 May 2001.

Armstrong, Pat. *Take Care: Warning Signals for Canada's Health System.* Aurora, ON: Garamond, 1994.

Armstrong, Patricia. "Unravelling the Safety Net: Transformations in Health Care and Their Impact on Women." Pp. 129–50 in *Women and Canadian Public Policy,* edited by Janine Brodie. Toronto: Harcourt Brace, 1996.

Armstrong, Pat, Carol Amaratunga, Jocelyne Bernier, Karen Grant, Ann Pederson, and Kay Willson. *Exposing Privatization: Women and Health Care Reform in Canada.* Aurora, ON: Garamond, 2002.

Armstrong, Pat, Hugh Armstrong, Ivy Bourgeault, Eric Mykhalovsky, and Jerry White. *Heal Thyself: Managing Health Care Reform.* Aurora, ON: Garamond, 2000.

Aslama, Minna, Anu Kantola, Ullamaija Kivikuru, Tuija Parikka, Inka Salovaara-Moring, and Sann Valtonen. "Suomen 1990-luvun talouskriisi: demokratian ja julkisen keskustelun koetinkivi." Pp. 9–22 in *Laman julkisivut. Media, kansa ja eliitit 1990-luvun talouskriisissä,* edited by Ullamaija Kivikuru. Helsingin yliopiston tutkimus- ja koulutuskeskus Palmenia, Palmenia-kustannus, Oppimateriaaleja 115, Tampere, 2002.

Attwood, Bain. *Rights for Aborigines.* Crows Nest, NSW: Allen and Unwin, 2003.

Ausschuss für Familie. "Ausschuss für Familie, Senioren, Frauen und Jugend, Anhörungsprotokoll, Deutscher Bundestag, Protokoll 14/77." 2001. www.bundestag.de/gremien/a13/a13_anh/a13_anh77.html (4 October 2002).

Austria's Fifth Report to the CEDAW Committee. Federal Ministry for Women. Vienna, September 1999.

Austria's National Report 1998 on the Implementation of the "Platform for Action" Fourth World Conference on Women Beijing 1995. 1998. www.womenwatch/confer/beijing (5 September 2003).

Bacchi, Carol Lee. *Women, Policy and Politics. The Construction of Policy Problems.* London et al.: Sage, 1999.

BÄK. "Der Diskussionsentwurf der Bundesärztekammer zu einer Richtlinie zur Präimplantationsdiagnostik." Pp. 157–68 in *Die Genkontroverse. Grundpositionen. Mit der Rede von Johannes Rau*, edited by Sigrid Graumann. Freiburg, Basel and Wien: Herder, 2001.

Baldini, Gianfranco, and Vassallo Salvatore. "Le regioni alla ricerca di una nuova identità istituzionale." Pp. 127–45 in *Politica in Italia. I fatti dell'anno e le interpretazioni. Edizione 2001,* edited by Mario Caciagli and Alan Zuckerman. Bologna: Il Mulino, 2001.

Banaszak, Lee Ann, Karen Beckwith, and Dieter Rucht, eds. *Women's Movements Facing the Reconfigured State.* Cambridge: Cambridge University Press, 2003.

Bane, Mary Jo. "Politics and Policies of the Feminization of Poverty." Pp. 381–96 in *The Politics of Social Policy in the United States*, edited by Margaret Weir, Ann Shola Orloff, and Theda Skocpol. Princeton: Princeton University Press, 1988.

Barlow, Maude, and Bruce Campbell. *Straight through the Heart.* Toronto: Harper-Collins, 1996.

Barrère-Maurisson, Marie-Agnès, Martine Buffier-Morel, and Sabine Rivier. *Partage des temps et des tâches dans les ménages.* Paris: La Documentation Française, 2001.

Bartenstein, Martin, and Wolfgang Schüssel. *Das ÖVP-Familienbuch für das 21. Jahrhundert. Ein familienpolitischer Wegweiser.* Wien: ÖVP-Bundespartei, 1999.

Bashevkin, Sylvia. "Road-Testing the Third Way: Welfare Reform in Canada, Britain and the United States." Public lecture at the Hebrew University of Jerusalem, December 21, 1999. Halbert Centre for Canadian Studies. Jerusalem, 2000.

Baude, Annika, ed. *Visionen om jämställdhet.* Stockholm: SNS Förlag, 1992.

Baudino, Claudie. "Parity Reform in France: Promises and Pitfalls" *Review of Policy Research* 20, no. 3 (Fall 2003): 385–401.

Beetham, David, Iain Byrne, and Pauline Ngan. *Democracy under Blair: A Democratic Audit of the United Kingdom.* London: Politicos Publishing, 2002.

Behning, Ute, Serrano Pascual, and Pascual Amparo, eds. *Gender Mainstreaming in the European Employment Strategy.* Brussels: European Trade Union Institute, 2001.

Behrendt, Larissa. *Achieving Social Justice.* Annnandale, NSW: Federation Press, 2003.

Belgian Chamber of Deputies (Kamer). K 50 1180 (handled in K 50 2389) voorstel van verklaring tot herziening van artikel 9 van de Grondwet 23 March 2001.

Belgian Senate (Senaat). 2–308 Wetsontwerp tot wijzingen van een aantal bepalingen betreffende de Belgische nationaliteit 29 November 1999.

Bell, Diane. "The Word of a Woman: Ngarrindi Stories and a Bridge to Hindmarsh Island." Pp. 117–38 in *Words and Silences. Aboriginal Women, Politics and Land,* edited by Peggy Brock. Sydney: Allen and Unwin, 2001.

Berg, Giselind. "Eizellspende—Eine notwendige Alternative?" Pp. 143–52 in *Fortpflanzungsmedizin in Deutschland. Wissenschaftliches Symposium des Bundesministeriums für Gesundheit in Zusammenarbeit mit dem Robert Koch-Institut vom 24.–26. Mai 2000 in Berlin,* edited by Bundesministerium für Gesundheit. Baden-Baden: Nomos, 2001.

Bergman, Solveig. "Naisliikehdinnän moninaisuus. 'Uusi' suomalainen naisliike yhteiskunnallisena liikkeenä." Pp. 165–86 in *Uudet ja vanhat liikkeet,* edited by Kaj Ilmonen and Martti Siisiäinen. Tampere: Vastapaino 1998.

Bergman, Solveig. *The Politics of Feminism. Autonomous Feminist Movements in Finland and West Germany from the 1960s to the 1980s.* Åbo: Åbo Akademi University Press, 2002.

Bergman, Solveig. "Women in New Social Movements." Pp. 97–117 in *Equal Democracies? Gender and Politics in the Nordic Countries,* edited by Christina Bergqvist et al. Oslo: Scandinavian University Press, 1999.

Bergqvist, Christina. "Childcare and Parental Leave Models." Pp. 121–34 in *Equal Democracies? Gender and Politics in the Nordic Countries,* edited by Christina Bergqvist et al. Oslo: Scandinavian University Press, 1999.

Bergqvist, Christina, and Anita Nyberg. "Welfare State Restructuring and Child Care in Sweden." Pp. 287–307 in *Child Care Policy at the Crossroads. Gender and Welfare State Restructuring,* edited by Sonya Michel and Rianne Mahon. New York: Routledge, 2002.

Bianchi, Marina, and Mormino Maria. "Militanti di se stesse. Il movimento delle donne a Milano." Pp. 127–73 in *Altri codici. Aree di movimento nelle metropoli,* edited by Alberto Melucci. Bologna: Il Mulino, 1984.

Bird, Karen. "Who Are the Women? Where Are the Women? And What Difference Can They Make? Effects of the Gender Parity in French Municipal Elections." *French Politics* 1, no. 1 (2003): 5–38.

Blommaert, Jan, and Jef Verschueren. *Debating Diversity: Analysing the Discourse of Tolerance.* London: Routledge, 1998.

Blomqvist, Paula, and Bo Rothstein. *Välfärdsstatens nya ansikte. Demokrati och marknadsreformer inom den offentliga sektorn.* Stockholm: Agora, 2001.

Blum, Catherine. *Les Situation respective des femmes et des hommes: Statistiques Pertinentes.* Report of the working group. Women's Rights Service and Deputy Ministry of Women's Rights and Job Training. 1999.

BMG. *Fortpflanzungsmedizin in Deutschland. Wissenschaftliches Symposium des Bundesministeriums für Gesundheit in Zusammenarbeit mit dem Robert Koch-Institut vom 24.–26. Mai 2000 in Berlin.* Schriftenreihe des Bundesministeriums für Gesundheit, Bd. 132. Baden-Baden: Nomos, 2001.

Bobbio, Luigi. *I governi locali nelle democrazie contemporanee.* Roma-Bari: Laterza, 2002.

Bogdanor, Vernon. *Power and the People: A Guide to Constitutional Reform.* London: Weidenfeld & Nicolson, 1997.

Bolaria, B. Singh, and Harley Dickinson, eds. *Health, Illness and Health Care in Canada.* 3rd ed. Scarborough and Ontario: Nelson, 2002.

Boles, Janet. "Form Follows Function: The Evolution of Feminist Strategies." *Social Policy* 23 (Summer 1993): 38–49.

Borchorst, Anette. "Equal Status Institutions." Pp. 167–89 in *Equal Democracies? Gender and Politics in the Nordic Countries,* edited by Christina Bergqvist et al. Oslo: Scandinavian University Press, 1999.

Boréus, Kristina. *Högervåg: Nyliberalismen och kampen om språket i svensk debatt 1969–1989.* Stockholm: Tiden, 1994.

Brock, Peggy, ed. *Words and Silences. Aboriginal Women, Politics and Land.* Sydney: Allen and Unwin, 2001.

Bryner, Gary. *Politics and Public Morality: The Great American Welfare Reform Debate.* New York: W.W. Norton & Co, 1998.

Buddingh, Hans. "Snelbelgwet als wapen in de strijd tegen xenophobie." *NRC Handelsblad,* 26 April 2000.

Budge, Ian, et al. *The New British Politics.* 2nd ed. London: Longman, 2001.

Bundesministerium des Innern. "Bericht der Unabhängigen Kommission Zuwanderung." Berlin, 4 July 2001. www.bmi.bund.de/dokumente/Artikel/ix_46877.htm (15 Aug. 2003).

Bundesministerium für Gesundheit und Frauen. *Sechster Bericht Österreichs an das Komitee für die Beseitigung der Diskriminierung der Frauen (CEDAW).* Wien: Bundesministerium für Gesundheit und Frauen, 2004.

Bundesministerium für Umwelt, Jugend und Familie, ed. *Österreichischer Familienbericht 1999.* Wien: Bundesministerium für Umwelt, Jugend und Familie, 1999.

Bürgerkonferenz 2001. http://www.buergerkonferenz.de (5 Sep. 2003).

Butt, Peter, Robert Eagleson, and Patricia Lane. *Mabo, Wik and Native.* Title Leichhardt (NSW): Federation Press, 2001.

Caestecker, Frank. "De geschiedenis van grensoverschrijdene migraties uit en in vlaanderen, weinig grensverleggend onderzoek." Pp. 69–82 in *Komende generaties: Wat weten wij (niet) over allochtonen in Vlaanderen?*, edited by Jan Vranken, Christiane Timmerman, and Katrien Van der Heyden. Leuven: Acco, 2001.

Caestecker, Frank, and Albert Martens. "De algemene beleidsontwikkelingen sinds 1984." Pp. 99–128 in *Komende generaties: Wat weten wij (niet) over allochtonen in Vlaanderen?*, edited by Jan Vranken, Christiane Timmerman, and Katrien Van der Heyden. Leuven: Acco, 2001.

Caestecker, Frank, and Andrea Rea. "De Belgische nationaliteitswetgeving in de twingtigste eeuw. Een terugkeer naar de zelfbewuste nati of het koesteren van het wantrouwen?" Pp. 69–120 in *Naar de Belgische nationaliteit: en jaar toepassing van het nieuwe wetboek van de Belgische nationaliteit (wet van 1 maart 2000),* edited by Marie Claire Foblets, René Foqué, and Michel Verwilghen. Brussels: Bruylant, 2002.

Caestecker, Frank, and Johan Wets. "Nieuwe migraties, oude wijn in nieuwe vaten?" Pp. 29–42 in *Komende generaties: Wat weten wij (niet) over allochtonen in Vlaanderen?*, edited by Jan Vranken, Christiane Timmerman, and Katrien Van der Heyden. Leuven: Acco, 2001.

Caine, Barbara, Moira Gatens, Emma Grahame, Jan Larbalestier, Sophie Watson, and Elizabeth Webby. *Australian Feminism. A Companion.* Melbourne: Oxford University Press, 1998.

Cameron, David. "National Interest, the Dilemmas of European Integration, and Malaise." Pp. 325–82 in *Chirac's Challenge: Liberalization, Europeanization, and Malaise in France,* edited by John T.S. Keeler and Martin Schain. New York: St. Martin's Press, 1996.

Cammisa, Anne Marie. *From Rhetoric to Reform? Welfare Policy in American Politics.* Boulder: Westview Press, 1998.

Canadian Health Coalition. *Found: Federal Funding; Missing: A Plan to Stem Privatization.* Analysis of the First Ministers' Health-Care Agreement. 28 September 2004. www.healthcoalition.ca (21 November 2004).

Casey, Kathleen J., and Susan J. Carroll. "Welfare Reform in the 104th Congress: Institutional Position and the Role of Women." Pp. 111–32 in *Women and Welfare: Theory and Practice in the United States and Europe,* edited by Nancy J. Hirschmann and Ulrike Liebert. New Brunswick: Rutgers University Press, 2001.

Castles, Stephen. *Here for Good: Western Europe's New Ethnic Minorities.* London: Pluto Press, 1984.

Castles, Stephen, and Mark J. Miller. *The Age of Migration: International Population Movements in the Modern World.* London: Macmillan, 1993.

Celis, Karen. "The Abortion Debates in Belgium 1974–1990." Pp. 39–61 in *Abortion Politics, Women's Movements and the Democratic State: A Comparative Study of State Feminism,* edited by Dorothy Stetson. Oxford: Oxford University Press, 2001.

Celis, Karen, and Petra Meier. "Do Women's Policy Agencies Empower Women? Investigating the Belgian Cases of Political Representation and Abortion." Paper for 1st ECPR General Conference Canterbury, September 2001.

Cento Bull, Anna. "Verso uno stato federale? Proposte alternative per la revisione costituzionale." Pp. 205–23 in *Politica in Italia. I fatti dell'anno e le interpretazioni. Edizione 2002,* edited by Paolo Bellucci and Martin Bull. Bologna: Il Mulino, 2002.

Centro de Investigaciones Sociológicas. *Barómetro de julio (Estudio Número 2.570)* [July Barometer (Study Number 2,570)]. Madrid: Centro de Investigaciones Sociológicas, 2004. www.cis.es (11 August 2004).

Centrum voor gelijkheid van kansen en voor racisme bestrijding. *1993 –2003: Van integratie naar Diversiteit:. Tien jaar Centrum.* Brussels: Centrum voor gelijkheid van kansen en voor racismebestrijding, 2003.

Centrum voor gelijkheid van kansen en voor racismebestrijding. *GelijkWaardig Balans 1993–1999 en perspectieven.* Brussels: Centrum voor gelijkheid van kansen en van racismebestrijding, 2000.

Centrum voor gelijkheid van kansen en van racisme bestrijding. *Naar Een Uitbreiding: Jaarverslag 2003.* Brussels: Centrum voor Gelijkheid van Kansen en Racismebestrijding, 2004.

Centrum voor gelijkheid van kansen en van racisme bestrijding. *Statistiek/ Demografisch overzicht van de Belgische bevolking.* 2005. www.antiracisme .be/nl/kader_nl.htm (April 2005).

Cerny, Philip G., and Martin A. Schain, eds. *French Politics and Public Policy.* London and New York: Methuen, 1980.

Cerny, Philip G., and Martin A. Schain, eds. *Socialism, the State and Public Policy in France.* London and New York: Methuen, 1985.

CNDF. *Propositions de revendications pour les femmes à transmettre à non élu-e-s.* Document transmis par le CNDF. July–August 1997.

Coester-Waltjen, Dagmar. "Elternschaft außerhalb der Ehe—Sechs juristische Prämissen und Folgerungen für die künstliche Befruchtung." Pp. 158–62 in

Fortpflanzungsmedizin in Deutschland. Wissenschaftliches Symposium des Bundesministeriums für Gesundheit in Zusammenarbeit mit dem Robert Koch-Institut vom 24.–26. Mai 2000 in Berlin, edited by Bundesministerium für Gesundheit. Baden-Baden: Nomos, 2001.

Colombo, Asher, and Sciortino Giuseppe. "La legge Bossi-Fini: estremismi gridati, moderazioni implicite e frutti avvelenati." Pp. 195–216 in *Politica in Italia. I fatti dell'anno e le interpretazioni, Edizione 2003,* edited by Jean Blondel and Paolo Segatti. Bologna: Il Mulino, 2003.

"Commissie Moest Achterstand Inhalen Na Verkiezingsjaar," *De Morgen,* 14 August 2004 (web archief).

Commissione Nazionale per la parità e le pari opportunità, Presidenza del Consiglio dei Ministri, Consulta delle Elette della Regione Piemonte. *La riforma della pubblica amministrazione: la parola alle donne. Atti del convegno,* Torino, 25 January 1999.

Commissione Nazionale per la parità e le pari opportunità, Presidenza del Consiglio dei Ministri. "Relazione al Presidente del Consiglio dei Ministri sull'attività svolta (1997–2000)." Typescript, Internal Document, Rome, 2000.

Commissione Nazionale per la parità e le pari opportunità, Presidenza del Consiglio dei Ministri. *Regioni: quali statuti e quali leggi elettorali.* (Typescript) Roma, 2003.

Committee report. *Pienten lasten hoitojärjestelmän kehittämistyöryhmän loppuraportti.* Sosiaali- ja terveysministeriön työryhmämuistioita 1994:11. Helsinki, 1994a.

Committee report. *Pienten lasten hoitojärjestelmän kehittämistyöryhmän väliraportti.* Sosiaali- ja terveysministeriön työryhmämuistioita 1994:1. Helsinki, 1994b.

Committee report. *Perhe- ja väestötoimikunnan mietintö.* KM 1995:4. Sosiaali- ja terveysministeriö, Helsinki, 1995.

Cook, Robin. *The Point of Departure.* London: Simon and Schuster, 2003.

Council of Europe. *Conference on Diversity and Cohesion: New Challenges for the Integration of Immigrants and Minorities 7–9 September.* Namur/Brussels: Council of Europe, 2000.

Curthoys, Ann. "Doing It for Themselves. The Women's Movement since 1990." Pp. 425–47 in *Gender Relations in Australia. Domination and Negotiation,* edited by Kay Saunders and Ray Evans. Sydney: Harcourt Brace Jovanovich, 1992.

D'Ercole, Marco Mira, and Terribile Flavia. "Spese pensionistiche: sviluppi nel 1996 e 1997." Pp. 219–42 in *Politica in Italia. Edizione 1998,* edited by Luciano Bardi and Martin Rhodes. Bologna: Il Mulino, 1998.

D'Haese, Reinoud, and Pol Van Den Driessche. "Overzicht van het Belgische politiek gebeuren in 1990." *Res Publica* 33 (1991): 375–95

Dackweiler, Regina-Maria. *Wohlfahrtsstaatliche Geschlechterpolitik am Beispiel Österreichs. Arena eines widersprüchlich modernisierten Geschlechter-Diskurses.* Opladen: Leske und Budrich, 2003.

Dahlerup, Drude. "From a Small to a Large Minority: Women in Scandinavian Politics." *Scandinavian Political Studies* 11, no. 11 (1988): 275–298.

Das Parlament. "Zu dieser Ausgabe." *Das Parlament,* edited by the Bundeszentrale für Politische Bildung, no. 11 (9 March 2001). www.das-parlament.de/2001/11/thema/2001_11_004_4828 (5 June 2003).

DATAR. *Seminaire: Mise en Oeuvre du Principe d'égalité des chances entre les hommes et les femmes*. Report of the Seminar. Mimeo. CNSAEA/ENGENDER. 1999.

Däubler-Gmelin. "Gespräch mit Herta Däubler-Gmelin. Die Würde des Embryos ist unbezweifelbar," *Frankfurter Allgemeine Zeitung,* 22 May 2001.

Day, Shelagh, and Gwen Brodsky. "Women and the Equality Deficit: The Impact of Restructuring Canada's Social Programs." Ottawa, ON: Status of Women Canada, March 1998.

Daylight, Phyllis, and Johnstone Mary. *Women's Business. Report of the Aboriginal Women's Taskforce*. Canberra: Australian Government Publishing Service, 1986.

DCE. Meerjarennota 2000. Van Vrouwenstrijd naar vanzelfsprekendheid, HTK 1999–2000, 27061, nr 1–2, maart. (2000a).

DCE. Meerjarenprogramma emancipatiebeleid 2000. HTK 2000–2001, 27061, nr 3 (15 November 2000). 2000b.

DCE/CBS. *Handboek Emancipatie 1999. Wie zorgt er in de 21e eeuw?* Den Haag: Elsevier, 1999.

Dearing, Albin, and Birgitt Haller, eds. *Das Österreichische Gewaltschutzgesetz.* Wien: Verlag Österreich, 2000.

Debate and discussion on 18, 19, and 20 January 2000 to be found in Handelingen 33 p. 5–31, Handelingen 34 p. 5–36, Handelingen 35 pp 5–20, Handelingen 36 p. 34–46.

Debate in Belgian Senate. Handeling 2–28 17 February 2000, Handeling 2–29 17 February 2000.

Decoo, Sybille. "Naturalisatieaanvragen stijgen spectaculair onder nieuwe wet," *De Morgen,* 5 August 2000.

Della Porta, Donatella. "The Women's Movement, the Left, and the State: Continuities and Changes in the Italian Case." Pp. 48–68 in *Women's Movements Facing the Reconfigured State,* edited by Lee Ann Banaszak, Karen Beckwith, and Dieter Rucht. Cambridge: Cambridge University Press, 2003.

Democratic Audit. *Making a Modern State: A New and Democratic Second Chamber for Britain*. Democratic Audit Paper No. 17. Colchester: Essex University, 1999.

Departementsserien no. 1993: 70. *Vårdnadsbidrag m.m.* Stockholm: Ministry of Social Affairs.

Deutsche Forschungsgemeinschaft. "Entscheidungen und Initiativen der DFG zum Thema Stammzellforschung 1997–2002." 2002. www.dfg.de/aktuelles_presse/themen_dokumentationen/stammzellen/entscheidungen_zur_stammzellforschung.html (4 September 2002).

Deutscher Ärztinnenbund. "Dammbruch-Effekt befürchtet: Ärztinnenbund lehnt in Ethik-Stellungnahme Präimplantationsdiagnostik ab." Köln, 21 January 2001. www.aerztinnenbund.de/Homepage/Presse/PID.html (28 September 2002).

Deutscher Bundestag. *Plenarprotokoll 14/173, Deutscher Bundestag, Stenographischer Bericht, 173. Sitzung*. Berlin, Donnerstag, den 31 May 2001.

Defalvard, Henri, Martine Lurol, and Evelyne Polzhuber. "Les inégalités de genre dans le passage aux 35 heures: sources et resistances." *Travail et Emploi,* no. 102 (2005).

Deweerdt, Mark. "Overzicht van het Belgische politiek gebeuren in 1993." *Res Publica* 36, no. 3–4 (1994): 233–68.

Deweerdt, Mark. "Overzicht van het Belgische politiek gebeuren in 1994." *Res Publica* 47, no. 3–4 (1995): 281–312.

Deweerdt, Mark. "Overzicht van het Belgische politiek gebeuren in 1996." *Res Publica* 39, no. 4 (1997): 468–521.

Deweerdt, Mark. "Overzicht van het Belgische politiek gebeuren in 1997." *Res Publica* 40, no. 3–4 (1998): 311–75.

Deweerdt, Mark. "Overzicht van het Belgische politiek gebeuren in 1998." *Res Publica* 41, no. 2–3 (1999): 165–238.

Deweerdt, Mark. "Overzicht van het Belgische politiek gebeuren in 1999." *Res Publica* 42, no. 2–3 (2000): 167–246.

Deweerdt, Mark. "Overzicht van het Belgische politiek gebeuren in 2000." *Res Publica* 43, no. 2–3 (2001): 215–315.

Deweerdt, Mark. "Overzicht van het Belgische politiek gebeuren in 2001." *Res Publica* 44, no. 2–3 (2002): 155–252.

DeWeerdt, Mark, and Rolf Falter. "Overzicht van het Belgisch politiek gebeuren in 1991." *Res Publica* 34, no. 3–4 (1992): 286–344.

DeWeerdt, Mark, and Rolf Falter. "Overzicht van het Belgisch politiek gebeuren in 1992." *Res Publica* 34, no. 3–4 (1993): 293–338.

Diamanti, Ilvo. "The Northern League: From Regional Party to Party of Government." Pp. 113–29 in *The New Italian Republic. From the Fall of the Berlin Wall to Berlusconi*, edited by Stephen Gundle and Simon Parker. London and New York: Routledge, 1996.

Dipartimento per le pari opportunità, Ufficio per le politiche comunitarie e internazionali. *Donne 2000, a 5 anni dalla Conferenza di Pechino, le cose fatte, gli ostacoli incontrati, le cose da fare*. Roma, 1999.

DMWRJT (Deputy Minister of Women's Rights and Job Training). *Conférence de Pekin, Cinq ans après: La Mise en oeuvre par la France des recommandations de la 4ième conférence mondial sur les femmes*. Paris: Documentation Française, 2000.

Dryzek, John, et al. *Green States and Social Movements: Environmentalism in the United States, United Kingdom, Norway, and Germany*. Oxford: Oxford University Press, 2003.

Duchen, Claire. *Feminism in France from May 1968 to Mitterrand*. London: Routledge and Kegan Paul, 1986.

Durán, María Ángeles, and María Teresa Gallego. "The Women's Movement in Spain and the New Spanish Democracy." Pp. 200–16 in *The New Women's Movement: Feminism and Political Power in Europe and the USA*, edited by Drude Dahlerup. London: Sage, 1986.

Ehrenreich, Barbara. *Fear of Falling: The Inner Life of the Middle Class*. New York: HarperCollins, 1989.

EK REM. Deutscher Bundestag, Referat Öffentlichkeitsarbeit, ed. "Enquete-Kommission Recht und Ethik der modernen Medizin, Stammzellforschung und die Debatte des Deutschen Bundestages zum Import von menschlichen embryonalen

Stammzellen." *Zur Sache* 1, 2002. Berlin: Publikationsreihe des Bundestags, 2002a.

EK REM. Deutscher Bundestag, Referat Öffentlichkeitsarbeit, ed. "Enquete-Kommission Recht und Ethik der modernen Medizin. Schlussbericht." *Zur Sache* 2, 2002. Berlin: Publikationsreihe des Bundestags, 2002b.

Emancipatieraad. *Met zorg naar nieuwe zekerheid. Advies over een geëmancipeerd inkomens- en sociale zekerheidsbeleid.* Den Haag: Emancipatieraad, 1996.

Emancipatieraad. *Oudere vrouwen: sekse telt.* Den Haag: Emancipatieraad, 1995.

Emancipatieraad. *Vrouwenmantel èn Mannentrouw in de thuiszorg.* Den Haag: Emancipatieraad, 1993.

Epstein, Barbara. "What Ever Happened to the Women's Movement?" *Monthly Review* 53, no. 1 (May 2001): 1–13.

Epstein, Cynthia Fuchs. "The Major Myth of the Women's Movement." *Dissent* 46, no. 4 (Fall 1999): 83–86.

Esping-Andersen, Gøsta. *The Three Worlds of Welfare Capitalism.* Cambridge: Polity Press, 1990.

Esping-Andersen, Gøsta. *Social Foundations of Postindustrial Economies.* Oxford: Oxford University Press, 1999.

Esping-Andersen, Gøsta. "After the Golden Age? Welfare State Dilemmas in a Global Economy." Pp. 1–31 in *Welfare States in Transition: National Adaptations in Global Economies,* edited by Gøsta Esping-Andersen. London: Sage, 2001.

Eurobarometer. *Racisme and Xenophobia in Europe: Eurobarometer Opinion Poll no 47.1.* Luxembourg, European Commission: European Year against Racism Closing Conference, 18–19 December 1997.

Evans, Robert G. "Two Systems in Restraint: Contrasting Experiences with Cost Control in the 1990s." Pp. 21–51 in *Canada and the United States: Differences That Count.* 2d Ed., edited by David M. Thomas. Peterborough, ON: Broadview, 2000.

Fagnani, Jeanne. "Family Policies and Working Mothers. A Comparison of France and West Germany." Pp. 126–37 in *Women of the European Union: The Politics of Work and Daily Life,* edited by Janice Monk and Dolors Maria García-Ramon. London, Routledge, 1996.

Fagnani, Jeanne. "Recent Changes in Family Policy in France: Political Trade-offs and Economic Constraints." Pp. 58–67 in *Women, Work and the Family in Europe,* edited by Emerek Drew and Evelyn Mahon. London: Routledge, 1998.

Falter, Rolf. "Forse stijging aanvragen naturalisaties," *De Standard* 2000.

Familie im Wandel. *Familie im Wandel, aber nicht in der Krise.* 2000. www.parlament.gv.at (August 2003).

"Familienministerin fordert mehr," *Kurier,* 18 November 1995.

Foblets, Marie-Claire, René Foqué, and Verwilghen Michel, eds. *Naar de Belgische nationaliteit: en jaar toepassing van het nieuwe wetboek van de Belgische nationaliteit (wet van 1 maart 2000).* Brussels: Bruylant, 2002.

Foqué, René. "Nationaliteit en burgerschap." Pp. 21–68 in *Naar de Belgische nationaliteit: en jaar toepassing van het nieuwe wetboek van de Belgische nationaliteit (wet van 1 maart 2000),* edited by Marie-Claire Foblets, René Foqué, and Michel Verwilghen. Brussels: Bruylant, 2002.

Fouquet, Annie, and Claude Rack. "Les Femmes et les Politiques d'Emploi." *Travail Genre, et, Sociétés,* no. 2 (November 1999): 47–70.

Franco, Ana, and Sylvain Jouhette. "Labour Force Survey: Principal Results 2002, EU and EFTA Countries." *Population and Social Conditions* (2003): 3–15.

Fränznick, Monika. "Statement." Pp. 385–86 in *Fortpflanzungsmedizin in Deutschland. Wissenschaftliches Symposium des Bundesministeriums für Gesundheit in Zusammenarbeit mit dem Robert Koch-Institut vom 24.–26. Mai 2000 in Berlin,* edited by Bundesministerium für Gesundheit. Baden-Baden: Nomos, 2001.

Freeman, Jo. "Change and Continuity for Women at the 1996 Republican and Democratic Conventions." *Off Our Backs* (January 1997): 2–3, 14–23.

Freeman, Jo. "Feminism vs. Family Values: Women and the 1992 Democratic and Republican Conventions." *Off Our Backs* (January 1992): 2–3, 10–17.

Freeman, Jo. "From Seed to Harvest: Transformations of Feminist Organizations and Scholarship." Pp. 397–408 in *Feminist Organizations: Harvest of the New Women's Movement,* edited by Myra Marx Ferree and Patricia Yancey Martin. Philadelphia: Temple University Press, 1995.

Frommel, Monika. "Status des Embryos: Juristische Aspekte." Pp. 67–75. in *Fortpflanzungsmedizin in Deutschland. Wissenschaftliches Symposium des Bundesministeriums für Gesundheit in Zusammenarbeit mit dem Robert Koch-Institut vom 24.–26. Mai 2000 in Berlin,* edited by Bundesministerium für Gesundheit. Baden-Baden: Nomos, 2001.

Fujimoto, Kazumi, et al. *Sekai no Seiji Kaikaku.* Tokyo: Toshindo, 1992.

Fukushima, Mizuho. *Tsukaikonasou ! Domesutikku Baiorensu Hou.* Tokyo: Akashi Shoten, 2001.

Fuller, Colleen. *Caring for Profit: How Corporations Are Taking Over Canada's Health Care System.* Vancouver: New Star Books, 1998.

Fusaro, Carlo. "La redistribuzione territoriale del potere politico nel dibattito parlamentare dalla Commissione Bozzi alla Commissione D'Alema (1983–1998)." Pp. 493–540 in *Stati nazionali e poteri locali,* edited by Silvio Gambino. Rimini: Maggioli, 1998.

Gakkai, Nihon Josei. "Kazoku Ho." Spacil Issue: Onnna ga Tou. *Joseigaku* 4 (1994).

Gamble, Andrew. *Remaking the Constitution. Developments in British Politics 7.* Houndsmills and Basingstoke: Palgrave, 2003.

Gauvin, Annie, and Henri Jacot. *Temps de travail, temps sociaux: Pour Une Approche Globale.* Paris: Economica, 1999.

Gelb, Joyce. *Feminism and Politics: A Comparative Perspective.* Berkeley: University of California Press, 1989.

Génisson, Cathérine. *Davantage de Mixité Professionnelle pour Plus d'égalité entre hommes et femmes.* Rapport pour le Premier Ministre, 1999.

Gerhard, Ute. "Atempause: Die aktuelle Bedeutung der Frauenbewegung für eine zivile Gesellschaft." Pp. 293–314 in *Feministische Perspektiven der Politikwissenschaft,* edited by Kathrin Braun, Gesine Fuchs, Christiane Lemke, and Katrin Töns. Tübingen: Oldenbourg, 2000.

Gertzog, Irwin. *Congressional Women: Their Recruitment, Integration, and Behavior.* 2nd ed. Westport, CT: Praeger, 1995.

Geyer, Christian, ed. *Biopolitik. Die Positionen*. Frankfurt a.M.: Suhrkamp, 2001.

Gilbert, Mark. "Le leggi Bassanini: una tappa intermedia nella riforma del governo locale." Pp. 161–80 in *Politica in Italia. I fatti dell'anno e le interpretazioni. Edizione 99*, edited by David Hine and Salvatore Vassallo. Bologna: Il Mulino, 1999.

Gilens, Martin. "'Race Coding' and White Opposition to Welfare." *American Political Science Review* 90, no. 3 (September 1995): 593–604.

Ginsborg, Paul. "Explaining Italy's Crisis." Pp. 19–39 in *The New Italian Republic. From the Fall of the Berlin Wall to Berlusconi*, edited by Stephen Gundle and Simon Parker. London and New York: Routledge, 1996.

Goelabdien, Roeland. *Van roeping tot beroep, verpleging en verzorging in historisch perspectief*. Utrecht: Landelijk Centrum Verpleging en Verzorging, 1995.

Goetz, Anne Marie. "The World Bank and Women's Movements." Pp. 24–66 in *Contesting Global Governance: Multilateral Economic Institutions and Global Social Movements*, edited by Robert O'Brien, Anne Marie Goetz, Jan Art Scholte, and Marc Williams. Cambridge: Cambridge University Press, 2002.

Goldberg, Christine. "Familie in der Postmoderne." Pp. 239–66 in *Postmodernes Österreich? Konturen des Wandels in Wirtschaft, Gesellschaft, Politik und Kultur*, edited by Max Preglau and Rudolf Richter. Wien: Signum-Verlag, 1998.

Goodall, Heather, and Jackie Huggins. "Aboriginal Women Are Everywhere. Contemporary Struggles" Pp. 298–424 in *Gender Relations in Australia. Domination and Negotiation*, edited by Kay Saunders and Ray Evans. Sydney: Harcourt Brace Jovanovich, 1992.

Goodman, Roger, and Ito Peng. "The East Asian Welfare States: Peripatetic Learning, Adaptive Change, and Nation-Building." Pp. 204–211 in *Welfare States in Transition: National Adaptations in Global Economies*, edited by Gøsta Esping-Andersen. London: Sage, 2001.

Gorce, Gaëtan. "Rapport d'Information déposé par la Commission des Affaires Culturelles, Famliales et Sociales sur l'application de la loi n° 98–461 du 13 juin 1998 d'orientation et d'incitation relative à la réduction du temps de travail." No. 1731. 6/22/99. National Assembly. 1999a. www.assemblee-nat.fr/dossiers/ttravail.asp (November 2005).

Gorce, Gaëtan. "Rapport fait Au Nom nom de la Commission des Affaires Culturelles, Familiales, et Sociales sur le projet de loi (n 1786) relatif à la réduction négociée du temps de travail." No. 1826. 10/1/99. National Assembly. 1999b. www.assemblee-nat.fr/dossiers/ttravail.asp (November 2005).

Gorton, Carla. "Women for Wik: The Groundswell Will Build" *Green Left Weekly*. 1997. www.greenleft.org.au/back/1997/298/298p16b.htm (26 October 2002).

Gov. prop. 211/1994: HE 211/1994 vp: *Hallituksen esitys eduskunnalle laeiksi lasten päivähoidosta annetun lain 11 a §:n väliaikaisesta muuttamisesta ja lasten kotihoidon tuesta annetun lain väliaikaisesta muuttamisesta annetun lain voimaantulosäännöksen muuttamisesta sekä lasten päivähoidosta annetun lain 31 §:n muuttamisesta*. Helsinki: Eduskunta.

Graumann, Sigrid, ed. *Die Genkontroverse. Grundpositionen. Mit der Rede von Johannes Rau*. Freiburg, Basel and Wien: Herder, 2001a.

Graumann, Sigrid. "Gesellschaftliche Folgen der Präimplantationsdiagnostik." Pp. 215–20 in *Fortpflanzungsmedizin in Deutschland. Wissenschaftliches Symposium des Bundesministeriums für Gesundheit in Zusammenarbeit mit dem Robert Koch-Institut vom 24.–26. Mai 2000 in Berlin,* edited by Bundesministerium für Gesundheit. Baden-Baden: Nomos, 2001b.

Graumann, Sigrid. "PID: Gen-Check vor der Schwangerschaft." *GID* 16, no. 139 (2000): 13–16.

Graumann, Sigrid. *Situation der Medienberichterstattung zu den aktuellen Entwicklungen in der Biomedizin und ihren ethischen Fragen.* Gutachten für die AG "Bioethik und Wissenschaftskommunikation" am Max-Delbrück-Centrum für Molekulare Medizin. Berlin, 2002.

Green Left Weekly, 1997. www.greenleft.org.au/back/1997/275/275p11b.htm (20 October 2002).

Gremmen, Ine. Ethiek in de gezinsverzorging — gender en de macht van zorg. Utrecht: jan van Arkel, 1995.

Guadagnini, Marila. "Limited Women's Policy Agencies Influence Produces Limited Results in Italy." Pp. 131–54 in *State Feminism, Women's Movements & Job Training. Making Democracies Work in a Global Economy,* edited by Amy Mazur. New York and London: Routledge, 2001.

Guadagnini, Marila. "Introduzione." Pp. 7–26 in *Da elettrici a elette. Riforme istituzionali e rappresentanza delle donne in Italia, in Europea e negli Stati Uniti,* edited by Marila Guadagnini. Turin: Celid, 2003.

Guadagnini, Marila. "Gendering the Debate on Political Representation in Italy: A Difficult Challenge." Pp. 85–105 in *State Feminism and the Political Representation,* edited by Joni Lovenduski. Cambridge: Cambridge University Press, 2005.

Guillén, Ana M. "Citizenship and Social Policy in Democratic Spain: The Reformulation of the Francoist Welfare State." *South European Society and Politics* 1, no. 2 (1996): 253–71.

Guillén, Ana M., and Manos Matsaganis. "Testing the 'Social Dumping' Hypothesis in Southern Europe: Welfare Policies in Greece and Spain during the Last 20 Years." *Journal of European Social Policy* 10, no. 2 (2000): 120–45.

Gunew, Sneja, and Anna Yeatman, eds. *Feminism and the Politics of Difference.* St. Leonards (NSW): Allen and Unwin, 1993.

Gustafsson, Gunnel, Maud Eduards, and Malin Rönnblom, eds. *Towards a New Democratic Order: Women's Organizing in Sweden in the 1990s.* Stockholm: Publica, 1997.

Gutiérrez, Rodolfo, and Ana M. Guillén. "Protecting the Long-Term Unemployed: The Impact of Targeting Policies in Spain." *European Societies* 2, no. 2 (2000):195–216.

Guyomarch, Alain, Howard Machin, Peter A. Hall, and Jack Hayward. *Developments in French Politics.* Basingstoke: Palgrave, 2002.

Hagel, Antje, and Antje Schuhmann. "Aufstieg und Fall der Frauenbewegung." Pp. 69–75 in *Gender Killer. Texte zu Feminismus und Politik,* edited by Cornelia Eichhorn and Sabine Grimm. Berlin and Amsterdam: Edition ID-Archiv, 1994.

Hall, Peter. "The Evolution of Economic Policy." Pp. 172–190 in *Developments in French Politics*, edited by Alain Guyomarch, Howard Machin, Peter A. Hall, and Jack Hayward. Basingstoke: Palgrave, 2001.

Hammond, Susan Webb. *Congressional Caucuses in National Policy Making*. Baltimore: Johns Hopkins University Press, 1998.

Hartmann, Heidi. "Feminism after the Fall." *Dissent* 42 (Spring 1995): 158–59.

Hauffe, Ulrike. "Statement." Pp. 382–83 in *Fortpflanzungsmedizin in Deutschland. Wissenschaftliches Symposium des Bundesministeriums für Gesundheit in Zusammenarbeit mit dem Robert Koch-Institut vom 24.–26. Mai 2000 in Berlin,* edited by Bundesministerium für Gesundheit. Baden-Baden: Nomos, 2001.

Hennig, Eike. "Die wichtigsten Probleme und die Parteineigung in der Bundesrepublik." 1999. www.uni-kassel.de/fb5/Politikwissenschaft/Demokratietheorie/wi_prob.html (30 June 2003).

Henry-Huthmacher, Christine. "Politik für Familien im europäischen Vergleich." *Politische Studien* 55, no. 396 (2004): 31–39.

Herik, Connie van den. *Functiewaardering van vrouwenfuncties in de gezinsverzorging. Reactie op het Functiewaarderingsonderzoek Gezinsverzorging 1990*. Utrecht and Amsterdam: Stichting Netwerk Gezinsverzorging (STING), 1991.

Hiilamo, Heikki. *The Rise and Fall of Nordic Family Policy? Historical Development and Changes during the 1990s in Sweden and Finland*. University of Turku, Department of Social Policy. STAKES (National Research and Development Centre for Welfare and Health): Research report 125. Saarijärvi: Gummerus, 2002.

Hiley, Graham. *The Wik Case: Issues and Implications*. Sydney: Butterworths, 1997.

Hinnfors, Jonas. *Familjepolitik. Samhällsförändringar och partistrategier 1960–1990*. Stockholm: Almqvist & Wiksell, 1992.

Hirschmann, Nancy J., and Ulrike Liebert. *Women and Welfare: Theory and Practice in the United States and Europe*. New Brunswick: Rutgers University Press, 2001.

Hochgeschurz, Marianne. "Zwischen Autonomie und Integration. Die neue (west-) deutsche Frauenbewegung." Pp. 155–84 in *Geschichte der deutschen Frauenbewegung,* edited by Florence Hervé. Köln: PapyRossa Verlag, 1998.

Hofmann, Heidi. *Die feministischen Diskurse über Reproduktionstechnologien. Positionen und Kontroversen in der BRD und den USA*. Frankfurt am Main and New York: Campus, 1998.

Hohe Akzeptanz für Kinderbetreuungsgeld in der Bevölkerung, edited by Österreichisches Institut für Fam ilienforschung, 2003, www.oif.ac.at.

Holland-Cunz, Barbara. "Wo steht die Frauenbewegung?" Pp. 24–48 in *Was uns bewegt. Beiträge aus der Frauenforschung*, edited by Elke Begander. Bielefeld: Kleine, 2000.

Holli, Anne Maria. "A Shifting Policy Environment Divides the Impact of State Feminism in Finland." Pp. 183–212 in *State Feminism, Women's Movements, and Job Training: Making Democracies Work in the Global Economy*, edited by Amy Mazur. New York and London: Routledge, 2001.

Holli, Anne Maria. *Discourse and Politics for Gender Equality in Late Twentieth Century Finland*. Acta Politica 23, Department of Political Science. Helsinki: Helsinki University Press, 2003.

Holli, Anne Maria. "Miehisestä tasa-arvosta kohti naisten käsitteellistä tilaa. Tasa-arvoasiain neuvottelukunnan tasa-arvopoliittinen diskurssi vv. 1972–86." Licenciate thesis, University of Helsinki, 1991.

Holli, Anne Maria. "Suomalainen tasa-arvopolitiikka vertailevan tutkimuksen valossa." Pp. 128–45 in *Tasa-arvopolitiikan haasteet*, edited by Anne Maria Holli, Terhi Saarikoski, and Elina Sana. Helsinki: WSOY and Tasa-arvoasiain neuvottelukunta, 2002.

Holli, Anne Maria. "'Tätä vääryyttä vastaan ei taistella kukkasin'? Yhdistys 9:n politiikan ja politiikkakäsityksen merkityksestä tasa-arvopolitiikan syntyhistoriassa." Master's thesis, University of Helsinki, 1988.

Holli, Anne Maria. "Towards a New Prohibitionism? State Feminism, Women's Movements and Prostitution Policies in Finland." Pp. 103–22 in *The Politics of Prostitution. Women's Movements, Democratic States and the Globalisation of Sex Commerce*, edited by Joyce Outshoorn. Cambridge: Cambridge University Press, 2004.

Holli, Anne Maria, and Johanna Kantola. "A politics for presence: state feminism, women's movements and political representation in Finland." Pp. 62–84 in *Feminism and Political Representation of Women in Europe and North America*, edited by Joni Lovenduski. Cambridge: Cambridge University Press, 2004.

Horie, Fukashi. *Seiji Kaikaku to Senkyo Seido*. Tokyo: Ashi Shobo, 1993.

Hosokawa, Morihiro. *Nihonshinto Sekinin aru Henkaku*. Tokyo: Tokei, 1993.

Huggins, Jackie. *Sister Girl*. St. Lucia: University of Queensland Press, 1998.

Inglehart, Ronald, and Pippa Norris. *Rising Tide: Gender Equality and Cultural Change around the World*. Cambridge: Cambridge University Press, 2003.

Institut für Ehe und Familie. *Stellungnahme zum Kinderbetreuungsgeldgesetz*. May 2001. www.parlament.gv.at (August 2003).

Instituto de la Mujer. *Gender Equality Plans and Evaluations*. Madrid: Instituto de la Mujer, 1988, 1990, 1993, 1996, 1997, 2003.

Italian Parliament. *Parliamentary Acts*. www.senato.it/leg/13/Bgt/Schede/Ddliter/13229.htm (November 2005).

Iwamoto, Misako. "1999nen Toitsu Chihosenkyo ni okeru Josei no Yakushin." *Ritsumeikan Daigaku, Seisaku Kagaku* 8, no. 3 (2001a): 23–38.

Iwamoto, Misako. "Domesutikku Baiorensu Boshi Ho (2001) Seitei no Seiji Katei." *Hosei Ronso (Mie Univ.)* 23, no.1 (2005): 1–25

Iwamoto, Misako. "Josei no Seijiteki Daihyo ni kansuru Seijiteki Gensetsu." *'Sei' to Seiji*, Japanese Political Science Association (2003): 15–44

Iwamoto, Misako. "Koizumi Just Another Sweet-talking Politician". *International Herald Tribune, Asahi Shinbun*, 6 October 2006.

Iwamoto, Misako. "The Madonna Boom: The Progress of Japanese Women into Politics in the 1980s." *PS: Political Science & Politics* 34, no. 2 (2001b): 225–26.

Iwamoto, Misako. "Nihon ni okeru Feminizumu to 'Seiji'." *Ritsumeika Daigaku Jinbunkagaku Kenkyuusyo Kiyo*, no. 78 (2001c): 31–54.

Iwamoto, Misako. "Onna no Inai Seiji Katei." *Joseigaku (Women's Study)* 5 (1997): 8–39.

Iwamoto, Misako. "Send a Far Greater Number of Women to Diet." *International Herald Tribune, Asahi Shinbun*, 9–10 October 2004.

Jacobs, Dirk. "(Geen) politieke participatie?" In *Komende generaties: Wat weten wij (niet) over allochtonen in Vlaanderen?*, edited by Jan Vranken, Christiane Timmerman, and Katrien Van der Heyden. Leuven: Acco, 2001.

Jacobs, Dirk. *Nieuwkomers in de politiek: het parlementaire debat omtrent kiesrecht voor vreemdelingen in Nederland en België 1970–1997*. Gent: Academia, 1998.

Jallinoja, Riitta. *Suomalaisen naisasialiikkeen taistelukaudet. Naisasialiike naisten elämäntilanteen muutoksen and yhteiskunnallis-aatteellisen murroksen heijastajana*. Porvoo: WSOY, 1983.

Jansen, Mechthild. "Was wird aus der Gleichheit der Geschlechter in einer ungleichen Gesellschaft? Perspektiven der Frauenbewegung." Pp. 212–28 in *Was Frauen bewegt und was sie bewegen*, edited by Ingeborg Mues. Frankfurt am Main: Fischer, 1998.

Jaroslovsky, Rich. "Washington Wire," *Wall Street Journal*, 13 December 1993.

Jenson, Jane. "Representations of Difference: The Varieties of French Feminism." Pp. 73–114 in *Mapping the Women's Movement: Feminist Politics and Social Transformation in the North*, edited by Monica Threlfall. London: Verso, 1996.

Jenson, Jane, Jacqueline Laufer, and Margaret Maruani. *The Gendering of Inequalities: Women, Men and Work*. London: Aldershot, 2000.

Jenson, Jane, and Rianne Mahon. "Representing Solidarity: Class, Gender and the Crisis in Social-Democratic Sweden." *New Left Review*, 201 (1993): 76–100.

Jenson, Jane, and Mariette Sineau. "France: Reconciling Republican Equality with 'Freedom of Choice'" Pp. 88–117 in *Who Cares? Women's Work, Childcare, and Welfare Redesign*, edited by Jane Jenson and Mariette Sineau. Toronto et al.: University of Toronto Press, 2001.

Jenson, Jane, and Celia Valiente. "Comparing Two Movements for Gender Parity: France and Spain." Pp. 69–93 in *Women's Movements Facing the Reconfigured State*, edited by Lee Ann Banaszak, Karen Beckwith, and Dieter Rucht. New York: Cambridge University Press, 2003.

Jonas, William. "Native Title Report 2002". *Canberra: Australian Human Rights & Equal Opportunity Commission*. 2002. www.hreoc.gov.au/social_justice/ntreport_02/index.html (13 September 2003).

Judge, David. *Political Representation*. London: Routledge, 1999.

Julkunen, Raija. *Suunnanmuutos. 1990-luvun sosiaalipoliittinen reformi Suomessa*. Tampere: Vastapaino, 2001.

Julkunen, Raija. "Timanttejakin parempi ystävä? Hyvinvointivaltion murroksen sukupuolittuneet seuraukset." Pp. 32–49 in *Tasa-arvopolitiikan haasteet,* edited by Anne Maria Holli, Terhi Saarikoski, and Elina Sana. Helsinki: WSOY, 2002.

Junter-Loiseau, Annie. "La Notion de Conciliation de la vie professionnelle et de la vie familiale: révolution temporelle ou métaphore des discriminations?" *Cahiers du Gedisst,* no. 23 (1999): 73–98.

Kaçar, Meryem. "Een radicale stap voorwaarts in de Belgische nationaliteitswet." Pp. 133–45 in *Naar de Belgische nationaliteit: en jaar toepassing van het nieuwe wetboek van de Belgische nationaliteit (wet van 1 maart 2000)*, edited by Marie-Claire Foblets, René Foqué, and Michel Verwilghen. Brussels: Bruylant, 2002.

Kaino, Tamie. *Domesutikku Baiorensu*. Tokyo: Fuma Shobo, 2002.

Kantola, Johanna. "Gender and the State: Comparisons of Feminist Discourses in Finland and Britain." PhD Thesis, University of Bristol, 2004.

Kaplan, Gisela. *Contemporary Western European Feminism*. London: UCL Press/Allen and Unwin, 1992.

Katzenstein, Mary Fainsod. *Faithful and Fearless: Moving Feminist Protest inside the Church and the Military*. Princeton: Princeton University Press, 1998.

Kautto, Mikko. *Two of a Kind? Economic Crisis, Policy Responses and Welfare during the 1990s in Sweden and Finland*. Forskningsraport från Kommittén Välfärdsbokslut. Statens Offentliga Utredningar. SOU 2000:83. Stockholm, 2000.

Keeler, John T.S., and Martin Schain, eds. *Chirac's Challenge: Liberalization, Europeanization, and Malaise in France*. New York: St. Martin's Press, 1996a.

Keeler, John T.S., and Martin Schain. "Mitterrand's Legacy, Chirac's Challenge." Pp. 1–22 in *Chirac's Challenge: Liberalization, Europeanization, and Malaise in France*, edited by John T.S. Keeler and Martin Schain. New York: St. Martin's Press, 1996b.

Kelly, Rita Mae, et al., eds. *Gender, Globalization, and Democratization*. Lanham, MD: Rowman and Littlefield, 2001.

Kettl, Donald F. *The Global Public Management Revolution*. Washington, DC: Brookings Institution, 2000.

Khol, Andreas, Günther Ofner, Günther Burkert-Dotolo, and Stefan Karner, eds. *Österreichisches Jahrbuch für Politik 1999–2002*. Wien and München: Verlag für Geschichte und Politik, 1999–2002.

Khol, Andreas, Günther Ofner, and Alfred Stirnemann, eds. *Österreichisches Jahrbuch für Politik 1990–1998*. Wien and München: Verlag für Geschichte und Politik, 1990–1998.

Kiander, Jaakko. *Laman opetukset. Suomen 1990-luvun kriisin syyt ja seuraukset*.VATT-julkaisuja 27:5. Helsinki: Valtion taloudellinen tutkimuskeskus, 2001.

Kingdom of Belgium. "Response to the Questionnaire on Implementation of the Beijing Platform for Action (1995) and the Outcome of the Twenty-third Special Session of the UN General Assembly (2000)." 30 April 2004.

Kino, Tamie. *Domesutikku Baiorensu Boshiho*. Tokyo: Syogakusya, 2001.

KKO. "Vantaan kaupunki korvausvastuuseen päivähoitokiistassa." *Korkeimman oikeuden tiedote*, no. 15 (2001).

Kobayashi, Yoshiaki. *Senkyo Seido*. Tokyo: Maruzen, 1994.

Koff, Harlan. "Immigrazione o integrazione? Dibattito pubblico e sviluppi concreti." Pp. 185–204 in *Politica in Italia. Edizione 2001*, edited by Mario Caciagli and Alan Zuckerman. Bologna: Il Mulino, 2001.

Kogoj, Traude, ed. *Lauter Frauen. Hintergründe und Perspektiven des Frauenvolksbegehren*. Wien: Turia und Kant, 1998.

Kolbert, Elizabeth. "New Arena for Campaign Ads: Health Care," *New York Times*, 20 March 1993.

Kollek, Regine. "Wegen der ethischen Brisanz nicht akzeptabel." *GID* 15, no. 131 (1999): 14–16.

Kollek, Regine. *Präimplantationsdiagnostik. Embryonenselektion, weibliche Autonomie und Recht*. Tübingen, 2000.

Kornbluh, Felicia. "Feminists in the Welfare Debate: Too Little? Too Late?" *Dollars and Sense* (November–December 1996): 24–25, 39–40

Kremer, Monique. *Geven en claimen. Burgerschap en informele zorg in Europees perspectief*. Utrecht: NIZW, 2000.

L'Etat de la France. Paris: Editions La Découverte & Syros, 1991–2001.

Lag 1994:553 om rätt till vårdnadsbidrag. (Legislation about the right to child care allowance.)

Lanquetin, Marie-Thérèse, Jacquelin Laufer, and Marie-Thérèse Letablier. "From Equality to Reconciliation in France." Pp. 68–88 in *Gendered Policies in Europe: Reconciling Employment and Family Life,* edited by Linda Hantrais. London: Macmillan, 2000.

Laufer, Jacqueline. "Equal Employment Policy in France: Symbolic Support and a Mixed Record." *Review of Policy Research* 20, no. 3 (Fall 2003): 423–42.

Laurent, Agnès. *Les 35 Heures: Un Nouveau Style de Vie*. Geneva: Minerva, 2000.

Lefebvre, Edwige Liliane. "Belgian Citizenship: Managing Linguistic, Regional and Economic Demands." *Citizenship Studies* 7, no. 1 (2003): 111–34.

Legislative Dossiers. Regeerakkoord 1999.

Lehtonen, Heikki. "Voiko suomalainen hyvinvointimalli muuttua?" *Sosiologia* 37, no. 2 (2000): 130–41.

Lemaître, Frédéric. *Les 35 Heures*. Paris: Flammarion, 1999.

Lenz, Ilse. "Bewegungen und Veränderungen. Frauenforschung und neue Frauenbewegungen in Deutschland." In *Zwischen Emanzipationsvision und Gesellschaftskritik. (Re)Konstruktion der Geschlechterordnung,* edited by Ursula Hornung, Sedef Gümen, and Sabine Weilandt. Münster: Westfälisches Dampfboot, 2001.

Lenz, Ilse, Helma Lutz, Mirjana Morokvasic, et al., eds. *Gender and Migration: Identities and Networks: Volume 2*. Opladen: Leske and Budrich, 2002.

Les dossiers thématiques. Hommes et femmes face á l'emploi. No. 17, 2000.

Levy, Jonah. "French Social Policy in the Age of High Unemployment." Pp. 191–210 in *Developments in French Politics*, edited by Alain Guyomarch, Howard Machin, Peter A. Hall, and Jack Hayward. Basingstoke: Palgrave, 2001.

Lewis, Neil. "The Health Care Debate: The Lobbyists; Vast Sum Spent to Sway Health Plan," *New York Times*, 22 July 1994. A 20.

LO. *Barnomsorg, förvärvsarbete och jämställdhet. Ett faktamaterial om förhållandena vid 1990-talets mitt*. Nr 29. Stockholm: LO, 1996.

Lovenduski, Joni. "Critical Mass or Minority Representation." *Parliamentary Affairs*, October 2001.

Lovenduski, Joni. *Feminising Politics*. London: Polity Press, 2005.

Lovenduski, Joni. "Gender Politics: A Breakthrough for Women." Pp. 200–212 in *Parliamentary Affairs*, October 1997.

Lovenduski, Joni, Petra Meier, Diane Sainsbury, Marila Guadagnini, and Claudie Baudino, eds. *State Feminism and Political Representation*. Cambridge: Cambridge University Press, 2005.

Lovenduski, Joni, and Vicky Randall. *Contemporary Feminist Politics*. Oxford: Oxford University Press, 1993.

Lucashenko, Melissa. "No Other Truth? Aboriginal Women and Australian Feminism." *Social Alternatives* 12, no. 4 (1994): 21–24.

Lupo, Salvatore. "The Changing Mezzogiorno: Between Representations and Reality." Pp. 247–62 in *The New Italian Republic. From the Fall of the Berlin Wall to Berlusconi*, edited by Stephen Gundle and Simon Parker. London and New York: Routledge, 1996.

Lurol, Martine. "35 Heures: Les Disparités entre hommes et femmes." *Quatre Pages: Centre d'Etude de l'Emploi*, 48 (November 2001b).

Lurol, Martine. "Le Travail des Femmes en France: Trente ans d'évolution des problématiques en sociologie (1970–2000)." *Documents de Travail: Centre d'Etudes de l'Emploi*, no. 7, (March 2001a): 4–33.

Lurol, Martine. "Quand les Institutions Se Chargent de La Quesion du Travail des Femmes, 197–1995." *Travail Genre, et, Sociétés*, no. 1 (April 1999): 179–199.

Lurol, Martine, and Jêrome Pélisse. "Les 35 heures des hommes et des femmes." *Travail, Genre et Société*, no. 8 (November 2002).

Lyke, Saskia van der. *Georganiseerde liefde. Publieke bemoeienis met zorg in de privésfeer*. Utrecht: Jan van Arkel, 2000.

Maessen, Pieter J.J. *Bezuinigingen op de gezinsverzorging. Besluitvorming in de verzorgingsstaat*. Leiden: Acco, 1989.

Mahon, Rianne. "Child Care in Canada and Sweden: Policy and Politics." *Social Politics* 4 (1997): 382–418.

Maino, Franca. "La ristrutturazione del servizio sanitario nazionale: la riforma Bindi e il federalismo fiscale." Pp. 147–66 in *Politica in Italia. I fatti dell'anno e le interpretazioni. Edizione 2001*, edited by Mario Caciagli and Alan Zuckerman. Bologna: Il Mulino, 2001.

Mairhuber, Ingrid. "Geschlechterpolitik im Sozialstaat Österreich seit Anfang der 80er Jahre." *Österreichische Zeitschrift für Politikwissenschaft* 28, no. 1 (1999): 35–47.

Majoni d'Intignano, Béatrice. *Égalité entre femmes et hommes: Aspect Economiques*. Report of the Prime Minister's Council on Economic Analysis. Paris: Documentation Française, 1999.

Manne, Robert. *In Denial: The Stolen Generations and the Right*. Melbourne: Schwartz Publishing, 2001.

Marchand, Marianne H., and Anne Sisson Runyan. "Introduction. Feminist Sightings of Global Restructuring: Conceptualizations and Reconceptualizations." Pp. 1–22 in *Gender and Global Restructuring: Sightings, Sites and Resistances*, edited by Marianne H. Marchand and Anne Sisson Runyan. London: Routledge, 2000

Maruani, Margaret. *Travail et Emploi des Femmes*. Paris: La Découverte, 2000.

Mattila, Mikko. *Policy Making in Finnish Social and Health Care. A Network Approach*. Acta Politica 12. Helsinki: Helsinki University Press, 2000.

Mazur, Amy G. *Gender Bias and the State: Symbolic Reform at Work in Fifth Republic France*. Pittsburgh: University of Pittsburgh Press, 1995a.

Mazur, Amy G. "Gender-Biased Universalism Resists State Feminist Approaches to Gendered Equality." In *Making Democracies Work: State Feminism, Women's Movements, and Job Training Policy*, edited by Amy Mazur. New York: Garland Publishing, Taylor & Francis Group, 2001.

Mazur, Amy G. "Gendering the Fifth Republic." Pp. 212–29 in *Developments in French Politics*, edited by Alistair Cole, Patrick Le Galès, and Jonah Levy. Basingstoke: Palgrave Macmillan, 2005.

Mazur, Amy, ed. *State Feminism, Women's Movements, & Job Training: Making Democracies Work in a Global Economy*. New York and London: Routledge, 2001.

Mazur, Amy G. "Strong State and Symbolic Reform in France: le Ministère des Droits de la Femme." Pp. 76–94 in *Comparative State Feminism*, edited by Dorothy McBride Stetson and Amy Mazur. Thousand Oaks, CA: Sage Publications, 1995b.

Mazur, Amy G. *Theorizing Feminist Policy*. Oxford: Oxford University Press, 2002.

Mazur, Amy G., and Andrew Appleton. "France at the Crossroads: An End to French Exceptionalism." Pp. 92–135 in *European Politics in the Age of Globalization*, edited by Howard J. Wiarda. Orlando, FL: Harcourt College Publishers, 2001.

McAdam, Doug, John D. McCarthy, and Mayer N. Zald. *Comparative Perspectives on Social Movements: Political Opportunities, Mobilizing Structures, and Cultural Framings*. Cambridge: Cambridge University Press, 1996.

McBride, Stephen, and John Shields. *Dismantling a Nation: The Transition to Corporate Rule in Canada*. Halifax: Fernwood, 1997.

McGlade, Hannah. "Aboriginal Women and the Commonwealth Government's Response to Mabo—An Internatioanl Human Rights Perspective." Pp. 139–56 in *Words and Silences. Aboriginal Women, Politics and Land*, edited by Peggy Brock. Sydney: Allen and Unwin, 2001.

McQuaig, Linda. *Shooting the Hippo: Death by Deficit and Other Canadian Myths*. Toronto: Viking Press, 1995.

Méda, Dominique. *Le Temps des Femmes*. Paris: Flammarion, 2000.

Méda. Dominique. *Qu'est-ce que la richesse?* Paris: Champs/Flammarion, 1999.

Meier, Petra. "The Belgian Paradox: Inclusion and Exclusion of Gender Issues in Politics." Pp. 41–61 in *State Feminism and Political Representation*, edited by Joni Lovenduski et al. Cambridge: Cambridge University Press, 2005.

Meier, Petra. "De kracht van de definitie. Quotawetten in Argentinië, België en Frankrijk vergeleken." *Res Publica* 46, no.1 (2004): 80–100.

Meloen, Jos. *Thuiszorg: het kind van de rekening. Organisatievernieuwing in nonprofit organisaties: een case studie van de wijkverpleegkunde, de gezinszorg en de thuiszorg in Nederland*. Leiden: Departement Bestuurskunde/Sociologie, 2000.

Mény, Yves. *La Corruption de la République*. Paris: Fayard, 1992.

Meyer, Mary K., and Elisabeth Prügl, eds. *Gender Politics in Global Governance*. Lanham, MD.: Rowman and Littlefield, 1999.

Mikanagi, Yumiko. "Jenda-no Seijigaku." Pp. 95–115 in *Political Science of New Politics* edited by Kensuke Kaku et al. Kyoto: Mineruva Shobo, 2000.

Miné, Michel. "La loi sure les 35 heures á l'épreuve des droits des femmes." *Travail Genre, et, Sociétés*, no. 2 (November 1999): 91–110.

Ministry of Social Affairs and Health, ed. *Trends in Social Protection in Finland 2002*. Ministry of Social Affairs and Health. Publications 2002:16. Helsinki: Edita, 2002.

Mink, Gwendolyn. *Welfare's End*. Ithaca: Cornell University Press, 1998.

Minkan-Seiji-Rincho. *Nihon Kaikaku no Bijon*. Tokyo: Kodansha, 1993.

Mitsui, Mariko. *Momoiro no Kenryoku*. Tokyo: Sanseido, 1992.

Morelli, Anne, Ludo Dierickx, and Dieter Lesage. *Racism: een element in het conflict tussen Vlamingen en Franstaligen*. Berchem: EPO, 1998.

Moreton-Robinson, Aileen. *Talkin' Up to to the White Woman. Indigenous Women and Feminism*. St. Lucia: University of Queensland Press, 2000.

Moynihan, Daniel Patrick. "The Negro Family: The Case for National Action." Pp. 39–124 in *The Moynihan Report and the Politics of Controversy*, edited by Lee Rainwater and William L. Yancey. Cambridge: M.I.T. Press, 1967.

MUA (Maritime Union of Australia). 2003. www.mua.org.au/war/invasion.html (24 May 2003).

Murray, Charles. *Losing Ground*. New York: Basic Books, 1984.

"Mütter sollen arbeiten können," *Kurier*, 11 March 1996

Naples, Nancy A. "The 'New Consensus' on the Gendered 'Social Contract': The 1987–1988 U.S. Congressional Hearings on Welfare Reform." *Signs: Journal of Women in Culture and Society* 22, no. 4. (1997): 907–45.

Nelen, Sarah, and Annie Hondeghem, eds. *Equality Oriented Personnel Policy in the Public Sector*. Amsterdam: International Institute of Administrative Sciences, IOS Press, 2000.

NER. "German National Ethics Council, Opinion on the Import of Human Embryonic Stem Cells. December 2001 (Document 001/01)." 2001. www.ethikrat.org/_english/publications/opinions.html (5 September 2003).

Nida-Rümelin, Julian. "Bioethik. Wo die Menschenwürde beginnt." *Tagesspiegel Berlin,* 3 January 2001.

"Nieuwe Belgen beslissen over vijf zetels in Antwerpen," *De Standaard,* 21 September 2005, p. 38.

Nihon, Josei Gakkai, Spacil Issue: Onnna ga Tou "Kazoku Ho," *Joseigaku* 4 (1994).

Nishio, Masaru. *Chiho Bunken*. Tokyo: Tokyo University Press, 1999.

NKO. www.bsk.utwente.nl/skon (9 May 2003).

Nohno, Chieko, et al. *Shokai DV Boshi Ho*.Tokyo: Gyosei, 2001.

Nohno, Chieko, et al. *Shokai Kaisei DV Boshi Ho*. Tokyo: Gyosei, 2005.

Nousiainen, Jaakko. "Suomalaisen parlamentarismin kolmas kehitysvaihe: konsensuaalinen enemmistöhallinta, vireytyvä eduskunta." *Politiikka* 42, no. 2 (2000): 83–96.

Nuita, Yoko. *Ano Toki, Kono Hito*. Tokyo: Domesu Shuppan, 2002.

Nupponen, Terttu. "Suomen puolueohjelmat ja sukupuoliroolit." Pp. 45–61 in *Miesten maailman nurjat lait,* edited by Katarina Eskola. Helsinki: Tammi, 1969.

Nüsslein-Vollhard, Christine. "Wann ist ein Tier ein Tier, ein Mensch kein Mensch?" *Frankfurter Allgemeine Zeitung,* 2 October 2001.

O'Connor, Alice. *Poverty Knowledge: Social Science, Social Poicy, and the Poor in Twentieth-Century U.S. History.* Princeton: Princeton University Press, 2001.

O'Shane, Pat. "Is There Any Relevance in the Women's Movement for Aboriginal Women?" *Refractory Girl,* no. 12 (September 1976): 31–34.

Oldersma, Jantine. "Het moderne feminisme en het sociaal kapitaal van Nederland." *Tijdschrift voor Sociologie* 20, no. 3–4 (1999): 415–40.

Oldersma, Jantine, Wil Portegijs, and Mia Janzen-Marquard. "The Iron Ring in Dutch Politics Revisited." *Public Administration* 77, no. 2 (1999): 335–60.

Oleaga, Ricardo. *El ama de casa, hoy* (Homemakers Today). Elorrio (Bizkaia): Eroski, 1990.

"Onkelinx laat snel-Belgwet evalueren," *De Standaard,* 28 April 2005, p. 9.

Orloff, Ann Shola. "Farewell to Maternalism: Welfare Reform, Ending Entitlement for Poor Single Mothers, and Expanding the Claims of Poor Employed Parents." Presented to the annual meeting of the American Political Science Association, San Francisco. 30 August 2001.

Ortbals, Candice D. "Embedded Institutions, Activisms, and Discourses: Untangling the Intersections of Women's Civil Society and Women's Policy Agencies in Spain." PhD dissertation, Indiana University, 2004.

Österreichische Kinderfreunde. "Stellungsnahme zum Kinderbetreuungsgeld." 2001. www.parlament.gv.at (August 2003).

Österreichische Volkspartei. *Grundsatzprogramm der ÖVP 1995.* 1995. www.övp.at (August 2003).

Österreichischer Amtskalender 1992–2002. Wien: Österreichische Staatsdruckerei, 1992–2002.

Österreichischer Bundesrat. *Protokoll der 650. Sitzung des österreichischen Bundesrats vom 19.2.1999.* www.parlament.gv.at (August 2003).

Österreichischer Nationalrat. Stenographisches Protokoll der 74. Sitzung des Nationalrats der Republik Österreich, XXI. Gesetzperiode, 6 June 2001. www.parlament.gv.at (August 2003).

Österreichisches Institut für Familienforschung. *Hohe Akzeptanz für Kinderbetreuungsgeld in der Bevölkerung.* 10 July 2003. www.oif.at/presse (24 October 2005).

Österreichisches Institut für Familienforschung. *Wahlfreiheit durch Kinderbetreuungsgeld?* 16 May 2005. www.oif.at/presse (24 October 2005).

Ostner, Ilona, and Jane Lewis. "Gender and the Evolution of European Social Policies." Pp. 159–93 in *European Social Policy. Between Fragmentation and Integration,* edited by Stefan Leibfried and Paul Pierson. Washington, DC: Brookings Institution, 1995.

Otake, Hideo. *Nihongata Popyurizumu.* Tokyo: Chuo Koron, 2003.

Outshoorn, Joyce. "Administrative Accommodation in the Netherlands: The Department for the Coordination of Equality Policy." Pp. 168–86 in *Comparative State Feminism,* edited by Dorothy McBride Stetson and Amy Mazur. Thousand Oaks, London, and New Delhi: Sage, 1995.

Outshoorn, Joyce. "Gendering the 'Graying'of Society'. A Discourse Analysis of the Care Gap." *Public Administration Review* 62, no. 2 (March/April 2002): 185–97.

Outshoorn, Joyce. "Op zoek naar de vrouwenbeweging in de jaren negentig." Pp. 32–49 in *Emancipatie en subcultuur. Sociale bewegingen in België en Nederland,* edited by Thijl Sunier et al. Amsterdam: IPP, 2000.

Outshoorn, Joyce. "Policy-making on Abortion: Arenas, Actors and Arguments in the Netherlands." Pp. 205–28 in *Abortion Politics, Women's Movements and the Democratic State,* edited by Dorothy McBride Stetson. Oxford: Oxford University Press, 2001.

Outshoorn, Joyce, ed. *The Politics of Prostitution: Women's Movements, Democratic States, and the Globalization of Sex Commerce.* Cambridge: Cambridge University Press, 2004.

Ozawa, Ichiro. *Nihon Kaizo Keikaku.* Tokyo: Kodansha, 1993.

Paloheimo, Heikki. "Pohjoismaiden EU-kansanäänestykset: puolueiden peruslinjat ja kansalaisten mielipiteet Suomessa, Ruotsissa ja Norjassa." Pp. 50–78 in *Suomen kansainväliset suhteet,* edited by Erkki Berndtson and Timo Kivimäki. Helsingin yliopisto, yleisen valtio-opin laitos, "Tutkimustietoa politiikasta ja hallinnosta," no. 9. Helsinki: Yliopistopaino, 1998.

Parikka, Tuija. "Kumppanuutta ja kaupankäyntiä: Hyvinvoinnin sukupuoli Helsingin Sanomissa 1988–97." Licenciate thesis, University of Helsinki, 2002.

Parliamentary Committee of Social Affairs and Health. *Eduskunnan sosiaali- ja terveysvaliokunnan mietintö 47/1994 vp.* Helsinki: Eduskunta, 1994.

Parliamentary documents. Eduskunta, Helsinki. 1994. www.eduskunta.fi (1 December 2002).

Pasquino, Gianfranco. *Il sistema politico italiano. Autorità, istituzioni, politica.* Bologna: Bononia University Press, 2002.

Pearce, Diana M. "The Feminization of Poverty: Women, Work and Welfare." *Urban and Social Change Review* 2 (February 1978): 28–36.

Pépin, Michel (coordinator). "Réduction de Temps du Travail: Une Chance pour l'égalité professionnelle." *ANACT: Travail et Changement* (October 1999): 7–17.

Picq, Françoise. *Les années-mouvement: libération des femmes.* Paris: Seuil, 1993.

Pigalle, Céline. *Femmes au travail. De qui se moque-t-on.* Issy-les Moulineaux: Prat Editions, 2000.

Pincus, Ingrid. *The Politics of Gender Equality Policy. A Study of Implementation and Non-Implementation in Three Swedish Municipalities.* Örebro: Örebro Studies in Political Science, 2002.

Platel, Marc. "Overzicht van het Belgische politiek gebeuren in 1995." *Res Publica* 38, no. 4 (1996): 501–25.

"PM, Provinces Sign \$41B Health Deal." *CBC News Online.* 16 September 2004. www.cbc.ca/news (23 October 2005).

Portegijs, Wil, Annemarie Boelens, and Saskia Keuzenkamp. *Emancipatiemonitor 2002.* Den Haag: SCP/CBS, 2002.

Potting, Marianne. *Van je familie . . . Zorg, familie en sekse in de mantelzorg.* Amsterdam: Aksant, 2001.

Proposition 1993/94:148 *Vårdnadsbidrag* (Bill from the government).

Proposition 1994/95:61. *Vårdnadsbidraget. Garantidagarna. Enskild barnomsorg.*

Raad voor Maatschappelijke Ontwikkeling/Raad voor de Volksgezondheid en Zorg. *Zorgarbeid in de toekomst. Advies over de gevolgen van demografische ontwikkeling van vraag en aanbod van (zorg)arbeid.* Den Haag: Zoetermeer, 1999.

Radcliff, Pamela. "Citizenship in Spain's Transition to Democracy." *Journal of Social History* (Fall 2002): 77–100.

Rai, Shirin M., ed. *Mainstreaming Gender, Democratizing the State? Institutional Mechanisms for the Advancement of Women.* Manchester: Manchester University Press, 2003.

Ramstedt-Silén, Viveca. *Riksdagsutskott eller kvinnoförening? Det kvinnliga nätverket I Finlands riksdag.* SSKH Notat 4/99. Svenska social- och kommunalhögskolan vid Helsingfors universitet, Helsingfors, 1999.

Randall, Vicky, and Georgina Waylen, eds. *Gender, Politics and the State*. London and New York: Routledge, 1998.

Rau, Johannes. "Wird alles gut?—Für einen Fortschritt nach menschlichem Maß." Pp. 14–29 in *Die Genkontroverse. Grundpositionen. Mit der Rede von Johannes Rau*, edited by Sigrid Graumann. Freiburg, Basel and Wien: Herder, 2001.

Rauch-Kallat, Maria. "Regierungsmitglieder werden Regierungsübereinkommen umsetzen." 2000. www.familienbund.at/body/volksbegehren (August 2003).

Raunio, Tapio, and Matti Wiberg, eds. *EU ja Suomi. Unionijäsenyyden vaikutukset suomalaiseen yhteiskuntaan*. Helsinki: Edita, 2000.

Reade, Katy. "Struggling to Be Heard." Tensions around Different Voices in the Australian Women's Liberation Movement in the 1970s and 1980s." Pp. 198–221 in *Contemporary Australian Feminism*, edited by Kate Pritchard Hughes. 1st ed. South Melbourne: Longman, 1994.

Reprokult. *Women's Forum for Reproductive Medicine, Reproductive Medicine and Genetic Engineering. Women between Self-Determination and Societal Standardisation*. Proceedings of the conference held in Berlin from 15 to 17 November 2001, edited by Reprokult Frauen Forum Fortpflanzungsmedizin. 2002.

Reynolds, Henry. *An Indelible Stain? The Question of Genocide in Australia's History*. Ringwood, Vic.: Penguin, 2001.

Rochon, Thomas R. *Culture Moves: Ideas, Activism, and Changing Values*. Princeton: Princeton University Press, 1998.

Rogers, Robert, and Rhodri Walters. *How Parliament Works*. 5th ed. London: Pearson Longman, 2004.

Rose, Deborah Bird. "Women and Land Claims." *Land Rights, Laws: Issues of Native Title*, no. 6 (January 1995).

Rosen, Ruth. *The World Split Open: How the Modern Women's Movement Changed America*. New York: Viking, 2000.

Rosenberger, Sieglinde Katharina. "Alles was Recht ist? Eine politikwissenschaftliche Einschätzung des FrauenVolksBegehrens." Pp. 202–26 in *Lauter Frauen. Hintergründe und Perspektiven des Frauenvolksbegehren*, edited by Traude Kogoj. Wien: Turia und Kant, 1998.

Rosenberger, Sieglinde. "Politik mit Familie: Debatten und Maßnahmen. Konflikt und Konsens." Pp. 754–72 in *Zur Situation von Familie und Familienpolitik in Österreich. 4. Österreichischer Familienbericht: Familie— zwischen Anspruch und Alltag*, edited by Maria Orthofer. Wien: Bundesministerium für Umwelt, Jugend und Familie, 1999.

Rosenberger, Sieglinde, and Daniela Schallert. "Politik mit Familie—Familienpolitik." *SWS-Rundschau* 40, no. 3 (2000): 249–61.

Rönnblom, Malin. *Ett eget rum? Kvinnors organisering möter etablerad politik*. Umeå: Statsvetenskapliga institutionens skriftserie, 2002, no. 3.

Rösslhumer, Maria, and Birgit Appelt. *Hauptsache Frauen. Politikerinnen in der Zweiten Republik*. Graz: Styria, 2001.

Rucht, Dieter, ed. *Protest in der Bundesrepublik: Strukturen und Entwicklungen*. Frankfurt am Main: Campus, 2001.

Ruß, Sonja, ed. *Frauenfakten 2004. Netzwerke.Organisaitonen. Institutionen von Business bis Feminismus*. Wien: Verlag Milena, 2004.

Russell, Meg. *Reforming the House of Lords: Lessons from Overseas*. Oxford: Oxford University Press, 2000.

Sainsbury, Diane. *Gender, Equality, and Welfare States*. Cambridge: Cambridge University Press, 1996.

Sainsbury, Diane, ed. *Gender and Welfare State Regimes*. Oxford: Oxford University Press, 1999.

Sainsbury, Diane. "Party Feminism, State Feminism and Women's Representation in Sweden." Pp. 195–215 in *State Feminism and Political Representation*, edited by Joni Lovenduski. Cambridge: Cambridge University Press, 2005.

Sasaki, Takeshi. *Rondan Jihyo January 1989–March 1992*. Tokyo: Asahi Shinbun, 1992a.

Sasaki, Takeshi. *Seiji ha Doko he Mukauno ka*. Tokyo: Chuo Koron, 1992b.

Sasaki, Takeshi. *Seiji ni Nani ga Dekiru noka*. Tokyo: Kodansha, 1991.

Sasaki, Takeshi. *Seijika no Joken*. Tokyo: Kodansha, 1995.

Sasaki, Takeshi, et al. *Seiji Kaikaku 1800 Nichi no Shinjitu*. Tokyo: Kodansha, 1999.

Sauer, Birgit. "Ein ewiges Pilotprojekt? Gender Mainstreaming in Österreich." Pp. 169–81 in *Gender Mainstreaming. Konzepte–Handlungsfelder–Instrumente*, edited by Michael Meuser and Claudia Neusüß. Bonn: Bundeszentrale für politische Bildung, 2005.

Saunders, Kay, and Ray Evans, eds. *Gender Relations in Australia. Domination and Negotiation*. Sydney: Harcourt Brace Jovanovich, 1992.

Savoie, Donald J. *Governing from the Centre: The Concentration of Power in Canadian Politics*. Toronto: University of Toronto Press, 1999.

Sawer, Marian. "The Life and Times of Women's Policy Machinery in Australia." Pp. 243–63 in *Mainstreaming Gender, Democratizing the State? Institutional Mechanisms for the Advancement of Women*, edited by Shirin M. Rai. Manchester: Manchester University Press, 2003.

Sawer, Marian. "Femocrats and Ecorats: Women's Policy Machinery in Australia, Canada and New Zealand." Pp. 112–37 in *Missionaries and Mandarins. Feminist Engagement with Development Institutions*, edited by Carol Miller and Shahra Razavi. London: Intermediate Technology Publications (in association with the United Nations Research Institute for Social Development), 1998.

Sawer, Marian. *Sisters in Suits. Women and Public Policy in Australia*. Sydney: Allen and Unwin, 1990.

Sawer, Marian. "The Watchers Within: Women and the Australian State." Pp. 36–53 in *Women, Public Policy and the State*, edited by Linda Hancock. South Yarra, Victoria: Macmillan, 1999.

Sawer, Marian, and Marian Simms. *A Woman's Place. Women and Politics in Australia*. 2nd ed. St. Leonards, NSW: Allen & Unwin, 1993.

Sawyers, Traci M., and David S. Meyer. "Missed Opportunities: Social Movement Abeyance and Public Policy." *Social Problems* 46, no. 2 (1999): 187–206.

Scalmer, Sean. "From Contestation to Autonomy: The Staging and Framing of Anti-Hanson Contention." *Australian Journal of Politics and History* 47, no. 2 (2001): 209–224.

Schain, Martin. "The Immigration Debate and the National Front." Pp. 169–98 in *Chirac's Challenge: Liberalization, Europeanization, and Malaise in France*, edited by John T.S. Keeler and Martin Schain. New York: St. Martin's Press, 1996.

Schattovits, Helmuth. "Kinderbetreuungsscheck in Österreich." Pp. 87–128 in *Aufwertung der Erziehungsarbeit,* edited by Christian Leipert. Opladen: Leske und Budrich, 1999.

Schäuble, Wolfgang. "Vergeßt die Mutter nicht." *Frankfurter Rundschau*, 21 May 2001.

Schmidt, Vivien. "Business, the State, and the End of Dirigisme." Pp. 105–42 in *Chirac's Challenge: Liberalization, Europeanization, and Malaise in France,* edited by John T.S. Keeler and Martin Schain. New York: St. Martin's Press, 1996.

Schneider, Ingrid. "Embryonale Stammzellforschung." Pp. 248–54 in *Fortpflanzungsmedizin in Deutschland. Wissenschaftliches Symposium des Bundesministeriums für Gesundheit in Zusammenarbeit mit dem Robert Koch-Institut vom 24.–26. Mai 2000 in Berlin,* edited by Bundesministerium für Gesundheit. Baden-Baden: Nomos, 2001.

SCP. *Sociaal en Cultureel Rapport 1994.* Rijswijk: Sociaal Cultureel Planbureau, 1994.

SCP. *Sociaal en Cultureel Rapport 2000.* Den Haag: Sociaal Cultureel Planbureau, 2000

Sevenhuijsen, Selma. *De zorg van het emancipatiebeleid. Een benadering vanuit de zorgethiek.* Utrecht: Universiteit Utrecht, Nederlands Genootschap Vrouwenstudies, 2001.

Shields, John, and Mitchell Evans. *Shrinking the State: Globalization and Public Administration "Reform."* Halifax: Fernwood, 1998.

Sidel, Ruth. *Women and Children Last.* New York: Penguin, 1986.

"Slechts één 'nieuwe Belg' op vijf kan op 8 oktober stemmen," *De Financieel Economische Tijd*, 8 August 2000.

"Snel-Belgwet lost niks op," *De Standaard,* 4 February 2004, p. 4.

Sörensen, Kerstin, and Christina Bergqvist. *Gender and the Social Democratic Welfare Regime. A Comparison of Gender-Equality Friendly Policies in Sweden and Norway.* Stockholm Work Life in Transition 2002:5.

Sozialdemokratische Partei Österreichs. *Grundsatzprogramm der SPÖ 1998.* 1998. www.spoe.at (August 2003).

Sozialdemokratische Partei Österreichs. "SPÖ-Forderungen zum Familien-Volksbegehren vom 19.5." 2000. www.parlament.gv.at (August 2003).

Statistik Austria. 2005. www.statistik.at (5 January 2005).

Steibl, Ridi. "Regierung setzt Forderungen des Familienvolksbegehrens Schritt für Schritt um." 2000. www.familienbund.at/body/volksbegehren (August 2003)

Stephens, John D. "The Scandinavian Welfare States: Achievements, Crisis, and Prospects." Pp. 33–66 in *Welfare States in Transition: National Adaptations in Global Economies,* edited by Gøsta Esping-Andersen. London: Sage, 2001.

Stetson, Dorothy McBride, ed. *Abortion Politics, Women's Movements and the Democratic State: A Comparative Study of State Feminism.* Oxford: Oxford University Press, 2001.

Stetson, Dorothy McBride. "The Oldest Women's Policy Agency: The Women's Bureau in the United States." Pp. 254–71 in *Comparative State Feminism,* edited by Dorothy McBride Stetson and Amy G. Mazur. Thousand Oaks, CA: Sage Publications, 1995.

Stetson, Dorothy McBride. *Women's Rights in France*. New York: Garland, 1987.

Stetson, Dorothy McBride, and Amy G. Mazur. *Comparative State Feminism*. Thousand Oaks, CA: Sage Publications, 1995.

Stichwort Newsletter 14. (2002).

STT. "Esko Aho: Päivähoitolaki oli kaataa hallituksen." *Suomen Tietotoimisto*, 24 December1994.

STTK. "Lausunto eduskunnan sosiaali- ja terveysvaliokunnalle hallituksen lakiesityksistä koskien lasten päivähoidon järjestämistä ja kotihoidon tukea (HE 210 ja HE 211)." Asiamies Riitta Työläjärvi, STTK. 15 November 1994.

"Studied to Death?" *CBC News Online*. 10 June 2005. www.cbc.ca/news (21 November 2005)

Summers, Anne. "The End of Equality? Australian Women and the Howard Government." *Pamela Denoon Lecture, Australian National University*. 6 March 2003 www.wel.org.au/announce/denoon/03lecture.htm (10 March 2003).

Sundman, Kerstin. *Between the Home and the Institutions: The Feminist Movement in Madrid, Spain*. Gothenburg: Acta Universitatis Gothoburgensis, 1999.

Svensson, Torsten. *Marknadsanpassningens politik. Den svenska modellens förändring 1980–2000*. Uppsala: Acta Universitatis Upsaliensis, 2001.

Sweden. Office of the Minister of Social Affairs. Kommittén Välfärdsbokslut. *Välfärd vid vägskäl. Utvecklingen under 1990-talet,* SOU 2000:3.

Sweden. Office of the Minister of Social Affairs. Kommittén Välfärdsbokslut. *Välfärdsbokslut för 1990-talet. Slutbetänkande.* SOU 2001:79

Sweden. Parliament. *Parliamentary minutes.* 1993/94:106.

Sweden. Parliament. *Parliamentary minutes.* 1993/94:108.

Swyngedouw, Marc, Jaak Billiet, Ann Carton, and Roeland Beerten. *De (on)Redelijke Kiezer. Onderzoek Naar De Politieke Opvattingen Van Vlamingen: Verkiezingen Van 21 Mei 1995*. Leuven: Acco, 1998.

Takemura, Masayoshi. *Chiisaku tomo Kirarito Hikaru Kuni Nihon*. Tokyo: Kobunsha, 1994.

Taylor, Malcolm G. *Insuring National Health Care: The Canadian Experience*. Chapel Hill, NC: UNC Press, 1990.

Taylor, Verta, and Nancy Whittier. "The New Feminist Movement." Pp. 544–61 in *Feminist Frontiers IV*, edited by Laurel Richardson, Verta Taylor, and Nancy Whittier. New York: McGraw-Hill, 1997.

Tazi-Preve, Irene Marjam. "Einstellungen der ÖsterreicherInnen zu Familie, Familienpolitik und dem Geschlechterverhältnis." *Österreichische Zeitschrift für Politikwissenschaft* 32, no. 4 (2003): 443–55.

Teramachi, Midori. *Shimin-ha Giin ninaru tameno Hon*. Tokyo: Gakuyo Shobo, 2002.

Thomas, David M, ed. *Canada and the United States: Differences That Count*. 2d ed. Peterborough, ON: Broadview, 2000.

Threlfall, Monica. "Feminist Politics and Social Change in Spain." Pp. 115–51 in *Feminist Politics and Social Transformation in the North*, edited by Monica Threlfall. London and New York: Verso, 1996.

Threlfall, Monica. "State Feminism or Party Feminism?: Feminist Politics and the Spanish Institute of Women." *The European Journal of Women's Studies* 5, no. 1 (1998): 69–93.

Threlfall, Monica. "The Women's Movement in Spain." *New Left Review* no. 151 (1985): 44–73.

Thuiszorg en zorg thuis, kansen voor de toekomst. "Verkenningen Ouderenzorg 1995–2010." *HTK*, 25351, no. 2 (1996–1997).

Thuiszorg in de jaren negentig. "Notitie over de toekomstige ontwikkeling en stimulering van de thuiszorg." *HTK*, 22300, 16, no. 44 (1991–1992).

Tiersky, Ronald. *France in the New Europe: Changing yet Steadfast.* Belmont, CA: Wadsworth, 1997.

Timmermans, J.M., ed. *Mantelzorg. Over de hulp van en aan mantelzorgers.* Den Haag: Sociaal en Cultureelplanbureau, 2003.

Tobias, Sheila. *Faces of Feminism: An Activist's Reflections on the Women's Movement.* Boulder: Westview Press, 1997.

Toinet, Marie-France. "The Limits of the Malaise in France." Pp. 279–300 in *Chirac's Challenge: Liberalization, Europeanization, and Malaise in France,* edited by John T.S. Keeler and Martin Schain. New York: St. Martin's Press, 1996.

Tolmein, Oliver. "Ein Recht auf fehlerfreie Babys?" *GID* 14, no. 125/126 (1998): 57–58.

Touissant, Sandy, Myrna Tonkinson, and David Trigger. "Gendered Landscapes: The Politics and Processes of Inquiry and Negotiating Interests in Land." Pp. 157–74 in *Words and Silences. Aboriginal Women, Politics and Land,* edited by Peggy Brock. Sydney: Allen and Unwin, 2001.

Trat, Josette, and Marie-Hélène Zylberberg-Hocquard. *La Participation des femmes aux instances de décision des syndicats à different niveaux.* Study conducted for the Women's Rights Service/GEDISST-CNRS. 2000.

Tuohy, Carolyn Hughes. *Accidental Logics: The Dynamics of Change in the Health Care Arena in the United States, Britain, and Canada.* New York: Oxford University Press, 1999.

Tyyskä, Vappu. *The Politics of Caring and the Welfare State. The Impact of the Women's Movement on Child Care Policy in Canada and Finland 1960–1990.* Sarja B/nide 277. Helsinki: Suomalainen Tiedeakatemia, 1995.

UCL Department of Political Science. Lord Wakeham. Royal Commission on Reform of the House of Lords. *A House for the Future.* London. Constitution Unit. HMSO, 2000. www.ucl.ac.uk/constitution-unit (1 August 2004).

Ulmanen, Petra. *(s)veket mot kvinnorna och hur högern stal feminismen.* Uddevalla: Atlas, 1998.

U.S. Congress. House of Representatives. *Beyond Public Assistance: Where Do We Go from Here?* Hearing before the Select Committee on Hunger. 25 March 1992.

U.S. Congress. House of Representatives. *Federal Policy Perspectives on Welfare Reform: Rhetoric Reality and Opportunities.* Hearing before the Domestic Task Force of the Select Committee on Hunger. 9 April 1992.

U.S. Congress. House of Representatives. *State and Local Perspectives on Welfare Reform: Rhetoric, Reality and Opportunities.* Hearing before the Domestic Task Force of the Select Committee on Hunger. 4 June 1992.

U.S. Congress. Senate. *Administration's Welfare Reform Proposal.* Hearing before the Subcommittee on Social Security and Family Policy of the Committee on Finance. 4 August 1992.

U.S. Congress. House of Representatives. *Rethinking Poverty Policy.* Hearing before the Select Committee on Hunger. 2 October 1992.

U.S. Congress. House of Representatives. *Ending Welfare As We Know It: Progress or Paralysis?.* Hearing before the Human Resources and Intergovernmental Relations Subcommittee of the Committee on Government Operations. 10 March 1994.

U.S. Congress. House of Representatives. *Hearing on H.R. 4605, Work and Responsibility Act of 1994.* Hearing before the Committee on Education and Labor. 2 August 1994.

U.S. Congress. House of Representatives. *Hearing regarding the Impact of Welfare Reform on Child Care Providers and the Working Poor.* Hearing before the Subcommittee on Human Resources of the Committee on Education and Labor. 20 September 1994.

U.S. Congress. House of Representatives. *Contract with America–Overview.* Hearings before the Committee on Ways and Means. 5, 10, 11, 12 January 1995.

U.S. Congress. House of Representatives. *Contract with America–Welfare Reform.* Hearings before the Committee on Ways and Means. 13, 20, 23, 27, 30, January and 2 February 1995.

U.S. Congress. House of Representatives. *Child Care and Child Welfare.* Joint Hearing before the Subcommittee on Human Resources of the Committee on Ways and Means and the Subcommittee on Early Childhood, Youth, and Families of the Committee on Economic and Educational Opportunities. 3 February 1995.

U.S. Congress. Senate. *Welfare Reform.* Hearings before the Subcommittee on Social Security and Family Policy of the Committee on Finance. 18 January and 25 February 1994.

U.S. Congress. Senate. *Broad Policy Goals of Welfare Reform.* Hearing before the committee on Finance. 9 March 1995.

U.S. Congress. Senate. *States' Perspective on Welfare Reform.* Hearing before the Committee on Finance. 8 March 1995.

U.S. Congress. Senate. *Teen Parents and Welfare Reform.* Hearing before the Committee on Finance. 14 March 1995.

U.S. Congress. Senate. *Child Support Enforcement.* Hearing before the Committee on Finance. 28 March 1995.

U.S. Congress. Senate. *Welfare Reform–Views of Interested Organizations.* Hearing before the Committee on Finance. 29 March 1995.

U.S. Congress. House of Representatives. *Earned Income Tax Credit.* Hearing before the Subcommittee on Oversight and the Subcommittee on Human Resources of the Committee on Ways and Means. 15 June 1995.

U.S. Congress. House of Representatives. *Causes of Poverty, with a Focus on Out of Wedlock Births.* 5 March 1996.

U.S. Congress. House of Representatives. *Welfare Reform.* Hearing before the Subcommittee on Human Resources of the Committee on Ways and Means. 22, 23 May 1996.

U.S. Congress. House of Representatives. *The Personal Responsibility and Work Opportunity Act of 1996.* Hearing before the Committee on Commerce. 11 June 1996.

U.S. Congress. Senate. *Welfare and Medicaid Reform.* Hearings before the Committee on Finance. 13, 19 June 1996.

Uusikylä, Petri. "Hyvinvointilainsäädännön verkostot. Sidosryhmäorganisaatio sosiaali- ja terveyslainsäädännön taustalla vuosina 1968–1995." Pp. 82–106 in *Verkostoyhteiskunta. Käytännön johdatus verkostoanalyysiin,* edited by Mikko Mattila and Petri Uusikylä. Helsinki: Gaudeamus, 1999.

Uusitalo, Hannu. "Tulonjako ja yhteiskunnalliset jaot." Pp. 26–42 in *Yhteiskunnalliset jaot. 1990-luvun perintö?,* edited by Timo Piirainen and Juho Saari. Helsinki: Gaudeamus, 2002.

Valiente, Celia. "A Closed Subsystem and Distant Feminist Demands Block Women-Friendly Outcomes in Spain." Pp. 111–30 in *State Feminism,Women's Movements, and Job Training: Making Democracies Work in a Global Economy,* edited by Amy G. Mazur. New York and London: Routledge, 2001a.

Valiente, Celia. "The Feminist Movement and the Reconfigured State in Spain (1970s–2000)." Pp. 30–47 in *Women's Movements Facing the Reconfigured State,* edited by Lee Ann Banaszak, Karen Beckwith, and Dieter Rucht. New York: Cambridge University Press, 2003b.

Valiente, Celia. "Gendering Abortion Debates: State Feminism in Spain." Pp. 229–45 in *Abortion Politics, Women's Movements, and the Democratic State,* edited by Dorothy McBride Stetson. New York: Oxford University Press, 2001b.

Valiente, Celia. "Mobilizing for Recognition and Redistribution on Behalf of Others? The Case of Mothers against Drugs in Spain." Pp. 239–59 in *Recognition Struggles and Social Movements: Contested Identities, Agency and Power,* edited by Barbara Hobson. Cambridge: Cambridge University Press, 2003a.

Valiente, Celia. "The Power of Persuasion: The *Instituto de la Mujer* in Spain." Pp. 221–36 in *Comparative State Feminism,* edited by Dorothy McBride Stetson and Amy Mazur. Thousand Oaks, CA: Sage, 1995.

Valiente, Celia. "State Feminism and Central State Debates on Prostitution in Postauthoritarian Spain." Pp. 205–24 in *The Politics of Prostitution:Women's Movements, Democratic States and the Globalization of Sex Commerce,* edited by Joyce Outshoorn. Cambridge: Cambridge University Press, 2004.

Valiente, Celia. "State Feminism and Gender Equality Policies: The Case of Spain (1983–1995)." Pp. 127–41 in *Sex Equality Policy in Western Europe,* edited by Frances Gardiner. London and New York: Routledge, 1997.

Välimäki, Anna-Leena. *Lasten hoitopuu. Lasten päivähoitojärjestelmä Suomessa 1800- ja 1900-luvuilla.* Helsinki: Suomen Kuntaliitto, 1999.

Van Eylen, Luk. "Snel-Belg-Wet is kaas met grote gaten," *De Standaard,* 5 June 2001.

Van Kersbergen, Kees. "The Declining Resistance of Welfare States to Change." Pp. 19–36 in *Survival of the European Welfare State,* edited by Stein Kuhnle. London and New York: Routledge, 2000.

Vassallo, Salvatore. "La terza bicamerale." Pp. 131–55 in *Politica in Italia. I fatti dell'anno e le interpretazioni. Edizione 1998,* edited by Luciano Bardi and Martin Rhodes. Bologna: Il Mulino, 1998.

Ventura, Sofia. *Il federalismo. Il potere diviso tra centro e periferia.* Bologna: Il Mulino, 2002.

Vincent, John. "All That Matters Is What Tony Wants." *London Review of Books* 22, no. 16 (March 2000): 6.

Vranken, Jan, Christiane Timmerman, and Katrien Van der Heyden, eds. *Komende generaties Wat weten we (niet) over allochtonen in Vlaanderen?* Leuven: Acco, 2001.

Vries, Petra de. "Feminism in the Netherlands." *Women's Studies International Quarterly* 4, no. 4 (1981): 389–409.

Vulto, Marij, and Marjolein Moree. *Thuisverzorging als professie. Een combinatie van hoofd, hand en hart.* Utrecht: De Tijdstroom, 1996.

Wahlfreiheit durch Kinderbetreuungsgeld? Zwischenbericht zur Evaluation des Kinderbetreuungsgeldes, edited by Österreichisches Institut für Famileinforschung, 2005, www.oif.ac.at.

Walter, Wolfgang. "Familienpolitik und Fertilität im europäischen Vergleich." *Politische Studien* 55, no. 396 (2004): 20–30.

Watson, Sophie, ed. *Playing the State. Australian Feminist Interventions.* Sydney: Allen and Unwin, 1990.

Weaver, R. Kent. "Ending Welfare As We Know It." Pp. 361–416 in *The Social Divide: Political Parties and the Future of Activist Government,* edited by Margaret Weir. Washington, DC: Brookings Institution Press, 1998.

Weaver, R. Kent. *Ending Welfare As We Know It.* Washington, DC: Brookings Institution Press, 2000.

Webb, Paul. *The Modern British Party System.* London: Sage, 2000.

Weir, Margaret, ed. *The Social Divide: Political Parties and the Future of Activist Government.* Washington, D.C.: Brookings Institution Press, 1998.

Weiss, Magdalene. "Statement." Pp. 383–85 in *Fortpflanzungsmedizin in Deutschland. Wissenschaftliches Symposium des Bundesministeriums für Gesundheit in Zusammenarbeit mit dem Robert Koch-Institut vom 24.–26. Mai 2000 in Berlin,* edited by Bundesministerium für Gesundheit. Baden-Baden: Nomos, 2001.

Wetboek van de Belgische nationaliteit. Officieuze coördinatie van de tekst ingevoerd bij wet van 28 juni 1984 en gewijzigd bij de wetten van 22 mei 1991, 13 juni 1991, 6 augustus 1993, 13 april 1995, 22 december 1998 en 1 maart 2000. (In werking getreden op 1 mei 2000).

Whittier, Nancy. *Feminist Generations: The Persistence of the Radical Women's Movement.* Philadelphia: Temple University Press, 1995.

"Wir waren schon weiter als heute: Dohnal wehrt sich gegen Rückschritt," *Kurier,* 24 February 1995.

Witte, Els. "Belgian Federalism: Towards Complexity and Asymmetry." *West European Politics* 15, no. 4 (1992): 95–117.

Witte, Els, Jan Craeybeckx, and Alain Meynen. *Political History of Belgium from 1830 Onwards*. Brussels: VUB Press, 2000.

Women for Wik. "Submission to the Joint Parliamentary Committee on the Native Title Amendment Bill 1997 from Women for Wik 16 October 1997." 1997. www.nwjc.org.au/womenforwik.html (26 Oct 2002).

"The Women's Movement at the Crossroads." *Social Policy* 23 (Summer 1993): 2–7.

Wright, Lisa. *Themes Emerging from the High Court's Recent Native Title Decisions*. National Native Title Tribunal Occasional Papers Series No. 1/2003. Perth (Western Australia): National Native Title Tribunal, 2003.

WRR. *Generatiebewust beleid*. Den Haag: Sdu Uitgevers, 1999.

WRR. *Doorgroei van arbeidsparticipatie*. Den Haag: Sdu Uitgevers (Wetenschappelijke Raad voor het Regeringsbeleid, rapport aan de regering, 57), 2000.

Yamaguchi, Jiro. *Seijikaikaku*. Tokyo: Iwanami Shoten, 1993.

Young, Lisa. *Feminists and Party Politics*. Vancouver, BC: UBC Press, 2000.

Zorg Nabij 2001. HTK, 2000–2001, 27401, nr. 65 (20 June 2001).

Zorgnota 2001. HTK, 2000–2001, 27401, nr. 1–2 (19 September 2000).

Zumstein, Monika. "Keimzellspende – Juristische Thesen." Pp. 134–42 in *Fortpflanzungsmedizin in Deutschland. Wissenschaftliches Symposium des Bundesministeriums für Gesundheit in Zusammenarbeit mit dem Robert Koch-Institut vom 24.–26. Mai 2000 in Berlin,* edited by Bundesministerium für Gesundheit. Baden-Baden: Nomos, 2001.

Index

abortion, 1, 4, 5, 35, 43, 44, 211, 286
abortion rights, 155, 195, 231; embryo
  protection vs., 156, 157, 161
adoption rights, 104
AFDC (Aid to Families with Dependent
  Children), 281, 287, 292; Clinton
  administration and, 289, 290;
  perceived failure of, 288, 291, 299,
  300n6; as perpetuating poverty, 299,
  300n6; PRWORA's elimination of,
  293, 294, 297; women's movement's
  support for, 299
affirmative action, 26, 53, 182–83, 201
Aid to Families with Dependent
  Children. *See* AFDC
Anti–Domestic Violence Act, 193–94,
  196
Armstrong, Patricia, 91, 92, 98n15–16,
  99n17
asylum: Austrian debate on, 21–22;
  Belgian debate on, 63, 67; German
  rights to, 148, 149–50
Aubry, Martine, 127, 129, 130, 135
Australia: Goods and Services Tax of,
  40; labor market deregulation in,
  40–41; *Mabo* High Court decision in,
  41, 46; monarchy vs. republic in, 41;
  national priority issues in, 40–42;

Office of Status of Women in, 51;
  Reconciliation in, 39, 46, 57n2; tax
  reform issues in, 40; *Wik* High Court
  decision in, 40, 47, 53–55; Women's
  Electoral Lobby of, 44, 53–54;
  women's policy agencies in, 51–53
Australian Indigenous people: feminist
  oppressors of, 55; historical
  injustices to, 45–46; literature on
  women of, 49; Stolen Children
  Inquiry and, 47
Australian native land rights, 41–42;
  debate framework for, 48; Document
  of Reconciliation and, 46, 57n2;
  gendering issue of, 40, 48–50, 55,
  56; *Mabo* High Court decision in, 41,
  46; matrilineal inheritance and, 49;
  policy environment of, 40, 55–56;
  policy outcome of, 50; public agenda
  development for, 45–48; *Wik* High
  Court decision in, 40, 47, 53–55;
  women's movement's impact on,
  56–57
Australian women's movement: actors
  for Indigenous people of, 54–55;
  agendas of groups in, 42–44;
  consolidation of, 53; co-optation of,
  50; government funding of, 43, 44;

363

About the Contributors

Terhi Aalto works as information officer at the Ministry of Social Affairs and Health in Finland. She has a master's degree in social sciences from the University of Helsinki with political science as her major subject. She wrote her master's thesis on the Finnish women's movement impact on children's day care and home care allowance policies in Finland.

Christina Bergqvist is associate professor at the Department of Government, Uppsala University, where she received a PhD in Political Science in 1994. Her main publications (in Swedish and English) deal with political representation, women's agency, and the welfare state. She was editior-in-chief of *Equal Democracies? Gender and Politics in the Nordic Countries* (Scandinavian University Press, 1999).

Kathrin Braun is a visiting professor for German and European Politics at the Jackson School of International Studies at the University of Washington, Seattle since fall 2004. She is a political scientist specialized on policy studies, particularly science policy, gender studies, political theory, and political philosophy. Kathrin Braun received her *Diplom* (1985) from the University of Oldenburg (Germany) and her PhD (1992) and *Habilitation* (1999) from the University of Hannover (Germany). She taught political science at different universities and graduate schools in Germany and Austria (Hannover, Goettingen, Innsbruck, Vienna). In 1999–2000 she was an expert member of the Parliamentary Study Commission on Law and Ethics of Modern Medicine of the German parliament. Her current research is on new forms of governance in the policy area of bioethics and the life sciences and on theoretical conceptions of biopolitics, particularly in Hannah Arendt, Michel Foucault, and

Giorgio Agamben. Her book *Menschenwürde und Biomedizin. Zum philosophischen Diskurs der Bioethik* was published in 2000.

Marila Guadagnini is associate professor of political science at the University of Turin. She is author of *Il sistema politico italiano. Temi per una discussione* (Il Segnalibro, Torino, 1997), *La stagione del disincanto? Cittadini, cittadine e politica alle soglie del 2000* (Il Segnalibro, Torino, 2001), co-author of *Il soffitto di cristallo? Le donne nelle posizioni decisionali in Europa* (Edizioni Fondazione Olivetti, Roma, 1999), and editor of *Da elettrici a elette. Riforme istituzionali e rappresentanza delle donne in Italia, in Europa e negli Stati Uniti* (Celid, Torino, 2003). She published numerous chapters and articles on gender and politics and wrote the chapters on Italy in the following books: *Comparative State Feminism* (edited by D. McBride Stetson and A. Mazur, Sage Publications, Thousand Oaks, CA, 1995), *State Feminism, Women's Movements and Job Training: Making Democracies Work in the Global Economy* (edited by A. Mazur, Routledge, New York, 2001), and *State Feminism and Political Representation* (edited by J. Lovenduski, Cambridge University Press, Cambridge, 2005).

Melissa Haussman is an Associate Professor of Political Science at Carleton University, Ottawa, Canada. In addition to co-editing the "hot issue" book, *Gendering the State in the Age of Globalization* and contributing the Canada chapter "New Federalism and Cracked Pillars," she wrote the Canadian abortion policy chapter in Dorothy Stetson's edited RNGS volume, *Abortion Politics* (Oxford University Press, 2001). She is the author of *Abortion Politics in North America* (Lynne Rienner, 2005), and the forthcoming *The Morning-After Pill: The Battle over Emergency Contraception* (Greenwood Press, 2007). She has written journal articles and edited volume chapters on U.S. women and the presidential nomination process, social movement organizations, and abortion policy.

Anne Maria Holli, PhD, is researcher at the Department of Political Science at the University of Helsinki, Finland. Her major areas of research are in the fields of public equality policies, women in the media, and women and politics in general. Her most recent publications include *Discourse and Politics for Gender Equality in Late Twentieth Century Finland* (Helsinki University Press, 2003) and a co-edited volume on Finnish gender equality policies, *Tasa-arvopolitiikan haasteet* (WSOY, 2002). She was also a co-author for *Equal Democracies? Gender and Politics in the Nordic Countries* (edited by Bergqvist et al.) (Scandinavian University Press, 1999), and wrote the chapters on Finland in the following RNGS-books: *State Feminism, Women's*

Movements and Job Training: Making Democracies Work in the Global Economy (edited by by A. Mazur) (Routledge, 2001) and T*he Politics of Prostitution. Women's Movements, Democratic States and the Globalisation of Sex Commerce* (edited by by J. Outshoorn) (Cambridge University Press, 2003).

Misako Iwamoto is a professor in the Faculty of Humanities and Social Sciences at Mie University, Japan. Her publications include a contribution to the American Political Science Association's Journal, *PS* online symposium, "The Mother's Body Protection Act and the Contraceptive Pill: Reproductive Rights and Policy Making in Japan," January 2004; "The Madonna Boom: The Progress of Japanese Women into Politics in the 1980s," *Political Science & Politics* 34, no. 2 (2001): 225–226; "Onna no Inai Seiji Katei [Political Process without Women], in *Joseigaku* (Women's Study) (Women's Studies Association of Japan, Vol. 5. 1997); and a paper presented at the Japanese Political Science Association, 2003, "Josei ni kansuru Seijiteki Gensetsu [Political Discourse on Women], 'Sei' to Seji [Sex, Sexuality and Politics]." She has been a member of the Executive Board of the Japanese Political Science Association since 2003, and a member of the Executive Board of the Japanese Society for Public Administration since 1998.

Joni Lovenduski is anniversary professor of politics at Birkbeck College, University of London. Her published work includes *Women and European Politics* (1986), *Contemporary Feminist Politics* (1993) (with Vicky Randall), *Political Recruitment: Gender, Race and Class in the British Parliament* (1995) (with Pippa Norris), and *High Tide or High Time for Labour Women* (1998) (with Maria Eagle MP). She was co-editor of *The Politics of the Second Electorate* (1981), *The New Politics of Abortion* (1986), *Gender and Party Politics* (1993), and *Gender and Political Participation* (2004) with Pippa Norris and Rosie Campbell. Recent books are *Feminizing Politics* with Polity Press and *State Feminism and Political Representation* (a jointly edited collection from the RNGS project).

Amy G. Mazur is professor in the Department of Political Science at Washington State University. Her research and teaching interests focus on comparative feminist policy issues with a particular emphasis on France. Her books include *Comparative State Feminism* (Sage, 1995) (editor, with Dorothy McBride Stetson); *Gender Bias and the State: Symbolic Reform at Work in Fifth Republic France* (Pittsburgh University Press, 1995); *State Feminism, Women's Movement, and Job Training: Making Democracies Work in the Global Economy* (Routledge, 2001) (editor); and *Theorizing Feminist Policy* (Oxford, 2002). She has published articles in *Political Research*

Quarterly, French Politics and Society, Policy Studies Journal, West European Politics, European Journal of Political Research, European Political Science, Review of Policy Research, Contemporary French Civilization, and *Travail Genre et Société* and *Espace-Temps*. She is co-convener of the Research Network on Gender, Politics and the State and convener of the French Politics Group of the APSA. She is co-editor of *Political Research Quarterly*. In fall 2001, she was the Marie-Jahoda Professor of International Feminist Studies at Ruhr University, Bochum and a Havens Center Visiting Scholar at the University of Wisconsin in spring 2003. In 2005–2006 she was an expert for the United Nations for the Expert Group Meeting on Equal Participation of Women and Men in Decision-making Processes and rapporteur of the final meeting report. She has received over $500,000 in research grants from the National Science Foundation, the European Science Foundation, and the French Ministry of Social Affairs.

Dorothy E. McBride (formerly Stetson) is Emeritus Professor of Political Science at Florida Atlantic University, where she was a founder of the women's studies program. She is co-convener (with Amy G. Mazur) of the Research Network on Gender, Politics and the State (RNGS). She is author of *Women's Rights in the U.S.A: Policy Conflict and Gender Roles* (3d ed.) (2004). She co-edited *Comparative State Feminism* (1995) and was editor and contributing author of *Abortion Politics, Women's Movements and the Democratic State: A Comparative Study of State Feminism* (2001). During 2006–2008 she is visiting scholar at the University of Washington.

Jantine Oldersma studied political science, teaches at the Department of Public Administration, and is an affiliate of the Joke Smit Research Center in Women's Studies, both at the University of Leiden. She has written on women in corporatist arrangements in the Netherlands, authored articles on public policy on political representation of women, and contributed to the RNGS volume on political representation (forthcoming). Other academic interests are political culture and political communication.

Joyce Outshoorn is professor of women's studies at the University of Leiden and head of the Joke Smit Research Center in Women's Studies; she is also affiliated with the Department of Political Science. She has written extensively on abortion politics, women's movements, and women's public policy. She is the editor of *The Politics of Prostitution. Women's Movements, Democratic States and the Globalisation of Sex Commerce* (Cambridge University Press, 2004). She is a co-director of the Research Network on Gender, Politics and the State. She is also co-editor of the forthcoming follow-up book on state feminist politics in the RNGS countries (under contract with Palgrave Press), and a contributing author of the forthcoming RNGS capstone book.

Birgit Sauer is professor of political science at the Department of Political Science, University of Vienna. Her PhD was on political rituals in the GDR (1993 at the Free University of Berlin), and her *Habilitation* on state and democratic theory in gender perspective (2000 at the University of Vienna). She is director of the Austrian RNGS team and co-director of the EU research project "VEIL" (Values, Equality, and Difference in Liberal Democracies. The Case of Muslim Headscarves). Recent publications include "Normalized Masculinities. Constructing Gender in Theories of Political Transition and Democratic Consolidation" (in Gabriele Jähnert et al., eds., *Gender in Transition in Eastern and Central Europe*); Proceedings, Berlin [*trafo verlag*], (2000, p. 26–36); "Conceptualizing the German State. Putting Women's Politics in its Place" (in Stuart S. Nagel and Amy Robb, eds., *Handbook of Global Social Policy*, New York: Marcel Dekker, 2000, p. 317–335); and "Die Asche des Souveräns. Staat und Demokratie" (in *der Geschlechterdebatte*, Frankfurt/New York: Campus, 2001).

Barbara Sullivan is a senior lecturer in the School of Political Science and International Studies at the University of Queensland, Australia. She teaches courses on the politics of gender and sexuality and feminist and political theory. Her research has spanned a number of areas including sexual citizenship, prostitution and trafficking, feminism, and liberal thought. Barbara's most recent publications include articles in the *International Feminist Journal of Politics* and *Law and Context*. She has published a monograph on prostitution in Australia *(The Politics of Sex*, Cambridge University Press, 1997) and edited three collections on prostitution, citizenship, and contractualism.

Celia Valiente is associate professor in the Department of Political Science and Sociology at Universidad Carlos III de Madrid (Madrid, Spain). Her main research interests are gender equality policies and the women's movement in Spain from a comparative perspective. Her most recent books are *Gendering Spanish Democracy* (with Monica Threlfall and Christine Cousins, Routledge, 2005) and *El feminismo de Estado en España: El Instituto de la Mujer (1983–2003)* [State Feminism in Spain: The Women's Institute (1983–2003)] (Valencia, Universitat de València, 2006). She has published articles in *Gender & Society*, *European Journal of Political Research*, and *South European Society & Politics*.

Alison E. Woodward has a PhD from the University of California at Berkeley. She is Professor and Chair of the International Affairs and Politics Program of Vesalius College at the Free University of Brussels (VUB) and cofounder of the Center for Women's Studies. She has held appointments at the universities of Uppsala, Antwerp, and Brussels, the Wissenschaftszentrum Berlin, and the Royal Institute of Technology in Stockholm among others. She held the M. Jahoda Chair at the Ruhr University in 2001 and a Senior Research Fellowship at Wayne State University in 2003. Her primary research interest is in the field of comparative European public policy and organization, especially in the areas of equal opportunities policies, housing, and alternative energy. Her current research is on transnational social movements and public policy and the role of regional parliaments in European governance. Recent publications include *Inclusions and Exclusions in European Societies* (edited with Martin Kohli) (Routledge, 2001) and *Going for Gender Balance* (Council of Europe, 2002).